Data Lake for Enterprises

Leveraging Lambda Architecture for building Enterprise Data Lake

Tomcy John
Pankaj Misra

BIRMINGHAM - MUMBAI

Data Lake for Enterprises

Copyright © 2017 Packt Publishing

First published: May 2017

Production reference: 1300517

Published by Packt Publishing Ltd.
Livery Place
35 Livery Street
Birmingham
B3 2PB, UK.

ISBN 978-1-78728-134-9

www.packtpub.com

Credits

Authors
Tomcy John
Pankaj Misra

Copy Editors
Shaila Kusanale
Vikrant Phadkay

Reviewers
Wei Di
Vivek Mishra
Ruben Oliva Ramos

Project Coordinator
Nidhi Joshi

Commissioning Editor
Amey Varangaonkar

Proofreader
Safis Editing

Acquisition Editor
Chaitanya Nair

Indexer
Mariammal Chettiyar

Content Development Editor
Aishwarya Pandere

Production Coordinator
Aparna Bhagat

Technical Editor
Karan Thakkar

Foreword

As organizations have evolved over the last 40 to 50 years, they have slowly but steadily found ways and means to improve their operations by adding IT/software systems across their operating areas. It would not be surprising today to see more than 250+ applications in each of our Fortune 200 companies. This has also slowly caused another creeping problem as we evolve from our level of maturity to another; silos of systems that don't interface well to each other.

As enterprises move from local optimization to enterprise optimization they have been leveraging some of the emerging technologies like Big Data systems to find ways and means by which they could bring data together from their disparate IT systems and fuse them together to find better means of driving efficiency and effectiveness improvement that could go a long way in helping enterprises save money.

Tomcy and *Pankaj,* with their vast experience in different functional and technical domains, have been working on finding better ways to fuse information from variety of applications within the organization. They have lived through the challenging journey of finding a ways to bring out changes (technological & cultural).

This book has been put together from the perspective of software engineers, architects and managers; so it's very practical in nature as both of them have lived through various enterprise grade implementation that adds value to the enterprise.

Using future proof patterns and contemporary technology concepts like Data Lake help enterprises prepare themselves well for the future, but even more given them the ability to look across data that they have across different organizational silos and derive wisdom that's typically lost in the blind spots.

Thomas Benjamin

CTO, GE Aviation Digital.

About the Authors

Tomcy John lives in Dubai (United Arab Emirates), hailing from Kerala (India), and is an enterprise Java specialist with a degree in engineering (B Tech) and over 14 years of experience in several industries. He's currently working as *principal architect* at *Emirates Group IT*, in their core architecture team. Prior to this, he worked with *Oracle Corporation* and *Ernst & Young*. His main specialization is in building enterprise-grade applications and he acts as chief mentor and evangelist to facilitate incorporating new technologies as corporate standards in the organization. Outside of his work, Tomcy works very closely with young developers and engineers as mentors and speaks at various forums as a technical evangelist on many topics ranging from web and middleware all the way to various persistence stores. He writes on various topics in his blog and *www.javacodebook.com*.

First and foremost, I would like to thank my savior and lord, Jesus Christ, for giving me strength and courage to pursue this project. It was a dream come true.
I would like to dedicate this book to my father (Appachan), Late C.O.John, and my dearest mom (Ammachi), Leela John, for helping me reach where I am today. I would also like to take this opportunity to thank my dearest wife, Serene and our two lovely children, Neil (son) and Anaya (daughter), for all their support throughout this project and also for allowing me to pursue my dream and tolerating not being with them after my busy day job.

It was my privilege working with my co-author, Pankaj. I take this opportunity to thank him for supporting me, when I first offloaded my dream of writing this book topic and then staying with me at all stages in completing this book. It wouldn't be possible to reach this stage in my career without mentors at various stages of my career. I would like to thank Thomas Benjamin (CTO, GE Aviation Digital), Rajesh R.V (chief architect, Emirates Group IT) and Martin Campbell (chief architect) for supporting me at various stages, with words of encouragement and wealth of knowledge.

Pankaj Misra has been a technology evangelist, holding a bachelor's degree in engineering, with over 16 years of experience across multiple business domains and technologies. He has been working with *Emirates Group IT* since 2015, and has worked with various other organizations in the past. He specializes in architecting and building multi-stack solutions and implementations. He has also been a speaker at technology forums in India and has built products with scale-out architecture that support high-volume, near-real-time data processing and near-real-time analytics.

This book has been a great opportunity for me and would always be an exceptional example of collaboration and knowledge sharing with my co-author Tomcy. I am extremely thankful to him for entrusting me with this responsibility and standing by me at all times. I would like to dedicate this book to my father B. Misra and my mother Geeta Misra who have always been one of the most special people to me. I am extremely grateful to my wife Priti and my kids, daughter Eva and son Siddhant, for their understanding, support and helping me out in every possible way to complete the book.

This book is a medium to give back the knowledge that I have gained by working with many of the amazing people throughout the years. I would like to thank Rajesh R.V. (chief Architect, Emirates Group IT) and Thomas Benjamin (CTO, GE Aviation) for always motivating, helping & supporting us.

About the Reviewers

Wei Di is currently a staff member in a business analytics data mining team. As a data scientist, she is passionate about creating smart and scalable analytics and data mining solutions that can impact millions of individuals and empower successful business.

Her interests also cover wide areas, including artificial intelligence, machine learning, and computer vision. She was previously associated with the eBay human language technology team and eBay research labs, with focus on image understanding for large-scale application and joint learning from both visual and text information. Prior to that, she was with Ancestry.com, working on large-scale data mining and machine learning models in the areas of record linkage, search relevance, and ranking. She received her PhD from Purdue University in 2011 with focus on data mining and image classification.

Vivek Mishra is an IT professional with more than 9 years of experience in various technologies like Java, J2ee, Hibernate, SCA4J, Mule, Spring, Cassandra, HBase, MongoDB, REDIS, Hive, Hadoop. He has been a contributor to open source software such as Apache Cassandra and lead committer for Kundera(a JPA 2.0-compliant object-datastore mapping library for NoSQL Datastores such as Cassandra, HBase, MongoDB, and REDIS).

Vivek, in his previous experience, has enjoyed long-lasting partnerships with the most recognizable names in SCM, banking and finance industries, employing industry-standard, full-software life cycle methodologies such as Agile and SCRUM. He is currently employed with Impetus Infotech.

He has undertaken speaking engagements in cloud camp and Nasscom big data seminars and is an active blogger at `mevivs.wordpress.com`.

Rubén Oliva Ramos is a computer systems engineer with a master's degree in computer and electronic systems engineering, teleinformatics, and networking specialization from University of Salle Bajio in Leon, Guanajuato, Mexico. He has more than 5 years of experience in developing web applications to control and monitor devices connected with Arduino and Raspberry Pi using web frameworks and cloud services to build Internet of Things applications.

He is a mechatronics teacher at the University of Salle Bajio and teaches students of master's in design and engineering of mechatronics Systems. He also works at Centro de Bachillerato Tecnologico Industrial 225 in Leon, Guanajuato, Mexico, teaching the following: electronics, robotics and control, automation, and microcontrollers at Mechatronics Technician Career. He has worked on consultant and developer projects in areas such as monitoring systems and datalogger data using technologies such as Android, iOS, Windows Phone, Visual Studio .NET, HTML5, PHP, CSS, Ajax, JavaScript, Angular, ASP .NET databases (SQlite, mongoDB, and MySQL), and web servers (Node.js and IIS). Ruben has done hardware programming on Arduino, Raspberry Pi, Ethernet Shield, GPS and GSM/GPRS, ESP8266, and control and monitor systems for data acquisition and programming.

He has written the book titled *Internet of Things Programming with JavaScript, Packt.*

His current job involves monitoring, controlling, and acquisition of data with Arduino and Visual Basic .NET for Alfaomega Editor Group.

> *"I want to thank God for helping me reviewing this book, to my wife, Mayte, and my sons, Ruben and Dario, for their support, to my parents, my brother and sister whom I love and to all my beautiful family."*

www.PacktPub.com

For support files and downloads related to your book, please visit www.PacktPub.com.

Did you know that Packt offers eBook versions of every book published, with PDF and ePub files available? You can upgrade to the eBook version at www.PacktPub.com and as a print book customer, you are entitled to a discount on the eBook copy. Get in touch with us at service@packtpub.com for more details.

At www.PacktPub.com, you can also read a collection of free technical articles, sign up for a range of free newsletters and receive exclusive discounts and offers on Packt books and eBooks.

https://www.packtpub.com/mapt

Get the most in-demand software skills with Mapt. Mapt gives you full access to all Packt books and video courses, as well as industry-leading tools to help you plan your personal development and advance your career.

Why subscribe?

- Fully searchable across every book published by Packt
- Copy and paste, print, and bookmark content
- On demand and accessible via a web browser

Customer Feedback

Thanks for purchasing this Packt book. At Packt, quality is at the heart of our editorial process. To help us improve, please leave us an honest review on this book's Amazon page at `https://www.amazon.com/dp/1787281345`.

If you'd like to join our team of regular reviewers, you can e-mail us at `customerreviews@packtpub.com`. We award our regular reviewers with free eBooks and videos in exchange for their valuable feedback. Help us be relentless in improving our products!

Table of Contents

Preface

Data is becoming very important for many enterprises and it has now become pivotal in many aspects. In fact, companies are transforming themselves with data at the core. This book will start by introducing data, its relevance to enterprises, and how they can make use of this data to transform themselves digitally. To make use of data, enterprises need repositories, and in this modern age, these aren't called data warehouses; instead they are called Data Lake.

As we can see today, we have a good number of use cases that are leveraging big data technologies. The concept of a Data Lake existed there for quite sometime, but recently it has been getting real traction in enterprises. This book brings these two aspects together and gives a hand-on, full-fledged, working Data Lake using the latest big data technologies, following well-established architectural patterns.

The book will bring Data Lake and Lambda architecture together and help the reader to actually operationalize these in their enterprise. It will introduce a number of Big Data technologies at a high level, but we didn't want to make it an authoritative reference on any of these topics, as they are vast in nature and worthy of a book by themselves.

This book instead covers pattern explanation and implementation using chosen technologies. The technologies can of course, be replaced with more relevant ones in future or according to set standards within an organization. So, this book will be relevant not only now but for a long time to come. Compared to a software/technology written targeting a specific version, this does not fall in that category, so the shelf life of this book is quite long compared to other books in the same space.

The book will take you on a fantastic journey, and in doing so, it follows a structure that is quite intuitive and exciting at the same time.

What this book covers

The book is divided into three parts. Each part contains a few chapters, and when a part is completed, readers will have a clear picture of that part of the book in a holistic fashion. The parts are designed and structured in such a way that the reader is first introduced to major functional and technical aspects; then in the following part, or rather the final part, things will all come together. At the end of the book, readers will have an operational Data Lake.

Part 1, *Overview*, introduces the reader to various concepts relating to data, Data Lake and important components . It consists of four chapters and as detailed below, each chapter well-defined goal to be achieved.

Chapter 1, *Introduction to Data*, introduces the reader to the book in general and then explains what data is and its relevance to the enterprise. The chapter explains the reasons as to why data in modern world is important and how it can/should be used. Real-life use cases have been showcased to explain the significance of data and how data is transforming businesses today. These real-life use cases will help readers to start their creative juices flowing and get thinking about how they can make a difference to their enterprise using data.

Chapter 2, *Comprehensive Concepts of a Data Lake*, deepens further into the details of the concept of a Data Lake and explains use of Data Lake in addressing the problems faced by enterprises. This chapter also provides a sneak preview around Lambda architecture and how it can be leveraged for Data Lake. The reader would thus get introduced to the concept of a Data Lake and the various approaches that organizations have adopted to build Data Lake.

Chapter 3, *Lambda Architecture as a Pattern for Data Lake*, introduces the reader into details of Lambda architecture, its various components and the connection between Data Lake and this architecture pattern. In this chapter the reader will get details around Lambda architecture, with the reasons of its inception and the specific problems that it solves. The chapter also provides the reader with ability to understand the core concepts of Lambda architecture and how to apply it in an enterprise. The reader will understand various patterns and components that can be leveraged to define lambda architecture both in the batch and real-time processing spaces. The reader would have enough background on data, Data Lake and Lambda architecture by now, and can move onto the next section of implementing Data Lake for your enterprise.

Chapter 4, *Applied Lambda for Data Lake*, introduces reader to technologies which can be used for each layer (component) in Lambda architecture and will also help the reader choose one lead technology in the market which we feel very good at this point in time. In this chapter, the reader will understand various Hadoop distributions in the current landscape of Big Data technologies, and how they can be leveraged for applying Lambda architecture in an enterprise Data Lake. In the context of these technologies, the reader will understand the details of and architectural motivations behind batch, speed and serving layer in an enterprise Data Lake.

Part 2, *Technical Building Blocks of Data Lake*, introduces reader to many technologies which will be part of the Data Lake implementation. Each chapter covers a technology which will slowly build the Data Lake and the use case namely Single Customer View (SCV). Almost all the important technical details of the technology being discussed in each chapter would be covered in a holistic fashion as in-depth coverage is out of scope of this book. It consists of six chapters and each chapter has a goal well defined to be achieved as detailed below.

Chapter 5, *Data Acquisition of Batch Data using Apache Sqoop*, delves deep into Apache Sqoop. It gives reasons for this choice and also gives the reader other technology options with good amount of details. The chapter also gives a detailed example connecting Data Lake and Lambda architecture. In this chapter the reader will understand Sqoop framework and similar tools in the space for data loads from an enterprise data source into a Data Lake. The reader will understand the technical details around Sqoop and architecturally the problems that it solves. The reader will also be taken through examples, where the Sqoop will be seen in action and various steps involved in using it with Hadoop technologies.

Chapter 6, *Data Acquisition of Stream Data using Apache Flume*, delves deep into Apache Flume, thus connecting technologies in purview of Data Lake and Lambda architecture. The reader will understand Flume as a framework and its various patterns by which it can be leveraged for Data Lake. The reader will also understand the Flume architecture and technical details around using it to acquire and consume data using this framework in detail, with specific capabilities around transaction control and data replay with working example. The reader will also understand how to use flume with streaming technologies for stream based processing.

Chapter 7, *Messaging Layer using Apache Kafka*, delves deep into Apache Kafka. This part of the book initially gives the reader the reason for choosing a particular technology and also gives details of other technology options. . In this chapter, the reader would understand Kafka as a message oriented middleware and how it's compared with other messaging engines. The reader will get to know details around Kafka and its functioning and how it can be leveraged for building scale-out capabilities, from the perspective of client (publisher), broker and consumer(subscriber). This reader will also understand how to integrate Kafka with Hadoop components for acquiring enterprise data and what capabilities this integration brings to Data Lake.

Chapter 8, *Data Processing using Apache Flink*, the reader in this chapter would understand the concepts around streaming and stream based processing, and specifically in reference to Apache Flink. The reader will get deep into using Apache Flink in context of Data Lake and in the Big Data technology landscape for near real time processing of data with working examples. The reader will also realize how a streaming functionality would depend on various other layers in architecture and how these layers can influence the streaming capability.

Chapter 9, *Data Storage using Apache Hadoop*, delves deep into Apache Hadoop. In this chapter, the reader would get deeper into Hadoop Landscape with various Hadoop components and their functioning and specific capabilities that these components can provide for an enterprise Data Lake. Hadoop in context of Data Lake is explained at an implementation level and how Hadoop frameworks capabilities around file storage, file formats and map-reduce capabilities can constitute the foundation for a Data Lake and specific patterns that can be applied to this stack for near real time capabilities.

Chapter 10, *Indexed Data Store using Elasticsearch*, delves deep into Elasticsearch. The reader will understand Elasticsearch as data indexing framework and various data analyzers provided by the framework for efficient searches. The reader will also understand how elasticsearch can be leveraged for Data Lake and data at scale with efficient sharding and distribution mechanisms for consistent performance. The reader will also understand how elasticsearch can be used for fast streaming and how it can used for high performance applications with working examples.

Part 3, *Bringing it all together*, will bring together technical components from part one and two of this book to give you a holistic picture of Data Lakes. We will bring in additional concepts and technologies in a brief fashion so that, if needed, you can explore those aspects in more detail according to your enterprise requirements. Again, delving deep into the technologies covered in this chapter is out of the scope of this book. But we want you to be aware of these additional technologies and how they can be brought into our Data Lake implementation if the need arises. It consists of two chapters, and each chapter has a goal well defined to be achieved, as detailed here.

Chapter 11, *Data Lake components working together*, after introducing reader into Data Lake, Lambda architecture, various technologies, this chapter brings the whole puzzle together and brings in a holistic picture to the reader. The reader at this stage should feel accomplished and can take in the codebase as is into the organization and show it working. In this chapter, the reader, would realize how to integrate various aspects of Data Lake to implement a fully functional Data Lake. The reader will also realize the completeness of Data Lake with working examples that would combine all the learning from previous chapters into a running implementation.

Chapter 12, *Data Lake Use Case Suggestions*, throughout the book the reader is taken through a use case in the form of "Single Customer View"; however while going through the book, there are other use cases in pipeline relevant to their organization which reader can start thinking. This provoking of thought deepens into bit more during this chapter. The reader will understand and realize various use cases that can reap great benefits from a Data Lake and help optimize their cost of ownership, operations, reactiveness and help these uses with required intelligence derived from data. The reader, in this chapter, will also realize the variety of these use cases and the extents to which an enterprise Data Lake can be helpful for each of these use cases.

What you need for this book

This book is for developers, architects, and product/project owners, for realizing Lambda-architecture-based Data Lakes for Enterprises. This book comprises working examples to help the reader understand and observe various concepts around Data Lake and its basic implementation. In order to run the examples, one will need access to various pieces of open source software, required infrastructure, and development IDE. Specific efforts have been made to keep the examples simple and leverage commonly available frameworks and components. The operating system used for running these examples is CentOS 7, but these examples can run on any flavour of the Linux operating system.

Who this book is for

- Java developers and architects who would like to implement Data Lake for their enterprise
- Java developers who aim to get hands-on experience on Lambda Architecture and Big Data technologies
- Java developers who would like to discover the world of Big Data and have an urge to implement a practical solution using those technologies.

Conventions

In this book, you will find a number of text styles that distinguish between different kinds of information. Here are some examples of these styles and an explanation of their meaning.

Code words in text, database table names, folder names, filenames, file extensions, pathnames, dummy URLs, user input, and Twitter handles are shown as follows: "Rename the completed spool file to `spool-1` as specified in the earlier example."

A block of code is set as follows:

```
agent.sources = spool-source
agent.sources.spool-source.type=spooldir
agent.sources.spool-source.spoolDir=/home/centos/flume-data
agent.sources.spool-source.interceptors=ts uuid
```

Any command-line input or output is written as follows:

```
${FLUME_HOME}/bin/flume-ng agent --conf ${FLUME_HOME}/conf/  -f
${FLUME_HOME}/conf/spool-fileChannel-kafka-flume-conf.properties  -n
agent -Dflume.root.logger=INFO,console
```

New terms and **important words** are shown in bold. Words that you see on the screen, for example, in menus or dialog boxes, appear in the text like this: " Without minimum or no delay (**NRT: Near Real Time or Real time**) the company wanted the data produced to be moved to Hadoop system"

Warnings or important notes appear in a box like this.

Tips and tricks appear like this.

Reader feedback

Feedback from our readers is always welcome. Let us know what you think about this book-what you liked or disliked. Reader feedback is important for us as it helps us develop titles that you will really get the most out of.

To send us general feedback, simply e-mail `feedback@packtpub.com`, and mention the book's title in the subject of your message.

If there is a topic that you have expertise in and you are interested in either writing or contributing to a book, see our author guide at `www.packtpub.com/authors`.

Customer support

Now that you are the proud owner of a Packt book, we have a number of things to help you to get the most from your purchase.

Downloading the example code

You can download the example code files for this book from your account at `http://www.packtpub.com`. If you purchased this book elsewhere, you can visit `http://www.packtpub.com/support` and register to have the files e-mailed directly to you.

You can download the code files by following these steps:

1. Log in or register to our website using your e-mail address and password.
2. Hover the mouse pointer on the **SUPPORT** tab at the top.
3. Click on **Code Downloads & Errata**.
4. Enter the name of the book in the **Search** box.
5. Select the book for which you're looking to download the code files.
6. Choose from the drop-down menu where you purchased this book from.
7. Click on **Code Download**.

Once the file is downloaded, please make sure that you unzip or extract the folder using the latest version of:

- WinRAR / 7-Zip for Windows
- Zipeg / iZip / UnRarX for Mac
- 7-Zip / PeaZip for Linux

The code bundle for the book is also hosted on GitHub at `https://github.com/PacktPublishing/Data-Lake-for-Enterprises`. We also have other code bundles from our rich catalog of books and videos available at `https://github.com/PacktPublishing/`. Check them out!

Errata

Although we have taken every care to ensure the accuracy of our content, mistakes do happen. If you find a mistake in one of our books-maybe a mistake in the text or the code-we would be grateful if you could report this to us. By doing so, you can save other readers from frustration and help us improve subsequent versions of this book. If you find any errata, please report them by visiting http://www.packtpub.com/submit-errata, selecting your book, clicking on the **Errata Submission Form** link, and entering the details of your errata. Once your errata are verified, your submission will be accepted and the errata will be uploaded to our website or added to any list of existing errata under the Errata section of that title.

To view the previously submitted errata, go to https://www.packtpub.com/books/content/support and enter the name of the book in the search field. The required information will appear under the **Errata** section.

Piracy

Piracy of copyrighted material on the Internet is an ongoing problem across all media. At Packt, we take the protection of our copyright and licenses very seriously. If you come across any illegal copies of our works in any form on the Internet, please provide us with the location address or website name immediately so that we can pursue a remedy.

Please contact us at copyright@packtpub.com with a link to the suspected pirated material.

We appreciate your help in protecting our authors and our ability to bring you valuable content.

Questions

If you have a problem with any aspect of this book, you can contact us at questions@packtpub.com, and we will do our best to address the problem.

Part 1 - Overview

This part of the book introduces the reader to various concepts in regards to Data, Data Lake and its important components . It consists of four chapters and as detailed below, each chapter has a goal well defined to be achieved.

Chapter 1, *Introduction to Data*, introduces the reader to the book in general and then takes the reader into explaining what data is and its relevance to the enterprise. The chapter explains the reasons as to why data in modern world is important and how it can/should be used. Real-life use cases have been showcased to explain the significance of data and how data is transforming businesses doing their business today. These real-life use case citations will help readers to start their creative juices flowing and in fact start thinking as to how they can make a difference to their enterprise using data.

Chapter 2, *Comprehensive Data Lake concepts*, further deepens into the details of the concept - Data Lake and explains use of Data Lake in addressing the problems faced by enterprises. This chapter also provides a sneak preview around Lambda architecture and how it can be leveraged for Data Lake. The reader would thus get introduced to the concepts of Data Lake and the various approaches that organizations have adopted to build Data Lakes.

Chapter 3, *Lambda Architecture as a Pattern for Data Lake*, introduces the reader into details of Lambda Architecture, its various components and the connection that it makes between Data Lake and this architecture pattern. In this chapter the reader will get into the details around Lambda architecture with reasons of its inception and the specific problems that it solves. It also provides the reader with ability to understand the core of Lambda architecture and how to apply it in an enterprise. The reader will understand various patterns and components that can be leveraged to define lambda architecture both in batch as well as real-time processing space. The reader would have enough background on Data, Data Lake and Lambda Architecture by now and can go onto the next section of implementing Data Lake for your enterprise.

`Chapter 4`, *Applied Lambda for Data Lake,* introduces reader to technologies which can be used for each layer (component) in Lambda Architecture and will also help the reader choose one lead technology in the market which we feel very good at this point in time. In this chapter, the reader will understand various Hadoop distributions in the current landscape of Big Data technologies and how it can be leveraged for applying Lambda architecture in an enterprise Data Lake. In context of these technologies, the reader will understand details and architectural motivations behind batch, speed and serving layer in an enterprise Data Lake.

Part 2 - Technical Building blocks of Data Lake

This part of the book introduces reader to many technologies which will be part of the Data Lake implementation. Each chapter covers a technology which will slowly build the Data Lake and the use case namely Single Customer View (SCV) in the due course. Almost all the important technical details of the technology being discussed in each chapter would be covered in a holistic fashion as in-depth coverage is out of scope of this book. It consists of six chapters and each chapter has a goal well defined to be achieved as detailed below.

Chapter 5, *Data Acquisition of Batch Data using Apache Sqoop*, delves deep into Apache Sqoop. It gives reasons for this choice and also gives the reader other technology options with good amount of details. The chapter also gives a detailed example connecting Data Lake and Lambda Architecture. In this chapter the reader will understand Sqoop framework and similar tools in the space for data loads from an enterprise data source into a Data Lake. The reader will understand the technical details around Sqoop and architecturally the problems that it solves. The reader will also be taken through examples, where the Sqoop will be seen in action and various steps involved in using it with Hadoop technologies.

Chapter 6, *Data Acquisition of Stream Data using Apache Flume*, delves deep into Apache Flume, thus connecting technologies in purview of Data Lake and Lambda Architecture. The reader will understand Flume as a framework and its various patterns by which it can be leveraged for Data Lake. The reader will also understand the Flume architecture and technical details around using it to acquire and consume data using this framework in detail, with specific capabilities around transaction control and data replay with working example. The reader will also understand how to use flume with streaming technologies for stream based processing.

Chapter 7, *Messaging Layer using Apache Kafka,* delves deep into Apache Kafka. This part of the book initially gives the reader the reason for choosing a particular technology and also gives details of other technology options. . In this chapter, the reader would understand Kafka as a message oriented middleware and how it's compared with other messaging engines. The reader will get to know details around Kafka and its functioning and how it can be leveraged for building scale-out capabilities, from the perspective of client (publisher), broker and consumer(subscriber). This reader will also understand how to integrate Kafka with Hadoop components for acquiring enterprise data and what capabilities this integration brings to Data Lake.

Chapter 8, *Data Processing using Apache Flink,* the reader in this chapter would understand the concepts around streaming and stream based processing, and specifically in reference to Apache Flink. The reader will get deep into using Apache Flink in context of Data Lake and in the Big Data technology landscape for near real time processing of data with working examples. The reader will also realize how a streaming functionality would depend on various other layers in architecture and how these layers can influence the streaming capability.

Chapter 9, *Data Storage using Apache Hadoop,* delves deep into Apache Hadoop. In this chapter, the reader would get deeper into Hadoop Landscape with various Hadoop components and their functioning and specific capabilities that these components can provide for an enterprise Data Lake. Hadoop in context of Data Lake is explained at an implementation level and how Hadoop frameworks capabilities around file storage, file formats and map-reduce capabilities can constitute the foundation for a Data Lake and specific patterns that can be applied to this stack for near real time capabilities.

Chapter 10, *Indexed Data Store using Elasticsearch,* delves deep into Elasticsearch. The reader will understand Elasticsearch as data indexing framework and various data analyzers provided by the framework for efficient searches. The reader will also understand how elasticsearch can be leveraged for Data Lake and data at scale with efficient sharding and distribution mechanisms for consistent performance. The reader will also understand how elasticsearch can be used for fast streaming and how it can used for high performance applications with working examples.

Part 3 - Bringing It All Together

This part of the books brings together technical components from part one and two of this book to give you a holistic picture of Data Lakes. We will bring in additional concepts and technologies in a brief fashion, so that you can explore those aspects in more detail according to your enterprise requirements. Again, delving deep into the technologies covered in this chapter is out of the scope of this book. But we want you to be aware of these additional technologies and how they can be brought into our Data Lake implementation if the need arises. It consists of two chapters, and each chapter has a goal well defined to be achieved, as detailed below.

`Chapter 11`, *Data Lake Components Working Together*, after introducing reader into Data Lake, Lambda Architecture, various technologies, this chapter brings the whole puzzle together and brings in a holistic picture to the reader. The reader at this stage should feel accomplished and can take in the codebase as is into the organization and show it working. In this chapter, the reader, would realize how to integrate various aspects of Data Lake to implement a fully functional Data Lake. The reader will also realize the completeness of Data Lake with working examples that would combine all the learnings from previous chapters into a running implementation.

`Chapter 12`, *Data Lake Use Case Suggestions*, throughout the book the reader is taken through a use case in the form of "Single Customer View"; however while going through the book, there are other use cases in pipeline relevant to their organization which reader can start thinking. This provoking of thought deepens into bit more during this chapter. The reader will understand and realize various use cases that can reap great benefits from a Data Lake and help optimize their cost of ownership, operations, reactiveness and help these uses with required intelligence derived from data. The reader, in this chapter, will also realize the variety of these use cases and the extents to which an enterprise Data Lake can be helpful for each of these use cases.

1
Introduction to Data

Through this book, we are embarking on a huge task of implementing a technology masterpiece for your enterprise. In this journey, you will not only have to learn many new tools and technologies but also have to know a good amount of jargon and theoretical stuff. This will surely help you in your journey to reach the ultimate goal of creating the masterpiece, namely Data lake.

This part of the book aims at preparing you for a tough road ahead so that you are quite clear in the head as to what you want to achieve. The concept of a Data lake has evolved over time in enterprises, starting with concepts of data warehouse which contained data for long term retention and stored differently for reporting and historic needs. Then the concept of data mart came into existence which would expose small sets of data with enterprise relevant attributes. Data lake evolved with these concepts as a central data repository for an enterprise that could capture data as is, produce processed data, and serve the most relevant enterprise information.

The topic or technology of Data lake is not new, but very few enterprises have implemented a fully functional Data lake in their organization. Through this book, we want enterprises to start thinking seriously on investing in a Data lake. Also, with the help of you engineers, we want to give the top management in your organization a glimpse of what can be achieved by creating a Data lake which can then be used to implement a use case more relevant to your own enterprise.

So, fasten your seatbelt, hold on tight, and let's start the journey!

Rest assured that after completing this book, you will help your enterprise (small or big) to think and model their business in a data-centric approach, using Data lake as its technical nucleus.

The intent of this chapter is to give the reader insight into data, big data, and some of the important details in connection with data. The chapter gives some important textbook-based definitions, which need to be understood in depth so that the reader is convinced about how data is relevant to an enterprise. The reader would also have grasped the main crux of the difference between data and big data. The chapter soon delves into the types of data in depth and where we can find in an enterprise.

The latter part of the chapter tries to enlighten the user with the current state of enterprises with regard to data management and also tries to give a high-level glimpse on what enterprises are looking to transform themselves into, with data at the core. The whole book is based on a real-life example, and the last section is dedicated to explaining this example in more detail. The example is detailed in such a manner that the reader would get a good amount of concepts implemented in the form of this example.

Exploring data

Data refers to a set of values of qualitative or quantitative variables.

> *Data is measured, collected and reported, and analyzed, whereupon it can be visualized using graphs, images or other analysis tools. Data as a general concept refers to the fact that some existing information or knowledge is represented or coded in some form suitable for better usage or processing.*

> *- Wikipedia*

Data can be broadly categorized into three types:

- Structured data
- Unstructured data
- Semi-structured data

Structured data is data that we conventionally capture in a business application in the form of data residing in a relational database (**relational database management system (RDBMS)**) or non-relational database (NoSQL - originally referred to as non SQL).

Structured data can again be broadly categorized into two, namely raw and cleansed data. Data that is taken in as it is, without much cleansing or filtering, is called raw data. Data that is taken in with a lot of cleansing and filtering, catering to a particular analysis by business users, is called cleansed data.

All the other data, which doesn't fall in the category of structured, can be called unstructured data. Data collected in the form of videos, images, and so on are examples of unstructured data.

There is a third category called semi-structured data, which has come into existence because of the Internet and is becoming more and more predominant with the evolution of social sites. The Wikipedia definition of semi-structured data is as follows:

> *Semi-structured data is a form of structured data that does not conform with the formal structure of data models associated with relational databases or other forms of data tables, but nonetheless contains tags or other markers to separate semantic elements and enforce hierarchies of records and fields within the data. Therefore, it is also known as self-describing structure.*

Some of the examples of semi-structured data are the well-known data formats, namely **JavaScript Object Notation (JSON)** and **Extensible Markup Language (XML)**.

The following figure (*Figure 01*) covers whatever we discussed on different types of data, in a pictorial fashion. Please don't get confused by seeing spreadsheets and text files in the structured section. This is because the data presented in the following figure is in the form of a record, which, indeed, qualifies it to be structured data:

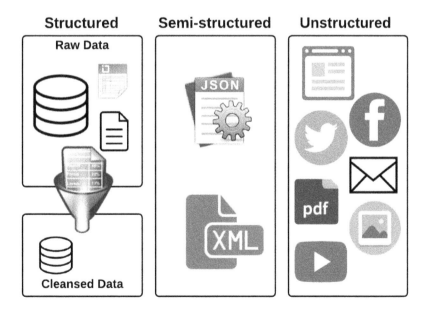

Figure 01: Types *of Data*

What is Enterprise Data?

Enterprise data refers to data shared by employees and their partners in an organization, across various departments and different locations, spread across different continents. This is data that is valuable to the enterprise, such as financial data, business data, employee personal data, and so on, and the enterprise spends considerable time and money to keep this data secure and clean in all aspects.

During all this, this so-called enterprise data passes the current state and becomes stale, or rather dead, and lives in some form of storage, which is hard to analyze and retrieve. This is where the significance of this data and having a single place to analyze it in order to discover various future business opportunities leads to the implementation of a Data lake.

Enterprise data falls into three major high-level categories, as detailed next:

- Master data refers to the data that details the main entities within an enterprise. Looking at the master data, one can, in fact, find the business that the enterprise is involved in. This data is usually managed and owned by different departments. The other categories of data, as follows, need the master data to make meaningful values of them.
- Transaction data refers to the data that various applications (internal and external) produce while transacting various business processes within an enterprise. This also includes people-related data, which, in a way, doesn't categorize itself as business data but is significant. This data, when analyzed, can give businesses many optimization techniques to be employed. This data also depends and often refers to the master data.
- Analytic data refers to data that is actually derived from the preceding two kinds of enterprise data. This data gives enough insight into various entities (master data) in the enterprise and can also combine with transaction data to make positive recommendations, which can be implemented by the enterprise, after performing the necessary due diligence.

The previously explained different types of enterprise data are very significant to the enterprise, because of which most enterprises have a process for the management of these types of data, commonly known as enterprise data management. This aspect is explained in more detail in the following section.

The following diagram shows the various enterprise data types available and how they interact with each other:

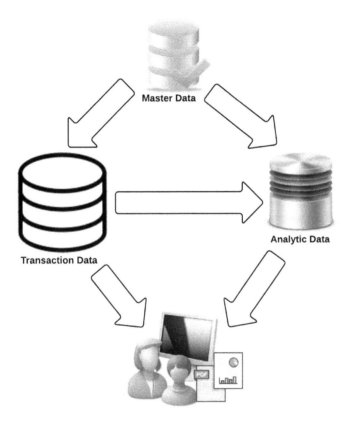

Figure 02: Different *types of Enterprise Data*

The preceding figure shows that master data is being utilized by both transaction and analytic data. Analytic data also depends on transaction data for deriving meaningful insights as needed by users who use these data for various clients.

Enterprise Data Management

Ability of an organization to precisely define, easily integrate and effectively retrieve data for both internal applications and external communication

- Wikipedia

EDM emphasizes data precision, granularity and meaning and is concerned with how the content is integrated into business applications as well as how it is passed along from one business process to another.

- Wikipedia

As the preceding wikipedia definition clearly states, EDM is the process or strategy of determining how this enterprise data needs to be stored, where it has to be stored, and what technologies it has to use to store and retrieve this data in an enterprise. Being very valuable, this data has to be secured using the right controls and needs to be managed and owned in a defined fashion. It also defines how the data can be taken out to communicate with both internal and external applications alike. Furthermore, the policies and processes around the data exchange have to be well defined.

Looking at the previous paragraph, it seems that it is very easy to have EDM in place for an enterprise, but in reality, it is very difficult. In an enterprise, there are multiple departments, and each department churns out data; based on the significance of these departments, the data churned would also be very relevant to the organization as a whole. Because of the distinction and data relevance, the owner of each data in EDM has different interests, causing conflicts and thus creating problems in the enterprise. This calls for various policies and procedures along with ownership of each data in EDM.

In the context of this book, learning about enterprise data, enterprise data management, and issues around maintaining an EDM are quite significant. This is the reason why it's good to know these aspects at the start of the book itself. In the following sections we will discuss big data concepts and ways in which big data can be incorporated into enterprise data management and extend its capabilities with opportunities that could not be imagined without big data technologies.

Big data concepts

Let me start this section by giving the Wikipedia definition for Big Data:

> *Big data is a term for data sets that are so large or complex that traditional data processing applications are inadequate to deal with them. The term "big data" often refers simply to the use of predictive analytics, user behaviour analytics, or certain other advanced data analytics methods that extract value from data, and seldom to a particular size of data set.*

> *- Wikipedia*

Let's try explaining, the two sentences that are given in the preceding Wikipedia definition. Earlier, big data referred to any data that is large and complex in nature. There isn't any specified size of data for it to be called big data. This data was considered so big that conventional data processing applications found it difficult to use it in a meaningful fashion. In the last decade or so, many technologies have evolved in this space in order to analyze such big data in the enterprise. Nowadays, the term big data is used to refer to any sort of analysis method that can comprehend and extract this complex data and make valuable use of it in the enterprise.

Big data and 4Vs

Whenever you encountered the term big data being overly used, you must have come across an important aspect with regard to it, called 4Vs (until recently, it was 3Vs, and then the fourth, very significant, V got introduced). The 4Vs, namely variety, velocity, volume, and veracity (in no particular order) determine whether the data we call Big Data really qualifies to be called big:

- **Variety**: In the context of big data, variety has a very important place. Variety refers to vivid types of data and the myriad sources from which these are arrived at. With the proliferation of technologies and the ever-growing number of applications (enterprise and different personal ones), there is high emphasis on data variety. This is not going to come down any time soon; rather, this is set to increase over a period of time, for sure. Broadly, data types can be categorized into structured and unstructured. Applications during this time deal mainly with structured data stored mostly in a **relational database management system (RDBMS)**. This is very common, but nowadays, there has been the need to look at more unstructured data, and some of the examples can be video content, image content, file content in the form of binaries, and so on.

- **Velocity**: In the context of big data, velocity is referred to in two aspects. First is the rate at which the data is generated, and second is the capability by which the enormous amount of data can be analyzed in real time to derive some meaningful conclusions. As the proverb goes, *Time is money*, this V is a very important aspect, which makes it easy to take quick decisions in real time. This aspect is one of the strongholds of some of the businesses, especially retail. Giving the customer a personalized and timely offer can be the deciding factor of the customer buying a product from you or ditching you to select a more favorable one.

- **Volume**: In the context of big data, volume refers to the amount/scale of data that needs to be analyzed for a meaningful result to be derived. There isn't a quantitative figure that categorizes a data to be falling into big data. But usually, this volume is definitely more than what a conventional application is handling as of now. So, in general, this is quite big and does pose a problem for a traditional application to deal with in a day-to-day fashion **(OLTP - OnLine Transaction Processing**). For many businesses, analyzing and making use of social data has become a necessity. These social apps (Facebook, Google+, LinkedIn, and so on) have billions of registered users producing billions of data (structured and unstructured) in a day-to-day fashion. In addition to this, there are applications that themselves produce a huge amount of data in the form of conventional transactions and other analytics (behavioral, location-based, and so on). Also, with the growing number of wearables and sensors that emit data every millisecond, the volume aspect is going to be very important, and this is not going to come down any time soon.

As detailed in the previous section, until recently, there used to be 3Vs. But quite recently, the fourth V was introduced by IBM, namely veracity. For data growing at an exponential rate and as deduced from different reliable and unreliable sources, the significance of this V is huge.

You must have already heard/read of fake news/material being circulated in various social media when there is something important happening in the world. This V brings this a very important aspect of accuracy in big data. With proliferation of data, especially in social channels, this V is going to be very important, and rather than 3Vs, it is leaning highly towards 4Vs of Big Data.

- **Veracity**: In the context of big data, veracity refers to accuracy of data being analyzed to get to a meaningful result. With a variety of sources, especially the not-so-reliable user-entered unstructured data, the data coming from some of these channels has to be consumed in a judicial manner. If an enterprise wants to use this data to generate business, its authenticity has to be verified to an even greater extent.

Big Data and its significant 4V's are shown in a pictorial representation, as follows:

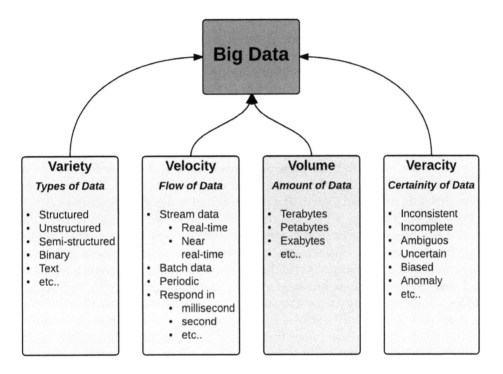

Figure 03: 4V's of Big Data

Figure 03 clearly shows what the 4V's are and what each of these V's means, with adequate bullet points for easy understanding.

Relevance of data

To any enterprise, data is very important. Enterprises have been collecting a good amount of past data and keeping it in a data warehouse for analysis. This proves the importance of data for enterprises for past data analysis and using this for future enterprise growth. In the last decade or so, with the proliferation of social media and myriads of applications (internal to the enterprise and external cloud offerings), the data collected has grown exponentially. This data is increasing in amount as the day goes by, but enterprises are finding it really difficult to make use of these high volumes of diverse data in an effective manner. Data relevance is at the highest for enterprises nowadays as they are now trying to make use of this collected data to transform or energize their existing business.

A business user when fed with these huge amounts of data and right tools can derive real good value. For example, if customer-related data from various applications flows into a place where this data can be analyzed, this data could give a good amount of valuable insights, such as who is the customer who engages with various website pages of the enterprise and how. These derivations can be used as a way in which they can look at either changing their existing business model or tweaking certain business processes to derive maximum profit for the enterprise. For example, looking at various insights from centralized customer data, a new business model can be thought through, say in the form of starting to look at giving loyalty points to such customers. This data can also be made use of, giving more personalized offers closer to customer recommendations. For example, looking at the customer behavior, rather than giving a general offer, more personalized offers suiting the customer's needs could be offered. However, these are fully dependent on the business, and there isn't one approach fitting all the scenarios. These data can, however, be transformed and cleansed to make them more usable for a business user through different data visualizations techniques available as of now in the form of different types of graphs and charts.

Data is relevant, but where exactly this data lives in an enterprise is detailed in the following section.

Vit Soupal (Head of Big Data, *Deutsche Telekom AG*) in one of his blogs defines these 4V's of big data as technical parameters and defines another three V's bringing in business into context. We thought that we would not cover these additional V's in our book, but these are definitely required for Data lake (Big Data) to be successful in an enterprise.

These additional 3 Vs (business parameters) are as follows:

- **Vision**: Every enterprise embarking on Big Data (Data lake) should have a well-defined vision and should also be ready to transform processes to make full use of it. Also, management in the enterprise should fully understand this and should be in a position to make decisions considering its merits.
- **Visualization**: Data lake is expected to have a huge amount of data. Some will make a lot of sense and some won't at certain points in time. Data scientists work on these data and derive meaningful deductions, and these need to be communicated in an effective manner to the management. For Big Data to be successful, visualization of meaningful data in various formats is required and mandated.
- **Value**: Big Data should be of value to the enterprise. These values could bring about changes in business processes or bring in new innovative solutions (say IoT) and entirely transform the business model.

Vit also gives a very good way of representing these 7 V's as shown in the following figure:

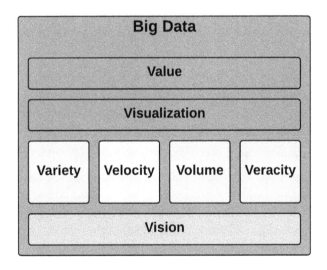

Figure 04: 7 V's of big data

Figure 04 shows that Big Data becomes successful in an enterprise only if both business and technical attributes are met.

The preceding figure (Figure 04) conveys that Data lake needs to have a well-defined vision and then a different variety of data flows with different velocity and volume into the lake. The data coming into the lake has different quality attributes (veracity). The data in Data lake requires various kinds of visualization to be really useful to various departments and higher management. These useful visualizations will derive various value to the organization and would also help in making various decisions helpful to the enterprise. Technical attributes in a Data lake are needed for sure (variety, velocity, volume, and veracity), but business attributes/parameters are very much required (vision, visualization, and value), and these make Data lake a success in the enterprise.

Quality of data

There is no doubt that high-quality data (cleansed data) is an irresistible asset to an organization. But in the same way, bad quality or mediocre quality data, if used to make decisions for an enterprise, cannot only be bad for your enterprise but can also tarnish the brand value of your enterprise, which is very hard to get back. The data, in general, becomes not so usable if it is inconsistent, duplicate, ambiguous, and incomplete. Business users wouldn't consider using these data if they do not have a pleasant experience while using these data for various analyzes. That's when we realize the importance of the fourth V, namely veracity.

Quality of data is an assessment of data to ascertain its fit for the purpose in a given context, where it is going to be used. There are various characteristics based on which data quality can be ascertained. Some of which, not in any particular order, are as follows:

- **Correctness/accuracy**: This measures the degree to which the collected data describes the real-world entity that's being captured.
- **Completeness**: This is measured by counting the attributes captured during the data-capturing process to the expected/defined attributes.
- **Consistency**: This is measured by comparing the data captured in multiple systems, converging them, and showing a single picture (single source of truth).
- **Timeliness**: This is measured by the ability to provide high-quality data to the right people in the right context at a specified/defined time.
- **Metadata**: This is measured by the amount of additional data about captured data. As the term suggests, it is data about data, which is useful for defining or getting more value about the data itself.
- **Data lineage**: Keeping track of data across a data life cycle can have immense benefits to the organization. Such traceability of data can provide very interesting business insights to an organization.

There are characteristics/dimensions other than what have been described in the preceding section, which can also determine the quality of data. But this is just detailed in the right amount here so that at least you have this concept clear in the head; these will become clearer as you go through the next chapters in this book.

Where does this data live in an enterprise?

The data in an enterprise lives in different formats in the form of raw data, binaries (images and videos), and so on, and in different application's persistent storage internally within an organization or externally in a private or public cloud. Let's first classify these different types of data. One way to categorize where the data lives is as follows:

- Intranet (within enterprise)
- Internet (external to enterprise)

Another way in which data living in an enterprise can be categorized is in the form of different formats in which they exist, as follows:

- Data stores or persistent stores (RDBMS or NoSQL)
- Traditional data warehouses (making use of RDBMS, NoSQL etc.)
- File stores

Now let's get into a bit more detail about these different data categories.

Intranet (within enterprise)

In simple terms, enterprise data that only exists and lives within its own private network falls in the category of intranet.

Various applications within an enterprise exist within the enterprise's own network, and access is denied to others apart from designated employees. Due to this reason, the data captured using these applications lives within an enterprise in a secure and private fashion.

The applications churning out this data can be data of the employees or various transactional data captured while using enterprises in day-to-day applications.

Technologies used to establish intranet for an enterprise include **Local Area Network (LAN)** and **Wide Area Network (WAN)**. Also, there are multiple application platforms that can be used within an enterprise, enabling intranet culture within the enterprise and its employees. The data could be stored in a structured format in different stores, such as traditional RDBMS and NoSQL databases. In addition to these stores, there lies unstructured data in the form of different file types. Also, most enterprises have traditional data warehouses, where data is cleansed and made ready to be analyzed.

Internet (external to enterprise)

A decade or so ago, most enterprises had their own data centers, and almost all the data would reside in that. But with the evolution of cloud, enterprises are looking to put some data outside their own data center into cloud, with security and controls in place, so that the data is never accessed by unauthorized people. Going the cloud way also takes a good amount of operational costs away from the enterprise, and that is one of the biggest advantages. Let's get into the subcategories in this space in more detail.

Business applications hosted in cloud

With the various options provided by cloud providers, such as **SaaS**, **PaaS**, **IaaS**, and so on, there are ways in which business applications can be hosted in cloud, taking care of all the essential enterprise policies and governance. Because of this, many enterprises have chosen this as a way to host internally developed applications in these cloud providers. Employees use these applications from the cloud and go about doing their day-to-day operations very similar to how they would have for a business application hosted within an enterprise's own data center.

Third–party cloud solutions

With so many companies now providing their applications/services hosted in cloud, enterprises needing them could use these as is and not worry about maintaining and managing on-premises infrastructure. These products, just by being on the cloud, provide enterprises with huge incentives with regard to how they charge for these services.

Due to this benefit, enterprises favorably choose these cloud products, and due to its mere nature, the enterprises now save their data (very specific to their business)in the cloud on someone else infrastructure, with the cloud provider having full control on how these data live in there.

Google BigQuery is one such piece of software, which, as a service product, allows us to export the enterprise data to their cloud, running this software for various kinds of analysis work. The good thing about these products is that after the analysis, we can decide on whether to keep this data for future use or just discard it. Due to the elastic (ability to expand and contract at will, with regard to hardware in this case) nature of cloud, you can very well ask for a big machine if your analysis is complex, and after use, you can just discard or reduce these servers back to their old configuration.

Due to this nature, **Google BigQuery** calls itself an*Enterprise Cloud Data Warehouse*, and it does stay true to its promise. It gives speed and scale to enterprises along with the important security, reliability, and availability. It also gives integration with other similar software products again in cloud for various other needs.

Google BigQuery is just one example; there are other similar software available in cloud with varying degrees of features. Enterprises nowadays need to do many things quickly, and they don't want to spend time doing research on this and hosting these in their own infrastructure due to various overheads; these solutions give all they want without much trouble and at a very handy price tag.

The list of such solutions at this stage is ever growing, and I don't think that naming these is required. So we picked BigQuery as an example to explain this very nature.

Similar to software as a service available in the cloud, there are many business applications available in cloud as services. One such example is Salesforce. Basically, Salesforce is a **Customer Relationship Management** (**CRM**) solution, but it does have many packaged features in it. It's not a sales pitch, but I just want to give some very important features such business applications in cloud bring to the enterprise. Salesforce brings all the customer information together and allows enterprises to build a customer-centric business model from sales, business analysis, and customer service.

Being in cloud, it also brings many of the features that software as a service in cloud brings.

Because of the ever-increasing impact of cloud on enterprises, a good amount of enterprise data now lives on the Internet (in cloud), obviously taking care of privacy and other common features an enterprise data should comply with to safeguard enterprise's business objectives.

Social data (structured and unstructured)

Social connection of an enterprise nowadays is quite crucial, and even though enterprise data doesn't live in social sites, it does have rich information fed by the real customer on enterprise business and its services.

Comments and suggestions on these special sites can indeed be used to reinvent the way enterprises do business and interact with the customers.

Comments in these social sites can damage the reputation and brand of an enterprise if no due diligence in taken on these comments from customers. The enterprise takes these social sites really seriously nowadays, because of which even though it doesn't have enterprise data, it does have customer reviews and comments, which, in a way, show how customer perceive the brand.

Because of this nature, I would like to classify this data also as enterprise data fed in by non-enterprise users. Its very important to take care of the fourth V, namely veracity in big data while analyzing this data as there are people out there who want to use these just as channels to get some undue advantages while dealing with the enterprise in the process of the business.

Another way of categorizing enterprise data is by the way the data is finally getting stored. Let's see this categorization in more detail in the following section.

Data stores or persistent stores (RDBMS or NoSQL)

This data, whether on premises (enterprise infrastructure) or in cloud, is stored as structured data in the so-called traditional RDBMS or new generation NoSQL persistent stores. This data comes into these stores through business applications, and most of the data is scattered in nature, and enterprises can easily find a sense of each and every data captured without much trouble. The main issue when data is stored in a traditional RDBMS kind of store is when the amount of data grows beyond an acceptable state. In that situation, the amount of analysis that we can make of the data takes a good amount of effort and time. Because of this, enterprises force themselves to segregate this data into production (data that can be queried and made use of by the business application) and non-production (data that is old and not in the production system, rather moved to a different storage).

Because of this segregation, analysis usually spans a few years and doesn't give enterprises a large span of how the business was dealing with certain business parameters. Say for example, if the production has five years of sales data, and 15 years of sales data is in the non-production storage, the users, when dealing with sales data analysis, just have a view of the last five years of data. There might be trends that are changing every five years, and this can only be known when we do an analysis of 20 years of sales data. Most of the time, because of RDBMS, storing and analyzing huge data is not possible. Even if this is possible, it is time consuming and doesn't give a great deal of flexibility, which an analyst looks for. This renders to the analyst a certain restricted analysis, which can be a big problem if the enterprise is looking into this data for business process tweaks.

The so-called new generation NoSQL (different databases in this space have different capabilities) gives more flexibility on analysis and the amount of data storage. It also gives the kind of performance and other aspects that analysts look for, but it still lacks certain aspects.

Even though the data is stored in an individual business application, it doesn't have a single view from various business application data, and that is what implementing a proper Data lake would bring into the enterprise.

Traditional data warehouse

As explained in the previous section, due to the amount of data captured in production business applications, almost all the time, the data in production is segregated from non-production. The non-production data usually lives in different forms/areas of the enterprise and flows into a different data store (usually RDBMS or NoSQL) called the data warehouse. Usually, the data is cleansed and cut out as required by the data analyst. Cutting out the data again puts a boundary on the type of analysis an analyst can do on the data. In most cases, there should be hidden gems of data that haven't flown into the data warehouse, which would result in more analysis, using which the enterprises can tweak certain processes; however, since they are cleansed and cut out, this innovative analysis never happens. This aspect is also something that needs correction. The Data lake approach explained in this book allows the analyst to bring in any data captured in the production business application to do any analysis as the case may be.

The way these data warehouses are created today is by employing an ETL (Extract, Transform, Load) from the production database to the data warehouse database. ETL is entrusted with cleaning the data as needed by the analyst who works with these data warehouses for various analyses.

File stores

Business applications are ever changing, and new applications allow the end users to capture data in different formats apart from keying in data (using a keyboard), which are structured in nature.

Another way in which the end users now feed in data is in the form of documents in different formats. Some of the well-known formats are as follows:

- Different document formats (PDF, DOC, XLS, and so on)
- Binary formats
    - Image-based formats (JPG, PNG, and so on)
    - Audio formats (MP3, RAM, AC3)
    - Video formats (MP4, MPEG, MKV)

As you saw in the previous sections, dealing with structured data itself is in question, and now we are bringing in the analysis of unstructured data. But analysis of this data is also as important nowadays as structured ones. By implementing Data lake, we could bring in new technologies surrounding this lake, which will allow us to make some good value out of this unstructured data as well, using the latest and greatest technologies in this space.

Apart from various file formats and data living in it, we have many applications that allow end users to capture a huge amount of data in the form of sentences, which also need analysis. To deal with these comments from end users manually is a Herculean task, and in this modern age, we need to decipher the sentences/comments in an automatic fashion and get a view of their sentiment. Again, there are many such technologies available that can make sense of this data (free flowing text) and help enterprises deal with it in the right fashion.

For example, if we do have a suggestion capturing system in place for an enterprise and (let's say) we have close to 1000 suggestions that we get in a day, because of the nature of the business, it's very hard to get into the filtering of these suggestions. Here, we could use technologies aiding in the sentiment analysis of these comments, and according to the rating these analysis tools provide, perform an initial level of filtering and then hand it over to the human who can understand and make use of it.

Enterprise's current state

As explained briefly in the previous sections, the current state of enterprise data in an organization can be summarized in bullets points as follows:

- **Conventional DW (Data Warehouse) /BI (Business Intelligence)**:
    - Refined/ cleansed data transferred from production business application using ETL.
    - Data earlier than a certain period would have already been transferred to a storage, which is hard to retrieve, such as magnetic tape storage.
    - Some of its notable deficiencies are as follows:
        - A subset of production data in a cleansed format exists in DW; for any new element in DW, effort has to be made
        - A subset of the data is again in DW, and the rest gets transferred to permanent storage
        - Usually, analysis is really slow, and it is optimized again to perform queries, which are, to an extent, defined

- **Siloed Big Data**:
    - Some departments would have taken the right step in building big data. But departments generally don't collaborate with each other, and this big data becomes siloed and doesn't give the value of a true big data for the enterprise.
    - Some of its deficiencies are as follows:
        - Because of its siloed nature, the analyst is again constrained and not able to mix and match data between departments.
        - A good amount of money would have been spent to build and maintain/manage this and usually over a period of time is not sustainable.

- **Myriad of non-connected applications**:
    - There is a good amount of applications on premises and on cloud.
    - Applications apart from churning structured data also produce unstructured data.

- Some of the deficiencies are as follows:
  - Don't talk to each other
  - Even if it talks, data scientists are not able to use it in an effective way to transform the enterprise in a meaningful way
  - Replication of technology usage for handling many aspects in each business application

We wouldn't say that creating or investing in Data lake is a silver bullet to solve all the aforementioned deficiencies. But it is definitely a step in the right direction, and every enterprise should at least spend some time discussing whether this is indeed required, and if it is a yes, don't deliberate over it too much and take the next step in the path of implementation.

Data lake is an enterprise initiative, and when built, it has to be with the consent of all the stakeholders, and it should have buy-ins from the top executives. It can definitely find ways to improve processes by which enterprises do business. It can help the higher management know more about their business and can increase the success rate of the decision-making process.

Enterprise digital transformation

Digital transformation is the application of digital technologies to fundamentally impact all aspects of business and society.

- infoworld.com

Digital transformation (**DX**) is an industry buzzword and a very strong initiative that every enterprise is taking without much deliberation. As the word suggests, it refers to transforming enterprises with information technology as one of its core pillars. Investing in technologies would definitely happen as part of this initiative, but data is one of the key aspects in achieving the so-called transformation.

Enterprises has known the importance of data and its analysis more and more in recent times, and that has definitely made every enterprise think out-of-the-box; this initiative is a way to establish data at the center.

As part of this business transformation, enterprises should definitely have Data lake as one of the core investments, with every department agreeing to share their data to flow into this Data lake, without much prejudice or pride.

Enterprises embarking on this journey

A Forrester Consulting research study commissioned by Accenture Interactive found that the key drivers of digital transformation are profitability, customer satisfaction, and increased speed-to-market.

Many enterprises are, in fact, already on the path of digital transformation. It is no more a buzzword, and enterprises are indeed making every effort to transform themselves using technology as one of the drivers and, you guessed it right, the other one being data.

Enterprises taking this path have clearly defined objectives. Obviously, this changes according to the enterprise and the business they are in. But some of the common ones, in no particular order, are as follows:

- Radically improve customer experience
- Reduce cost
- Increase in revenue
- Bring in differentiation from competitors
- Tweak business processes and, in turn, change the business model

Some examples

There are a number of clear examples about what enterprises want to achieve in this space, some of which are as follows:

- Ability to segment customers and give them personalized products. Targeting campaigns to the right person at the right time.
- Bringing in more technologies and reducing manual work, basically digitizing many aspects in the enterprise.
- Using social information clubbed together with enterprise data to make some important decisions.
- Predicting the future in a more quantitative fashion and taking necessary steps and also preparing accordingly, well in advance, obviously.
- Taking business global using technology as an important vehicle.

The next section details one of the use cases that enterprises want to achieve as part of digital transformation, with data as the main contributor. Understanding the use case is important as this is the use case we will try to implement in this book throughout.

Data lake use case enlightenment

We saw the importance of data in an enterprise. What enterprises face today is how to mine this data for information that can be used in favor of the business.

Even if we are able to bring this data into one place somehow, it's quite difficult to deal with this huge quantity of data and that too in a reasonable time. This is when the significance of Data lake comes into the picture. The next chapter details, in a holistic fashion, what Data lake is. Before getting there, let's detail the use case that we are trying to achieve throughout this book, with Data lake taking the center stage.

Data lake implementation using modern technologies would bring in many benefits, some of which are given as follows:

- Ability for business users, using various analyzes, to find various important aspects in the business with regard to people, processes, and also a good insight into various customers
- Allowing the business to do these analytics in a modest time frame rather than waiting for weeks or months
- Performance and quickness of data analysis in the hands of business users to quickly tweak business processes

The use case that we will be covering throughout this book is called Single Customer View. **Single Customer View** (**SCV**) is a well-known term in the industry, and so it has quite a few definitions, one of which is as follows:

> *A Single Customer View is an aggregated, consistent and holistic representation of the data known by an organisation about its customers.*

> *- Wikipedia*

Enterprises keeps customer data in varying degrees siloed in different business applications. The use case aims at collating these varying degrees of data from these business applications into one and helping the analysts looking at this data create a single customer view with all the distinct data collected. This single view brings in the capability of segmenting customers and helping the business to target the right customers with the right content.

The significance of this use case for the enterprise can be narrowed down to points as listed next:

- Customer segmentation
- Collating information
- Improving customer relations and, in turn, bringing is retention
- Deeper analytics/insight, and so on

Conceptually, the following figure (*Figure 05*) summarizes the use case that we plan to implement throughout this book. Structured, semi-structured, and unstructured data is fed into the Data lake. From the Data lake, the **Single Customer View** (**SCV**) is derived in a holistic fashion. The various data examples are also depicted in each category, which we will implement in this book. Doing so gives a full use of a Data lake in an enterprise and is more realistic:

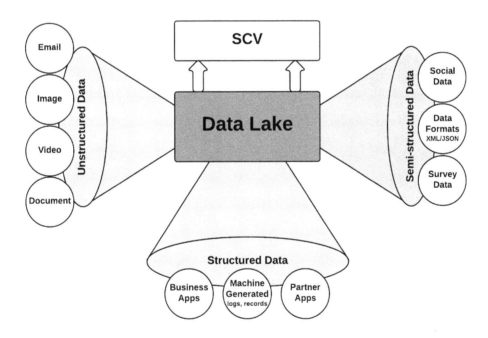

Figure 05: Conceptual *view of Data lake use case for SCV*

Figure 05 shows that our Data lake acquires data from various sources (variety), has different velocities and volumes. This is more a conceptual high-level view of what we will be achieving after going through the whole book.

We are really excited, and we hope you are, too!

Summary

In this chapter, we delved deep into some of the common terminologies in the industry. We started the chapter by understanding data, enterprise data, and all important big data. We then dealt with the relevance of data, including various data quality attributes. After that, we went into the details of the different types of data classification and where the data lives in an enterprise.

In the sections that followed, we dealt with digital transformation and finished the chapter with the use case that we will be implementing throughout this book in more detail.

After completing this chapter, you will have clearly grasped many terminologies and will also have a good understanding of the significance of data and Data lake to an enterprise. Along with that, you will have a very good idea about the use case and its relevance.

In the next chapter, we will delve deep into Data lake and also the pattern that we will use in implementing Data lake in more detail.

2

Comprehensive Concepts of a Data Lake

The concept of a Data Lake in an enterprise was driven by certain challenges that enterprises were facing with the way the data was handled, processed and stored. Initially, all the individual applications in the enterprise, via a natural evolution cycle, started maintaining huge amounts of data themselves with almost no reuse in other applications in the same enterprise. These created information silos across various applications. As the next step of evolution, these individual applications started exposing this data across the organization as a data mart access layer over the central data warehouse. While Data Mart solved one part of the problem, other problems still persisted. These problems were more about data governance, data ownership and data accessibility, which were required to be resolved so as to have better availability of enterprise relevant data. This is where a need was felt to have Data Lakes which could not only make such data available but also store any form of data and process it so that data can be analyzed and kept ready for consumption by consumer applications. In this chapter, we will look at some of the critical aspects of a Data Lake and understand how it matters for an enterprise.

What is a Data Lake?

If we need to define the term Data Lake, it can be defined as a vast repository of a variety of enterprise-wide, raw information that can be acquired, processed, analyzed and delivered.

A Data Lake acquires data from multiple sources in an enterprise in its native form and may also have internal, modeled forms of this same data for various purposes. The information thus handled could be any type of information, ranging from structured or semi-structured data to completely unstructured data. A Data Lake is expected to be able to derive enterprise-relevant meanings and insights from this information using various analysis and machine learning algorithms.

Relevance to enterprises

A Data Lake brings a variety of capabilities to the enterprise by centralizing the data. With data being centralized, the enterprise can tap into capabilities that have not yet been explored. This data can help enterprises with a lot more meaningful business insights when compared to any single system in the enterprise. Additionally, with a lot more advancements in Data Science and Machine Learning, a Data Lake can help with many more optimized operating models for the enterprise as well as specialized capabilities like predictive analysis, recommendations and so on for future growth.

These are hidden capabilities and have never seen the light of day until this point as the so-called important data is out of reach from people who can see relevant insights to make or transform the business in a better way.

How does a Data Lake help enterprises?

Organizations have been aspiring for a long time to achieve a unified data model that can represent every entity in an enterprise. This has been a challenge due to various reasons, some of which have been listed here:

- An entity may have multiple representations across the enterprise. Hence there may not exist a single and complete model for an entity.
- Different enterprise applications may be processing the entities based on specific business objectives, which may or may not align with expected enterprise processes.
- Different applications may have different access patterns and storage structures for every entity.

These issues have been bothering enterprises for a long time; limiting standardization of business processes, service definition and their vocabulary.

In Data Lake perspective, we are looking at the problem the other way around. Bringing Data Lake would mean implicitly achieving a unified data model to a good extent without really impacting the business applications, which are good at solving very specific business problems. A Data Lake may represent an entity to its fullest based on the information captured from various systems that owns this data.

With entities being represented with much better and complete details, Data Lakes do present a lot of opportunities to the enterprise to handle and manage data in a way that can help the enterprise grow and derive business insights to achieve enterprise goals. An interesting article by *Martin Fowler* is worth mentioning here, as he summarizes some of the key aspects around Data Lake in an enterprise at the following link: `https://martinfowler` `.com/bliki/DataLake.html`.

Data Lake benefits

Organizations generate a huge amount of data across their business systems and as they grow bigger, they also need to get smarter in handling data across disparate systems.

One of the most basic approaches is to have a single domain model that accurately describes their data and represents the most significant data for their overall business. Such information may be referred to as enterprise data.

An organization that has well-defined enterprise data also has some ways to manage that data so that changes to the definition of data are always consistent and it is well known as to how systems are sharing this information.

In such a case, the systems may be broadly classified as data owners and data consumers. For enterprise data, there needs to be an owner, and that owner defines how the data becomes available to other consuming systems that play the role of data consumers.

Once organisations have this clear definition of data and systems, they can leverage a lot of information with such mechanisms. Nowadays, one of the common ways to envisage this entire model of enterprise data is by building an enterprise-wide Data Lake responsible for capturing, processing, analyzing and serving this data to the consuming systems. Consistent knowledge of this central model can help the organisations with the following:

- Data Governance and Lineage
- Applying machine learning and artificial intelligence to derive business intelligence
- Predictive Analysis, such as a domain-specific recommendation engine
- Information traceability and consistency

- Historical Analysis to derive dimensional data
- A centralized data source for all enterprise data results in data services primarily optimized for data delivery
- Helping organizations take more informed decisions for future growth

In this section, we discussed what a Data Lake is capable of? A definitive follow-on in this chapter would be to discuss and summarize how a Data Lake works and can be realized.

How Data Lake works?

In order to realize the benefits of a Data Lake, it is important to know how a Data Lake may be expected to work and what components architecturally may help to build a fully functional Data Lake. Before we pounce on the architectural details, let us understand the life cycle of data in the context of a Data Lake.

At a high level, the life cycle of a data lake may be summarized as shown here:

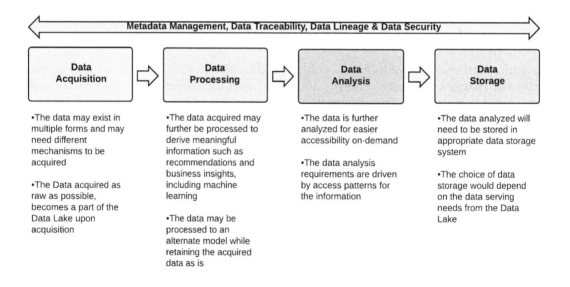

Figure 01: Data *Lake life cycle*

These can also be called various stages of data as it lives within the Data Lake. The data thus acquired can be processed and analyzed in various ways. The processing and data analysis could be a batch process or it could even be a near-real-time process. Both of these kinds of processing are expected to be supported by a Data Lake implementation as both of these patterns serve very specific use cases. The choice between the type of processing and analysis (batch/near-real-time) may also depend on the amount of processing or analysis to be performed, as it may not be feasible to perform extremely elaborate operations for near-real-time expectations, while there could be business use cases that cannot wait for long-running business processes.

Likewise, the choice of storage would also depend on the requirements of data accessibility. For instance, if it is expected to store the data such that it could be accessed via SQL queries, the choice of storage must support a SQL interface. If the data access requirement is to provide a data view, it may involve storing the data in such a way that the data may be exposed as a view and allows for easy manageability and accessibility of data. A more prominent requirement that has been evident in recent times is that of providing data as a service, which involves exposing data over a lightweight services layer. Each of those exposed services accurately describes and delivers the data. This mode also allows for service-based integration of data with systems that can consume data services.

While the data flows into a Data Lake from the point of acquisition, its metadata is captured and managed along with data traceability, data lineage, and security aspects based on data sensitivity across its life cycle.

> *Data lineage is defined as a data life cycle that includes the data's origins and where it moves over time. It describes what happens to data as it goes through diverse processes. It helps provide visibility to the data analytics pipeline and simplifies tracing of errors back to their sources.*
>
> *Traceability is the ability to verify the history, location, or application of an item by means of documented recorded identification.*
>
> *- Wikipedia*

Differences between Data Lake and Data Warehouse

Many a times, Data Lakes are also perceived as Data Warehouses. Both Data Lake and Data Warehouse have different objectives to be achieved in an enterprise. Some of the key difference are shown here:

Data Lake	Data Warehouse
Captures all types of data and structures, semi-structured and unstructured in their most natural form from source systems	Captures structured information and processes it as it is acquired into a fixed model defined for data warehouse purposes
Possesses enough processing power to process and analyze all kinds of data and have it analyzed for access	Processes structured data into a dimensional or reporting model for advanced reporting and analytics
A Data Lake usually contains more relevant information that has good probability of access and can provide operational needs for an enterprise	A Data Warehouse usually stores and retains data for long term, so that the data can be accessed on demand

As evident from the above differences, a Data Lake and Data Warehouse would ideally complement each other in an enterprise, and in no way should a Data Lake be seen as a replacement for a Data Warehouse as they play absolutely distinct roles in an enterprise.

Approaches to building a Data Lake

Different organizations would prefer to build the data lake in different ways, depending on where the organisation is in terms of the business, processes, and systems.

A simple data lake may be as good as defining a central data source, and all systems may use this central data source for all the data needs. Though this approach may be simple and look very lucrative, it may not be a very practical way for the following reasons:

- This approach would be feasible only if the organizations are building their information systems from scratch
- This approach does not solve the problems of existing systems
- Even if organization decides to build the data lake with this approach, there is a lack of clarity of responsibility and separation of concerns
- Such systems often try to do everything in a single shot, but eventually lose out with increasing demand of data transactions, analysis, and processing

A better way to build a data lake would be to look at the organization and its information systems as a whole, classify the data ownership, and define a unified enterprise model. This approach, while it may have process-specific challenges and may take more effort to get defined, will nonetheless provide the required flexibility, control, and clear data definition and separation of concerns between the entities of various systems in an enterprise. Such Data Lakes can also have independent mechanisms to capture, process, analyze and serve enterprise data to the consuming applications.

Lambda Architecture-driven Data Lake

As we discussed in earlier sections, there exist multiple ways of processing data, however they can be broadly classified into batch and real-time data processing. While there can be scenarios where one of them provides the desired outcomes, there can be additional scenarios that may need data from both batch as well as real-time data processing components. This drives us to a problem of merging batch data with real-time data. This problem is addressed by the Lambda Architecture pattern, which will be discussed in further detail in the next chapter. Here, we are discussing the initial view of a Lambda-Architecture-driven data lake.

Lambda Architecture, as a pattern, provides the ways and means to perform highly scalable and performant distributed computing on large sets of data and yet (eventually) provides consistent data with the required processing, both in batch as well as in near real time. Lambda Architecture defines the ways and means to enable scale-out architecture across various data load profiles in an enterprise, with low latency expectations.

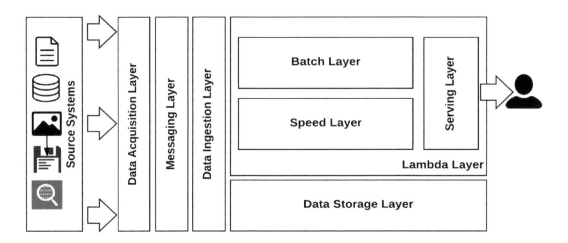

Figure 02: Layers *in a Data Lake*

The way the Lambda Architecture pattern achieves this is by dividing the overall architecture into layers. Each of these layers are covered on high-level in below sections of this chapter.

Data ingestion layer - ingest for processing and storage

A fast ingestion layer is one of the key layers in the Lambda Architecture pattern. This layer needs to control how fast data can be delivered into the working models of the Lambda Architecture. Some of the key specifications of this layer are:

- It must be highly scalable with on-demand scalability to be able to scale based on varying load conditions
- It must be fault tolerant with both fail-safety (recovery) as well as fail-over (resiliency)
- This layer must be able to support multi-thread and multi-event execution

- This layer must be able to quickly transform the acquired data structure into the target data formats as needed by the processing layers of the Lambda Architecture
- This layer must ensure that all of the data delivered is in its purest form for further processing

Batch layer - batch processing of ingested data

The batch processing layer of a Lambda Architecture is expected to process the ingested data in batches so as to ensure optimum utilization of system resources; at the same time, long-running operations may be applied to the data to ensure high quality of data output, which is also known as modeled data. The conversion of raw data to modeled data is the primary responsibility of this layer, wherein the modeled data is the data model that can be served by the serving layers of the Lambda Architecture. The primary specifications for this layer can be defined as follows:

- The batch layer must be able to apply data cleaning, data processing, and data modeling algorithms on the raw data ingested
- It must have mechanisms in place to replay/rerun the batches for recovery purposes
- The batch layer must be able to support machine learning and data science based processing on the raw ingested data to produce high quality of modeled data
- This layer may also have to perform some other operations to improve the quality of the overall modeled data by de-duplication, detecting erroneous data, and providing a view of the data lineage

Speed layer - near real time data processing

This layer is expected to perform near-real-time processing on the data received from the ingestion layer. Since the processing is expected to be in near real time, such data processing will need to be quick, fast, and efficient, with support and design for high-concurrency scenarios and an eventually consistent outcome. A lot of factors play a role in making this layer fast, which will be discussed in detail later in this book. Broadly, the specifications for such a layer can be summarized as follows:

- Must support fast operation on very specific data streams ingested.
- Must be able to produce a data model relevant to near-real-time processing needs. All long-running processes must be delegated to batch mode.

- Must be supported by fast access and storage layers so as to have no backlog/pile-up of events to be processed.
- Must be decoupled like the batch process from the ingestion layer.
- Must produce output model in a way that it can be merged with the batch-processed dataset to provide enriched enterprise data.

Data storage layer - store all data

The data storage layer is very eminent in the Lambda Architecture pattern as this layer defines the reactivity of the overall solution to the incoming event/data streams. As per the theory of connected systems, a system is only as fast as the slowest system in the chain. Hence, if the storage layer is not fast enough, the operations performed by the near-real-time processing layer would be slow, thus hampering the near-real-time nature of the architecture.

In the overall Lambda Architecture, there are broadly two kinds of active operations on the ingested data: Batch processing and Near-Real-Time processing. The data needs for batch and Near-Real-Time processing are very different. For instance, a batch mode, in most cases, would need serial read and serial write operations, for which a Hadoop storage layer may suffice. However, if we consider Near-Real-Time Processing, which would need quick lookups and quick writes, Hadoop storage may not be the right fit. For supporting Near-Real-Time processing, it is required that the data layer supports some kind of indexed data storage.

Batch Mode	Near-real-time processing
Serial read and serial write operation	Quick lookups and quick writes
Hadoop storage layer (yes)	Hadoop storage layer (no)

Typical specifications for a storage layer in a Lambda Architecture can be summarized as given here:

- Must support both serial as well as random operations
- Must be tiered based on the usage pattern with appropriate data solutions
- Must be able to handle large volumes of data for both batch as well as near-real-time processing
- Must be flexible and scalable for multiple data structure storage

Serving layer - data delivery and exports

The Lambda Architecture also emphasizes the criticality of how the data is served or delivered to the consuming application. Data, as we know, can be delivered in multiple ways between systems. However, one of the most common ways to deliver data is via services. In the context of a Data Lake, these services may be called Data Services that may deliver primarily data.

One of the other ways to deliver data is via exports. The data in its final form can be exported as messages, files, data dumps, and so on for other systems to consume.

The primary focus while delivering/serving data is to have the data in the desired form. This form can be enforced as a data contract whether the data is served by services or by exports. However, during data delivery operations, it is very important to have a merge between the batch data and the data from near real-time processing, as both of these streams would hold key information from an organizational domain perspective. The data serving/delivery layer will need to ensure that the data is consistent as adhering to an agreed contract with the consuming application.

Overall, high-level specifications for the data serving/delivery layer can be summarized as follows:

- It must support multiple mechanisms to serve data to the consuming application
- For every mechanism supported for serving the data, there should be adherence to a contract in agreement with the consuming application
- It must support merged views of both batch-processed and near real time processed data
- It must be scalable and responsive to the consuming application

With the serving layer having its key responsibility to serve the data out of the Data Lake, this layer may also optionally merge the data for enrichment.

While these are primarily specifications of Lambda Architecture layers, there are other layers too such as data acquisition, messaging, and the data ingestion layer that feed the data into the Lambda Architecture for processing, which we will discuss later in this chapter.

Data acquisition layer - get data from source systems

In an organization, data exists in various forms, which can be classified as structured data, semi-structured data, or unstructured data.

Some of the examples of structured data are relational databases, XML/JSON data, messages across systems and so on. Semi-structured data is also very prevalent from an organization perspective, particularly in the form of e-mails, chats, documents and so on. Unstructured data also exists in a workplace in the form of images, videos, raw texts, audio and so on.

For all of these types of data, it may not be possible to always define a schema. Schemas are very useful while translating data into meaningful information. While defining the schema of structured data would be very straightforward, a schema cannot be defined for semi-structured or unstructured data.

One of the key roles expected from the acquisition layer is to be able to convert the data into messages that can be further processed in a Data Lake; hence the acquisition layer is expected to be flexible to accommodate a variety of schema specifications. At the same time, it must have a fast connect mechanism to seamlessly push all the translated data messages into the data lake.

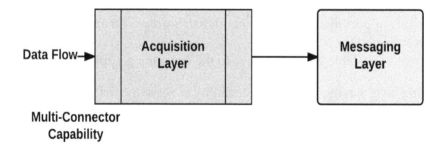

Figure 03: Data *acquisition components*

A Data acquisition layer may be composed of multi-connector components on the acquisition side and push the acquired data into a specific target destination. In the case of Data Lakes, the target destination would be the messaging layer.

There are specific technology frameworks that enable low-latency acquisition of data from various types of source systems; for every data type, the acquisition connectors are generally required to be configured/implemented depending on the framework used. The data acquisition layer is expected to perform limited transformation on the data acquired so as to minimize the latency. The transformation within the data acquisition layer should be performed only to convert the acquired data into a message/event so that it can be posted to the messaging layer.

 In the event that the messaging layer is not reachable (either due to a network outage or downtime of the messaging layer), the data acquisition must also support the required fail-safety and fail-over mechanisms.

For this layer to be fail-safe, it should be able to support local and persistent buffering of messages such that, if needed, the messages can be recovered from the local buffer as and when the messaging layer is available again. This component should also support fail-over and if one of the data acquisition processes fails, another process seamlessly takes over.

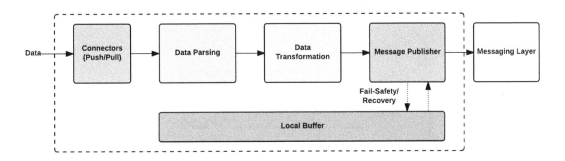

Figure 04: Data Acquisition Component Design

For this layer to support low-latency acquisition, it needs to be built on fast and scalable parsing and transformation components.

As shown in the preceding figure, an acquisition layer's simplified component view comprises connectors, data parsers, data transformers, and a message publisher. We will be discussing these components in detail in specific chapters in the context of the specific technologies and frameworks.

Messaging Layer - guaranteed data delivery

The messaging layer would form the **Message Oriented Middleware (MOM)** for the data lake architecture, and hence would be the primary layer for decoupling the various layers with each other, but with guaranteed delivery of messages.

In order to ensure that the delivery of messages is guaranteed, the messages will need to be persistent. This persistence of messages is usually done on a storage drive. The storage drive used for persisting these messages should be fit for the purpose based on number and size of the messages to be stored. Fundamentally, since the nature of message oriented middleware is to queue up the messages, for both writes and reads, this fits well into the characteristics of serial access (writes and reads), for which spinning disks may be adequate. However, for a very large scale application with millions of messages streamed per second, SSD could provide better IO rates.

The other aspect of a messaging layer is its ability to enqueue and dequeue messages, as is the case with most messaging frameworks. Most messaging frameworks provide enqueue and dequeue mechanisms to manage publishing and consumption of messages respectively. Every messaging framework provides its own set of libraries to connect to its resources (queues/topics).

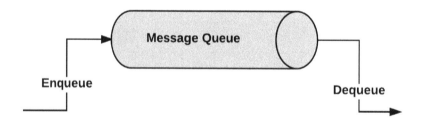

Figure 05: Message queue

Any message-oriented middleware generally supports two types of communication with queue and topic messaging structures. They are as follows:

- Queues are mostly used for point-to-point communication, with every message consumed only once by one of the consumers

- Topics are mostly used for publish/subscribe mechanisms, wherein a message is published once but is consumed by multiple subscribers (consumers). Hence a message is consumed multiple times, once by every consumer. Internally, topics are based on queues; however, these internal queues are managed differently by the messaging engine to provide a publish/subscribe mechanism.

Both queues and topics can be configured to be non-persistent or persistent. For the purpose of guaranteed delivery, it is imperative to have persistent queues such that messages are never lost.

At a high level, the message-oriented middleware can be abstracted with components such as message broker, message store, and queues/topics with a messaging framework/engine.

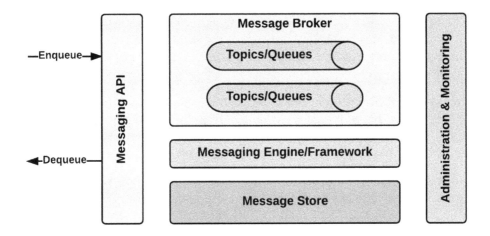

Figure 06: A messaging framework

Shown here are the high-level components of a messaging framework. Please note, the details have been abstracted to provide a simplified view. These components will be discussed in greater detail in Chapter 7, *Messaging Layer using Apache Kafka* later in this book.

Exploring the Data Ingestion Layer

The data ingestion layer is responsible for consuming messages from the messaging layer and performing the required transformation to ingest them in the lambda layer such that the transformed output conforms to the expected storage or processing formats. This layer must also make sure that the messages are consumed in a consistent way, such that no message is lost and every message is processed at least once.

This layer is expected to have multiple consumers/threads for parallel consumption of messages. Every such consumer in this layer must be stateless and must have fast streaming capability. These streams must be drawn from the messaging layer and the generated output must also be streamed into the lambda layer. The data ingestion layer must ensure that the rate of message consumption is always more than or equal to the message ingestion rates, such that there is no latency to process the messages/events. A lower processing rate or latency in this layer will result in a pile-up of messages in the messaging layer and hence would compromise the near-real-time processing capability of the messages/events. This layer should also support a fast consumption approach for recovery from such pile-ups if required.

Hence there is an implicit need that this layer is always in near real time with minimum latency such that there are no messages are piled up in the messaging layer. In order to be near real time, this layer must have capability to continuously consume the messages/events and have enough resiliency for fail-over.

The message consumers here play a vital role of delivering the messages to the lambda layer for further processing. Hence the internal components of message consumers is similar to the data acquisition layer with the differentiation that the message consumers are aware of the message format from the messaging layer (source) and the format in which the messages need to be delivered to the lambda layer (destination). The message consumption may be done in micro-batches to achieve the required resource optimization and achieve better system efficiency.

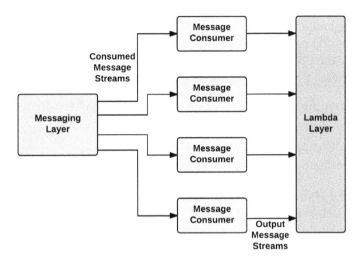

Figure 07: Message consumers

The message consumers, however, may need to push the output stream for both batch as well as speed layer processing in the lambda layer.

Exploring the Lambda layer

As mentioned before, the lambda layer typically comprises two layers, a batch layer as well as a near real time processing layer known as the speed layer.

Batch layer

Batch processing has been one of the most traditional ways of processing large amounts of data and are usually long-running processes. With the advent of many recent big data technologies, these Batch processes have become much more efficient and performant; this has greatly helped in reducing processing times.

The batch process is usually aware of the expected data to be consumed and the expected output. Historically, these processes were monolithic in nature and would process the entire dataset in a single run and some level of multi-threading, with specific mechanisms for handling failure scenarios and operational procedures to maintain such processes in production.

Hadoop, as a big data technology, provided all of the required framework and technology support for building batch processes that were more efficient and scalable than traditional batch processes. Hadoop came with two major components required for executing batch processes, primarily the process and the storage. Hadoop batch processes proved to be faster than regular batch processes primarily due to the following reasons:

1. Fast and optimized execution of processes using the Map-Reduce paradigm.
2. Sequential storage for fast sequential reads and writes.
3. Replicated storage for higher availability of data.
4. Runtime execution of processes near the data managed by job schedulers.

These capabilities of a Hadoop-based batch process provided immense improvements over traditionally built batch processes, wherein the data distribution and process distribution was managed by the underlying Hadoop framework, while the mapper and reducer jobs are focused on specific data processing.

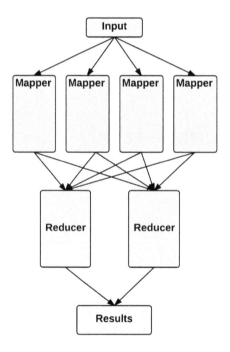

Figure 08: The Map-Reduce paradigm - batch processing

A Map-Reduce paradigm of process execution is not a new paradigm; rather it has been used in many applications ever since mainframe systems came into existence. It is based on *Divide and Rule* and stems from the traditional multi-threading model. The primary mechanism here is to divide the batch across multiple processes and then combine/reduce output of all the processes into a single output. This way, each and every process is running in parallel but independent of each other on partitions of data. This ensures that the data is processed at least once and the output of each of these processes are combined and results de-duplicated if any. With built-in framework capabilities, this execution of a batch proved to be highly optimized and helped Hadoop technology to get into solving mainstream batch problems. Such Batch processes also provided good window to derive more business intelligence from data processing and are also embedded with more sophisticated capabilities like data science and machine learning to serve batch oriented analytical needs. But then there were always questions around: what can be done for real-time needs?

As an answer to the near real time needs of data processing, multiple frameworks originated. These were aimed at solving this problem. Lambda Architecture also provides mechanisms to use some of these frameworks mainly in its speed layer.

Some of the early attempts made to achieve real-time processing is by triggering frequent batch processes. However, the processing could never get closer to near real time expectations.

Speed layer

The speed layer attributes to the near real time processing layer of Lambda Architecture, where the messages/data are processed as soon as they are ingested and the processed data is stored in the storage layer.

Since the primary need for the speed layer is to make data available in near real time, one has to ensure that the processing, storage and data availability meets the near real time expectation.

This would be possible only if the processing layer, storage layer, and serving layer are all operating at equal velocities to ensure that the data is not getting halted at any point in the flow.

Some of the initial streaming technologies used were Flume with HDFS, which did solve some part of the problem; however, it constrained the overall solution to having data converted to logs and these logs would get ingested into HDFS with almost no processing. The processing ultimately was done using batch processes that were not real time in nature.

It was soon realized that reliance on Hadoop batch processing would not fit into the expectation on near real time processing, hence there were separate frameworks built that specialized in near real time processing and these frameworks would constitute the speed layer in Lambda Architecture.

The initial frameworks were standalone frameworks, which did not integrate well into the Hadoop ecosystem; however, as there was more usage and maturity around these capabilities, it was evident that the systems needs to be integrated such that operability and manageability are simplified.

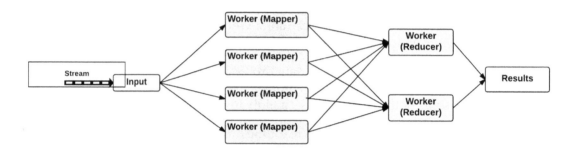

Figure 09: Near Real-Time Processing Pipeline

The mechanism implemented by these frameworks was same as that of Hadoop, that is, the Map-Reduce paradigm. However, it was implemented for real-time processing. Every framework had their own way of handling streaming data and resource management. Many of these frameworks were built on fast in-memory messaging capabilities which was a very effective way to decouple one component from another in real time processing yet have minimal latency.

The real-time processing was often dependent on data like the look-up data and reference data; hence there was a need to have a very fast data layer such that any look-up or reference data does not adversely impact the real-time nature of the processing. Here, some of the NoSQL technologies played that role well which we will discuss in later sections and chapters.

Serving layer

The serving layer in a Lambda Architecture plays the role of delivering data to the consumers. The serving layer could support various protocols for data delivery. All of these protocols could be classified as a push or a pull from a data consumer perspective.

A serving layer must be able to consume the required data from the data lake's data storage layer and deliver that data to the consuming application in adherence to the interface agreed.

Data push

Any mechanism used to push data out of the Data Lake can be defined as a Data Push mechanism. These can be of various types; however, here we are discussing some of the most common mechanisms:

- **Data Exports**: A serving layer must have the required tools, controls, and manageability to export the data in desired format for consumer applications. A part of this layer does indicate similar roles to that of an ETL; however, it is more driven by what the consumer application requires and how. These may be driven by internal batch processes scheduled at the serving layer such that the data from Data Lake can be extracted, transformed, and loaded to the destination. This part of the serving layer may also leverage some of the embedded ETL tools for the purpose.
- **Data Publish**: A serving layer may also publish the data to the required queues/topics for consumption by consumer applications as subscribers. This gets us to point-to-point data delivery and publish/subscribe models. Since these data had to be publishable messages, the size of these messages needs to be as small as possible for optimal performance.

Data pull

Any mechanism used to pull the data from Data Lake can be considered as Data Pull mechanism. Here, we will discuss, some of the most common data pull mechanisms.

- **Services**: One of the most popular mechanisms of data delivery are the data services. This comprises of building web services (REST/SOAP) over the Data Lake, such that the data can be exposed via services to the consuming applications. This works very well for consuming relatively small volumes of data over HTTP for near real time application requirements. This also stems from the notion of data as a service, wherein the entire data is ready and available over services. Such service requests and response definitions must be concise and clearly defined so that these are generic enough for multiple consumers to consume. This also implicitly means that the data access must be highly optimized so as to guarantee sub-second response times or large dataset, with the capability of random access. These services are more geared towards read-only services for data and should not be used for data mutations.

- **Data Views**: A Data Lake can also potentially have data delivery mechanisms based on data views that can be connected from various applications and the data can be fetched/pulled. This mechanism of serving data has been very common as it combines simplicity with ease of maintenance and access. Once data is exposed from a data view, any of the authorized applications can directly connect to such a data view using standard drivers and any additional data processing can be performed by the consuming application itself. These views are generally materialized views to keep them performant and isolate any query impact that may occur on underlying participating tables. However materialized views also need data refreshes to be performed which can be done incrementally or may also involve reconstruction of the entire data view, also known as refresh cycles. If a refresh cycle is involved in rebuilding the entire materialized view, the required mechanisms must be in place, such that while the refresh cycle are executed the data serving is not impacted. Traditionally this was done using synonyms; for some recent technologies, the same is achieved via replicated datasets.

Data storage layer

The data storage layer in a Lambda Architecture must provide a flexible access mechanism and at the same time should be highly optimized for both batch as well as near real time operations. In other words, the storage must support both sequential as well as random access of data. In a typical Lambda Architecture, the following layers are directly dependent on the storage.

Batch process layer

A batch process, from the perspective of data access, requires sequential access of data and the storage layer should be optimized for this operation. Hadoop as a technology reads and writes data as blocks and each of these blocks contains data in a sequence. Even the block level access in Hadoop is in a sequence to make sure that any batch to disk operation is fast enough even on spinning disks (commodity hardware).

Speed layer

The speed layer needs to perform its operation in near real time on the received data message and hence it needs to access the storage that supports random access to be able to quickly look up the required information and write back the processed data.

Serving layer

The serving layer consists of various operations that require both sequential and random access to disk depending on the nature of the data delivery. For instance, if an export is required to be performed for large datasets, the serving layer would mostly trigger a batch process to export the required data, which will largely depend on sequential data access. But if the data delivery is in the form of data services, the required disk access must support random data access to ensure that the response time service expectations are met.

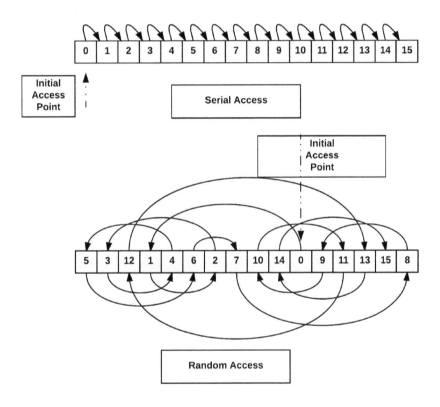

Figure 10: Data Access Patterns

Thus, the data in a Data Lake can be broadly classified into two categories on the basis of accessibility, that is, Non-Indexed Data and Indexed Data.

- **Indexed Data**: In the context of maintaining indexed data in a Data Lake, we are looking at maintaining data that can be randomly addressed and accessed. The underlying hardware also plays a vital role in supporting the storage and access patterns for random data. As mentioned before, SSD would surely be a good fit here. But there are other things associated like cost, failure frequency, availability, storage volume, power consumption and so on, which motivates us to think about the spinning disks. In this context, there is a trade-off expected in I/O rates. At the same time, one can also think about tiered storage here such that the high IO/transaction data indexes stay in SSD while the rest falls to spinning disk.

  Today, almost all data indexing frameworks support both SSD as well as Spinning disks. Some of the leading frameworks in this space, who have been widely used in the context of Big Data technology and Lambda Architecture are Solr and Elastic. Both of these frameworks are based on the Lucene engine and depend on the open source Lucene engine for core indexing capabilities with added capabilities around data indexing and access. These frameworks guarantee sub second response time over large volumes of data which fits well into the need for speed layer for fast lookups and persistence. Both Elastic and Solr store indexes of the data and can optionally also store the data for fast lookup.

- **Non-indexed Data**: The raw data as ingested into a data lake is stored sequentially and in blocks of data generally. These blocks of data form a unit of data for processing. Since the non-indexed data is stored sequentially, it is used for batch data processing and the output data is also stored sequentially. Since this is sequential data, there is limited lookup capability based on keys that few of the storage formats support. Some of the data storage also support some level of indexing and partitioning of data such that the data can be located as fast as possible. This data is generally used for batch processing and in order to make the batch process execute fast, the batch process runs near to the data such that movement of data for processing is minimized, taking advantage of data localization. This is one of the key reasons for a fast map-reduce process in Hadoop ecosystem.

- **Storage-Based Classification:** While these differences are related more to access patterns, the data stores can also be classified based on storage mechanisms.

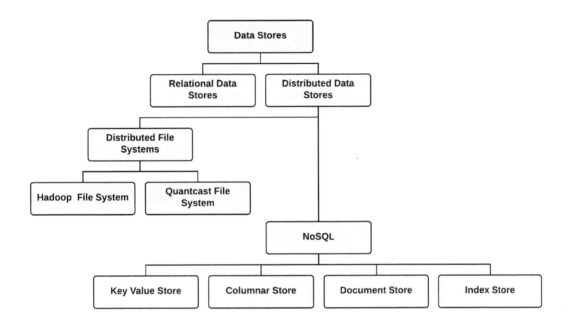

Figure 11: Data Stores

Relational data stores

These data stores have been most popular since last many decades and most commonly represent structured data with relationships between data entities. The relational data stores have matured since years and have been widely used across enterprises. Until a few years ago, these stores used to form the primary storage layer of every enterprise and almost all of the enterprise data would exist in these relational data stores as they provided a very logical way to organize and manage data.

Distributed data stores

While relational data stores were very efficient in handling relational datasets, soon it was realized that they may not be the best fit for other types of data storage. These types of data included semi-structured and unstructured data. Keeping relational data stores scalable at very high volumes for data storage and access also involved complicated processes and practices. These challenges were recently addressed by a range of distributed data stores which came into existence as distributed file systems and NoSQL (Not only SQL) data stores. Hadoop has been one of the most popular distributed file systems, while there have been a number of NoSQL data stores that have come into existence, each one of them solves a very specific problem. All NoSQL databases are inherently implemented on similar concepts of distributed data management, but they can be further classified into the following categories:

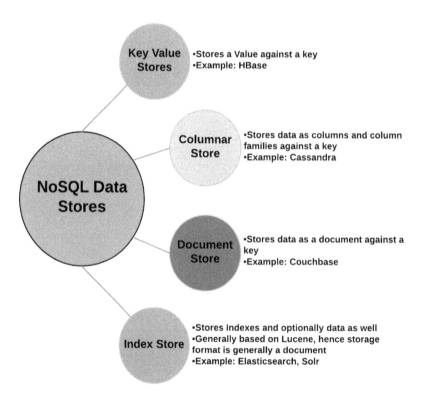

Figure 12: NoSQL Data Stores Classification

Shown here is a broad classification of NoSQL data stores as of their current state. Each of these types specializes in solving a particular problem related to data access and data management.

For instance, a key value store could be most appropriate while capturing ticks or machine data and where accessibility requirement can be done via key based access. Likewise columnar storage provides a denormalized storage mechanism, wherein the data is stored as columns or family of columns, instead of rows, which solves the problem of a read heavy use case and is expected to support write heavy scenarios as well. Document stores are mostly suited for storing an entire document against a key. Most often these documents are of JSON format and these stores can store JSON as is and provide a JSON-friendly query engine for supporting queries. An index store generally is preferred where there are heavy search scenarios to be implemented across large datasets in sub second, taking advantage of indexing capabilities.

Each of these stores has numerous books published as each of them has a vast landscape of capabilities when it comes to large-scale data handling and management in an enterprise. With respect to Data Lakes, we would be picking some of these data stores to demonstrate various aspects of the data serving layer in future chapters. In `Chapter 5`, *Data Acquisition of Batch Data with Apache Sqoop,* we will cover HBase and in chapter 10 we will cover Elasticsearch as NoSQL stores used in our Data Lake.

Summary

In this chapter, we went through various parts of a data lake and the Lambda Architecture at a high level and established a foundation for chapters later in this book. There, we will dive into greater technical details towards realizing this architecture. This chapter introduced the concept of data lake, some high-level concepts around data acquisition, messaging layer, ingestion layer, and Lambda Architecture layers, namely speed and batch. We also discussed, to some extent, the concepts around data storage and differences between storing data for random access and sequential access.

3

Lambda Architecture as a Pattern for Data Lake

In the previous chapter, while going through the concepts of Data Lakes, you were introduced a bit to Lambda Architecture. In this chapter, we will go into a bit of detail on Lambda Architecture and also try to explain the significance of this important architecture pattern in this book's Data Lake implementation.

This chapter, though it tries to cover this architecture paradigm in detail, doesn't give any technology implementation. This is intentional to make sure that you understand the concepts of these patterns first; once that is achieved, the following chapters will detail this pattern with technology backing.

After going through this chapter, you will learn the Lambda Architecture pattern in detail. Once you learn this pattern, you will also see how it forms an integral part of our Data Lake construction.

What is Lambda Architecture?

Lambda Architecture is not technology dependent; rather it is agnostic of technology and defines some practical and well-versed principles to handle and cater to big data. It is a very generic pattern that tries to cater to common requirements raised by most big data applications. The pattern allows us to deal with both historical data and real-time data alongside each other. We used to have two different applications catering to transactional — **OnLine Transaction Processing (OLTP)** and analytical — **OnLine Analytical Processing (OLAP)** data, but we couldn't mix these together; rather they live separately and don't talk to each other.

These bullet points describe what a Lambda Architecture is:

- Set of patterns and guidelines. This defines a set of patterns and guidelines for the big data kind of applications. More importantly, it allows the queries to consider both historical and newly generated data alike and gives the desired view for the analysts.
- Deals with both historical (batch) and real-time data.
- Technology agnostic and generic in nature. Not at all dependent on technologies, this is a pattern that is generic, and any technology can be used so long as the main layer and its responsibilities are met.
- It clearly separates responsibilities into distinct layers. It does separate responsibilities between layers and complies with the Separation of concerns principle of architecture beautifully.
- It's domain agnostic. It can be applied to different types of business domains as it is a pattern that is generic.

History of Lambda Architecture

Nathan Marz coined the term **Lambda Architecture** (**LA**) to describe a generic pattern for data processing that is scalable and fault-tolerant. He gathered this expertise working extensively with big-data-related technologies at **BackType** and Twitter. The pattern is conceptualized to handle/process a huge amount of data by using two of its important components, namely batch and speed layer. Nathan generalized his findings and experience in the form of this pattern, which should cater to some of the important architecture principles, such as these:

- **Linear scalable**: It should scale out and not up and should cater to different kinds of use cases
- **Fault-tolerant**: Capable of a wide range of workloads, it should also shield the system from hardware and software failure and inherent human mistakes
- **Backtype**: Reads and updates
- Extensibility: Manageable, easy to extend, and easy to keep adding new features and data elements

There is a wealth of details documented at `http://lambda-architecture.net/`. The architecture pattern became significant with the emergence of big data and the enterprises' focus on real-time analytics and digital transformation. Why the pattern was named **Lambda** (symbol λ) is not very clearly detailed.

However, we have always thought the greek letter in association with the pattern to be a way by which data comes from two places. Batch and Speed data (layer) pipeline represents the curved parts of the lambda Symbol, which then combine and serve through the serving layer (the line merging from the curved part), as shown in the following figure:

Figure 01: The Lambda Symbol

Principles of Lambda Architecture

Nathan Marz, in his Big Data book, has given full-fledged details on the Lambda Architecture pattern. The following are the three main principles on which his pattern has been developed. Some of these have been briefly covered in the previous section.

- Fault-tolerant
    - Hardware
    - Software
    - Human
- Immutable Data
- Re-computation

Lets detail each one of these principles in the next sections.

Fault-tolerant principle

Hardware, software, and human fault tolerance should be part of this pattern. The pattern is for catering to big data, and because of this, any of these faults can be a big problem to recover from. So, data loss and data corruption don't have any place in this pattern because of the data vastness. If it does have this, in most cases, it is irrecoverable; so this principle is quite a strong need.

One of the important parts of this is human fault tolerance. Some of the very common mistakes are typical operational mistakes made in day-to-day operations; the next most common mistakes are bugs introduced over a period of time (releases) into the production system. The system should indeed be designed to cater to and address these aspects.

Immutable Data principle

The data should be stored in a raw format from the different source systems. More importantly, the data stored should be immutable in nature. By making it immutable, it inherently takes care of human fault tolerance to at least some extent and takes away errors with regards to data loss and corruption. It allows data to be selected, inserted, and not updated or deleted. To cater to fundamental fast processing/performance, the data is usually stored in a denormalized fashion. Data being immutable makes the system in general simpler and more manageable.

Re-computation principle

Since raw data is always available in the lake, it's always possible to cater to new requirements by running or re-computing functions against the raw data. In addition to this, it's apt to store this data in a schema-less structure because tying data to a schema brings its own issue of re-computation. Tying data to schema also brings overhead to development and maintenance.
While implementing the Data Lake with this pattern as one of the main layers, we will see how these principles described before are realized.

Components of a Lambda Architecture

We have been talking about the various components of Lambda Architecture in multiple sections of this book already, and I am sure you will have some idea after going through those sections. This section and the following section detail each and every component of the Lambda Architecture. But this will avoid any dependency on technologies because we need to go under this layer, and once we are through, we can use any technology available in the market and create this pattern without much trouble. Understanding each layer and its significance along with the lead function that it has to take care of is very much required, as this is the basis that you would get when going through future chapters. In the context of Data Lake, the components of Lambda Architecture just form one of the layers, which is termed as the Lambda Layer. We will now go through various layers in this Lambda Layer in detail. The main layers constituting the Lambda Layer are as follows:

- Batch layer
- Speed layer
- Serving layer

A pictorial view of a Lambda Architecture is shown next. The figure shows these important layers in the pattern:

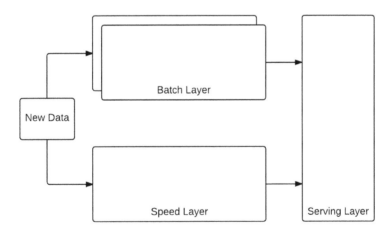

Figure 02: Components of a Lambda Architecture

As you can see very clearly from this diagram, new data is fed to both the batch and speed layers. The batch layer keeps producing and re-computing views for every set batch interval. The speed layer also creates the relevant real-time/speed views. The serving layer orchestrates the query by querying both the batch and speed layers, merges it, and sends the result back.

Whenever new batch views are created, the speed view in place is discarded and only the new data after that batch is taken into consideration for generating the speed views. Also, old batch views are kept and archived or discarded according to the use case or implementation.

In a generic fashion, the new way of handling big data is to follow a data pipeline as shown in the next figure, in which data is taken from the source of truth in the rawest format. Then we create an appropriate view out of it, catering to a business requirement; we use these views as needed. The core working of Lambda Architecture does follow these footsteps by allowing the batch and speed layers to produce appropriate views. Then the serving layer comes in between and does the necessary orchestration of these created views.

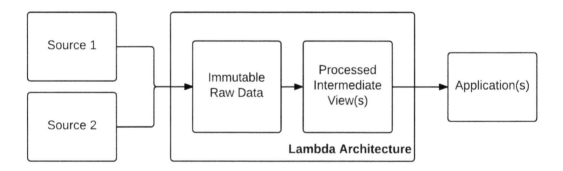

Figure 03: Big Data pipeline

Batch layer

The batch layer is where raw data is stored as is in the rawest format possible. Since no omission nor transformation happens while storing, many different use cases with different perspectives can be derived from these at different stages. This is the store where master data in an immutable state is also available and used by various analyses going forward. Since the data is immutable, update and even delete are forbidden operations. Data is always appended (added) with a timestamp so that when some data is required, it can be queried with the highest timestamp to get the latest record. Delete is also forbidden because then many analyses would require these deleted record details.

The queries, when run against raw data, would result in lot of processing time. To avoid these delays while querying the required details, in a periodic fashion, views aligning closer to the required format (result) is generated and stored, called batch views. Whenever a new batch view is regenerated (by taking in data that has come after the last batch processing), the old batch view is discarded. As one of the principles of this architecture is fault tolerance, this regeneration of batch view every time, even though it is really time consuming, takes away the various errors that could have got introduced as explained earlier. There are different approaches that can be used to make sure that this data processing takes less time as opposed to conventional batches, which take hours and even days to complete.

pure function (Lambda) = function (all data)

Figure 04: Lambda Architecture - batch layer

The persistence store requirement for a batch layer catering to a very large amount of data is that it should support high-scale random reads. However, it need not support random writes as the data is bulk-loaded in a set frequency.

With respect to the single customer view use case, the following figure shows how the batch layer can be realized, by producing a so-called batch view (intermediate view) from the customer master dataset.

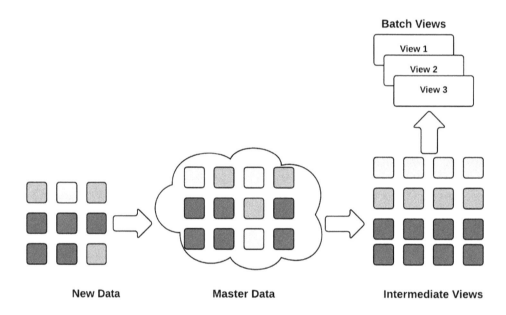

New Data   **Master Data**   **Intermediate Views**

Figure 05: Single customer view - batch layer

For our use case of a single customer view, the customer data flows into the batch layer, where the master dataset is maintained; and then, at a set batch process interval, batch views are created. The serving layer, when required, will query these views, merge with the speed views, and send the results across.

Speed layer

Speed layer is also known as the Real-time Layer and (as the name suggests) caters to real-time analysis requirements. The batch layer operates in specified intervals and between the completion of one batch execution and start of another; the business users still wants analysis to be conducted on the data. The responsibility of merging the batch view along with real-time data is the role of the Speed layer. Now, the batch processing window can be reduced, but since batch deals with a good amount of data, processing by the batch layer usually takes time and the business cannot wait for this lag in processing of the batch layer. For achieving near real-time data for analysis, data is incremented to the speed layer in a low latency fashion. Once the batch layer is executed and catches up with the data in the speed layer, the speed layer views are discarded and the process continues.

The query, when fired by the user, queries both the batch and speed layer. It merges the result to get the results for the user according to the desired parameters sent.

To achieve fault tolerance and to recover from the errors introduced, both the batch and speed layer at any moment can resort to re-computation (batch layer from the raw data) or roll back (to a previous state for batch layer) and just flush (for speed layer and regenerating the view).

There are some important concepts that this layer complies with to achieve its basic objective, which are as follows:

- **Incremental computation**: A new real-time view is created using an existing real-time view and new data. As detailed before, this is done so as to reduce the time taken to make the data available for analysis in near real time.
- **Eventual consistency**: To achieve some of the computations in real time is really complex and time consuming. In that case, the system goes for approximations (closer or more approximate to correct answer). After some time (usually not too much), the data becomes correct.

The store requirements for speed layer should support both random read and write to cater to incremental updates. The speed layer does allow mutation as against the batch layer but deals with a very small dataset (say, a day as the batch process frequency) compared to the batch layer, which does deal with a huge amount of data (spanning months or years).

Following the generic approach as explained in the previous section, the speed layer also creates a so-called speed view (intermediate view) catering to the requirement, as shown in this diagram:

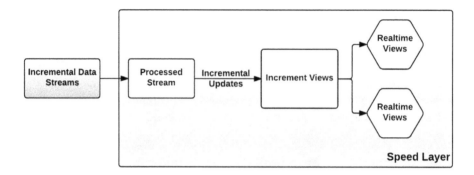

Figure 06: Lambda Architecture - speed layer

With respect to the single customer view, this is how the speed layer can be realized:

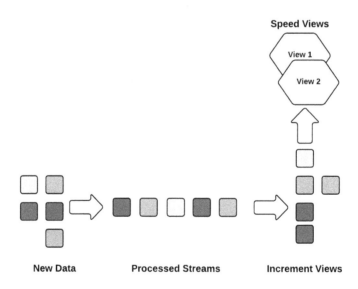

Figure 07: Single customer view - speed layer

The new data flows to the speed layer, where the appended data is processed and appropriate speed views are created. When required by the serving layer, the speed view gets merged with the batch views and results are sent across.

CAP Theorem

In the previous section, we did give some very important aspects such as eventual consistency (the next section dives deep into this) and other aspects in brief. Before explaining this aspect in more detail, it is apt to explain a very important theorem called CAP theorem.

> *CAP (Consistency, Availability, Partition Tolerance) Theorem, also named Brewer's theorem after computer scientist Eric Brewer, states that it is impossible for a distributed computer system to simultaneously provide all three (Consistency, Availability, Partition Tolerance) guarantees.*

> *- Wikipedia*

Out of three guarantees, a distributed system can only have one of **C (Consistency)** or **A (Availability)** when the distributed data is partitioned. A distributed system is bound to have network failures, and in this case, network partitioning would have to be tolerated. Let's detail these three important aspects in a concise manner in this table:

Consistency	• When data is partitioned (distributed), all the nodes see the same data at a given time, and this should be true for all times • When queried, each node will return the latest data. If not, the system will just error out
Availability	• At all times, every request being fired at the system generates a valid response • While doing this, it doesn't mean that every request will receive a response with the latest information (data)
Partition tolerance	• The system is able to perform continuously even if a network failure or data loss occurs

The Data Lake using Lambda Architecture works with this theorem in a context. Usually in such a context, Availability is chosen as against Consistency. Because of this aspect, consistency of data would be achieved eventually, and more often than not, data goes with approximations. This is known as eventual consistency. We will go into a bit more detail of this aspect in the following section:

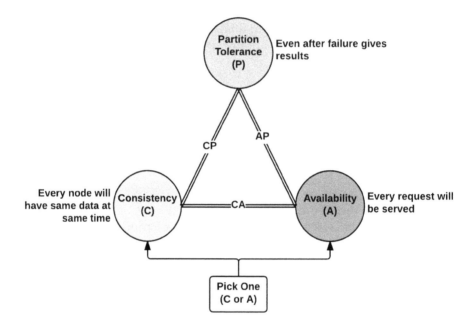

Figure 08: CAP theorem

The traditional **ACID (Atomicity, Consistency, Isolation, Durability)** based stores such as RDBMSes choose Consistency over Availability. NoSQL-based stores, which are more common for Data Lake because of their features, choose the **BASE** (**Basically Available, Soft state, Eventual consistency**) philosophy and choose Availability over Consistency.

Eventual consistency

Eventual consistency is a consistency model used in distributed computing to achieve high availability that informally guarantees that if no new updates are made to a given data item, eventually all accesses to that item will return the last updated value.

- Wikipedia

In the previous section, you would have clearly got the notion behind the guarantees, namely consistency versus availability.

Its expected that data in a distributed system will become eventually consistent but always available. For a Data Lake, the availability guarantee is more important than consistency, but it purely depends on the use case. We cannot show/use bad data to the end user as this would have a huge impact on the company's brand. So, use cases need to be carefully validated you take this as a generic principle for your Data Lake.

In the context of Data Lakes (Lambda Layer), if the speed layer becomes corrupted (data loss or data corruption), eventually the batch and serving layer would correct these mistakes and have the queries served fine through the serving layer. The speed layer in the pattern just keeps the data for a period of time so that the batch and serving layers can process the data from scratch and ensure consistency; once done, the speed layer views get discarded.

Serving layer

The core task of the serving layer is to expose the views created by both the batch and speed layer for querying by other systems or users.

Apart from this, there is a good amount of orchestration work done by this layer. The speed layer needs to keep looking at the batch layer to see if the necessary batch operation is done. If so, the batch layer store needs to be updated soon after the batch operation is conducted from the batch view. Soon after this, the existing speed layer view will be discarded and this is also a bookkeeping activity which keeps the speed layer store size in control.

The following figure shows the two layers namely batch and serving in action:

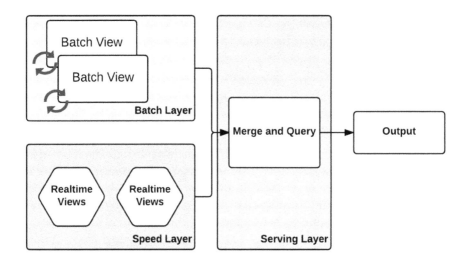

Figure 09: Lambda Architecture - serving layer

When a query comes to the serving layer, it in turn forms and fires two queries to the two different layers namely batch and speed. The queries fired look into the timestamp of records and fetches the results according to the parameters supplied. Once it gets the records from both the layers, it merges and applies various application logic and produces the final output in the desired format by the system or user. Because of the quality of data, the batch layer is more reliable (recomputation aspect when each batch operation is completed), in case of conflicts, the batch view results overrides that of speed layer.

Complete working of a Lambda Architecture

The following figure pictorially shows the complete working of Lambda Architecture:

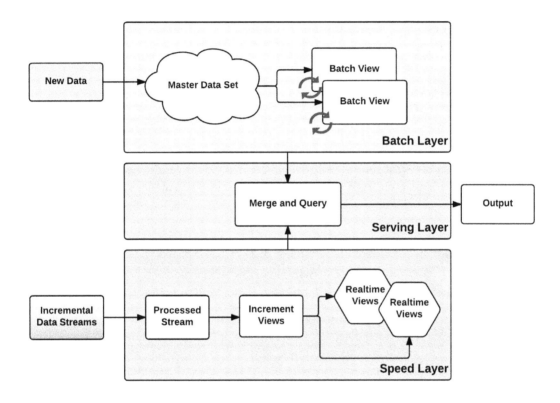

Figure 10: Complete working of Lambda Architecture

As briefly explained earlier, the master data set is maintained and managed in the batch layer. When new data arrives, it is despatched to both, batch and speed layer. Once it reaches the batch layer, at regular batch interval batch views are generated and recomputed from scratch each time. Similarly, the speed layer using the new data generates the speed view whenever the new data arrives in the layer. The serving layer when queried, merges both the speed and batch layer views to generate the appropriate query results.

Once the batch view is generated, the speed view is discarded and till the time new data arrives only bath view needs to be queried as all the data is available in the batch layer itself.

Batch Layer	• Stored immutable data • Constantly growing in size • Recomputes views all the time
Speed Layer	• Constant stream of data • Stores mutable data • Less in size/ volume • Views live for a specified period and discarded at intervals
Serving Layer	• Responsible for indexing and making sure exposed batch views perform well • Exposes real-time views created incrementally by the speed layer • Merges result from both batch and speed views in a consistent fashion

Advantages of Lambda Architecture

There are various advantages because of which we chose Lambda Architecture for construction Data Lake for the enterprise. Some of these advantages can be given as:

- Data stored is in raw format. Because of this, at any time, new algorithms, analytics, or new business use cases can be applied to the Data Lake by simply creating new batch and speed views. This is one of the biggest advantages of traditional data warehouses in which data is cleansed and stored. Because of this, new use cases would need to change the data schema, and this is usually time and effort consuming.

- One of its very own important principles, namely recomputation, helps correct fault tolerance without much trouble. As more and more data comes into the lake, data loss and corruption can be something that cannot be afforded. Because of this recomputation, at any moment we can recompute, roll back, or flush data to correct these errors.

- Lambda Architecture separates different responsibilities into well-defined and bounded layers. By doing so, these layers can have different technologies and different optimization techniques can be employed to make it function better without any effect on that other layers. Some of the technologies used in these layers, including stores, can be swapped with a better one without much trouble.

- It provides a pluggable architecture. Adding a new type of source data or similar one already plugged in, the architecture is built to take in these source systems without many changes at all.

Disadvantages of Lambda Architectures

Choosing a Lambda Architecture to develop a Data Lake for your enterprise does incur some inherent disadvantages if some of its aspects are not fully thought through. Some of these are as follows:

- Due to its different layers, it is generally considered to be complex. Keeping sync between these two layers incurs cost and effort, and this has to be thought through and handled.
- Because of these two distinct and fully distributed layers (batch and speed), maintenance and support activities are quite hard.
- There are a good number of technologies that have to be mastered to construct a Lambda-Architecture-driven Data Lake. Getting people who have expertise in these technologies can be troublesome for your recruitment division.
- Implementing a Lambda Architecture with open sources technologies and then deploying in the cloud can be troublesome. To avoid this, you could very well use cloud technologies to implement Lambda Architecture, but by doing so, the enterprise automatically gets itself tied to a particular cloud provider and that inherently is considered a disadvantage.
- Even though the architecture pattern has been around for quite some time now, the tools are still immature and evolving. Cloud evolution has surely accelerated and innovated in this space so it won't be long before we get mature solutions and tools in this space.
- CI/ CD is now a requirement and not at all a luxury. As tools in this space are still not that mature, tools in regards to CI/ CD also fall into the same category, making it hard to do many automations.
- The setup could require a good amount of hardware components. Technically, low end hardware components can be used but for enterprise grade, usually high end is considered with a well-defined support model with vendors.
- The architecture pattern has always been criticized for implementing the same job twice (batch and speed layer).

Technology overview for Lambda Architecture

As explained briefly earlier, Lambda Architecture is a pattern with well defined guidelines and is technology agnostic. Looking at its various components/layer, any technology can be brought in to do the required job.

With, emergence of various cloud providers, you could even get ready-made components in cloud (many are cloud dependent) which actually implements the Lambda Architecture. In this book, we are marching ahead to actually create a Data Lake in which the lambda pattern just covers one layer, called Lambda Layer.

Since there are so many choices for technologies, the future chapters are a bit opinionated. When we make each technology, we would give the rationale for our choice, but keeping it as open as possible. We would also give our other technology choices, so that if needed, these technologies can indeed be swapped by the reader if required. Having said that, we will actually implement the Data Lake using the selected technology. The next part of the book details each technologies in detail, and once done in the following part, we will bring these technologies together and build the Data Lake.

Applied lambda

Enterprise-level Data Lake is one of the applications of the Lambda Architecture pattern. In this book, we are going to cover this in more detail. However, there are other use cases where this pattern can be applied and this section tries to cover these.

Enterprise-level log analysis

One of the very common use cases for this pattern is log ingestion and various analytics that surround it. The **ELK** (**Elasticsearch**, **Logstash**, **Kibana**) stack is a leading one in this space, but this pattern could very well be used. The logs can vary from conventional application logs to different types of logs produced by various software and hardware components. If we need to have an enterprise level log management and analytical capability this pattern is indeed a good choice. These logs are produced in large quantities and at very high velocity. Also these are immutable in nature and does need to have an order in place for analyst (may be a developer of an application or a security data scientists making use of this data to decipher any security threat) to make use of these.

Using the important layer in Lambda Layer (batch and speed layer which we will explain in detail in next coming sections) helps validate these real-time logs and also can comprehend past logs to give a real-time insight. These insights can result in some actions which can be proactively assigned to a development team. For instance, application bugs can be assigned to application developer and threat reviews can be assigned to security analysts.

In addition to log analysis to detect certain anomalies, we can also use this data as a analysis methodology and auditing. For example website like, Google Analytics data when fed to lake and analyzed can be used to derive some trends, which can be advantageous to the business running the website.

Capturing and analyzing sensor data

With the ever-increasing **Internet of Things** (**IoT**) use cases, more and more sensors are expected to be used by enterprises. With more sensors, comes huge amount of data. With huge amount of data from these sensors, making out useful information can be really hard and tricky. Using Data Lake with Lambda Layer can help users with a scalable solution for such real-time analytics for these huge volume sensor data.

Real-time mailing platform statistics

For an enterprise, mailing platform plays a very important component these days. With huge amount of data from business applications and social platforms, the e-mail marketing platform role is significant. Many e-mail platforms gives a good amount of tracking information for each e-mail sent in the form of different tracking statuses like opened, link clicked, and so on. Making use of this huge amount of tracking data and making it available as a real-time statistics will help refine the marketing team to better target the emails and also with different content. These days, e-mail platforms have the capability of A/B testing on the content and this is quite important data for the marketing team to better prepare marketing email material according to the target audience.

Real-time sports analysis

Analysis and statistics of various games in a real-time fashion using the historic batch view and real-time data from a current game to show the viewers different statistics and analysis.

The batch layer can keep doing various batch operations and prepare the various batch views and these can be mixed with the current game and various milestones achieved in this current game could be deduced and shown. In the game of cricket, for example, the current game when played, the current player could achieve various milestones. For example, achieve 1000 runs in Test Cricket, during this time these special milestones can be shown to the viewers watching the match/ game.

Recommendation engines

Various business-related recommendation engines using both historic and current real-time data from various business applications, most of the time, end user operated website.

Analyzing security threats

Logs can be captured from various hardware and software components including business applications and analyzed for security threats by comparing with past datasets. According to various analyses conducted, different mechanisms of authentication (for example) can be done. Say, for example, we can step up authentication (two-factor); The request is coming from *Nigeria* repeatedly within a span of few minutes to be stepped up or altogether blocked for being reviewed by a human and then for authorizing the transaction.

Multi-channel consumer behaviour

Lambda Architecture can be used to analyze multi-channel customer behavior. It can be used to analyze customer purchase behaviors, their past purchases, their social connect and so on. and then use this data for a targeted marketing campaign. Also, various A/B testing results can be analyzed, and then you can appropriately take action on how a campaign e-mail has to be triggered.

Working examples of Lambda Architecture

Here are some of the working examples where Lambda Architecture has been used as a way by which certain use cases have been handled:

- **Multiple use cases on Twitter**: One of the use cases where modified lambda is used in the area of sentiment analysis of tweets.
- **Multiple use cases in Groupon**.
- **Answers by Crashlytics**: Deals with mobile analytics, use Lambda Architecture layers of batch and speed effectively to produce meaningful analytics.
- **Stack Overflow**: A well-known question-answer forum with a huge user community and plenty of activity. For a logged-in user, recommended questions make a new section, where the Lambda Architecture is used. There are other analytics too, such as voting, which uses batch views.
- **Flickr Magic View**: Revised Lambda Architecture to create a magic view by combining bulk and real-time compute (courtesy: `code.flickr.com`).

Kappa architecture

This book is about building Data Lakes using Lambda Architecture as one of the main layers (Lambda Layer). However, we feel that the readers also need to learn about another minimalist Lambda Architecture under active discussion, namely Kappa architecture. It is more or less similar to lambda, but for the sake of simplicity, the batch layer is removed and only the speed layer is kept. The main idea is to avoid having to compute a batch layer from scratch all the time and try doing almost all of these in real-time or the speed layer. One of the disadvantages of the Lambda Architecture, as detailed above, is to have to keep coding and executing the same logic twice, and this is avoided in the Kappa Architecture.

An image speaks more than a thousand words, and the next diagram compares both the Kappa and Lambda Architectures side by side. In this, you can clearly see that in Kappa, the only missing part is the all-important batch layer:

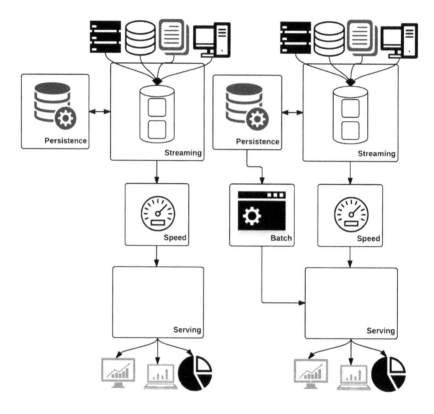

Figure 11: Kappa (left) and Lambda (right) architectures side by side

We strongly feel that for building a Data Lake, even though complex, Lambda Architecture is the way to go and that's the reason for choosing this pattern. We really wanted to give you readers another perspective was shown in the previous figure, you dive deep into implementation mode and that's the only reason to explain the Kappa architecture briefly.

The Batch layer in Lambda exists for a reason and to address this aspect, Kappa brings in newer technology frameworks capable of handling a huge amount of data and do the relevant processing. We do feel that in Kappa, the responsibility taken care of by both batch and speed layers in Lambda is diluted and combined. In fact, we can make use of newer technologies in Lambda and keep these layers separate having well-defined responsibilities set.

Summary

In this chapter, you learned about the Lambda Architecture in detail. In our Data Lake implementation, the Lambda Layer (an implementation of the Lambda Architecture) forms an integral part.

We have taken care to introduce only the theoretical aspects of Lambda Architecture in this chapter, and stayed away from all technologies; we want you to understand that this is a pattern and any technology can be used to implement various parts of this architecture without much trouble. In the next chapter, however, we will start introducing technologies and will introduce places where it can be used.

The first few sections of this chapter introduced you to this pattern and later sections detailed a bit more of each of the components/layers forming a Lambda Architecture. We stated the advantages and disadvantages associated with this pattern and gave a full picture of this pattern in detail before wrapping up.

We hope you now have enough of a background on Data, Data Lake, and Lambda Architecture; you can go to the next chapter to actually implement a Data Lake for your enterprise.

4
Applied Lambda for Data Lake

As introduced in the initial chapters, big data is defined as four Vs, that is, Variance, Velocity, Volume, and Varsity. We also got introduced to Lambda architecture and how it can possibly enable merge outputs from two distinctive processing pipelines. In order to leverage big data technologies to solve processing problems, it may be a good idea to marry Lambda architecture with these Big Data architectures such that we can reap the benefits of both. Though big data refers to an end-to-end solution to handle, process, and manage information across all the four Vs, it has become quite synonymous with the Hadoop Big Data framework. While the initial implementation of Hadoop was introduced by the open source Apache community, its immediate demand brought in a lot of commercial offerings for support. Over a period of time, the community witnessed a number of customized distributions of Hadoop. Some of the most popular ones today are **Cloudera**, **Hortonworks**, and **MapR.** As we know, Hadoop as a framework was initially implemented by Yahoo! for internal Big Data scenarios and was later open sourced as Hadoop under an Apache license. Horton works as a spin-off from Yahoo! and continues to maintain its commercial offering in this space, competing closely with Cloudera and MapR. In this chapter, we will have a quick overview of the technologies in the Hadoop landscape and how can they conceptually help us realize a Data Lake.

Here we want to establish certain grounds in terms of the overall landscape of big data and the specific technologies chosen in this book for forthcoming chapters. As far as possible, this book will refer to standard open source distributions so that the examples and concepts are distribution agnostic and can be run on any distribution of your choice. Hence, the content of this book will lean more towards open source distributions.

Knowing Hadoop distributions

A Big Data ecosystem consists of multiple capabilities, and for every capability in the ecosystem, there are one or more frameworks. Different distributions realize these capabilities in their own specific ways and also have some additional edge over other competitors in the same space.

cloudera   MAPR

HORTONWORKS

Figure 01: Hadoop distributions

Shown here are some of the leading distributions of Hadoop framework, wherein Cloudera, Hortonworks, and MapR are the leaders in commercial space while Apache Hadoop is an open source distribution. These commercial offerings, while having their own specific capabilities, are largely based on the specifications of the open source Hadoop framework.

Just to put a few things into the perspective of why a Hadoop distribution should be chosen, unfortunately there is no straight answer for it. However, we can compare these distributions across various dimensions that we may be interested in for evaluation.

Selection factors for a big data stack for enterprises

For any enterprise to adopt a particular Hadoop Distribution that is commercially supported, there are a few key factors that the enterprise would generally need to evaluate against these distributions in context of its maturity and culture of adoption. Here, we will briefly touch upon some of these key factors.

Technical capabilities

Each of the distributions has its own unique capabilities as well as many other capabilities which are similar to each other. At the minutest details, we can always have a big list of capabilities, but we can focus on some of the prominent ones for the purpose of comparison and evaluation.

Ease of deployment and maintenance

Many Hadoop distributions, while using common core components, do differentiate themselves from others in terms of ease of deployment and maintenance. This may vary from automation and monitoring interfaces to alerts and upgrades, and so on.

Integration readiness

Many of these distributions provide specific capabilities for integration with other data systems, both inbound as well as outbound. This, at times, becomes a crucial factor for selection of a particular Hadoop distribution:

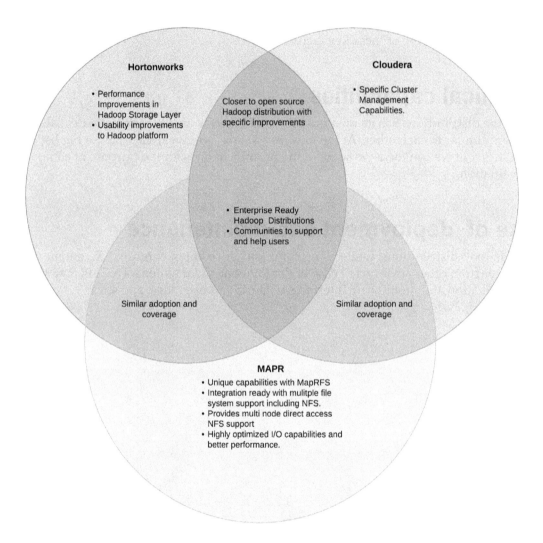

Figure 02: Hadoop distributions and their features

While we see Apache Hadoop as a great open source framework for big data processing, it may be critical for enterprises to get professional services around these capabilities. For that purpose, every enterprise should evaluate these Hadoop distributions for fitment into their organizations, since every organization would have its own processes, standards, monitoring, and alerting expectations, and above all, its own skill set. However, for the purpose of this book, we prefer to keep the understanding to be very neutral around building a Data Lake with a Lambda Architecture; hence we will resort to open source Apache Hadoop for all examples and samples.

Batch layer for data processing

The core of Hadoop technology has been its ability to perform faster, performant, and optimized batch processes. It proved to be a big success in solving some of the more complex problems of long-running batch processing within organizations. The initial implementations of Hadoop were based on open source Hadoop distributions; however, with the inherent need to make it professionally supported, there were a number of features that were incorporated to make it feasible for enterprise use in terms of provisioning, management, monitoring, and alerting. This resulted in some of the more customized distributions led by MapR, Cloudera, and Hortonworks:

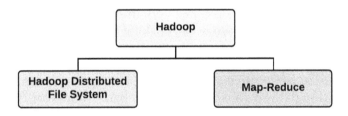

Figure 03: The Hadoop 1 framework

As shown in this image, the *Hadoop 1 framework* can be broadly classified into Storage and Processing. Storage here is represented by **Hadoop Distributed File System (HDFS)** while processing is represented as a **MapReduce** API. *Hadoop 2* included many of the improved capabilities with the introduction of YARN, and this representation changed as shown here:

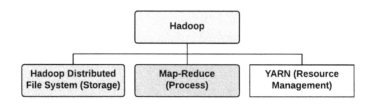

Figure 04: The Hadoop 2 framework

There could be a number of other frameworks that could have been considered here like **Pig scripts**, Hive queries, **Impala** queries, and so on. However, all of these are internally executed as MapReduce batch jobs and can be additionally orchestrated with actions, stages, and parameters in an **Oozie** workflow or cascade.

Let's have a closer look at how Hadoop MapReduce batch jobs work. The functioning of a Hadoop MapReduce consists of various key components that were introduced as part of the initial Hadoop framework. The Hadoop framework itself has undergone an evolution with Hadoop 1 and Hadoop 2. Hadoop 1, while establishing the Hadoop capability of MapReduce batch jobs, it did suffer from a single point of failure. With the introduction of Hadoop 2, this single point of failure was eliminated and a few other key capabilities were added. From a discussion perspective, we will cover Hadoop 2 and compare it with Hadoop 1 as we go through the details. Hadoop 2, for batch frameworks, consists of the following key components:

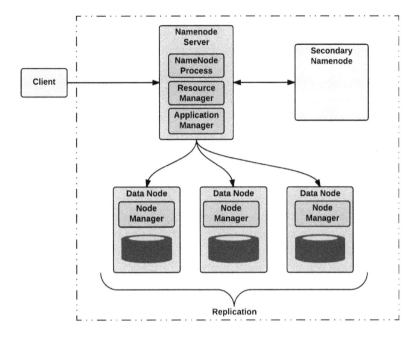

Figure 05: A typical Hadoop cluster

The NameNode server

This component has the responsibility of scheduling and tracking jobs spread across the cluster. Until Hadoop 1, it was a single point of failure, but with Hadoop 2, this responsibility was delegated to YARN, which creates multiple job trackers across the cluster and ensures failover.

The secondary NameNode Server

This component is used for snapshotting of the in-memory state of a Hadoop cluster and to keep track of write-ahead logs and transactional attributes. It is often used to replicate the cluster state. This is not a backup node for the NameNode server, but is for snapshotting purposes.

Yet Another Resource Negotiator (YARN)

Yet Another Resource Negotiator (YARN) was introduced in Hadoop 2 is the primary resource manager for the whole of the Hadoop cluster. This eliminated the single point of failure that existed in Hadoop 1 by spawning multiple job trackers in a Hadoop cluster such that failure of a job tracker does not affect other jobs and ensures re-scheduling of failed jobs to resume from the point of failure.

Data storage nodes (DataNode)

A Data node's primary role in a Hadoop cluster is to store data, and the jobs are executed as tasks on these nodes. The tasks are scheduled in a way that the batch job processing is done near the data by allocating tasks to those nodes which would be having the data for processing in most certainty. This also ensures that the batch jobs are optimized from execution perspectives and are performant with near data processing.

Please see the details and inner working of a typical Hadoop batch process here:

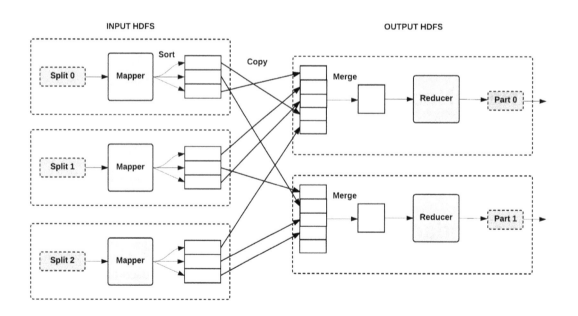

Figure 06: MapReduce in action

Here, we see that the job, when initiated, is divided into a number of mapper jobs. The number of mapper jobs spawned typically depends on the block size and the amount of data to be processed. From a job process perspective, one can always specify the maximum number of mapper jobs, however the number of mappers would always be limited by the maximum number of mappers specified. This is very helpful when we want to limit the amount of cores that can be utilized for batch jobs.

As stated before, the block size plays a vital role in the batch process since the unit of work for a mapper depends on the block size, and the job is distributed across the mappers as blocks of data as inputs.

At a high level, a typical batch job is executed in the following sequence:

1. The job driver program, which sets the job context in terms of mapper, reducer, and data format classes, is executed.
2. The mapper jobs are fed with blocks of data, as read from job execution.
3. The output produced by the mapper is sorted and shuffled before it is fed to reducers.
4. The reducer performs the reduce function on the intermediate data produced by mappers and stores the output back on HDFS as per data format definitions defined in the job driver program.

While this may seem to be very simple and straight forward, the actual job execution consists of multiple stages. At this point, we just want to provide a context for the Hadoop Batch processing hence limiting the information to a level that is required to understand the concept.

 We will be discussing this subject again in much greater detail in later chapters on the batch layer.

The overall expectation of the batch layer in a Lambda Architecture is to provide high-quality, processed data that can be correlated with near-real-time processing of the speed layer, resulting in considerably dependable and consistent information reflected in near-real-time.

Speed layer

The speed layer in a Lambda Architecture provides near real-time processing of events. Since the expectation is to process the events in near-real-time there is a limited amount of processing that can be done on a limited size of information. This may also include machine learning or complex event processing algorithms that can be run for near-real-time scenarios.

The term near-real-time processing is a relative term and may mean different things for different people and different scenarios. For instance, for a customer reservation, this may mean of the order of 2-3 seconds, however for a use case such as recommendation engine, it may mean a few minutes.

In terms of Lambda Architecture, this layer should receive the same event/message which otherwise is also captured by the batch layer, but both of these layers would give very different meaning to the data once processed, complementing their respective purposes for realizing a use case.

Speed layer generally comprises of stream processing of the event received from acquisition layer, and generally there is a presence of a messaging middleware for guaranteed delivery as well as loosely coupled integration with the acquisition layer.

Some of the early frameworks in this space have been Apache Storm, Flume, and Apache Kafka with consumer-based stream processing. Flume has remained a popular choice in this space, but recently Spark Streaming and Flink have been gaining a good adoption for their support and simplicity when it comes to deploying parallel processing and pipeline processing with support for scale-out architecture. There are very specific differences in the way each of these frameworks operates, some of which are explained next.

Flume for data acquisition

Flume plays a very important part in the data acquisition capability in our Data Lake implementation. Below figure pictorially shows how Flume's stream processing works.

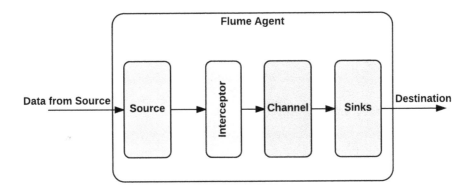

Figure 07: Flume stream processing

Shown here is a very-high-level component architecture of the Flume process, which consists of **Source**, **Interceptors**, **Channels**, and **Sinks**. Each one of these components has a very specific responsibility when handling events/messages.

While we will be dwelling on this. In much more detail in later chapters, please check out a summary of these components now.

Source for event sourcing

This component captures data from source systems in the form of Flume events/messages. Flume has a number of built-in source connectors that can connect to a variety of systems with multiple protocol supports.

Interceptors for event interception

Interceptors transform flume events/messages en route to channels. These typically consist of event serializers and are applied before the event/messages reaches the channel.

Channels for event flow

Flume supports persistent as well as in-memory channels. A channel provides a layer of indirection for flume events/messages and supports multiple patterns for the way the events/messages are relayed to the sink from the channel.

Sink as an event destination

Sink represents the target system connectors from a Flume perspective. Flume has built-in sink connectors for connecting to various systems in an enterprise over various protocols, in a very similar way to that of the source.

While Flume was the initial approach for near real-time stream processing, it did lack from being a true near-real-time that could accommodate custom processing of events/messages, and had develop custom component for the same. The set up and deployment of flume was static at a given point in time, with a given configurations. For any changes required, the configurations needed changes and the Flume process had to be restarted. This posed a limitation for near-real-time use cases.

These limitations were soon addressed by frameworks such as Storm, Spark Streaming, and so on. For the context of this book and to apply the Lambda architecture to Data Lakes, we will be primarily considering Spark Streaming and the Flink framework.

Spark Streaming

Shown in the next image is a very simplified view of the Spark streaming process. Spark was originally designed for faster processing of batches of data from Hadoop and was translated for near-real-time use cases as Spark streaming, retaining some of the fundamental building blocks and patterns in both the scenarios. One of the primary building blocks of Spark Streaming is DStreams, Receivers, and **Resilient Distributed Datasets** (**RDD**). While Spark started with optimizing batch processing and was translated for near-real-time use cases, the fundamental behavior remained somewhat similar. Even for near-real-time use cases, Spark streaming works with micro-batches with a batch interval. This batch interval also introduces some latency in Spark stream-based processing, limiting the near-real-time behavior to a few seconds rather than a fraction of a second.

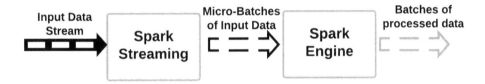

Figure 08: Spark streaming

As shown here, the overall Spark streaming approach works with data streams having real-time data inflow for near-real-time processing. The Spark streaming components divide the incoming data stream into multiple micro-batches. These micro-batches are then submitted to the core Spark Engine, which processes these micro-batches to produce batches of processed data.

DStreams

Streams represent discrete sets of **RDDs (Resilient Distributed Datasets)** for both input and output data streams. Spark streaming provides many of the Streams as part of the Spark streaming framework, while various frameworks supporting Spark streaming, provide their own implementations of RDDs that can be used for DStreams.

These DStreams are divided into micro-batches before getting submitted to the core Spark Engine for processing:

Figure 09: Spark streaming streams

Data Frames

Data Frames represent a window of time that allows for executing operations on the time-windowed dataset. One of the most common of such operations is executing SQL queries on the specific windowed dataset or Data Frame via a Spark session. This allows a quick analysis of data streamed into a given time window and performing of windowing operations. A Data Frame is generally seen as a set of columns that can be logically considered as a table but with optimizations to perform quick operations with a SQL-like interface provided by the Spark framework.

Checkpointing

Spark streaming supports both metadata checkpointing as well as data checkpointing in order to provide the required fault tolerance for critical 24/7 applications. Metadata checkpointing includes configurations, DStream operations, and batches to recover the overall process, while data checkpointing includes persisting the in-flight RDDs to a reliable storage. Checkpointing can be enabled for operations that involve data transformations. However, for simple processing, where certain failure levels can be tolerated, it may not be required.

Apache Flink

Flink as a framework overcomes these limitations of Spark streaming also supports exactly once processing which good consistency. It processes data iteratively row by row and is not limited by constraints of micro-batching as in the case of Spark streaming. It also supports time based windowing functions that are very helpful while performing event correlations, while keeping the processing pipeline very flexible and scalable.

The primary feature of Flink which makes it different and very suitable for iterative processing is generally attributed to its near-real-time processing capability. However, it also supports batch processing. Some of the important features of Flink are as follows:

1. **Exactly once** processing makes it a reliable candidate for performing accurate aggregations while the streams are processed. This is generally not the case with Flume. It also supports checkpoint mechanism to keep it tolerant with respect to failures as well.

2. **Out of order processing** is supported which provides excellent capability in the streaming layer to have the processing done in the expected order with respect to event timelines. In a typical multi-threaded environment, it is very obvious that the events may arrive out of order to downstream systems. This is further elaborated here:

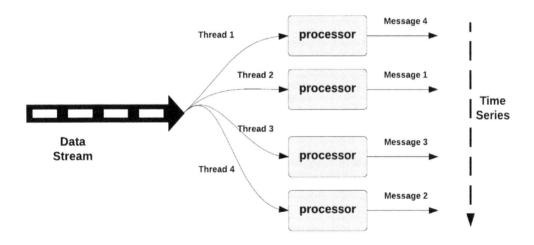

Figure 10: Out of order scenario

3. Provides out-of-the-box **windowing** capability for a streamed event, not only on the basis of event time but also on the basis of counts and sessions. This is particularly useful when such events need to be categorized/grouped together.

4. Failure recovery is supported with no data loss, with a very light-weight process state management such that the processing is resumed from the point of failure:

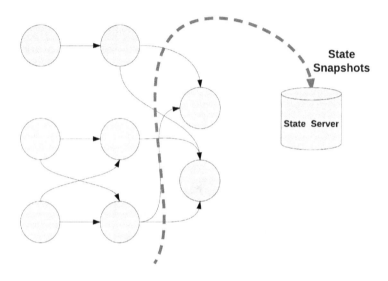

Figure 11: Apache Flink failure recovery

5. Flink is proven for **high-throughput and low-latency processing**. As mentioned earlier, since it is not dependent on micro-batching constraints, latency is very low compared to Spark Streaming and it happens to be the most appropriate near-real-time event processing framework.

6. It **works with YARN and MESOS** as resource managers, and scheduling event processing on the available nodes and for failure recoveries.

Flink is designed and implemented to be run on a large node cluster. It also supports standalone cluster deployment with dynamic pipeline processing, as shown in this sample execution:

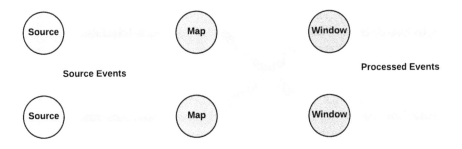

Figure 12: Flink stream processing

If we look at the overall Flink architecture, it is built to support both bounded as well as unbounded dataset processing, with APIs supporting both the modes. An architecture layout as depicted on `flink.apache.org` can be seen here:

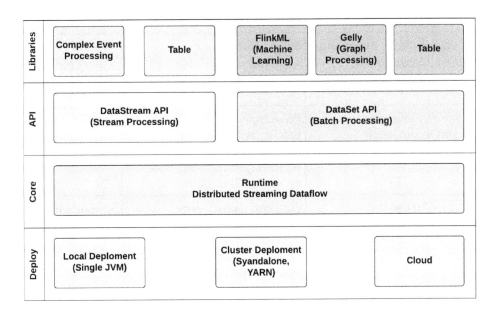

Figure 13: Apache Flink architecture

When we refer to bounded and unbounded datasets, we are typically referring to batch and stream processing respectively. Since Flink is fundamentally a stream processing framework, it can also perform batch operations effectively as batch data is nothing but a subset of streaming data. Any near-real-time framework in general can be leveraged for batch processing. But it is not true the other way round; that is, pure batch based processing such as a Hadoop MapReduce batch process cannot perform the role of a stream processing framework since its capabilities are built for batch processing, which cannot be used for stream processing. Even if we minimize the interval between various batch jobs, it will always have a lag to prepare, process, and load the results of the batch process.

Here are the key differences between all the three frameworks that we have discussed in this chapter, namely Flume, Spark Streaming, and Apache Flink:

Flume	Spark Streaming	Apache Flink
Flume is mostly used as an event producer for data acquisition. However, it can be leveraged for stream processing as well with custom sink implementations.	Provides stream processing capability as part of Hadoop framework, and provides for stream processing across a topology of nodes.	This is an in-memory, near-real-time processing framework across nodes.
Scalability is achieved by increasing the number of sinks in flume configurations and is generally static in nature.	Supports dynamic scaling with nodes based topology.	Support for dynamic scaling with nodes-based processing topology.
Processes data as flume events, supporting single and batch processing for real-time scenarios.	Processes data as micro batches only. Hence it introduces certain latency which may not be expected for few critical use cases.	Processes events in near-real-time.
Flume processes an event at least once, and in case of exceptions, it replays the events. This can cause duplicate processing.	Supports exactly once processing but can result into data loss. At least Once processing is also supported and will not cause data loss.	Supports Exactly once processing.

In addition to parallel processing, complex event processing has also been used in near-real-time processing very effectively, along with Natural Language Processing and machine learning. Some of these algorithms are appropriate for near-real-time execution, while many are not. Any latency in processing affects the overall processing time frames since the such processing is as slow as the slowest component in the component orchestration.

One of the other areas that does greatly influence the throughput is the data compressions that play a vital role in processing speeds. While compression in a **Remote Procedure Call (RPC)** may seem to be an overhead from the processing perspective, they do save on costly IO operations and can provide considerable performance gains across near-real-time processing. It is important to have the right compression codec supported for such processing. For instance, a simple ZIP-based compression may introduce more lags than performance gains since it is a transformation-based compression and does not support parallel compression techniques. In this space **SNAPPY** and **LZO** are more suitable compression codecs that can provide required performance gains. However, the choice of these codecs also depends on the support provided by the parallel processing framework being used.

The output of the Speed Layer is captured generally in the serving layer having high performance data repositories. Some of examples would be **HBase**, **Elasticsearch**, in-memory cache, and so on. Since this layer perform near-real-time processing, these data technologies also provide viable means for quick lookup and for reference data purposes.

Serving layer

The serving layer consists of data that can be readily served to consumer applications. Hence this is mostly the processed data. The processed data in this layer could be exposed via any of the data repositories and multiple protocols.

From the perspective of customer SCV, the processed customer data may exist in a materialized data view, a data service, as an export ready to be served or via direct access to tables for BI/reporting use cases. There could be multiple use cases, every use case may demand it's own data representation and accessibility.

A typical serving layer can be represented as follows:

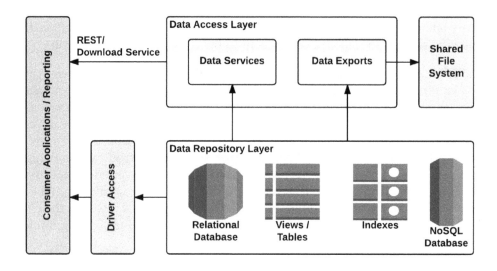

Figure 14: Serving layer

As seen from this representation, a serving layer as well may have multiple moving parts, but broadly they would be Data Repository and Data Access or Data Delivery Layer.

Data repository layer

The Data repository layer may be composed of multiple types of databases. The reason for this is that different data types may need to be represented for different purposes and usually a single choice of database would not suffice. The idea behind the serving layer is that it should be able to serve the data as per the requirement, hence multiple databases do find a good use here. In general the serving layer would serve a combined view of data both from the batch layer as well as from the speed layer.

Relational databases

This would still find a lot of utility in the serving layer as integrations may be required with various reporting and BI tools, which works on standard database drivers based access. This may involve populating data into this store at scheduled intervals from the batch layer.

Big data tables/views

Few applications need to integrate directly with the data from table or views, hence these tables/views need to be kept up to date with data in the serving layer. Access to these is again via data drivers as well as being accessible via native connectivity libraries in cases of Hive and Impala.

Data services with data indexes

The data indexes are used for quick searches for data and are generally used by data services in the data access layer. These can optionally also be exposed as **REST/SOAP** endpoints. This indexing layer is generally based on *Lucene* based indexing engines and are very fast when it comes to searches that need to reflect the changes in near-real-time. The indexes could optionally also serve the complete data and in certain time critical use cases that is helpful as well. It needs to be ensured that these indexes are built to support performance and scalability since these handle more of the real time service load.

The most common framework to build data services is Spring Boot, closely followed by Dropwizard. All of these frameworks support **JAX-RS 2.0** specifications and integrate well with service definition tools such as Swagger, providing a well rounded capability for building and publishing REST services in general.

In order to maintain the data consistency of the Data Lake, it is important to consider that these services are all read-only services, since their primary role is to deliver data, and should not ideally expose endpoints to change the data, since the data should only be altered by data processing cycles in a Lambda Architecture as discussed earlier.

NoSQL databases

These databases are of great use for applications who want to consume this data directly via native NoSQL drivers, for high performance lookups and access. This access can also be wrapped behind data services like in case of Data Indexes. The processes data will need to be modelled in a way that provides for optimized storage and supports the expected access patterns. This should also support high performance and scale out architecture such as data indexes as this repository can also play a vital role for near-real-time use cases.

Data access layer

The Data access layer in any application has the responsibility to access the data from underlying data repositories based on the access patterns expected. Here we can broadly categorize the data access layer to be performing either a pull or a push of data with respect to the serving layer.

At a high level, a data push refers to outflow of the data from the serving layer wherein the data is pushed out to other systems by the serving layer.

A Data Pull however refers to outflow of the data from the serving layer wherein the external systems pull the data from the serving layer, if the data is in the available format and the serving layer supports the expected data definition and protocols for data exchange.

Data exports

The data can be exported from the data repository as a scheduled export with a `cron` job. Many applications prefer to get a scheduled data dump once in a while for their operation requirements. The serving layer must have the required tools, processes, and schedulers to support data export use cases. Such data exports have been very prominent; however to get the best results, it needs to be ensured that more and more streaming formats (text files, comma separated values, Extensible Markup Language, JavaScript Object Notation, and so on) are used for these exports for consistent performance rather than transformational formats (`.doc`, `.pdf`, `.xlsx`, and so on).

Data publishing

The serving layer may also need to publish the processed data. This is more of a case with the output from near-real-time processing in which other downstream systems may be interested. Here the serving layer may play the role of an event hub. Most often it is good to expose such events over a topic such that multiple consumers could consume these events. However, a slow or unavailable consumer could potentially cause a pile up of messages on the data lake side. Hence this component should also be built for failure scenarios so that smooth recovery can be ensured, while keeping serving layer healthy and functional.

As discussed before as well, if we need to ever classify data based on Push or Pull, this can be classified as:

Push	Pull
Data Exports Data Publish	Relation Database Access Tables/Views NoSQL and Indexes via Data Service

For the purpose of this book, the various technologies that we will be considering to build a **Data Serving Layer** are the following:

Data Serving Layer Component	Technology
Relational Database	PostgreSQL
Tables and Views	Hive, Impala
Indexes	Elasticsearch
NoSQL Database	HBase, Couchbase
Data Services	Spring Boot Service
Data Exports	Hadoop MapReduce, Sqoop, Pig Scripts
Data Publish	JMS, Kafka

Summary

In this chapter, we discussed how we plan to apply a Lambda Architecture by choosing specific frameworks and technologies. With the suggested set of of frameworks and technologies, we will realize the use case as discussed in `Chapter 1`, *Introduction to Data* to have a fully functional data lake as we progress through later chapters of this book. Just to summarize, the following image demonstrates the selection of technologies as discussed in this chapter in various layers of a Data Lake with a Lambda Architecture applied:

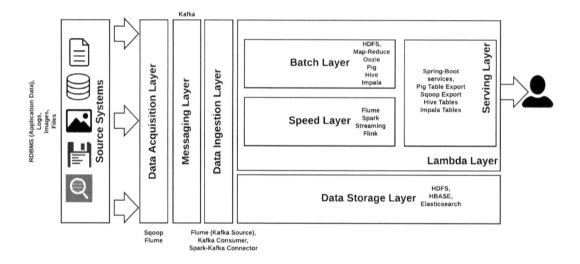

Figure 15: Technology mapping

5

Data Acquisition of Batch Data using Apache Sqoop

Now that we have discussed some of the essential elements of a data lake in the context of Lambda Architecture, it is imperative that the complete story around data lake starts from capturing the data from source systems, which we are referring to as Data Acquisition.

Data can be acquired from various systems, in which data may exist in various forms. Each of these data formats would need a specific way of data handling such that the data can be acquired from the source system and put to action within the boundaries of data lake.

In this chapter, we would be specifically looking at acquiring data from relational data sources, such as a **Relational DataBase Management System** (**RDBMS**) and discuss specific patterns for the same. When it comes to capturing data specifically from relational data sources, **Apache Sqoop** is one of the primary frameworks that has been widely used as it is a part of the Hadoop ecosystem and has been very dominant for this capability.

Various technologies would now be mentioned at various points (not that you should know or we will discuss everything in this book) throughout this part of the book and the following parts as we are now in the process of actually implementing the Data Lake using various technologies.

Context in data lake - data acquisition

The process of inducting data from various source systems is called data acquisition. In our data lake, we have a layer defined (in fact, the first one) which has only this responsibility to take care of.

One of the main technologies that we see doing the main job of inducting data into our data lake is using Apache Sqoop. The following sections of this chapter aim at covering Sqoop in detail so that you get a clear picture of this technology as well as get to know the data acquisition layer in detail.

Data acquisition layer

In Chapter 2, *Comprehensive Concepts of a Data Lake* you got a glimpse of the data acquisition layer. This layer's responsibility is to gather information from various source systems and induct it into the data lake. This figure will refresh your memory and give you a good pictorial view of this layer:

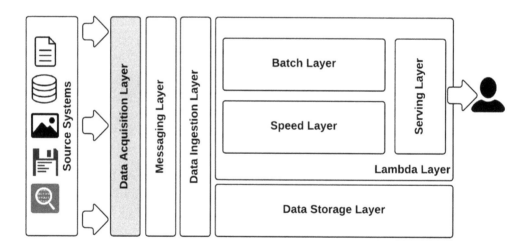

Figure 01: Data lake - data acquisition layer

The acquisition layer should be able to handle the following:

- **Bulk data:** Bulk data in the form of regular batches or micro-batches, as the case may be. Sqoop is able to handle huge amounts of bulk data and integrate it with the legacy applications datastore residing in traditional RDBMS. Micro-batch refers to more frequent bulk loads with less records to handle in each load. Sqoop is not the right choice here, rather Apache Flume (discussed in detail in the subsequent chapters, as we do have cases which require this) is a more apt choice.

- **High-velocity data:** Data varying from a few megabytes to terabytes in the form of regular batches and micro-batches needs to be handled by this layer efficiently without any bottleneck. One aspect is the speed at which this data comes (micro-batches can come more frequently and randomly as against regular batches which happen in a specified time interval), and another is the amount at which data comes into this layer.

- **Different formats of data (disparate data):** Different types of file formats (XML, JSON, TEXT, and so on) and different structured and unstructured data formats. Non-relational formats, such as various binary data, from various sources, such as IoT sensors, server logs, machine generated logs, image data, video data, and so on also has to be handled efficiently.

- **Structured/unstructured data:** The previous point covered this aspect but this point demands a separate mention because of its significance. Also, it has to cater semi-structured data, which falls in between structured and unstructured data. Chapter 1, *Introduction to Data* did cover these different data types in a bit more detail, so we wouldn't want to repeat ourselves here.

- **Integration with diverse technologies and systems**: With different types of business applications and Internet applications available in the enterprise, this layer has to integrate well with different technology applications and data stores with ease and ingest data into the data storage layer in our data lake.

Data acquisition of batch data - technology mapping

To cover our use case and to build data lakes, we use two different technologies in this layer, namely Apache Sqoop and Apache Flume. This chapter dives deep into Sqoop and Chapter 7, *Messaging Layer with Apache Kafka* dives deep into Flume.

The following figure brings in the technology aspect to the conceptual architecture that we will be following throughout this book. We will keep explaining each technology and its relevance in the overall architecture before we bring all the technologies together in the final part of this book (*Part 3*).

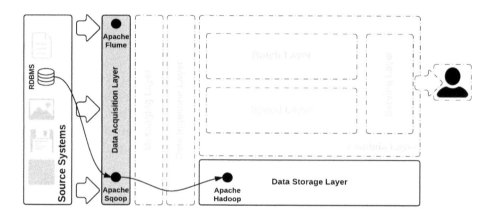

Figure 02: Technology mapping for acquisition layer

In line with our use case, we will be connecting to some of the business applications data store based on a traditional RDBMS. We will be using PostgreSQL as our RDBMS database holding customer data. We will connect to an intranet (B2B) application and an Internet (B2C) application which holds different sets of customer profile information within itself. Our data lake will have a consolidation of profile information from these disparate business applications, from which we will derive SCV.

Business to Business (B2B) applications are applications used by various departments within the organization and between organizations/businesses.

Business to Consumer (B2C) applications are applications used by organizations to interact with their consumers.

Why Apache Sqoop

One of the very commonly used tools for data transfer for Apache Hadoop.

In the data acquisition layer, we have chosen Apache Sqoop as the main technology. There are multiple options that can be used in this layer. Also, in place of one technology, there are other options that can be swapped. These options will be discussed in detail to some extent in the last section of this chapter.

Apache Sqoop is one of the main technologies being used to transfer data to and from structured data stores such as RDBMS, traditional data warehouses, and NoSQL data stores to Hadoop. Apache Hadoop finds it very hard to talk to these traditional stores and Sqoop helps to do that integration very easily.

Sqoop helps in the bulk transfer of data from these stores in a very good manner and, because of this reason, Sqoop was chosen as a technology in this layer.

Sqoop also helps to integrate easily with Hadoop based systems such as **Apache Oozie**, **Apache HBase**, and **Apache Hive**.

Apache Oozie is a server-based workflow scheduling system to manage Hadoop jobs.

HBase is an open source, non-relational distributed database modeled after Google's BigTable and is written in Java.

Apache Hive is a data warehouse infrastructure built on top of Hadoop for providing data summarization, query, and analysis.

- Wikipedia

History of Sqoop

Sqoop was initially developed and maintained by Cloudera, and later incubated as an Apache project on 23 July, 2011. In April 2012, the Sqoop project was promoted as Apache's top-level project. Since then, all releases have been managed by Apache committee members. As of the writing of this book, 1.4.6 is the stable release for Sqoop, released on May 11, 2015.

Due to some inherent challenges in Sqoop 1 (version 1.x.x), fresh thought came in this regard and this brought Sqoop 2 into existence. In this book, we will be using Sqoop 1 instead of Sqoop 2. However, we will make sure that you are introduced, in more detail, both the versions of Sqoop so that you have a fair bit of knowledge and clearly know the distinction between the two versions and when to use what.

Advantages of Sqoop

Below are the advantages of Apache Sqoop, which is also the reason for choosing this technology in this layer.

- Allows the transfer of data with a variety of structured data stores like Postgres, Oracle, Teradata, and so on.
- Since the data is transferred and stored in Hadoop, Sqoop allows us to offload certain processing done in the **ETL** (**Extract**, **Load** and **Transform**) process into low-cost, fast, and effective Hadoop processes.
- Sqoop can execute the data transfer in parallel, so execution can be quick and more cost effective.
- Helps to integrate with sequential data from the mainframe. This helps not only to limit the usage of the mainframe, but also reduces the high cost in executing certain jobs using mainframe hardware.
- Data from other structured data stores can be Sqooped into Hadoop, which is mainly for unstructured data stores. This process allows us to combine both types of data for various analysis purposes in a more cost effective and fast manner.
- Has an extension mechanism, using which different connectors can be built and hooked. This can be used to customize existing connectors, and can also be tweaked according to use case requirements. There are a number of in-built connectors for stores such as MySQL, PostgreSQL, Oracle, and a number of well-known ones. Because of its capability of writing extensions, many companies have written custom connectors that are well supported and enterprise grade. For example, Oracle connector is developed by Quest Software and VoltDB connector is developed by VoltDB itself.
- In addition to JDBC based connectors (for various RDBMS systems), it also has direct connectors which uses native tools for better performance.
- Sqoop also supports a variety of file formats such as Avro, Text, and SequenceFile.

Avro is a remote procedure call and data serialization framework developed within Apache's Hadoop project. It uses JSON for defining data types and protocols, and serializes data in a compact binary format.

- Wikipedia

SequenceFile is a flat file consisting of binary key/value pairs. It is extensively used in MapReduce as input/output formats.

- Hadoop wiki

Disadvantages of Sqoop

Even though Sqoop has very strong advantages to its name, it does have some inherent disadvantages, which can be summarized as:

- It uses a JDBC connection to connect with RDBMS based data stores, and this can be inefficient and less performant.
- For performing analysis, it executes various map-reduce jobs and, at times, this can be time consuming when there are lot of joins if the data is in a denormalized fashion.
- Being used for bulk transfer of data, it could put undue pressure on the source data store, and this is not ideal if these stores are heavily used by the main business application.

Workings of Sqoop

For your data lake, you will definitely have to ingest data from traditional applications and data sources. The ingested data, being big, will definitely have to fall into the Hadoop store. Apache Sqoop is one technology that allows you to ingest data from these traditional enterprise data stores into Hadoop with ease.

SQL to Hadoop = SQOOP

The figure below (*Figure 03*) shows the basic workings of Apache Sqoop. It gives tools to export data from RDBMS to the Hadoop filesystem. It also gives tools to import data from a Hadoop filesystem back to RDBMS.

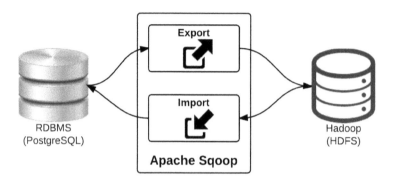

Figure 03: Basic workings of Sqoop

In our use case, we will be exporting the data stored in RDBMS (PostgreSQL) to the **Hadoop File System** (**HDFS**). We will not be looking at Sqoop's import capability in detail, but we will briefly cover that aspect also in this chapter so that you have pretty good knowledge of the different capabilities of this great tool.

As of writing this book, Sqoop has two variations (flavours) called by its major versions as **Sqoop 1** and **Sqoop 2**. We have detailed sections below which explain both Sqoop 1 and 2, jotting down comparisons between the two for easy understanding. In this book, as detailed earlier, we will be working with Sqoop 1, as Sqoop 2 is still a work in progress and we wouldn't want to start solving its inherent problems while constructing the code for our use case.

Below is a figure taken from official Sqoop documentation, and it shows the architecture view for Apache Sqoop 1.

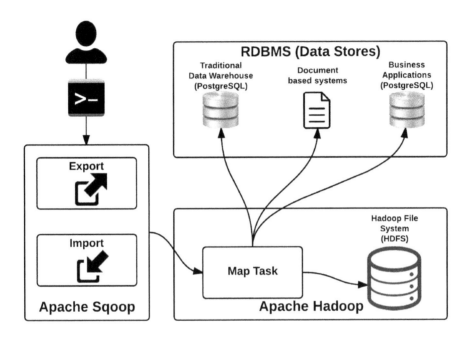

Figure 04: Conceptual architecture of Sqoop 1

The workings of Sqoop are pretty straightforward, as detailed conceptually in the preceding figure. The user interacts with Sqoop using command prompts using various commands. These commands, when executed, kick off map tasks in Hadoop, which connects with the supplied RDBMS (using **JDBC - Java DataBase Connectivity**) and then connects to the Hadoop filesystems and stores data. One of the inherent problems with Sqoop 1 is very fundamental and this is due to the usage of JDBC for connectivity, as this can be quite clunky for different use cases.

> *JDBC is an application programming interface (API) for the programming language Java, which defines how a client may access a database. It is part of the Java Standard Edition platform, from Oracle Corporation.*

- Wikipedia

The next section gives the reader a glimpse of Sqoop 2, as this is logically the next step in the upgrade process for Sqoop 1.

Sqoop 2 architecture

The workings of Sqoop 2 are very much in line with Sqoop 1. However, Sqoop 2 brings in more user-friendly and easy-to-use features by taking difficult parts of Sqoop 1 away from the user. It brings in a new web browser based tool along with the client (this is the only option in Sqoop 1) and also helps the user install Sqoop once on a machine, giving provision for the user to access it from multiple places. It also gives a good amount of RESTful API's (more details can be found in the Apache Sqoop documentation at `https://sqoop.apache.org/docs/1.99.5/RESTAPI.html`), which aids in many of the integrations that Sqoop needs to support for effective use in the context of a data lake.

The following figure (*Figure 05*) shows the detailed architecture of how Sqoop 2 works as compared to Sqoop 1. To bring in comparison between Sqoop 1, additional parts brought in by Sqoop 2 are shaded. The architecture figure is referred from the Sqoop documentation (`https://sqoop.apache.org/docs/1.99.5/`) and changed to decipher the context of this book.

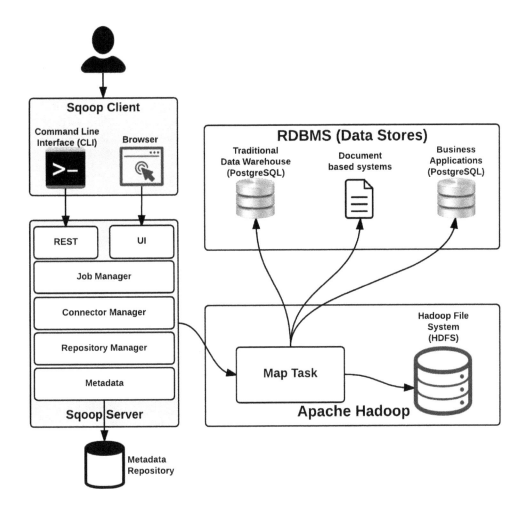

Figure 05: Conceptual architecture of Sqoop 2

As shown in *Figure 05*, the shaded sections are new in Sqoop 2. Sqoop 2 has introduced a server component and has also given a new client in the form of a browser, using which users can now interact with Sqoop and this interface shields the user from clunky commands and hides the complexity behind the browser interface. Due to the server component, users can now interact with Sqoop from other machines as well, as opposed to Sqoop 1. There are a number of components inside Sqoop the server component, enabling this new set of features, and these are shown in the above figure. Also, with that, a new block in the server, namely **Metadata**, which stores so-called data for data so that it is quite easy for the user, takes away much of the commonly repeated stuff, and allows us to use this data stored in the repository.

Sqoop 1 versus Sqoop 2

It's important to understand the difference between the two flavours of Sqoop, and this sections aims to cover that in some detail. It will first explain the main design thoughts on which Sqoop 2 was designed and then compare each of these with regards to Sqoop 1.

As detailed in blogs on the Apache website on Sqoop, below are the main design thoughts on which the newly-developed and ever-evolving Sqoop 2 architecture design is based. They are:

- Ease of use
- Ease of extension
- Security

The subsections below will delve into the above design thoughts and compare both Sqoop 1 and Sqoop 2.

Ease of use

Adding the layer between the client and Hadoop is the reason for a lot of the ease which Sqoop 2 brings as compared to Sqoop 1. The following table compares this design though between the two versions.

Sqoop 1	Sqoop 2
Command line is the only client option	Command line along with browser interface (via Hue) are the client options
Client only architecture	Client-server architecture

Client works only on the same machine where Sqoop is installed	Server setup allows access to Sqoop from different machines
Tight coupling between other tools (Apache Oozie) when integration is brought about.	Integration is quite easy using the exposed REST API's
Connectors and drivers need to be configured for each client installation separately. Each of the clients need to have connection details with them to connect and execute.	Because of server component, connectors and JDBC drivers would be configured in one place
No well defined role-based access possible.	Role-based access and execution is possible because of the central access by the server component.
More error prone, as many options are to be filled in manually by the user by reading various available documentation.	Having a browser-based interface makes sure that the user is advised when they make mistakes and that all necessary options are filled in before actually using Sqoop.

Table 01: Sqoop 1 and Sqoop 2 - Comparison based on Ease of Use

> *Hue (Hadoop User Experience) is an open-source Web interface that supports Apache Hadoop and its ecosystem, licensed under the Apache v2 license.*

- Wikipedia

Quite clearly, this design thought scores well with Sqoop 2 as against Sqoop 1 and most of the advantages come in by default for Sqoop 2 because of the central one-time server component installation.

Ease of extension

Let's now get into the second design thought based on which Sqoop 2 was designed. This aspect is quite crucial for modern day enterprises with varying types of applications in which data lives.

Sqoop 1	Sqoop 2
Only JDBC style connector possible	Apart from JDBC, other connectors can be built and used. Because of this, it is quite flexible and other data stores can easily write and maintain their own connectors.

Common connector functionality not abstracted away, making it complex to write connectors and they are forced to know the nitty-gritties of Sqoop	Common connector functionality abstracted away and providers need to only write the core aspects. This allows the shielding of unwanted complexities while writing the connector.
Complexity of writing a connector is quite high.	Complexity has reduced considerably as low-level working details of Sqoop have been abstracted away and the connector provider only writes core logic of data transfer.
Explicit selection of connector is not mandated nor validated, paving way for errors. Connector selection is implicit.	Explicit connector selection is mandated reducing errors resulting due to selection of wrong connector.

Table 02: Sqoop 1 and Sqoop 2 - Comparison based on ease of extension

The table above summarized the differences between Sqoop 1 and 2 with regard to writing a connector. Clearly, Sqoop 2 brings in good advantages as against Sqoop 1.

Security

One of the key design thoughts which Sqoop 2 considered when it was being designed and developed is security. For modern day enterprises, utmost care is given to data security, and Sqoop 2 does aid in having a granular and fine grained access control.

The following table summarizes this very important aspect between the two Sqoop versions.

Sqoop 1	Sqoop 2
No role-based access control	Role-based access control possible because of the single Sqoop server component.
Only Hadoop security available	Hadoop security along with role-based security available.
Limited security support (username/password) when integrating with external systems	External system security using role-based access control.
Client requires direct access to Hive and HBase	Server only needs to have access and the client having access is defined using well defined roles.

Each client makes distinct connections which are never reused	Connections are made first class objects and they are pooled and used multiple times. Users having Admin role creates connection objects and users having Operator role uses these connections for executing various jobs.
Does not possess resource management policy	Possesses resource management policy. The above point allows how connections can be used and how each role can be used during execution of job (import or export).

Table 03: Sqoop 1 and Sqoop 2 - Comparison based on security

Clearly, Sqoop 2 scores well against Sqoop 1 in one of the key aspects, namely, security. For modern day enterprises, security plays a key role, especially in regard to data and how it can be accessed and used by different parties in the organization.

When to use Sqoop 1 and Sqoop 2

At the time of writing this book Sqoop 2 is still not fully complete in all aspects and not fully in a stable state. That's the core reason for us to choose Sqoop 1 for implementing the chosen use case for this book. However, clearly Sqoop 2 brings in good advantages (detailed in subsections above) as against Sqoop 1 and when fully ready should be used or favored in place of Sqoop 1.

Functioning of Sqoop

Let's get into a bit more detail on the actual working of Sqoop in this section. When a command is entered in the command line, these in turn execute a map task to connect to the desired RDBMS (using appropriate connector) and then retrieve the required/relevant data. After the map task, it hands over the data to the reduce task, which has the responsibility of persisting this retrieved data to HDFS/HBase/Hive.

Data import using Sqoop

The import tool within Sqoop when given commands imports individual or all tables from RDBMS using various available connector API's into HDFS. When importing data, each row in an RDBMS table is imported into HDFS as a record. According to the type of data, it is either stored as text files for text data or as sequence files and Avro files in case of binary data.

The following figure (*Figure 06* - our interpretation of Sqoop Export inspired from Apache Sqoop blogs) details the Sqoop import tool functioning by importing data from PostgreSQL to HDFS:

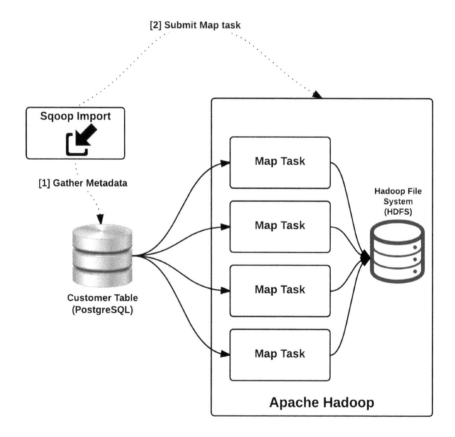

Figure 06: Working of Sqoop Import

Before the actual Sqoop import function executes, the tool analyses the database and forms relevant metadata. The formed metadata is then used to execute the import function from the database of the required table or the whole table as the case may be.

Sqoop does provide different options based on which the import function can take place. The data imported from a table is stored as single or multiple HDFS files (according to size of data from source) in the form of comma separated values (for each column) and each row in the table is separated using a new line. Sqoop also provides options while importing to specify file format (Avro or text files).

Later in this chapter we will actually run you through the Sqoop command which will be used to get data from PostgreSQL to HDFS. This section just gives the import Sqoop functioning and its actual working under the hood.

Data export using Sqoop

The working of the Sqoop export tool is very much similar to the Sqoop import tool. When the export command is executed, Sqoop gathers the metadata required for the export function and then churns the appropriate map tasks depending on the size and nature of the data; then it transfers the data to the appropriate RDBMS. It does use the available connectors to actually persist/write the data to the database. Some connectors have a concept of staging table where data is first collected (staged) and then actually moved to the target database. This staged table approach is good in one aspect where there is a failure while export and because of this staged data availability, the whole job doesn't have to be redone, rather it could very well be reused.

The following figure (*Figure 07* - our interpretation of Sqoop Export inspired from Apache Sqoop blogs), very much similar to Sqoop import (*Figure 06*) gives the inner working of Sqoop when exporting data using Sqoop:

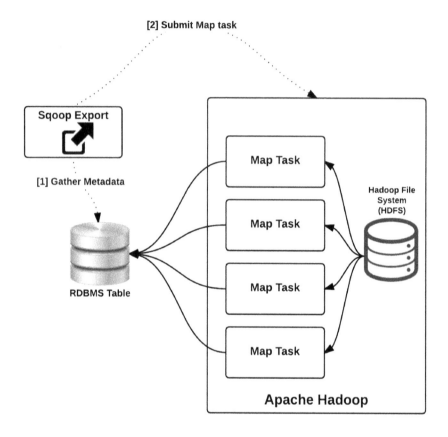

Figure 07: Working of Sqoop Export

Our use case does not demand showing the export function of Sqoop; however, we will just give you the important Sqoop export commands in the next sections of this chapter so that you as a reader have a complete understanding of Sqoop.

Sqoop connectors

Sqoop connector allows Sqoop job to:

- Connect to the desired database system (import and export)
- Extract data from the database system (export) and
- Load the data to the database system (import)

Apache Sqoop allows itself to be extended in the form of having the capability of plugin codes, which is specialized in data transfer with a particular database system. This capability is a part of Sqoop's extension framework and can be added to any installation of Sqoop. Sqoop 1 does have this capability and Sqoop 2 extends this aspect even further and adds many new features (the comparison section before has covered this aspect). Sqoop 2 has better integration using well defined connector API's.

For transferring data when Sqoop is invoked, two components come into play, namely:

- **Driver**: JDBC is one of the main mechanisms for Sqoop to connect to a RDBMS. The driver in purview of Sqoop refers to JDBC driver. JDBC is a specification given by **Java Development Kit** (**JDK**) consisting of various abstract classes and interfaces. Any RDBMS for connecting to them provides drivers complying with the JDBC specification. These drivers are proprietary and often have licenses associated with it, based on which this could be used. For Sqoop to work, these drivers need to be installed as the case may be by individual users and then used. Since these drivers are written by the database system providers it would be written with utmost care to be highly performant and efficiency in mind.

- **Connector:** For a Sqoop job to run, it requires metadata of the data which needs to be transferred. Connector helps to retrieve these metadata and aids in transferring data (import and export) in the most efficient manner possible. JDBC is one of the main mechanisms and uses SQL language for data extraction and load; but each database systems would have certain hacks called as dialects. Connector uses these dialects to efficiently transfer data. Sqoop ships with a default JDBC connector (generic), which works with JDBC and SQL-compliant database systems; but due to its generic nature, it may not be the most optimal way of transferring data. There are other built-in connectors and external specialized connectors, which will be discussed in detail in the following subsection.

The figure (*Figure 08*) shows how these components are used by the Sqoop client to get a connection and thereafter use this connection object to transfer data from and to the database system:

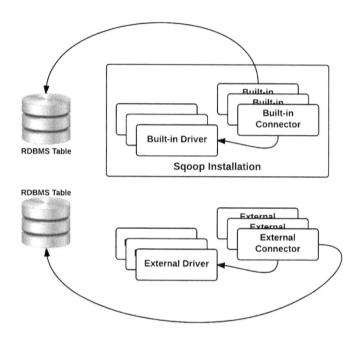

Figure 08: Sqoop Connector components and its working

In the case of Sqoop 1, when a command is executed, Sqoop first analyses the command-line arguments and scans the Sqoop installation for the most apt (efficient and better performing) connector. It does scan both the built-in and manually installed connectors while choosing the best possible option. If it is not able to find right connector, as a last resort, it uses the built-in generic JDBC connector. Once it selects a connector, it looks for the best driver, and mostly there is a specialized driver tagged to a connection and database system to choose from. In case of generic JDBC driver, however, the driver has to be explicitly supplied using the command-line parameters.

One of the difference between Sqoop 2 is that in Sqoop 2, the connector has to be explicitly selected as against implicit selection in Sqoop 1.

Types of Sqoop connectors

Sqoop connectors can be broadly classified as below:

- **Built-in connectors**: Connectors which ship along with the default Sqoop installation are categorized in this. Built-in connectors can again be sub-categorized as follows:
    - **Generic JDBC connector**: This connector can be used to connect to any database system complying with JDBC and SQL. Sqoop chooses this connector as a last resort when it is not able to find any other connector (default or manually installed).
    - **Specialized connectors**: These are connectors included by default along with Sqoop installation for all the popular database management systems. Some of the example connectors falling into this category are Oracle, MySQL, PostgreSQL and so on.
    - **Fast-path connectors:** Specialized built-in connector which use database specific tools to better perform the data transfer option fall into this category. MySQL and PostgreSQL have such native tool based connectors which does have better performance and throughput purely by the merit of being native.
- **Pluggable external connectors**: As against built-in default connectors, Sqoop does allow plugging in external connectors dealing with appropriate datasource to better do the data transfer and these connectors fall into this category. These are specialized connectors, mostly supplied and maintained by the database providers. Being managed by the provider themselves, these usually are highly performant and use different database native tools to do the data transfer job. Connectors dealing with different NoSQL databases are readily available, such as Couchbase connector.

Sqoop support for HDFS

Sqoop is natively built for HDFS export and import; however, architecturally it can support and source and target data stores for data exports and imports. In fact, if we observe the convention of the words Import and Export it is all with respect to whether the data is coming into HDFS or going out of HDFS respectively. Sqoop also supports incremental data exports and imports with having an additional attribute/fields for tracking the database incrementals.

Sqoop also supports a number of file formats for optimized storage such as Apache Avro, orc, parquet, and so on. Both parquet and Avro have been very popular file formats with respect to HDFS while orc offers better performance and compression. But as a tradeoff, parquet and Avro formats are relatively more preferred formats due to maintainability and recent enhancements for these formats in HDFS, supporting multi-value fields and search patterns.

> *Avro is a remote procedure call and data serialization framework developed within Apache's Hadoop project. It uses JSON for defining data types and protocols, and serializes data in a compact binary format. Its primary use is in Apache Hadoop, where it can provide both a serialization format for persistent data, and a wire format for communication between Hadoop nodes, and from client programs to the Hadoop services.*

> *- Wikipedia*

Sqoop working example

We will be using **Google Cloud Platform** for running the whole use case that we will be covering in this book. Screenshots and code would be covered throughout this book with this in mind so that the reader at the end of this book would have a fully functioning Data Lake in the cloud which slowly could be connected to the real database existing in the enterprise.

Being the first chapter, which is now dealing with installation and code, this chapter will install certain softwares/tools/technologies/libraries that will be referred to in subsequent chapters. In the context of Sqoop, some installations and commands won't be required but are needed for running all of these in the cloud having a clean node with nothing installed on it.

These examples have been prepared and tested on *CentOS 7*, and this would be our platform for all the examples covered in this book.

Installation and Configuration

For all the installations discussed in this book, we are following some basic conventions and assumptions:

1. The user is assumed to be a non-root, but `sudo` user configured with no password.

2. All downloads are assumed to be downloaded into a single directory, referred to as `${DOWNLOAD_DIR}`. This should be configured as an environment variable using the following command and the same must be added into `~/.bashrc`:

```
export DOWNLOAD_DIR=<path of download directory>
```

3. All the installations are assumed to done in user directories, except for RPMs, hence any system level changes, package installations, and so on will have to be done using sudo.

Now let's get our hands dirty with some code. This section details each and every point as a step for easy reading and understanding. Let's dig in.

Step 1 - Installing and verifying Java

1. For the purpose of the examples covered in this book, it is recommended to go with Oracle JDK only.
2. Please copy the download link to the latest Java JDK from the Oracle website. For Linux distributions, RPM download is recommended. At the time of writing this book, this is the Oracle JDK download page (`http://www.oracle.com/technetwork/java/javase/downloads/jdk8-downloads-2133151.html`), however this changes often, hence may require some fresh search and exploration on search engines.
3. In order to download from the copied link, please run this command in CentOS shell. Here the copied link is the one pointing to the `download.oracle.com`, however since this link is dynamic, it will need to be copied for every download.

```
wget --header "Cookie: oraclelicense=accept-securebackup-
cookie"
http://download.oracle.com/otn-pub/java/jdk/8u131-b11/d54c1d3a0
95b4ff2b6607d096fa80163/jdk-8u131-linux-x64.rpm
```

4. Once downloaded, run the setup to complete the installation with the following commands:
5. Install the downloaded RPM file by running the following command:

```
rpm --install <JDK_RPM_FILE>
```

6. Set the `JAVA_HOME` environment variable, pointing to the directory where JDK is installed; usually it is in the subdirectories of `/usr/java`.

   export JAVA_HOME=/usr/java/default

7. Configure the `PATH` variable as:

   export PATH=$PATH:$JAVA_HOME/bin

8. Put the above export statements in `~/.bashrc`
9. Verify the install by executing the following command and observing that `PATH` has the location of JAVA folder installed:

   echo $PATH

Even now, `java -version` would show Open JDK but that can be ignored as various components make use of `JAVA_HOME` as a reference point for JAVA install.

Step 2 - Installing and verifying Hadoop

1. As mentioned before we would be using open source Apache Hadoop distribution for all the samples in this book, specifically version 2.7.3.
2. Download the Hadoop Distribution from the following location in `${DOWNLOAD_DIR}` using `wget` command:

   ```
   wget
   http://www-eu.apache.org/dist/hadoop/common/hadoop-2.7.3/hadoop-2.7
   .3.tar.gz
   ```

3. Once the download is complete, using the shell change into any user directory, let us refer it as `${HADOOP_HOME}`, where we want to install, and run the following command to extract the contents:

   ```
   tar -xzvf ${DOWNLOAD_DIR}/ hadoop-2.7.3.tar.gz
   ```

4. Also, please disable the firewall from within the shell using the following command and reboot the VM:

   ```
   systemctl stop firewalld
   systemctl disable firewalld
   ```

5. We will be setting up Hadoop in pseudo distributed mode for the examples, while in production Hadoop is setup in distributed mode (in `Chapter 09`, *Data Store using Apache Hadoop* we are covering Hadoop deployment options in a bit more detail). Change into the `${HADOOP_HOME}` directory and perform the changes as mentioned here: `https://goo.gl/x6TC9q`

6. In case of `HOST KEY VERIFICATION FAILURE`, while setting up Hadoop in Pseudo distributed mode, please run the following commands in the shell:

```
ssh-keyscan -H -t rsa localhost  >> ~/.ssh/known_hosts
ssh-keyscan -H -t rsa 0.0.0.0  >> ~/.ssh/known_hosts
ssh-keyscan -H -t rsa 127.0.0.1  >> ~/.ssh/known_hosts
```

8. Once the DFS is up and running, the installation completion can be confirmed by navigating to the following URL: `http://localhost:50070`.

9. This pseudo-distribution setup is a reasonably complete setup that will be required for running various examples covered in this book.

10. As of now, we may just run DFS, however we will delve into other services like YARN, Hive, Hbase, and so on in later chapters in this book. For running Sqoop examples we just need dfs running.

11. Please set the environment variable `HADOOP_HOME` to point to the Hadoop installation directory, using the export command in `~/.bashrc`. Also configure the PATH environment variable:

```
export HADOOP_HOME=<Hadoop-Installation-Directory>
export PATH=$PATH:$JAVA_HOME/bin:$HADOOP_HOME/sbin:$HADOOP_HOME/bin
```

Step 3 - Installing and verifying Hue

Hue provides a complete UI based access to various Hadoop services, orchestrations, workflows and even a browser for HDFS. Hue setup is very straightforward, and can be done by compiling the hue from source. In order to install Hue, the following steps may be followed:

1. Please download Hue 3.11 using the following command for its tarball release:

```
wget
https://dl.dropboxusercontent.com/u/730827/hue/releases/3.11.0/hue-
3.11.0.tgz
```

2. Extract the contents of the tarball in a user directory by using the following command:

```
tar -zxvf ${DOWNLOAD_DIR}/hue-3.11.0.tgz
```

3. Hue setup has dependency on Python 2.7 and many of the other packages, which need to be installed the OS specific package installer. For the purpose of this book, we have tried all the installs on CentOS 7, and we ended up with the following packages to be specifically installed:

```
sudo yum install libffi-devel
sudo yum install gmp-devel
sudo yum install python-devel mysql-devel
sudo yum install ant gcc gcc-c++ rsync krb5-devel mysql openssl-
devel cyrus-sasl-devel cyrus-sasl-gssapi sqlite-devel openldap-
devel python-simplejson
sudo yum install libtidy libxml2-devel libxslt-devel
sudo yum install python-devel python-simplejson python-
setuptools sudo yum install maven
```

4. As per Hue's README.txt, which has the installation steps, please run the following command from the HUE source directory (the directory where we extracted tarball):

```
PREFIX=~/ make install
```

5. Here PREFIX is considered to be the installation directory, but it can be any of the user directories as well. Hue setup would create a directory, hue, under that PREFIX.

6. Once the install completes, configure the ${PREFIX}/hue/desktop/conf/hue.ini with the correct HDFS URL as shown:

```
fs_defaultfs=hdfs://localhost:9000
```

7. Set the environment variable ${HUE_HOME} using the following command, and add the same to ~/.bashrc.

```
export HUE_HOME=~/hue
```

(assuming that this is the folder path created in the previous step).

8. Configure `${HADOOP_HOME}/etc/hadoop/hdfs-site.xml` with the following properties:

```
<property>
  <name>dfs.webhdfs.enabled</name>
  <value>true</value>
</property>
<property>
  <name>hadoop.proxyuser.hue.hosts</name>
  <value>*</value>
</property>
<property>
  <name>hadoop.proxyuser.hue.groups</name>
  <value>*</value>
</property>
```

9. Once Hue is setup, please change to the `${HUE_HOME}` and start the hue server with the following command:

   `${HUE_HOME}/build/env/bin/supervisor`

10. To run it as a daemon process, so that the process does not terminate if your console gets disconnected, you may use the following command:

    `${HUE_HOME}/build/env/bin/supervisor -d`

11. Navigate to `http://localhost:8888` and create the user account for Hue. After login, we can also see HDFS file view from hue (located at top right corner).

Once we login into the Hue console, some errors or misconfiguration may be reported, but these can be ignored, as we will be setting up these configurations with every framework we integrate with Hue.

Step 4 - Installing and verifying Sqoop

Sqoop has been changing in its form and features very rapidly since the Hadoop platform release. As mentioned before, the Sqoop framework, as it stands today, comes as Sqoop and Sqoop 2. While Sqoop is the older generation of the ETL framework in the Hadoop world, it is complete. On the other hand, Sqoop 2 is a more recent advancement with a REST-based interface but it is still not complete. For the purpose of installation, we'll cover the installation of the Sqoop version specifically.

Sqoop binary packages can be downloaded and extracted as given below:

1. Download the binary package of sqoop with hadoop2 compatibility with the following command:

   ```
   wget
   https://www-eu.apache.org/dist/sqoop/1.4.6/sqoop-1.4.6.bin__hadoop-
   2.0.4-alpha.tar.gz
   ```

2. Extract this tarball in any of the user directories, let us refer to it as `${SQOOP_HOME}`, with the following command:

   ```
   tar -zxvf <DOWNLOAD_LOCATION>/sqoop-1.4.6.bin__hadoop-2.0.4-
   alpha.tar.gz
   ```

3. Configure the **${SQOOP_HOME}** environment variable with the following command and add the same to `~/.bashrc`:

   ```
   export SQOOP_HOME=${SQOOP_HOME}
   export PATH=$PATH:$SQOOP_HOME/bin
   ```

4. Verify by invoking `sqoop --help` in the CentOS shell.

Alternatively, to build and install Sqoop from source, please follow the following steps:

1. Download the latest version of Sqoop from:

   ```
   wget http://www-eu.apache.org/dist/sqoop/1.4.6/sqoop-1.4.6.tar.gz
   ```

2. Extract this tarball in any of the user directories; let's refer to it as `${SQOOP_HOME}`, with the following command:

   ```
   tar -zxvf <DOWNLOAD_LOCATION>/sqoop-1.4.6.tar.gz
   ```

3. Follow instructions in `COMPILING.txt` to compile the source code, or alternatively using ssh change into `${SQOOP_HOME}` and run the following command:

   ```
   ant release
   ```

4. During the install, if any executables are reported to be missing, please install them using package installer (`yum install <required package>`). The ones we encountered on CentOS 7 were, **AsciiDoc**, **LSB** and xmlto.

5. After the install, copy the `bin` folder of Sqoop source into build/bin and copy the build folder to an independent folder.

6. Configure the `${SQOOP_HOME}` environment variable with the following command and add the same to `~/.bashrc`:

```
export SQOOP_HOME=${SQOOP_HOME}
export PATH=$PATH:$SQOOP_HOME/bin
```

7. Verify by invoking `sqoop -help` in the CentOS shell.

Step 5 - Installing and verifying PostgreSQL (RDBMS)

We have selected PostgreSQL as our relational database, which we would be using both as a metastore as well as a data store for relational information. While the sample described in this chapter may correspond to Sqoop, the installation will be reused across the chapter.

PostgreSQL provides ready packages for almost all the common operating systems. For Linux, the PostgreSQL is available as a standard package that can be installed using native package installer. On CentOS 7, we followed the following steps.

1. Run the following command in terminal:

```
sudo yum install postgresql-server*
```

2. Once the database is installed, please initialize the database by running the following:

```
sudo service postgresql initdb
sudo chkconfig postgresql on
```

3. Start postgres server with the following command:

```
sudo service postgresql start
```

4. By this time, a Postgres user (non-interactive) has been created on the system. The database password for this user may be altered with the following commands:

```
sudo -u postgres psql postgres
```

This would take you into Postgres shell which would be indicated as `postgres=#`. Use the following command to enter the new password:

```
postgres=# password postgres
```

5. Exit the Postgres shell by entering the following command:

    ```
    postgres=# q
    ```

6. Next, we will need to alter configurations in the data directory of the newly created database. Invoke the following command to see the data directory and the port on which PostgreSQL is running. Default port is *5432*. As a reference, it can be seen something similar to /usr/bin/postgres -D /var/lib/pgsql/data -p 5432 after the command is executed:

    ```
    sudo service postgresql status
    ```

7. Set the permissions to modify the pgsql data files with the following command:

    ```
    sudo chmod 777 -R /var/lib/pgsql
    ```

8. Now go to data directory of Postgres and alter the pg_hba.conf (/var/lib/pgsql/data/pg_hba.conf) to allow local and remote users connect to the database using postgres user credentials. A typical modified file of pg_hba.conf looks as given:

```
# TYPE   DATABASE         USER              ADDRESS
                   METHOD
# "local" is for Unix domain socket connections only
local    all              all
                                              md5
# IPv4 local connections:
host     all              all               127.0.0.1/32
         md5
# IPv6 local connections:
host     all              all               ::1/128
              md5
# remote connections
host     all              all               0.0.0.0/0
              md5
# Allow replication connections from localhost, by a user with the
# replication privilege.
#local   replication      postgres
                              peer
#host    replication      postgres          127.0.0.1/32
              ident
#host    replication      postgres          ::1/128
              ident
```

9. The lines highlighted above have been changed from their original values to enable a normal username/password based login.

10. Now, we will need to modify the `/var/lib/pgsql/data/postgresql.conf` file with the following:

```
# - Connection Settings -

listen_addresses = '*'          # what IP address(es) to listen on;
                                # comma-separated list of addresses;
                                # defaults to 'localhost'; use '*' for all
                                # (change requires restart)
```

11. Set the permissions back onto the folder `/var/lib/pgsql` with the following command:

    ```
    sudo chmod 0700 -R /var/lib/pgsql
    ```

12. Start/Restart the PostgreSQL service with the following command:

    ```
    sudo service postgresql restart
    ```

This completes the database setup. In order to be able to remotely access this database please ensure the following:

- The database port is open and accessible
- A client application is installed to help run the query on Postgre database. We would recommend installing `pgAdmin4` as the PostgreSQL client.

Step 6 - Installing and verifying HBase (NoSQL)

1. Download **HBase** binary version 0.98.24 from the following URL using the command:

    ```
    wget
    https://archive.apache.org/dist/hbase/0.98.24/hbase-0.98.24-hadoop2
    -bin.tar.gz
    ```

At the time of authoring this book, the stable version of HBase was 1.2.4, but we were forced to fallback to 0.98.x vesion of HBase due to compatibility issues of Sqoop 1 with newer versions of HBase.

2. Extract the above binary with tar command as shown below, from the directory where you would want to extract it, let us refer to it as `${HBASE_HOME}`:

```
tar -zxvf downloads/hbase-0.98.24-hadoop2-bin.tar.gz
```

3. Set an environment variable `HBASE_HOME` pointing to the directory where the files have been extracted with following command and add the same to `~/.bashrc` file:

```
export HBASE_HOME=${HBASE_HOME}
export PATH=$PATH:$HBASE_HOME/bin
```

4. Once extracted, we can observe that the HBase configuration files are placed in `${HBASE_HOME}/conf` directory.

5. Lookup `hbase-site.xml` in `<HBASE_HOME>/conf` directory, and please modify the following as shown below (`centos` is the username used in this sample configuration, this can be replaced with the username on the VM. Also, replace the localhost with IP address of HDFS).

```xml
<configuration>
  <property>
    <name>hbase.rootdir</name>
    <value>hdfs://localhost:9000/user/centos/hbase</value>
  </property>
  <property>
    <name>hbase.zookeeper.property.dataDir</name>
    <value>/home/testuser/zookeeper</value>
  </property>
</configuration>
```

6. Please start HBase by executing `<HABSE_HOME>/bin/start-hbase.sh`, which would start the Hbase service which can be monitored at `http://localhost:60010`:

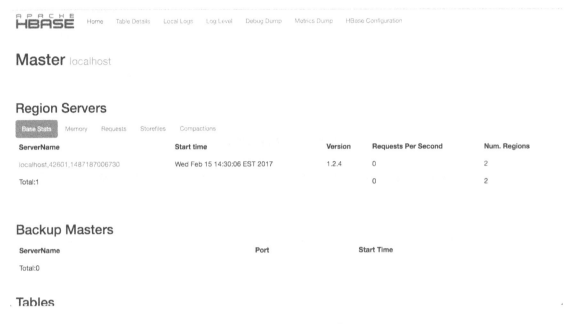

Figure 09: HBase Service Console

7. We may verify the HBase install by launching it's shell and running some basic HBase queries:
    1. Launch the shell by executing `<HBASE_HOME>/bin/hbase` shell command.
    2. Create a test table by executing the following query inside the shell:

    ```
    create 'test', 'cf'
    ```

3. If the above table gets created successfully, it indicates that the basic setup is successful and refreshing the HBase Service home page lists the table created as shown:

Tables

| User Tables | System Tables | Snapshots |

1 table(s) in set. [Details]

Namespace	Table Name	Online Regions	Offline Regions	Failed Regions	Split Regions	Other Regions	Description
default	test	1	0	0	0	0	'test', {NAME => 'cf'}

Figure 10: HBase Install Verification

8. Also, alternatively, please consider referring to the `Get Started` page of HBase of further reference.

This is the basic setup of HBase and would be sufficient for us to run a few Sqoop examples.

Configure data source (ingestion)

In this section we will see how to configure our data source which will be considered as a source for data ingestion into our Data Lake.

1. Login into PostgreSQL database using a client (`pgAdmin4`) with the user postgres and respective credentials.
2. Create the source database that would have customer profile information. This database can be created using `pgAdmin4` UI, let us name it as `sourcedb`.
3. Execute the following script to create the table:

```
CREATE TABLE public."customer"(
    id integer NOT NULL,
    first_name character varying COLLATE pg_catalog."default",
    last_name character varying COLLATE pg_catalog."default",
    dob date,
    CONSTRAINT "customer_pkey" PRIMARY KEY (id)
)
WITH (
    OIDS = FALSE
)
TABLESPACE pg_default;
```

```
ALTER TABLE public."customer"
OWNER to postgres;
```

4. Insert a few rows of data into this table with a script as given below:

```
INSERT  INTO public."customer"
values(0,'tomcy','john','1985-10-20');
INSERT  INTO public."customer"
values(1,'rahul','dev','1989-08-15');
INSERT  INTO public."customer"
values(2,'pankaj','misra','1982-08-10');
INSERT  INTO public."customer" values(3,'devi','lal','1990-05-06');
INSERT  INTO public."customer" values(4,'john','doe','1992-06-25');
```

With the above steps completed we are ready with our source data that we would want to import into HDFS. The table in postgresql should now look as shown in the figure (*Figure 11*):

id [PK] inte...	first_name character...	last_name character...	dob date
0	tomcy	john	1985-10-20
1	rahul	dev	1989-08-15
2	pankaj	misra	1982-08-10
3	devi	lal	1990-05-06
4	john	doe	1992-06-25

Figure 11: Loaded sample data in RDBMS

Sqoop configuration (database drivers)

In order to configure Sqoop with required database drivers, please follow the following steps:

1. Since the database of our choice is postgresql, please download the postgresql JDBC driver from the following location (the latest driver at the time of authoring this book) from within the VM (CentOS) using the following command:

```
wget
https://jdbc.postgresql.org/download/postgresql-9.4.1212.jre6.jar
```

2. Place the JDBC driver inside `${SQOOP_HOME}/lib` folder.

Configuring HDFS as destination

Sqoop's natural destinations are HDFS and RDBMS for import and export respectively. However, Sqoop 2 also supports few more connectors to the list, namely Kafka and Kite.

> *Kite is a high-level data layer for Hadoop. It is an API and a set of tools that speed up development. You configure how Kite stores your data in Hadoop, instead of building and maintaining that infrastructure yourself.*

- http://kitesdk.org/docs/current/

With respect to Sqoop 1, both the source and destination are provided as part of the command line parameters, as would be evident in the examples covered in this chapter.

Sqoop Import

Sqoop when compiled comes with a set of shell scripts that invoke the Sqoop jobs. All the Sqoop operations are performed via a single shell script, which can be found inside `${SQOOP_HOME}/bin`, i.e. `sqoop.sh`.

In order to perform a data import from the configured sources, i.e. postgresql database into HDFS, the shell command can be run as given:

```
bin/sqoop import --connect
jdbc:postgresql://<DB_SERVER_ADDRESS>/<DB_NAME>?schema=<SCHEMA> --table
<TABLE_NAME> --m 1 --username <DB_USER_NAME> --password <DB_PASSWORD>
Where:
    <DB_SERVER_ADDRESS> → Address (hostname/IP) of the database
    <DB_NAME>             → Database Name
    <SCHEMA>              → Database Schema where the source table exists
    <TABLE_NAME>          → Name of the table to be imported
    <DB_USER_NAME>        → Name of the postgresql user who has access to the
                            table
    <DB_PASSWORD>         → Database password for the user
    --me                  → Indicates number of map tasks
```

In our case, the filled-in command is as shown:

```
sqoop import --connect jdbc:postgresql://<CentOS_IP>/sourcedb?schema=public
--table customer --m 1 --username postgres --password <password>
```

Once the import is complete, the imported files can be viewed via Hue or by Namenode UI (**Utilities** | Browse the file system), as shown in the screenshots.

The figure shows the HDFS view in Hue:

Figure 12: HDFS View in Hue (HDFS Browser menu in top right)

The figure (*Figure 13*) shows the same HDFS view in the Namenode UI:

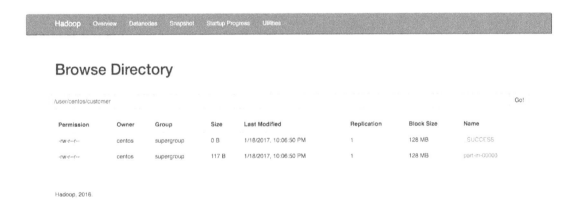

Figure 13: HDFS View in Namenode UI (Utilities/Browse the filesystem menu)

If we look into the file, we see that this file has the contents which we had initially inserted into the sourcedb database in PostgreSQL:

Figure 14: File Contents via Hue

This file written into HDFS has been written in text format, which is the default format until and unless specified. Alternatively, the same Sqoop import could be run to import the data into HDFS as binary Avro data files as well, by making a small change to the import parameters as shown below.

```
bin/sqoop import --connect
jdbc:postgresql://<DB_SERVER_ADDRESS>/<DB_NAME>?schema=<SCHEMA> --table
<TABLE_NAME> --m 1 --username <DB_USER_NAME> --password <DB_PASSWORD> --as-
avrodatafile --append
```

The resulting difference can be seen in the following screenshots. The figure below shows the Avro file uploaded to HDFS viewed using Hue in the HDFS File browser.

Figure 15: Import as Avro Data File via Hue

In the previous screenshot, clicking on the Avro part file would show the content stored in HDFS as shown in following screenshot:

Figure 16: Avro Data File Contents via Hue

As seen in previous figure, the Avro representation of data is slightly different from text representation. An Avro file is also compressed, hence provides the benefits of compression at storage levels.

Import complete database

Sqoop executable also comes with the capability to import all tables from a relational database to HDFS. The typical syntax to perform this is as given:

```
sqoop import-all-tables (generic-args) (import-args)
```

With respect to the previous import command, the only difference here would be to use the `import-all-tables` option of Sqoop command. A sample command is as shown:

```
bin/sqoop import-all-tables --connect
jdbc:postgresql://<DB_SERVER_ADDRESS>/<DB_NAME>?schema=<SCHEMA> --m 1 --
username <DB_USER_NAME> --password <DB_PASSWORD> --as-avrodatafile
```

As we come to this point, we also realize that in order to see this command in action, we should have multiple tables in the relational database. Hence, I would suggest creating an additional table of addresses related to customers:

```
CREATE TABLE public.address
(
    id integer NOT NULL,
    custumer_id integer NOT NULL,
    street1 character varying COLLATE pg_catalog."default",
    street2 character varying COLLATE pg_catalog."default",
    city character varying COLLATE pg_catalog."default",
    state character varying COLLATE pg_catalog."default",
    country character varying COLLATE pg_catalog."default",
    zip_pin_postal_code character varying COLLATE pg_catalog."default",
    CONSTRAINT address_pkey PRIMARY KEY (id),
    CONSTRAINT customer_fkey FOREIGN KEY (custumer_id)
    REFERENCES public.customer (id) MATCH SIMPLE
    ON UPDATE NO ACTION
    ON DELETE NO ACTION
)
WITH (
    OIDS = FALSE
)
TABLESPACE pg_default;

ALTER TABLE public.address
    OWNER to postgres;
```

Once the table is created, the following scripts may be used to load sample data:

```
INSERT INTO address (id, custumer_id, street1, street2, city, state,
country, zip_pin_postal_code)
VALUES (0, 0, 'd-40', 'chavez street', 'trivandrum', 'kerala', 'india',
'778908');
```

```
INSERT INTO address (id, custumer_id, street1, street2, city, state,
country, zip_pin_postal_code)
VALUES (1, 1, '1-90', 'cooper street', 'mumbai', 'maharashtra', 'india',
'400056');
INSERT INTO address (id, custumer_id, street1, street2, city, state,
country, zip_pin_postal_code)
VALUES (2, 2, 'a-47', 'sector-11', 'noida', 'uttar pradesh', 'india',
'201311');
INSERT INTO address (id, custumer_id, street1, street2, city, state,
country, zip_pin_postal_code)
VALUES (3, 3, 'r-98', 'sector-37', 'gurgaon', 'haryana', 'india',
'122021');
INSERT INTO address (id, custumer_id, street1, street2, city, state,
country, zip_pin_postal_code)
VALUES (4, 4, '201', 'high street', 'austin', 'texas', 'us', '41101');
```

If we want to see the import-all-tables in action, we will have to remove existing files in HDFS otherwise this command would fail with a message similar to: `Output directory hdfs://localhost:9000/user/<username>/customer already exists.`

In order to remove the contents from HDFS, we may run the following command in the shell:

```
hdfs dfs -rm -r /user/<username>/*
```

After the import of tables are done, we see that the tables were traversed in a cascading manner to retrieve all the information as shown in the following screenshot:

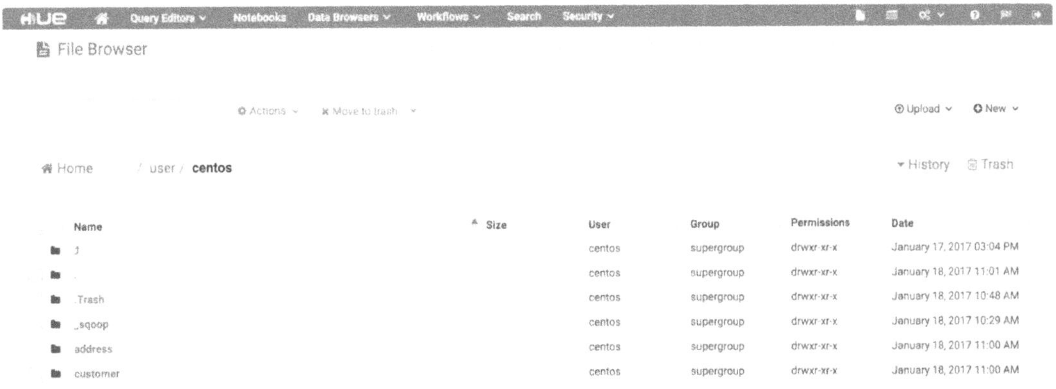

Figure 17: Import all tables in a database into HDFS

Import selected tables

In order to import selected tables, there is no direct mechanism in Sqoop, however it can be achieved by scripting. Sqoop does support getting a list of all tables, and then these tables can be looped over to import selective tables into HDFS.

Import selected columns from a table

Sqoop does provide a command line option to import selected columns into HDFS. This be done either by using the `--columns` option or by using free form query capability of Sqoop. Both of these variations are shown as follows:

- Using `--columns` options:

```
bin/sqoop import --connect
jdbc:postgresql://<DB_SERVER_ADDRESS>/<DB_NAME>?schema=<SCHEMA> --
table customer --columns id,first_name,last_name --m 1 --username
<DB_USER_NAME> --password <DB_PASSWORD> --as-avrodatafile --append
```

- Using free form query capability

```
sqoop import  --query 'SELECT c.*, a.* FROM customer c JOIN address
a on (c.id == a.id) WHERE $CONDITIONS'  -m 1 --target-dir
/user/foo/joinresults
```

Import into HBase

As indicated earlier during the installation steps, Sqoop can also import/export data with HBase as destination/source respectively. Here we shall see how to initiate data import from RDBMS into HBase using Sqoop.

```
bin/sqoop import --connect
jdbc:postgresql://<DB_SERVER_ADDRESS>/<DB_NAME>?schema=<SCHEMA> --table
<TABLE_NAME> --m 1 --username <DB_USER_NAME> --password <DB_PASSWORD>  -
hbase-table <HBASE_TABLE_NAME> --column-family <HBASE_COLUMN_FAMILY_NAME> -
hbase-create-table
```

An example with filled-in values for the above command is as shown as follows:

```
sqoop import --connect jdbc:postgresql://<CentOS_IP>/sourcedb?schema=public
--table customer --m 1 --username postgres --password <password> -hbase-
table customer --column-family h_cust_col1 -hbase-create-table
```

As we see here, there are a few new arguments used specific to HBase. HBase is a NoSQL data store with primary capability to support key value pairs and column families, the arguments used here are specified for table name and column family definition.

After we run the above Sqoop import command, we observe the data to be imported in HDFS storage area of HBase.

In order to view the data in HBase, we can use hbase shell, which can be launched by running the following command in the VM (CentOS) shell:

```
${HBASE_HOME}/bin/hbase shell
```

Once the hbase shell is initialized, run the command as shown in the following screenshot:

```
hbase(main):002:0> scan 'customer'
ROW                              COLUMN+CELL
 0                               column=h_cust_col1:dob, timestamp=1487190691627, value=1985-10-20
 0                               column=h_cust_col1:first_name, timestamp=1487190691627, value=tomcy
 0                               column=h_cust_col1:last_name, timestamp=1487190691627, value=john
 1                               column=h_cust_col1:dob, timestamp=1487190691627, value=1989-08-15
 1                               column=h_cust_col1:first_name, timestamp=1487190691627, value=rahul
 1                               column=h_cust_col1:last_name, timestamp=1487190691627, value=dev
 2                               column=h_cust_col1:dob, timestamp=1487190691627, value=1982-08-10
 2                               column=h_cust_col1:first_name, timestamp=1487190691627, value=pankaj
 2                               column=h_cust_col1:last_name, timestamp=1487190691627, value=misra
 3                               column=h_cust_col1:dob, timestamp=1487190691627, value=1990-05-06
 3                               column=h_cust_col1:first_name, timestamp=1487190691627, value=devi
 3                               column=h_cust_col1:last_name, timestamp=1487190691627, value=lal
 4                               column=h_cust_col1:dob, timestamp=1487190691627, value=1992-06-25
 4                               column=h_cust_col1:first_name, timestamp=1487190691627, value=john
 4                               column=h_cust_col1:last_name, timestamp=1487190691627, value=doe
5 row(s) in 0.0940 seconds

hbase(main):003:0>
```

Figure 18: Imported Table into HBase as seen in "HBase shell"

There is no direct way to export data from HBase using Sqoop; however, it can be achieved by making a Hive view over HBase tables. We will discuss Sqoop export from HDFS in detail in the next section.

Sqoop Export

Similar to the Sqoop import function, Sqoop also can export data from HDFS to a relational database. The precondition, however, is that the table must be already existing in the target database:

```
sqoop export (generic-args) (export-args)

sqoop export --connect
jdbc:postgresql://<DB_SERVER_ADDRESS>/<DB_NAME>?schema=<SCHEMA> --table
```

```
<TABLE_NAME> --m 1 --username <DB_USER_NAME> --password <DB_PASSWORD> --
export-dir <HDFS_SOURCE_PATH>
```

Here `<HDFS_SOURCE_PATH>` is the Hadoop filesystem path as a source that would be exported to a target database:

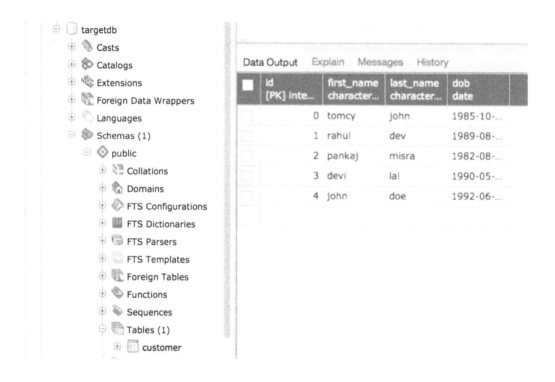

Figure 19: Export to RDBMS from HDFS using Sqoop Export

Sqoop Job

The Sqoop framework also supports concept of Jobs. A Sqoop job may be defined and saved for reusability of Sqoop commands. A Sqoop job typically consists of a source and a destination defined with a few other optional parameters. A Sqoop job is saved in Sqoop metadata for reusability and remote access.

Job command

A job is stored as a metadata entity within Sqoop metastore. The primary objective of creating a job is to define a one-time configuration between source and target systems and reuse it multiple times to perform export or import. Like any other entity, even job supports lifecycle methods such as create, get, update, and delete with a few other functions. We will discuss these functions in the next sections.

Create job

A typical syntax for creating a Sqoop job execution can be defined as:

```
sqoop job (generic-args) (job-args)
   [-- [subtool-name] (subtool-args)]

bin/sqoop job --create <JOB_NAME> -- <OPERATION_NAME> --connect
jdbc:postgresql://<DB_SERVER>/sourcedb?schema=public --table <TABLE_NAME> -
-m 1 --username <DB_USER> --password <DB_PASSWORD> --as-avrodatafile

Where,
<JOB_NAME>                    → Name of the job to be created
<OPERATION_NAME>             → Name of the sqoop operation to be defined,
e.g. import
<DB_SERVER>                  → DB Server address or IP
<TABLE_NAME>                 → Name of the table to be imported
<DB_USER>                    → Username of the DB containing data to be
imported
<DB_PASSWORD>                → Password of the DB containing data to be
imported
```

Please observe the spaces around --. These spaces are interpreted as separators of one segment of command from the other.
For simplicity, the embedded default datastore, namely HSQLDB, is considered here as Sqoop 1 metastore.

HSQLDB is a relational database engine written in Java, with a JDBC driver, conforming to ANSI SQL:2011. A small, fast, multithreaded engine and server with memory and disk tables, LOBs, transaction isolation, multiversion concurrency and ACID.

- https://sourceforge.net/projects/hsqldb/

List Job

The configured jobs can be listed by using the following command:

```
bin/sqoop job --list
```

Run Job

Running the job would always require accessing the stored job and then executing it, hence meta connect (connection to Sqoop 1 metastore where job metadata is stored) would be required here as well. The following command would execute a stored job.

```
bin/sqoop job --exec <JOB_NAME>
```

If prompted for password, please enter your PostgreSQL user password.

Create Job

A typical syntax for creating a Sqoop job execution can be defined as:

```
sqoop job (generic-args) (job-args)
   [-- [subtool-name] (subtool-args)]

bin/sqoop job --create <JOB_NAME> -- <OPERATION_NAME> --connect
jdbc:postgresql://<DB_SERVER>/sourcedb?schema=public --table <TABLE_NAME> -
-m 1 --username <DB_USER> --password <DB_PASSWORD> --as-avrodatafile

Where,
    <JOB_NAME> → Name of the job to be created
    <OPERATION_NAME> → Name of the sqoop operation to be defined, e.g.
import
    <DB_SERVER> → DB Server address or IP
    <TABLE_NAME> → Name of the table to be imported
    <DB_USER> → Username of the DB containing data to be imported
    <DB_PASSWORD> → Password of the DB containing data to be imported
```

Sqoop 2

Sqoop 2 contains all the capabilities as described above in the context of Sqoop 1, as well as many of the new capabilities which do not exist in Sqoop 1. These include Sqoop-shell, metadata support for multiple databases as repositories, as well as concept of links and remotability of Sqoop jobs.

Sqoop 2 runs from within an embedded container and depends on Hadoop environment variables to locate all dependencies.

Here, we are referring to v 5 of Sqoop 2 primarily because it worked slightly better than the latest versions of Sqoop 2 at the time of authoring this book.

In order to install Sqoop 2, the following steps are required to be performed:

1. Download the Sqoop 1.99.5 (yes, this officially called as Sqoop 2) binary distribution for Hadoop 2 using the following command:

   ```
   wget
   http://archive.apache.org/dist/sqoop/1.99.5/sqoop-1.99.5-bin-hadoop
   200.tar.gz
   ```

2. Once the download is complete, extract the contents of the tarball into a user directory with the following command. Let us refer to the extracted Sqoop folder as ${SQOOP2_HOME} and update the ~/.bashrc file accordingly.

   ```
   tar -zxvf ${DOWNLOAD_DIR}/sqoop-1.99.5-bin-hadoop200.tar.gz
   ```

3. Configure the file located at ${SQOOP2_HOME}/server/conf/catalina.properties to contain all the absolute classpath directories of our Hadoop install. A sample of such a configuration in our case is given below for reference (/data1/home/centos/hadoop-2.7.3 below refers to ${HADOOP_HOME} and makes sure absolute path is given, as it doesn't resolve environment variables correctly):

   ```
   common.loader=${catalina.base}/lib,${catalina.base}/lib/*.jar,${cat
   alina.home}/lib,${catalina.home}/lib/*.jar,${catalina.home}/../lib/
   *.jar,/data1/home/centos/hadoop-2.7.3/share/hadoop/common/lib/*.jar
   ,/data1/home/centos/hadoop-2.7.3/share/hadoop/common/*.jar,/data1/h
   ome/centos/hadoop-2.7.3/share/hadoop/hdfs/*.jar,/data1/home/centos/
   hadoop-2.7.3/share/hadoop/hdfs/lib/*.jar,/data1/home/centos/hadoop-
   2.7.3/share/hadoop/mapreduce/*.jar,/data1/home/centos/hadoop-2.7.3/
   share/hadoop/mapreduce/lib/*.jar,/data1/home/centos/hadoop-2.7.3/sh
   are/hadoop/yarn/*.jar,/data1/home/centos/hadoop-2.7.3/share/hadoop/
   yarn/lib/*.jar
   ```

4. Configure `${SQOOP2_HOME}/server/conf/sqoop.properties` to point to the Hadoop configurations as shown:

```
org.apache.sqoop.submission.engine.mapreduce.configuration.director
y=/data1/home/centos/hadoop-2.7.3/etc/hadoop
```

5. Set the permissions to the Sqoop 2 scripts with the following command:

```
chmod +x ${SQOOP2_HOME}/bin/*
```

6. Verify the Sqoop 2 configuration with the following command (if there is an error *Caused by: java.sql.SQLNonTransientConnectionException: No current connection,* ignore it and the configuration is all good):

```
${SQOOP2_HOME}/bin/sqoop2-tool verify
```

7. Launch the sqoop 2 server with the following command:

```
${SQOOP2_HOME}/bin/sqoop2-server start
```

Hue comes with native integration with Sqoop 2, and at the time of authoring this book, there were incompatibilities found between Hue and Sqoop 2. These incompatibilities have been raised and are currently bugs registered in Hue JIRA. Once such link is provided for reference: https://issues.cloudera.org/browse/HUE-5128.

However, we observed that once we have Sqoop 2 set up and working, we could use Sqoop 2 shell and view the configured jobs and connectors in Hue. Some of the screenshots have been provided as an indicative reference. Once we have the issues fixed in Hue for Sqoop 2, we will see that this would be a very strong capability for actively managing Sqoop 2 via Hue.

In the images below, we see a few configurations for resource links that can be configured via Hue for Sqoop 2 (in the `Data Browser` menu item, click on `Sqoop Transfer`). Here, we are configuring a database link and an HDFS link.

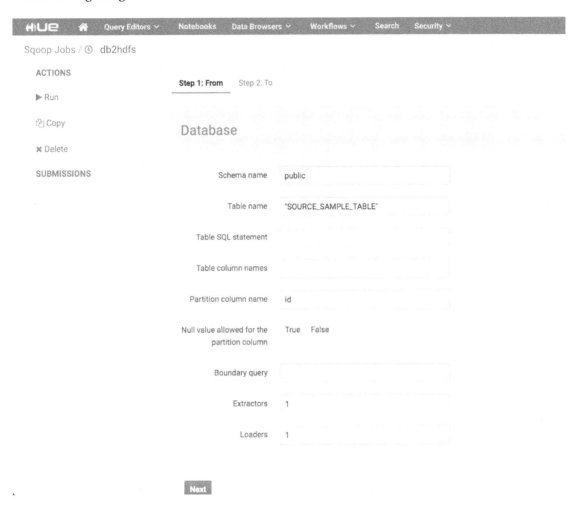

Figure 20: RDBMS to HDFS via Sqoop 2 and Hue

Clicking on next navigates Hue to the next screen which captures the database connection details to finally save the database link to the database repository.

Figure 21: RDBMS Link

Similarly, an HDFS link can also be configured with **hdfs** link name and **HDFS URI** as shown:

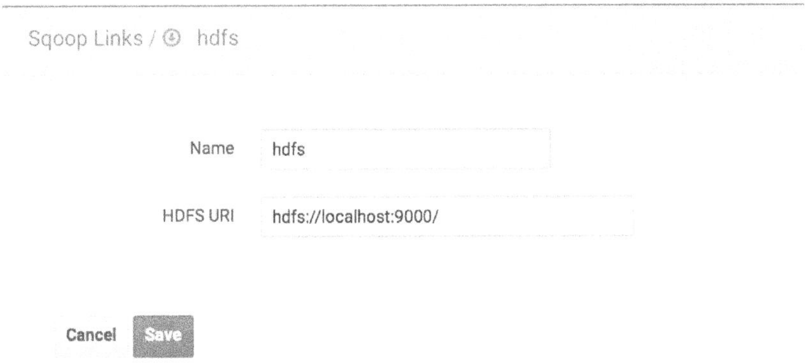

Sqoop Links / ④ hdfs

Name   hdfs

HDFS URI   hdfs://localhost:9000/

Cancel Save

Figure 22: HDFS Link

Like Sqoop 1, Sqoop 2 also needs a metadata repository. By default, Sqoop 2 uses an embedded **Apache Derby** database (`https://db.apache.org/derby/`); however, external databases can also be configured via `sqoop.properties` file. A sample of this file is provided in the following code block highlighting the Sqoop 2 repository configuration:

```
# External connectors load path
# "/path/to/external/connectors/": Add all the connector JARs in the
specified folder
#
org.apache.sqoop.connector.external.loadpath=
org.apache.sqoop.repository.jdbc.handler=org.apache.sqoop.repository.postgr
esql.PostgresqlRepositoryHandler
org.apache.sqoop.repository.jdbc.maximum.connections=4
org.apache.sqoop.repository.jdbc.url=jdbc:postgresql://192.168.43.28/sqoop?
schema=SQOOP
org.apache.sqoop.repository.jdbc.driver=org.postgresql.Driver
org.apache.sqoop.repository.jdbc.user=sqoop
org.apache.sqoop.repository.jdbc.password=sqoop
org.apache.sqoop.repository.jdbc.transaction.isolation=READ_COMMITTED
```

As shown in the code snippet above, we would need to create a user `sqoop` for the above configuration to work. Cloudera provides a reference page on how to set up this user at the following location: `https://goo.gl/F6iJsb`.

We have also referred (from Cloudera) to those setup instructions below, with very minor modifications with respect to the specific PostgreSQL version we are working with in this book. Full setup and detailing of Sqoop 2 is outside the scope of this book:

```
$ psql -U postgres
Password for user postgres: *****
postgres=# CREATE ROLE sqoop LOGIN ENCRYPTED PASSWORD 'sqoop'
NOSUPERUSER INHERIT CREATEDB NOCREATEROLE;
CREATE ROLE

postgres=# CREATE DATABASE "sqoop" WITH OWNER = sqoop
ENCODING = 'UTF8'
TABLESPACE = pg_default
LC_COLLATE = 'en_US.UTF-8'
LC_CTYPE = 'en_US.UTF-8'
CONNECTION LIMIT = -1;
CREATE DATABASE

postgres=# q
```

Sqoop in purview of SCV use case

As we have seen here, Sqoop covers a substantial part of building a single customer view, as we discussed in `Chapter 1`, *Introduction to Data*. Sqoop covers one of the most prominent channels for data acquisition, i.e. data transfer from relational databases to the HDFS layer. Most business and partner apps fall into this category and amount to a majority of structured information.

Hence, from the perspective of building a single customer view:

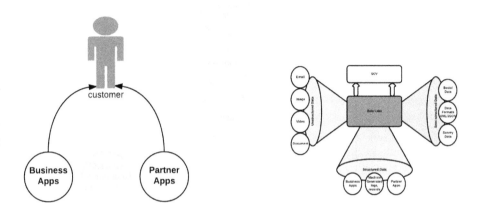

Figure 23: Sqoop in purview of SCV use case

As seen from the above, out of the entire single customer view, we still have various other types of information to be captured, which we will be covering in the chapters to follow.

From the perspective of single customer view, we discussed in this chapter various import and export mechanisms of data. As we start building a complete data lake for single customer view, we can visualize various architecture layers and components getting introduced.

From the Sqoop usage perspective, the layers being introduced here are data acquisition and can be visualized as shown:

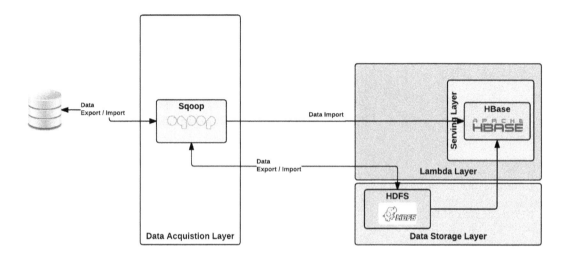

Figure 24: Acquisiton Layer with Sqoop for Single Customer View

When to use Sqoop

Apache Sqoop could be employed for many of the data transfer requirements in a data lake, which has HDFS as the main data storage for incoming data from various systems. These bullet points give some of the cases where Apache Sqoop makes more sense:

- For regular batch and micro-batch to transfer data to and from RDBMS to Hadoop (HDFS/Hive/HBase), use Apache Sqoop. Apache Sqoop is one of the main and widely used technologies in the data acquisition layer.
- For transferring data from NoSQL data stores like MongoDB and Cassandra into the Hadoop filesystem.
- Enterprises having good amounts of applications whose stores are based on RDBMS, Sqoop is the best option to transfer data into a Data Lake.
- Hadoop is a de-facto standard for storing massive data. Sqoop allows you to transfer data easily into HDFS from a traditional database with ease.

- Use Sqoop when performance is required, as it is able to split and parallelize data transfer.
- Sqoop has a concept of connectors and, if your enterprise has diverse business applications with different data stores, Sqoop is an ideal choice.

When not to use Sqoop

Sqoop is the best suited tool when your data lives in database systems such as Oracle, MySQL, PostgreSQL, and Teradata; Sqoop is not a best fit for event driven data handling. For event driven data, it's apt to go for Apache Flume (`Chapter 7`, *Messaging Layer with Apache Kafka* in this book covers Flume in detail) as against Sqoop. To summarize, below are the points when Sqoop should not be used:

- For event driven data.
- For handling and transferring data which are streamed from various business applications. For example data streamed using JMS from a source system.
- For handling real-time data as opposed to regular bulk/batch data and micro-batch.
- Handling data which is in the form of log files generated in different web servers where the business application is hosted.
- If the source data store should not be put under pressure when a Sqoop job is being executed, it's better to avoid Sqoop. Also, if the bulk/batch have high volumes of data, the pressure that it would put on the source data store would be even greater, which is usually not desirable.

Real-time Sqooping: a possibility?

For real-time data ingestion we don't think Sqoop is a choice. But for near real-time (not less than 5 mins, no particular reason for choosing the time as 5 mins), Sqoop could be used for transferring data. Since these are more frequent, the volume of data should also be in such a way that Sqoop can handle and complete it before the next execution starts.

Other options

For the bulk/batch transfer of data from RDBMS to the Hadoop filesystem there aren't many options in the open source world. However, there are possible choices whereby we could transfer data from RDBMS to Hadoop, and this section tries to give you the reader some possible options so that, according to enterprise demands, they can be evaluated and brought into the data lake as technologies if found suitable.

Native big data connectors

Most of the popular databases have connectors, using which data can be extracted and loaded onto the Hadoop filesystem. For example, if your RDBMS is Oracle, Oracle provides a suite of products which integrate the Oracle database with Apache Hadoop. The figure below (*Figure 09*) shows the full suite of Oracle Big Data connector products and what they do (details taken from www.oracle.com).

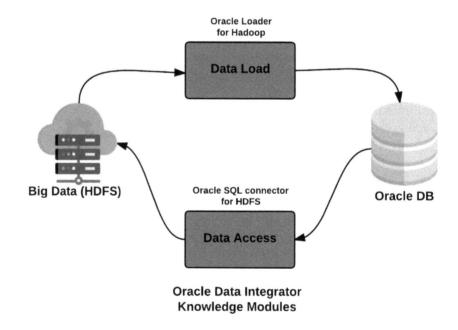

Figure 25: Oracle Big Data connector suite of products

Similar to Oracle, MySQL RDBMS has MySQL Applier, which is the native big data connector which can be used to load data from MySQL to Hadoop filesystem. MySQL Applier is also capable of incremental data transfer (real-time) as against the traditional batch by Sqoop. The following figure (*Figure 10*) shows the MySQL native connector to transfer data to HDFS.

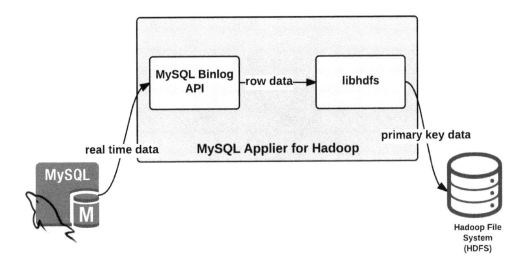

Figure 26: MySQL Applier for Hadoop

Talend

Talend is an open source ETL development (graphical), monitoring and scheduling tool. In purview of this chapter, we are only taking the ETL capability of Talend into discussion but it has a suite of products having different capabilities ideal for big data. Talend is supported by a very large community and has a huge amount of connectors (800+, largest connector library), using which you will be able to do the integration work with a variety of tools and technologies with ease. Talend is a mature product and supports a variety of big data technologies.

Having a rich set of connectors, Talend can integrate and transfer data from a variety of database systems to Hadoop without much trouble and is a viable alternate to Sqoop. Talend also has a graphical user interface, using which the data pipelines can be authored and executed, making it very user-friendly to operate. It also has a Sqoop connector, using which Sqoop's advantages can also be brought into your big data landscape.

A reference transformation graph taken from `talendexpert.com` is as shown in the following figure (*Figure 11*):

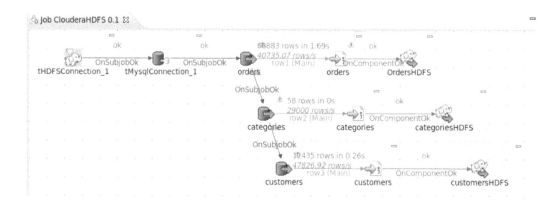

Figure 27: Talend graphical user interface for ETL development

Pentaho's Kettle (PDI - Pentaho Data Integration)

Pentaho is an open source (commercial offering also available) **Business Intelligence** (**BI**) suite comprising of a variety of products, one among it being called Kettle, capable of data integration. **Kettle** is now called **Pentaho Data Integration** (**PDI**). It's a Java based tool and supports cross platform, having support for a variety of database technologies.

Pentaho comes with inbuilt readers and writes for both HDFS and relational databases and provides a rich graphical user interface to enable data movement and transformation.

Summary

In this chapter, we started introducing or rather mapping technologies into the various data lake layers. In this chapter, we started with the technology introduction in the data acquisition layer. We started the chapter with the layer definition first, and then listed down reasons for choosing Sqoop by detailing both its advantages and disadvantages. We then covered Sqoop and its architecture in detail. While doing so, we covered two important versions of Sqoop, namely version 1 and 2. Soon after this theoretical section, we delved deep into the actual workings of Sqoop by giving the actual setup required to run Sqoop, and then delved deep into our SCV use case and what we are achieving using Sqoop.

After reading this chapter, you should have a clear understanding of the data acquisition layer in our data lake architecture. You should have also gotten in-depth details on Apache Sqoop and what are the reasons for choosing this as a technology of choice for implementation. You would also have gained knowledge on the actual working of Sqoop and how we can use it in action by going through the working example. You would by now have also implemented data acquisition functionality from PostgreSQL to HDFS using Sqoop, which kickstarts our SCV use case using Data Lake.

In the next chapter, we will move on to the next layer in our Data Lake, namely the Messaging Layer, and introduce the technology choices that we have chosen in detail, similar to what we have done in this chapter.

6

Data Acquisition of Stream Data using Apache Flume

To continue with the approach of exploring various technologies and layer in Data Lakes, this chapter aims to cover another technology being used in the data acquisition layer. Similar to the previous chapter (and, in fact, every other chapter in this part of the book), we will first start with the overall context in purview of Data Lake and then delve deep into the selected technology.

Before delving deep into the chosen technology, we will give our reasons for choosing this technology and also will familiarize you with adequate details so that you are acquainted with enough details to go back to your enterprise and start actually using these technologies in action.

This chapter deals with Apache Flume, the second technology in the data acquisition layer. We will start off lightly on Apache Flume and then dive deep into the nitty-gritties. Finally we will show you a working Flume example--linking with our SCV use case. The final section of the chapter is chosen to familiarize you with other similar technologies that can be used in place of Flume to realize the capability in your Data Lake architecture.

After reading this chapter, you will have a clear idea of Flume's usage in the architecture and will also have gained enough details on the full working of Flume. You will also have hands-on experience with Flume and will have progressed further in our journey to implement Data Lake and realize the SCV use case.

This is really exciting; let's dive in!!

Context in Data Lake: data acquisition

One of the V's of Big Data makes this chapter significant in all aspects in the modern era of any enterprise, namely Velocity. Traditionally, analytics was all done on data collected in the form of data (slow data), but nowadays analytics is done on data flowing in real time and then acted upon in real time to make a meaningful contribution to the business. The business outcome can be in the form of acting on a live Twitter stream of a customer to enhance customer experience or showing up a personalized offer by looking at some of his recent actions on your website. In this chapter, we will be covering mainly the Data Acquisition part of real-time data in our Data Lake.

In Chapter 5, *Data Acquisition of Batch Data with Apache Sqoop* we have detailed what the Data Acquisition layer is, so I won't be covering that in this section. However there is a significant difference between the data handled in Chapter 5, *Data Acquisition of Batch Data with Apache Sqoop* (which was batch data) and real-time data (in this chapter). Let's understand these data types in a bit more detail before delving into the technical aspects.

What is Stream Data?

Stream data is the data generated by a variety of business applications and external applications (these days, almost all social media) continuously and in a fast pace, usually having a small payload. There is a variety of data that falls into this category, some which are as follows:

- Log data generated by various web and application servers where your application is hosted
- Data generated by user behaviour (page impression, link clicks and so on) on your company's website
- Loads of data generated by your customers on various social network platforms
- In recent times, data generated by various sensors as part of your enterprise's vision to go to IoT platforms

These are real time data which comes one after the other and makes sense when processed in a sequential manner. For an enterprise analysing these data and then responding appropriately can be a business model and this can indeed transform their way of working. Looking at these data in real time fashion and then personalizing according to customer needs can indeed be very rewarding for the customer, but will also bring financial gains to the business and can improve customer experience (intangible benefits).

The following figure shows the stream data from various so called sources which will eventually come as is into the Data Lake or gets processed and persisted in the data store:

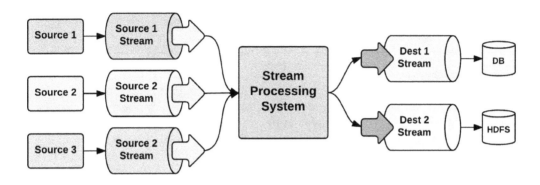

Figure 01: Data Streaming in action

Enterprise should start using these data initially for bear minimum use cases, for example, collect log data and see if there are errors which can be proactively looked upon and corrected. Over a period of time, complex use cases can be derived, say analyse user behaviour (from the behavioural data by your user on your site) and serve the user in a real-time fashion appropriate offers.

It's better to stream these data into the Hadoop file system as is without any processing but we can also have an approach of putting data as is in Hadoop and can also have some processing making real sense for business. These processed data can then flow to a visual analytic tool and then showcase necessary details for business to use these in real time business decision making. Say, keep analysing booking data for your ecommerce site and if not meeting the target, make necessary adjustments in the prices of each item (may be give discounts for items having huge inventory and not really selling).

One of the very fundamental issues with analysing stream data is to handle message received in order. If the order if not maintained the analysis can result in wrong interpretations which can have adverse negative impact on business. The amount of data coming along can vary and it can be that when the system is in load velocity of data can be very huge for the various components to handle. Architecture principles like scalability, durability and other aspects should be considered and dealt with.

Batch and stream data

The following table (*Table 01*) summarizes the main difference which exist between batch and stream data. Our use case does have both these types of data. For handling batch data we selected and used Sqoop as the technology and for stream data handling and transfer to Hadoop we have selected Flume as the choice.

Batch Data	Stream Data
Mostly the volume of data is quite high and deal with a chunk of data in defined period of time. Batch consisting of thousands of records.	The volume of data is not that great. But, deal with high velocity data and it comes continuously but does not have defined period in which they come. Stream data consist of single or few record. Few records are sometimes also called as micro-batch as the batch record size is quite small compared to conventional batch.
Analysis or processing is done on a very large period or all the data.	Analysis and processing is done on a small dataset over a moving time window in a continuous manner.
Period of operation spans from minutes to hours usually.	Operation period spans from milliseconds to seconds in most of the cases.
Since the data set is huge, complex analysis can be performed deriving usual deductions for business decision making.	Simple analysis can be performed and in usual case done with batch analysis to derive usual information.
Example, customer who has purchased more electronic items past month when the sale was going on.	Example, detection of credit card fraud as and when a purchase happens OR RBA (Risk Based Analysis) for important transactions in your ecommerce website. According to risk, step up authentication to multi factor (say One Time Password) mechanism.

Table 01: Details *summarizing difference between Batch and Stream data*

The preceding table does state quite clearly the varying difference between batch and stream data. This means, these two data need to be handled accordingly when ingesting into the Data Lake.

Data acquisition of stream data - technology mapping

The following figure brings in technology aspect to the conceptual architecture that we will be the following throughout this book.

We have chosen Apache Flume as the real time data transfer technology and this does come in the data acquisition layer of our Data Lake implementation.

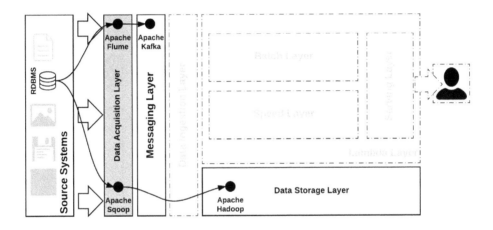

Figure 02: Technology mapping for Acquisition Layer

Inline with our use case of SCV, the real time data from various business applications will flow into the Flume and then transferred to the Hadoop file system for storage and later analysis. The real time data from business application that we are going to handle is the customer's behavioural data when dealing with the enterprise's website. Data such as page visits, link clicks, location details, browser details and so on will flow into Flume and then stored in HDFS.

The following figure (*Figure 03*) shows only the aspect that we will be delving deep in this chapter, rest of the layers and other aspects from Data Lake is intentionally taken away from this diagram. However it does show Sqoop also so that we are building onto our full-fledged Data Lake architecture as we navigate through chapters one by one.

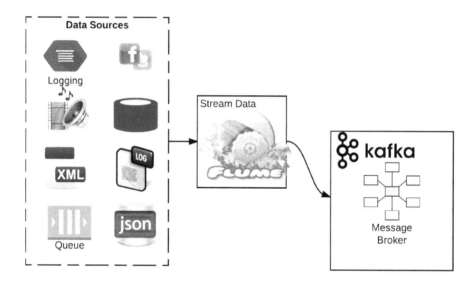

Figure 03: Working of Flume in the Data Lake

What is Flume?

Flume (not technical) is constructed to transfer logs down a mountain by using the shear capability of water flowing through a constructed channel. These channels can be build over a large distance and enables to transfer these logs quickly, effectively and in a very cost effective manner. These flumes can be used for transferring variety of materials, although initially the main intent was to transfer logs and lumber.

Standing by its name Flume, it's a piece of technology which enables to transfer huge amount of data from a source to its intended destination. Similar to its physical counterpart (log Flume), this was also constructed initially for transfer of log data accumulated in each servers (and other software components), aggregate it and give a holistic analytical capability. Later on it was extended for different sources and different destinations.

The following figure (*Figure 04*) gives the conceptual view of how Flume functions. In our use case (Data Lake implementation with SCV in mind), we will be using to capture log data (collected from various web servers) as well as event data (mainly behavioural data) and channelling into the common data storage (Hadoop system) as shown earlier in *Figure 03*:

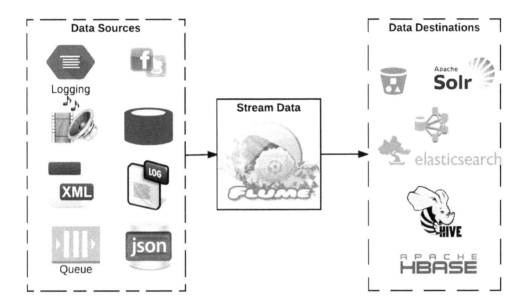

Figure 04: Conceptual view of working of Flume

Sqoop and Flume

In this section, we are not going to compare the features of Sqoop and Flume; rather we are doing this to bring out the difference between the two technologies and what features these bring onto the table. For realizing our Data Lake we do need two technical capabilities as offered by these technologies for sure.

To put you reader at ease comparing these technologies and bring out its capabilities, the following table has summarized information as points and some details to elaborate the point. It's important to note that each row is not a one on one comparison between the two, rather it summarizes capability of each in a tabular, easily readable format.

Sqoop	Flume
Batch data handling.	Stream data (real time data) handling.
Works on high volume of data. Size of data can be of the range of gigabytes to terabytes.	Works on low volume data with high velocity. Data is usually messages and of the range of kilobytes to megabytes.
Main capability is to transfer data from RDBMS to Hadoop (HDFS).	Main capability is to transfer data in motion (stream) data into Hadoop (HDFS).
Works really well with variety of RDBMS, mainly using the JDBC technique. Vendors of RDBMS does have provision of writing their own connector and can use many optimization techniques (using native) to achieve the best results.	Apart from message type of data, Flume works well in bringing log data into Hadoop.
Has capability to parallelize data transfer operation.	N/A
Most apt for data at rest (data residing in RDBMS).	Most suitable for data in motion.
Acts on data which is more or less static in nature.	Acts on data which changes often. Because it is event driven, the order in which these events reaches is quite important to make sure that data integrity is kept while bringing to the Hadoop environment.
Works on data which is already aggregated and collected.	Collection and aggregation of data possible, it deals with the most recent data.
	Inherently reliable, highly available and distributed in nature.
Being batch, it can put undue pressure on the source system from where data is being transferred to HDFS.	Does Not put any pressure on the source system and works completely disconnected manner.

Table 02: Sqoop and Flume difference summarized in a table

The following figure quite well summarizes the capability which Sqoop and Flume brings in purview of the capability requirement required in implementing the Data Lake.

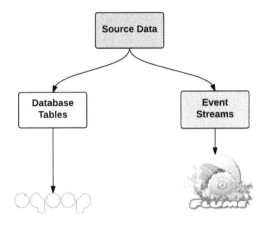

Figure 05: Sqoop and Flume

Why Flume?

This section is dedicated explain you why we have chosen Flume as our technical choice in the technical capability that we look to realize Data Acquisition layer for handling stream/real time data.

With the following subsections, we will first dive into the history and then into Flume's advantages as well as disadvantages. The advantages detailed are the main reasons for our choice of this technology for dealing with transfer of real-time data into Hadoop.

History of Flume

Apache Flume was developed by Cloudera for handling and moving large amount data produced into Hadoop. Without minimum or no delay (**NRT: Near Real Time or Real time**) the company wanted the data produced to be moved to Hadoop system, for various analysis to be carried. That was how this beautiful came into existence.

As detailed in previous section, it was initially conceived and developed to take care of a particular use case of collecting and aggregating log data from various source (web servers) into Hadoop for performing various analytics useful for proactive maintenance. Later on it was redesigned and refactored to include different sources and destinations and also design was taken into account for pluggability and extensibility in mind.

Very much similar to Sqoop, Flume also has two major flavours. They are:

- Flume OG (Old Generation: pre 1.0)
- Flume NG (New Generation)

As the name suggests, **Flume OG** was the initial Flume distribution, which then underwent complete rewrite and refactoring giving rise to **Flume NG**. Flume NG is the current supported and active Apache project and this is the flavor we will use in our book. As of writing this book, the latest version of Flume NG is 1.7.0, which was released on October 17, 2016. Flume got into Apache Incubator with version 1.0.0 and 1.1.0.

Advantages of Flume

Some of the core advantages of Apache Flume which made this technology chosen are as detailed here in bullet points:

- Open source.
- Very good documentation, with many examples and patterns of how these can be applied, is available.
- High throughput with low latency.
- Declarative configuration.
- Inherently distributed.
- Highly reliable, available, and scalable (horizontally).
- Highly extensible and customizable.
- Less costly installation, operation and maintenance.
- Contextual routing aspect has a dedication subsection in this chapter. But for you to have a heads-up, this is an aspect of Flume to look at the payload (stream data or event) and construct a routing which is apt.
- Build-in support for a variety of source and destination systems.
- Inherently highly pluggable.
- Feature rich.

- Transaction support is built in.
- Capability of getting data from multiple servers into Hadoop easily
- Supports different data flows like multiple-hop, fan-out, fan-in and so on.
- Good integration support with a variety of existing monitoring tools.

Disadvantages of Flume

Although Flume has good advantages attached to it, it does have some disadvantages pulling it down on certain aspects. They are as follows:

- Weak ordering guarantee.
- Does Not guarantee that message reaching is unique (duplicate messages might pop in at times, in many scenarios).
- For an enterprise, sizing the hardware of a typical Flume can be tricky, and in most cases, it's trial and error. Because of this, its scalability aspect is often put under a lens.
- The throughput that Flume can handle depends on the backing store of the channel. So, scalability and reliability is under question when the choice of backing store is not chosen wisely considering all factors.

Clearly Flume's advantages overweight its disadvantages and that's one of the main reason for our choice. Second aspect is it popularity (which is relative) and that the reason not mentioned in the advantages but this aspect really matters for an enterprise (easy recruitment, good community with answers for every question).

Flume architecture principles

Any technology piece to be successful, should have clearly defined architecture principles based on which its design is created and then evolved throughout. Flume also comes in one such software and up next are some of the architecture principles based on which Flume was designed (some of those got introduced as part of Flume NG):

- **Reliability**: The capability of continuously accepting stream data and events without losing any data, in a variety of failure scenarios (mostly partial failures). One of the core architecture principles taken very seriously by Flume is fault-tolerance, which means that even if some components fail or misbehave, some hardware issues pop up, or if bandwidth or network behaves bad, Flume will accept these as facts of life in most cases and carry on doing its main job without shutting down completely. Flume does guarantee that the data reaching the Flume Agent will eventually be handed over to other components as long as the agent is kept running. There are settings that can be set to control the reliability level. Good to know that higher the reliability, lower will be the scalability.

- **Scalability**: Flume has the ability to handle more stream data with mere changes in hardware topology. Flume scales horizontally by allowing to add additional machines to cater to the load of increased message throughput. In the architecture section we will cover various components which needs change when scaled horizontally. The scalability does however depend on the destination system's ability to keep taking data coming out of the pipeline and that at times can be a defining aspect of how much your flume can scale.

- **Manageability**: Ability to manage various components as part of the solution centrally in all aspects is key to success installation of any architecture in production. Apache Flume, using Flume master (will explain in next section in detail) component allows managing all components in a central fashion using defined settings controlled through a web interface or Flume command line interface.

- **Extensibility**: One of the very important principle which allows integration of this technology with various source and destination systems. This is a mandatory requirement and definitely one of the core principles how Flume was designed and architected. This is achieved mainly by writing new or using built-in connectors to connect to Flume in both input and output.

These are some of the core architecture principles on which Flume was made and in the following sections many of these aspects will get clarified more.

The Flume Architecture

We discussed in previous section, the architecture principles based on which Flume was conceived, now let's deep dive into the architecture. Let's start off with a very basic diagram detailing the architecture of Flume (*Figure 06*) and then in the following sections keep diving deep.

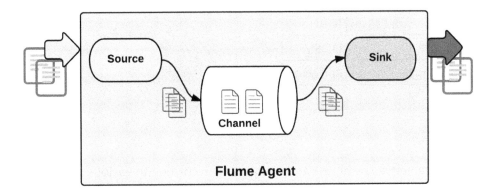

Figure 06: Basic Flume Architecture

A simple Flume architecture has three important components, which work together to transfer a data from source to destination in real time fashion (stream or log data). They are:

- **Source**: The responsibility of listening to stream data or events and then putting it to the channel
- **Channel**: A pipe where events are stored until it has been taken by someone else
- **Sink**: The responsibility of taking away events from the channel for further processing (sending to another source) or persisting to a data store. If sink operation fails, it will keep trying until success.

The following table summarizes some of examples for each of the components in the Flume architecture namely **Source**, **Channel** and **Sink**:

Source	Channel	Sink
Console	Memory	Memory
Exec	File	JDBC
Syslog	JDBC	File
Avro	and so on	Null
JMS		HDFS
Spooling Directory		and so on
and so on		

Table 03: Some examples of source, channel, and sink

Figure 06 depicts a very basic Flume architecture but according to various setup or arrangements of these core components different topologies can be setup and used according to the requirement. Some of the well known arrangements are:

- Distributed pipeline
- Fan Out
- Fan In

The following subsections gives you a very detailed description for these arrangements. Also, it has another section which details advanced Flume architecture by bringing in some more components into the basic one.

Distributed pipeline - Flume architecture

The source, channel, sink unit can chain one after the other accomplishing what is called as Distributed pipeline architecture, as shown in *Figure 07*:

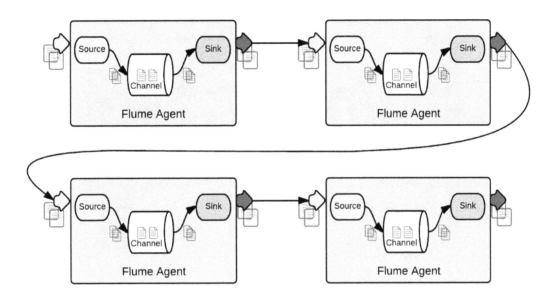

Figure 07: Distributed pipeline Flume architecture

Fan Out - Flume architecture

Arrangement of the Flume components namely source and channel in such a way that there is one source which is fed to many channels is termed as Fan Out Flume architecture. The following figure (*Figure 08*) shows the Fan Out architecture:

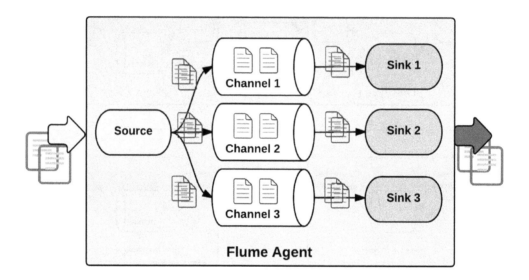

Figure 08: Fan Out Flume architecture

Fan In - Flume architecture

The arrangement of Flume's components, namely source and channel, in such a way that there are many sources fed to one channel is termed as a Fan In Flume architecture. The following figure (*Figure 09*) shows this architecture:

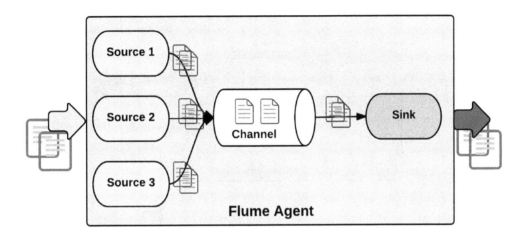

Figure 09: Fan In Flume Architecture

Next is a figure (*Figure 10*) that combines these Flume components in a more complex manner, and it is more functionally suited to a particular use case. This is shown to you to make you understand that according to your use case, you are free to arrange these components:

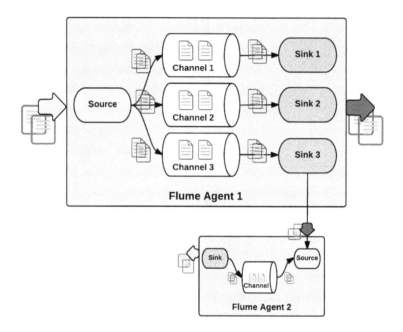

Figure 10: Typical Flume Architecture arrangement catering to a use case

Three tier design - Flume architecture

Most of the Flume deployments follow a well documented three tier design. The three main tiers of this design are:

- **Agent Tier**: This is the tier where the Flume agents are located along with sources which contains data which have to be moved.
- **Collector Tier**: This is the tier where the data from the agent tier is collected using multiple collectors and then these are forwarded to the next layer.
- **Storage Tier**: This is the tier where data from collector tier flows finally and stored. This will have file systems like HDFS where the data is stored.

The following figure (*Figure 11*) shows the three tier design of a Flume Architecture in action:

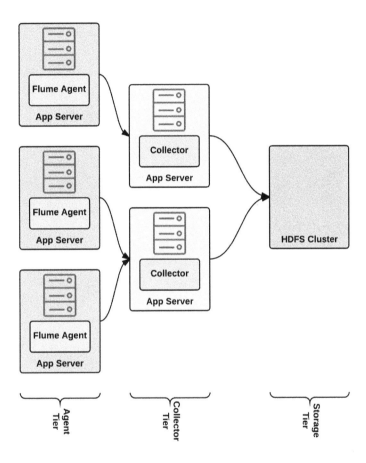

Figure 11: The three-tier design of Flume architecture

Advanced Flume architecture

The Flume architecture in an enterprise setting will have one more important component namely Flume master, whose main responsibility is to serve as a centralized authority for all the configurations of all nodes in the overall architecture. Every machine participating in the architecture is termed as node. Each node depends on the master to retrieve the configurations which dictates as to how the Flume should perform its actions.

The entire Flume topology can be configured or reconfigured dynamically by sending relevant commands using Thrift API to the Flume master.

The following figure (*Figure 12*) shows an advanced Flume architecture arrangement, which shows the all-important Flume master controlling the configuration and dictating the overall working and topology of Flume:

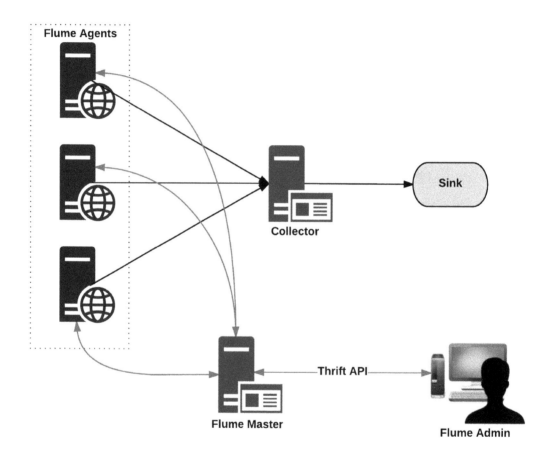

Figure 12: Advanced Flume architecture

Flume reliability level

Reliability is one of the core architecture principle based on which Flume architecture was designed. To achieve this level of reliability, Flume provides its user with configurable reliability levels. They are classified as follows:

- **End-to-end**: When this reliability level is set, the event sent to Flume will surely make it to the other end as long as the originating agent (the agent which accepted the **venet**) is alive. To achieve this reliability level, the agent when receiving an event stores/writes in the disk in **WAL** (**Write Ahead Log**). When the event reaches the defined endpoint and acknowledgement is sent all the way to the originating agent and then the written event is erased. This level can withstand failure of any component after the originating agent. As pointed out earlier, higher the reliability lower is it scalability and this falls into highest reliability level offered by Flume.

- **Store on failure**: When this reliability level is set, the event when traversing through different agents (hops), the originating agent of the event will only store/write to the disk only if the agent to whom the event was sent fails. In principal agent only write to disk the detail of event if there is no acknowledgement from the next hop on agent. This is a more practical reliability level but if there are silent failures, events can be lost forever.

- **Best-effort**: This reliability level is the weakest and the most lightweight in which the vent is sent to the next hop without writing to the disk and does not rely on any acknowledgement or failure coming back from the next agent where the event was sent to.

Choose the right reliability level what your use case demands and always keep in mind that more the reliability, less is the scalability and more is the cost of maintenance.

Flume event - Stream Data

Event is the unit of data which is send across the Flume pipeline. The structure of the event is quite simple and had two parts to it namely:

- **Event header**: A Key/Value pair in the form `Map<String, String>`. These headers are meant to add more data about the event. For example, these headers can hold severity and priority aspects of this event, and so on. These headers can also contain UUID or event ID which distinguishes one event from the other.

- **Event payload**: An array of bytes (byte array) in the form `byte[]`. 32 KB is the default body size, which is usually truncated after that figure but this is a configurable value in Flume.

This figure shows the internal structure of the Flume event, which hops from one agent to another in Flume:

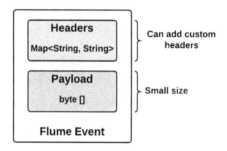

Figure 13: Anatomy of a Flume event

Flume agent

Flume agent is the smallest possible deployment comprising of Source, Channel and Sink as its main components. The following figure shows a typical Flume agent deployment:

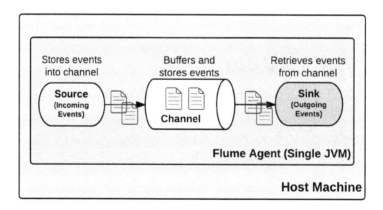

Figure 14: Flume Agent components

Flume agent is a Java daemon which received event from a source and then passes onto a channel, where it is usually written to the disk (according to reliability level set) and then moves the event to the sink. When the sink receives the event it sends acknowledgement back to channel and channel erases the event from its store. The agent has a very small memory footprint (*-Xmx20m*) and can be controlled declaratively using configurations.

Flume agent configurations

Some of these aspects have been unintentionally discussed in details in the Flume architecture section, however we thought that separate section for these agent configuration is required. Since we don't want to repeat ourselves, we will be referring some aspects back to that section.

The following are main configurations using which agents can be arranged:

- **Multi-hop (multi-agent flow)**: Similar to the one given in the preceding section *Distributed pipeline - Flume architecture*. One agent feeds the event to another (called as a hop) and this carries on according to use case demand. *Figure 15* shows multi-hop flume agent configuration:

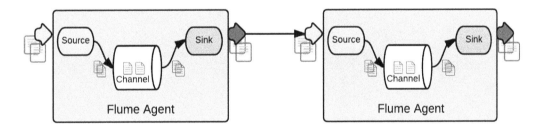

Figure 15: Multi-hop flume agent configuration

- **Consolidation (converging flow)**: Similar to one given in the preceding section, *Three tier design - Flume architecture*. Multiple agents consolidates the events and sends it across to other set of agents. *Figure 16* shows this setup of agent configuration in action:

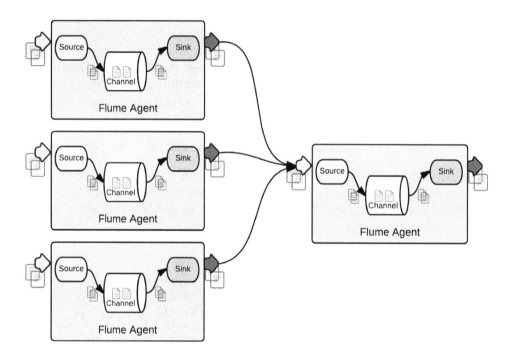

Figure 16: Consolidation flume agent configuration

- **Multiplexing**: Similar to *Figure 10* in which inside an agent a source fans out to multiple channels and one of the channel feeds to another agent's source. This is one such setup and varied kinds of setup is possible as demanded by the use case.

Flume source

Flume agent can have multiple sources, but it is mandatory to have at least one source for it to function. The source is managed by Source Runner which controls the threading aspect and execution models namely:

- Event-driven and
- Polling

In event-driven execution model the source listens and consumes events. In polling execution model the source keeps polling for events and then deal with it.

The event (as detailed earlier) can take a variety of content satisfying the event schema (header and payload). The source, complying with the architecture principle of extensibility, works on plugin approach. The source requires mandated name and type. According to the type, source will demand additional parameters and accordingly configurations have to set for it to work fine. The source can accept single event or a batch of event (mostly and in ideal case micro-batch as opposed to regular batch). Built-in sources in Flume can be broadly classified as:

1. **Asynchronous sources**: Client sending the events doesn't handle the failure. Once the event is sent the client forget it (fire and forget). Some of the examples are as follows:
    - **Exec** executes the command and ingest the output as data. Configuration looks as shown in the code block:

      ```
      agent.sources.http.type=http
      agent.sources.http.port-8080
      ```

    - **Syslog** (spooling directory) parses the file and ingests the data. The following configuration is just an example of how a spooling directory can be configured:

      ```
      agent.sources.spool.type = customerDataDir
      agent.sources.spool.spoolDir = /data/lake/customerdata
      agent.sources.spool.deletePolicy = immediate
      ```

2. **Synchronous sources**: After the event is sent and if the source doesn't acknowledge to the client, the client can deal with the failure scenarios gracefully. Some of the examples are:

- **JMS**, these are events produced and handled by Java Messaging Service (Queues and Topics). Sample configuration for connecting to an AMQP queue is as follows:

```
agent.sources.jms.type = jms
agent.sources.jms.initialContextFactory =
org.apache.activemq.jndi.ActiveMQInitialContextFactory
agent.sources.jms.providerURL =
tcp://datalakeserver:61616
agent.sources.jms.destinationName = customerData
agent.sources.jms.destinationType = customerDataQueue
```

- **HTTP** inherently starts a web server to handle REST API. This is an example configuration:

```
agent.sources.execSource.type=exec
agent.sources.execSource.command='ps -ef | grep java'
```

Custom Source

If your use case demands a special source, a custom source can be written by implementing source interface. An example of how this custom source (`class com.datalakebook.CustomSource`) can be configured for an agent `ag1` is as follows:

```
ag1.sources = src1
ag1.channels = ch1
ag1.sources.src1.type = com.datalakebook.CustomSource
ag1.sources.src1.channels = ch1
```

Flume Channel

A channel is a mechanism used by the Flume agent to transfer data from source to sink. The events are persisted in the channel and until it is delivered/taken away by a sink, they reside in the channel. This persistence in channel allows sink to retry for each event in case there is a failure while persisting data to the real store (HDFS).

Channels can be broadly categorized into two:

1. **In-memory**: The events are available until the channel component is alive:
   - Queue: In-memory queues in the channel. This has the lowest latency time for processing because the events are persisted in memory.

2. **Durable:** Even after the component is dead, the event persisted is available, and when the component becomes online, these events will be processed:
   - **File (WAL or Write-Ahead Log)**: The most used channel type. It's durable and requires disk to be RAID, SAN or similar.
   - **JDBC**: A proper RDBMS backed channel that provides ACID compliance.
   - **Kafka**: stored in Kafka cluster.

There is another special channel called **Spillable Memory Channel**, which stores data in-memory and on disk. When the capacity of in-memory is full, rest of the events are stored to disk (embedded file channel).

You will be clearly remembering the reliability section that has been discussed earlier in this chapter. The reliability aspect depends on the channel type which is being configured as detailed before. Channels also takes care of the event ordering and also helps in transaction guarantee for the agent.

RAID (originally redundant array of inexpensive disks, now commonly redundant array of independent disks) is a data storage virtualization technology that combines multiple physical disk drive components into a single logical unit for the purposes of data redundancy, performance improvement, or both.

A **storage area network** (**SAN**) is a network which provides access to consolidated, block level data storage. SANs are primarily used to enhance storage devices, such as disk arrays, tape libraries, and optical jukeboxes, accessible to servers so that the devices appear to the operating system as locally attached devices.

In computer science, **write-ahead logging** (**WAL**) is a family of techniques for providing atomicity and durability (two of the ACID properties) in database systems. In a system using WAL, all modifications are written to a log before they are applied. Usually both redo and undo information is stored in the log.

In computer science, **ACID** (**Atomicity, Consistency, Isolation, Durability)** is a set of properties of database transactions. In the context of databases, a single logical operation on the data is called a transaction.

- Wikipedia

Custom channel

The pluggable aspect of Flume can be used to write custom channel according to your requirement satisfying the use case. For this, the class has to be written implementing the channel interface. A sample configuration of a custom channel for an agent `ag1` for a custom channel class `com.datalakebook.CustomChannel` is as follows:

```
ag1.channels = ch1
ag1.channels.ch1.type = com.datalakebook.CustomChannel
```

Flume sink

Similar to the source, the sink is managed by **SinkRunne**, which manages the thread and execution model. Unlike a source, however, a sink is polling-based and polls the channel for events. The sink is the component that outputs (according to type of output required) it from the agent to an external or other source. Sinks also participate in transaction management, and when the output from a sink is successful, an acknowledgement is passed back to the channel. The channel then takes the event away from the persistence mechanism. Transaction management will be covered in detail in a separate section.

There are a variety of existing sinks available, as follows:

- **HDFS**: Write to HDFS. This currently supports writing text and sequence files (in compressed format as well). The following is a sample HDFS sink configuration (taken from Flume user guide) for an agent named a1. The full configuration can be found in the Flume user guide (https://flume.apache.org):

```
a1.channels = c1
a1.sinks = k1
a1.sinks.k1.type = hdfs
a1.sinks.k1.channel = c1
a1.sinks.k1.hdfs.path = /flume/events/%y-%m-%d/%H%M/%S
a1.sinks.k1.hdfs.filePrefix = events-
a1.sinks.k1.hdfs.round = true
a1.sinks.k1.hdfs.roundValue = 10
a1.sinks.k1.hdfs.roundUnit = minute
```

- **HBase**: Writes to HBase
- **AsyncHBase**: Writes to HBase asynchronously
- **Hive**: Writes text or JSON to Hive tables and partitions
- **Null & Logger**: For debugging
- **Kafka:** This can publish the event to a Kafka topic. For our use case, we will definitely be using this sink
- And so on

For a complete list of **Flume Sinks** and its configuration details, please go through the Flume user guide (https://goo.gl/U8pS35) as covering this in all aspects is outside the scope of this book.

Custom sink

Custom sink can be written taking advantage of its pluggable nature. You need to implement the Sink interface according to your requirement to write custom sink. Here is a sample configuration of how custom sink can be configured for an agent ag1 for which com.datalakebook.CustomSink class is written implement the Sink interface:

```
ag1.channels = ch1
ag1.sinks = cus1
ag1.sinks.cus1.type = com.datalakebook.CustomSink
ag1.sinks.cus1.channel = ch1
```

Flume configuration

Flume can be fully configured using the flume configuration file. A single image speaks more than thousand words, so we will like to explain Flume configuration using the following figure. An exhaustive flume configuration is out of scope of this book, but will explain some core aspects of how the flume can be configured and this can be base for understanding a full-fledged configuration.

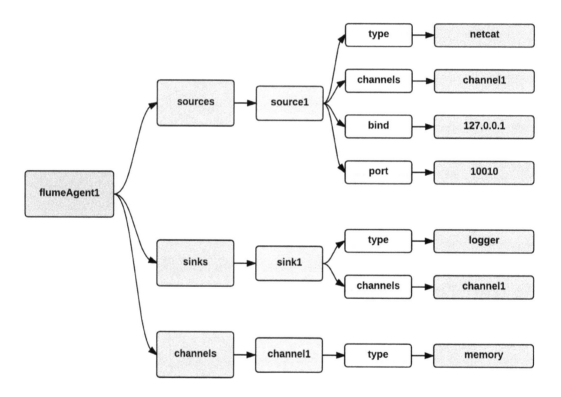

Figure 17: Flume Configuration Tree (sample)

The next code block shows the preceding configuration tree figure:

```
# Active Flume Components
flumeAgent1.sources=source1
flumeAgent1.channels=channel1
flumeAgent1.sinks=sink1

# Define and Configure Source 1
flumeAgent1.sources.source1.type=netcat
flumeAgent1.sources.source1.channels=channel1
flumeAgent1.sources.source1.bind=127.0.0.1
flumeAgent1.sources.source1.port=10010

# Define and Configure Sink 1
flumeAgent1.sinks.sink1.type=logger
flumeAgent1.sinks.sink1.channels=channel1

# Define and Configure Channel 1
flumeAgent1.channels.channel1.type=memory

# Other Flume Agent configurations
flumeAgent2.sources=source2
...
```

When a configuration is loaded by Flume for actual execution, it follows some defined rules. Some of which are as given next:

- Every agent should have at least one channel
- Every source should have at least one channel
- Every sink should have only one channel
- Agents should be named and only these named agents configurations are loaded
- Within a named agent, only active components are loaded
- Every component defined should have its type defined

Flume transaction management

Throughout the previous sections we have indeed transaction aspects at various stages. The following figure summarizes these discussions in a more pictorial fashion:

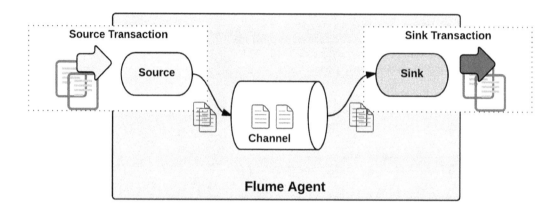

Figure 18: Transaction management in Flume (Source Tx and Sink Tx)

This figure shows that incoming data from a client or previous sink starts the present agent transaction and this is termed as **Source Tx** in the figure. The Source Tx ends soon after the event is persisted in the channel and acknowledgement received.

In purview of an agent a second transaction kicks in termed as **Sink Tx** which start with the data being polled by the sink and when the data is successfully transferred, channel uses the acknowledgement to remove the data in the channel.

Flume does have transaction management in all aspects and according to use case various reliability levels can be set in channel which decides how the transaction behaviour (Sink Tx) is realized.

Other flume components

In addition to main components in Flume, there are other very important components. These components will be discussed in some detail in this section. The following figure shows all of these components working together:

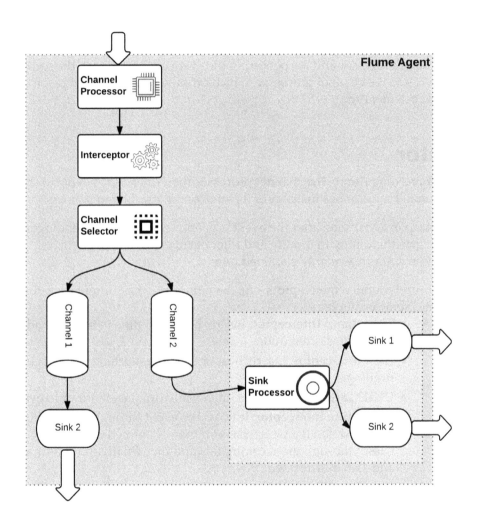

Figure 19: Other Flume components working together

The following subsection gets deep into working and responsibility of each of the components in the preceding figure (*Figure 19*). Let's get started and understand how these components will help you in designing the right Flume component arrangement to execute your use case successfully.

Channel processor

As shown in *Figure 19* the source sends the events to the channel processor. Every source has its own channel processor and for persisting the event in the channel, the source delegates the work to the channel processor, which actually does the job of persisting according to the channel type.

Interceptor

As seen in the preceding figure, the channel processor then passes the events to the interceptor. Channel selector has instance of its interceptor attached to it.

Interceptors act upon event soon after the event is generated and before sending it to the channel. Flume gets this ability to modify and filter events with help from these interceptors. Interceptors are mainly classified into:

1. Built-in/predefined interceptors - As the name says these interceptors built-in in Flume. Some examples are:
    - **Timestamp Interceptor**: Inserts header of time in milliseconds when the event is acted upon.
    - **Host Interceptor**: Inserts host or IP of the machine where agent is running.
    - **UUID Interceptor**: Inserts universally unique identifier to every event.
    - **Morphline Interceptor**: It floats the event through a morphline configuration file which has commands defined and all these events passes through these commands and then finally the events are filtered and also transformed.
    - **Search and Replace Interceptor**: Based on regular expressions it gives the functionality of search and replace functionality and so on.
2. Custom interceptors:
    - By looking at the event, it can insert headers or transform the event. It's plain Java code of writing a custom interceptor.

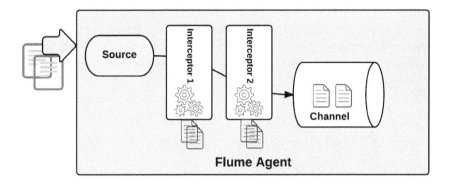

Figure 20: Interceptor chain in action

Channel Selector

As shown in the preceding figure, channel selector helps in selecting the right channel based on set criteria. Very much similar to interceptors, channel selector is classified into two main categories:

1. **Built-in channel selector**:
   - Replicating channel selector
       - Default channel selector if explicitly not specified
       - If more than one channel is specified for a source, each channel gets a copy of the event.
   - Multiplexing Channel Selector
       - According to header value a channel is selected.
       - Can say that this provides dynamic routing based on the specified header values.
       - Context Routing

2. **Custom Channel Selector**: For handling dynamic criteria you can write your own custom implementation for `ChannelSelector` class.

Sink Groups

Reliability is one of the core architecture principle on which Flume was built on. To take care of failures, flume components can be arranged in a variety of fashion. In case of failures when transferring data from channel to sink, sink can be setup in a load balanced or failover fashion. For achieving this prerequisite is to configure a Sink Group. A Sink Group, as its name suggests, is a logical grouping of of sinks. The defined or these named group participates in load balancing or failover case.

Some of the aspects of a Sink Group which are worth noting down is as follows:

- A sink can only be associated with one Sink Group at a time.
- All sinks has their own default Sink Group where it belongs to.
- If not specified each sink belongs to this default Sink Group and it behaves as a pass through for events.
- The Sink Group can be deactivated at any point but deactivating it doesn't have any impact on the sinks participating in that Sink Group.
- In the Flume configuration, Sink Group is a top level element.

Sink Processor

Sink Processor dictates how the Sink Group will function and achieve the load balancing or failover scenarios required by the reliability guarantee agreed for your Flume setup. Sink Processor is also a top level component in the Flume configuration. Broadly Sink Processor is classified into two:

1. **Built-in Sink Processor**: These are processors present by default with Apache Flume.
   - Default Sink Processor:
     - Accepts only one sink.
     - Doesn't have to be explicitly put as a single sink has this processor by default.
   - Failover Sink Processor:
     - Keeps a prioritized list of sinks
     - Uses that priority to select the sink and makes sure that there is always a sink to process an event.
     - If an event fails while sending to a sink, the next event automatically selects the next sink in the priority list.

- Load Balancing Sink Processor:
  - Keeps an indexed list of sink
  - When events come along it uses conventional load balancing approach of looking at the load and then distributing the load evenly as possible.
  - Round robin load balancing is defaulted
  - Apart from round robin Flume has another algorithm namely random.

2. **Custom Sink Processor**: Does have support for this but not yet in there with the latest Flume release.

Event Serializers

To convert the event into format of your choice serializers can be a handy component whipped with the Flume installation. Only a very few sinks support serializers at the moment namely `File_Roll` sink and HDFS Sink. There are few serializers in the default installation of Flume as follows:

1. **Body text terializer**:
   - Writes the body of the event as is into an output stream
   - Event headers are however ignored while the stream is written

2. **Flume event - avro event serializer**:
   - Writes the event to an Avro container file

3. **Avro event serializer**:
   - This is similar to the preceding serializer but has configurable control over the record schema of the Avro container file

Context Routing

As explained earlier, event has two main parts namely Header and Payload. Header (Key/Value pair) values can be used and accordingly routing defined. Two components where the routing selection can be decided are:

- **Channel**: A channel can be selected according to the header values. Custom component namely Channel Selector can be written which can have code written to select the channel desired for achieving your use case.

- **Sink**: As before, header values can be used to make decisions to select the right sink. Also, within the sink different operations can be performed by writing custom sink which can do whatever your use case require. There are some default header values which can also be used to do sophisticated stuff for your use case selected.

Basically you can introduce any number of headers and using which your components can do the right stuff. Doing this, the flume components behaves dynamically in all aspects.

Flume working example

In this section, as always throughout this part of the book, we will cover a full working example for the technology; towards the end of this section, there will be a dedicated section that covers how in our use case SCV is implemented, showing real code snippets.

Installation and Configuration

This step details most of the installation stuff that has to be done to make Flume working. This is a pre-requisite to be dealt with.

Step 1: Installing and verifying Flume

In this section we will install Apache Flume and then verify its installation. Follow the given steps for complete installation:

1. Download the Apache Flume binary distribution with the following command; we will be using the current version of Apache Flume, which is 1.7.0.

   ```
   wget http://www-us.apache.org/dist/flume/1.7.0/apache-flume-1.7.0-b
   in.tar.gz
   ```

2. Once downloaded, change the directory to a location where you will want to extract contents by using the following command:

   ```
   tar -zxvf ${DOWNLOAD_DIRECTORY}/apache-flume-1.7.0-bin.tar.gz
   ```

3. Let us refer to the extracted flume folder as `${FLUME_HOME}`. Set `${FLUME_HOME}` as an environment variable as well as in the `~/.bashrc` file with the following command, where `${FLUME_HOME}` should be replaced with the complete path:

```
export FLUME_HOME=${FLUME_HOME}
```

4. Once extracted, getting started with flume is as simple as putting in the required configuration in `conf/flume-conf.properties`. The next section will detail out various parts of this configuration.

Step 2: Configuring Flume

The `conf` folder in the Flume configuration folder comes with templates for configuration files. These templates are well documented and provide a jumpstart for users. If we look into `conf/flume-conf-template.properties`, we see the following:

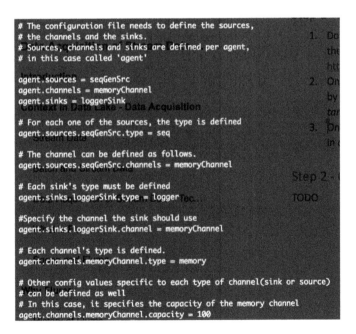

Figure 21: Flume Configuration Template

In the *Flume Configuration* section covered before, more details on various configuration aspects have already been covered with examples; so we will not repeat ourselves here. With regards to configuring Flume to cater to our SCV use case, it will be covered in the following sections.

Step 3: Start Flume

The flume agent can be started with the `flume-ng` command as shown next (sample only, and for reference). Again, these will be detailed in later sections:

```
bin/flume-ng agent -n $agent_name conf -f conf/flume-conf.properties

Here,
agent      → The instance of Flume agent
-n $agent_name → Name of the agent as defined in the configuration file
-f conf/flume-conf.properties → configuration file with flume component
definitions
```

Flume in purview of SCV use case

As discussed with the overall data lake architecture in previous chapters and the Single Customer View use case, it is evident that capabilities of Flume can be leveraged in multiple ways. Flume can be used for data acquisition as well as can play a role in data ingestion as well. For the context of this chapter we will focus on data acquisition capabilities of flume from various sources in context of SCV use case.

While we may discuss the messaging layer in a greater detail in later chapters, in order to complete the data acquisition mechanisms for flume, we will also cover in the examples some basic parts of messaging engine, Apache Kafka.

Kafka Installation

We will perform a basic, bare minimum setup of Kafka, only as a message broker (message going in an out of a component), playing a primary role of a Flume sink. We will go ahead with default configurations for now.

1. Download the Kafka binaries with the following command:

```
wget http://redrockdigimark.com/apachemirror/kafka/0.10.1.1/kafka_2
.11-0.10.1.1.tgz
```

2. Change directory to a user directory, where we will want to extract the contents of the kafka tarball using the following command:

```
tar -xzvf <DOWNLOAD_DIRECTORY>/kafka_2.11-0.10.1.1.tgz
```

3. Let us refer to the extracted Kafka folder as ${KAFKA_HOME} and configure the same using the following command and add the same to ~/.bashrc file. Also, as with other installations, you can optionally update $PATH with ${KAFKA_HOME}/bin:

```
export KAFKA_HOME=${KAFKA_HOME}
```

4. Change the directory into the extracted Kafka folder, ${KAFKA_HOME} and run the following commands to start the Kafka server:

```
${KAFKA_HOME}/bin/zookeeper-server-start.sh
${KAFKA_HOME}/config/zookeeper.properties
```

And then, in a separate bash shell, start the kafka server with the following command

```
${KAFKA_HOME}/bin/kafka-server-start.sh
${KAFKA_HOME}/config/server.properties
```

5. On successful start of the Kafka server, you should be able to see the message started (kafka.server.KafkaServer) on the shell console.

6. This Kafka instance is started based on the default server.properties file which is bundled within the Kafka binary. For the purpose of Flume as an acquisition layer, this will be good enough.

In the following sections we will be detailing a number of examples required for completion of SCV scenarios. One such scenario will be to load the data from database while the other will be to load the data from unstructured data source, such as a spool file. We will see how to realize these scenarios with these examples.

Example 1 - RDBMS to Kafka

As we have created some data with earlier chapters for Sqoop export/import, we will reuse the same data for streaming them as events into Kafka using Flume in this example. Database Source Configuration:

1. Copy the PostgresSQL driver jar, downloaded in previous chapters (Chapter 5, *Data Acquisition of Batch Data with Apache Sqoop*), into ${FLUME_HOME}/lib folder:

   ```
   cp ${SQOOP_HOME}/lib/postgresql-9.4.1212.jre6.jar
   $F{LUME_HOME|/lib
   ```

2. SQL as a source is not a standard source which gets bundled with flume distribution. Hence a third party source needs to be downloaded and installed:
   1. Download the source from the following location, using this command:

      ```
      wget https://github.com/keedio/flume-ng-sql-source/archive/
      1.4.2.tar.gz
      ```

   2. Rename file as sql-source-1.4.2.tar.gz:

      ```
      mv ${DOWNLOAD_DIR}/1.4.2.tar.gz
      ${DOWNLOAD_DIR}/sql-source-1.4.2.tar.gz
      ```

   3. Extract the contents of tarball into a user folder using the following command

      ```
      tar -zxvf ${DOWNLOAD_DIRECTORY}/sql-source-1.4.2.tar.gz
      ```

   4. Change directory into the extracted contents and compile the source code using the following command. The binary JAR will be compiled into the target folder:

      ```
      mvn install -DskipTests
      ```

   5. Create the plugins.d with sql-source as its subdirectory and other directories using the following command:

      ```
      mkdir -p ${FLUME_HOME}/plugins.d/sql-source/lib
      ```

6. Copy the jar from target folder to the `plugins.d/sql-source/lib` folder using the following command:

```
cp ${DOWNLOAD_DIR}/flume-ng-sql-source-1.4.2/target/flume-ng-
sql-source-1.4.2.jar
${FLUME_HOME}/plugins.d/sql-source/lib
```

3. Change directory back to `${FLUME_HOME}` and create a new flume configuration file `db-kafka-flume-conf.properties`. Make the following configuration changes:

   - **Source Configuration**: The source can be configured with the following properties. Please change the properties as per your VM setup. The directory pointed by `agent.sources.sql-source.status.file.path` should be an existing directory before executing Flume agent, here as per the following properties, it will be `mkdir ~/db-kafka`. In the flume configuration, we will need to specify the full path for all directory and file locations:

```
agent.sources = sql-source
agent.sources.sql-
source.type=org.keedio.flume.source.SQLSource
agent.sources.sql-
source.hibernate.connection.url=jdbc:postgresql://<ip_addre
ss>/sourcedb?schema=public
agent.sources.sql-source.hibernate.connection.user=postgres
agent.sources.sql-
source.hibernate.connection.password=<db_password>
agent.sources.sql-source.table=customer
agent.sources.sql-source.columns.to.select=*
agent.sources.sql-source.status.file.path=/home/centos/db-
kafka
agent.sources.sql-source.status.file.name=sql-source.status
```

The properties set just now can be explained as given in tabular format (*Table 04*):

Property	Description
`agent.sources`	Set a logical reference name for the source
`agent.sources.sql-source.type`	The class declaring the type of source being configured. Here it belongs to the open source GitHub project for SQL source.
`agent.sources.sql-source.hibernate.connection.url`	Set the JDBC URL
`agent.sources.sql-source.hibernate.connection.user`	Set the connection user
`agent.sources.sql-source.hibernate.connection.user`	Set the connection user password
`agent.sources.sql-source.table`	Set the table name
`agent.sources.sql-source.columns.to.select`	Set the columns to be selected. Here it is set to * which means all.
`agent.sources.sql-source.status.file.path`	Set it to a location where we want to keep the status file for source
`agent.sources.sql-source.status.file.path`	Set the name of status file

Table 04: Flume source configuration

- **Channel Configuration**:

```
# The channel can be defined as follows.
agent.channels = memoryChannel
agent.sources.sql-source.channels = memoryChannel
agent.channels.memoryChannel.type = memory
agent.channels.memoryChannel.capacity = 100
```

- **Sink Configuration**:

```
# Each sink must be defined
agent.sinks = kafkaSink
agent.sinks.kafkaSink.type=org.apache.flume.sink.kafka.KafkaSink
agent.sinks.kafkaSink.brokerList=localhost:9092
agent.sinks.kafkaSink.topic=db
agent.sinks.kafkaSink.channel = memoryChannel
```

4. Overall Configuration should now look as:

```
agent.sources = sql-source
agent.sources.sql-source.type=org.keedio.flume.source.SQLSource
agent.sources.sql-
source.hibernate.connection.url=jdbc:postgresql://<ip_address>/sour
cedb?schema=public
agent.sources.sql-source.hibernate.connection.user=postgres
agent.sources.sql-
source.hibernate.connection.password=<db_password>
agent.sources.sql-source.table=customer
agent.sources.sql-source.columns.to.select=*
agent.sources.sql-source.status.file.path=/home/centos/db-kafka
agent.sources.sql-source.status.file.name=sql-source.status

# The channel can be defined as follows.
agent.channels = memoryChannel
agent.sources.sql-source.channels = memoryChannel
agent.channels.memoryChannel.type = memory
agent.channels.memoryChannel.capacity = 100

# Each sink  must be defined
agent.sinks = kafkaSink
agent.sinks.kafkaSink.type=org.apache.flume.sink.kafka.KafkaSink
agent.sinks.kafkaSink.brokerList=localhost:9092
agent.sinks.kafkaSink.topic=db
agent.sinks.kafkaSink.channel = memoryChannel
```

5. Launch the flume agent with the following command:

```
${FLUME_HOME}/bin/flume-ng agent --conf ${FLUME_HOME}/conf/  -f
${FLUME_HOME}/conf/db-kafka-flume-conf.properties  -n agent -
Dflume.root.logger=INFO,console
```

6. **Observations**:

- The following statements in status file indicate the last index read and meta information of the source:

cat ~/db-kafka/sql-source.stat

{"SourceName":"sql-source","URL":"jdbc:postgresql:\/\/192.168.43.28\/sourcedb?schema=public","LastIndex":"5","ColumnsToSelect":"*","Table":"customer"}[centos@localhost apache-flume-1.7.0-bin]$ ▮

Figure 26: Source last index read and meta information

- The following Kafka logs indicate the events that were queued:

cat /tmp/kafka-logs/db-0/00000000000000000000.log

[centos@localhost apache-flume-1.7.0-bin]$ cat /tmp/kafka-logs/db-0/00000000000000000000.log
5??qS????????????"0","tomcy","john","1985-10-20"4??b????????????"1","rahul","dev","1989-08-15"7?N??????
???????!"2","pankaj","misra","1982-08-10"3??@????????????"3","devi","lal","1990-05-06"3?`????????????"
4","john","doe","1992-06-25"[centos@localhost apache-flume-1.7.0-bin]$ ▮

Figure 27: Kafka log showing events queued

- The following consumer command launches a consumer and shows the events consumed from Kafka:

```
${KAFKA_HOME}/bin/kafka-console-consumer.sh
${KAFKA_HOME}/config/consumer.properties --topic db -
bootstrap-server localhost:9092 --from-beginning
```

[[centos@localhost kafka_2.11-0.10.1.1]$ bin/kafka-console-consumer.sh ./config/consumer.properties --t]
opic db -bootstrap-server localhost:9092 --from-beginning
[2017-02-16 07:24:37,025] INFO [GroupCoordinator 0]: Preparing to restabilize group console-consumer-47
468 with old generation 0 (kafka.coordinator.GroupCoordinator)
[2017-02-16 07:24:37,029] INFO [GroupCoordinator 0]: Stabilized group console-consumer-47468 generation
 1 (kafka.coordinator.GroupCoordinator)
[2017-02-16 07:24:37,057] INFO [GroupCoordinator 0]: Assignment received from leader for group console-
consumer-47468 for generation 1 (kafka.coordinator.GroupCoordinator)
"0","tomcy","john","1985-10-20"
"1","rahul","dev","1989-08-15"
"2","pankaj","misra","1982-08-10"
"3","devi","lal","1990-05-06"
"4","john","doe","1992-06-25"

Figure 28: Consumer command showing events consumed from Kafka

Example 2: Spool messages to Kafka

A Spool file, in simple words, is a file containing data to be processed. Most of the times, such files contain delimited information (information separated by a character), and is read line by line for processing, wherein each line represents a record. Optionally, each of these line may also contain XML/JSON data structure.

One of the sources of data can be spool files emitted by other systems, which may contain user data and these spool files may work as integration points into the Data Lake.

Flume framework supports a number of variations of spool formats, here we are considering the most common spool format which contains data as JSON messages.

A spool source may be configured with the following steps:

1. Create another configuration file, `${FLUME_HOME}/conf/spool-kafka-flume-conf.properties` file, the same way as done for `db-kafka` integration.
2. Perform source, channel and sink configuration as follows:
   - **Source Configuration**:
     1. Provide Spooler file configuration, as a source. Please create data user directory with command `mkdir ~/flume-data`. This directory will contain the spool file to be processed:

        ```
        agent.sources = spool-source
        agent.sources.spool-source.type=spooldir
        agent.sources.spool-
        source.spoolDir=/home/centos/flume-data
        ```

     2. Make sure that the spooler directory exists and is accessible and flume process can access it

3. Create a spool file and populate the spool file with the following data, and save it in ~/data directory with the filename as spool-1 for reference:

```
{"id":0,"firstName":"tomcy","lastName":"john","dob
":"1985-10-20"}{"id":1,"firstName":"rahul","lastNa
me":"dev","dob":"1989-08-15"}{"id":2,"firstName":"
pankaj","lastName":"misra","dob":"1982-08-10"}{"id
":3,"firstName":"devi","lastName":"lal","dob":"199
0-05-06"}{"id":4,"firstName":"john","lastName":"do
e","dob":"1992-06-25"}
```

- **Channel Configuration**: Channel configuration is not very different than in the previous example with just one minor change as we continue to use the memory channel.

```
agent.channels = memoryChannel
agent.sources.spool-source.channels = memoryChannel
agent.channels.memoryChannel.type = memory
agent.channels.memoryChannel.capacity = 100
```

- **Sink Configuration**: Minor changes required in sink configuration since most of the sink configuration remains the same except the Kafka topic, as given next:

```
# Each sink   must be defined
agent.sinks = kafkaSink
agent.sinks.kafkaSink.type=org.apache.flume.sink.kafka.Kafk
aSink
agent.sinks.kafkaSink.brokerList=localhost:9092
agent.sinks.kafkaSink.topic=spooled
agent.sinks.kafkaSink.channel = memoryChannel
```

3. Launch the flume agent with the following command:

```
${FLUME_HOME}/bin/flume-ng agent --conf ${FLUME_HOME}/conf/  -f
${FLUME_HOME}/conf/spool-kafka-flume-conf.properties  -n agent -
Dflume.root.logger=INFO,console
```

4. Verification and Observations:
   - The spool file got renamed as `spool-1.COMPLETED` since it was processed.
   - Kafka logs contain the data streamed from spool file, as shown next:

   ```
   cat /tmp/kafka-logs/spooled-0/00000000000000000000.log
   ```

```
[centos@localhost apache-flume-1.7.0-bin]$ cat /tmp/kafka-logs/spooled-0/00000000000000
000000.log
W?T\?????????????A{"id":0,"firstName":"tomcy","lastName":"john","dob":"1985-10-20"}V?Mx
????????????@{"id":1,"firstName":"rahul","lastName":"dev","dob":"1989-08-15"}Y?????????
???????C{"id":2,"firstName":"pankaj","lastName":"misra","dob":"1982-08-10"}Uu?D{???????
??????{"id":3,"firstName":"devi","lastName":"lal","dob":"1990-05-06"}U)V??????????????{
"id":4,"firstName":"john","lastName":"doe","dob":"1992-06-25"}????????????????[centos@lo
```

Figure 31: Kafka log revisited

   - Running Kafka consumer consumes the queued messages in Kafka logs:

   ```
   ${KAFKA_HOME}/bin/kafka-console-consumer.sh
   ${KAFKA_HOME}/config/consumer.properties --topic spooled -
   bootstrap-server localhost:9092 --from-beginning
   ```

```
[centos@localhost kafka_2.11-0.10.1.1]$ bin/kafka-console-consumer.sh ./config/consumer
.properties  --topic spooled -bootstrap-server localhost:9092 --from-beginning
[2017-02-16 09:08:09,863] INFO [GroupCoordinator 0]: Preparing to restabilize group con
sole-consumer-88710 with old generation 0 (kafka.coordinator.GroupCoordinator)
[2017-02-16 09:08:09,863] INFO [GroupCoordinator 0]: Stabilized group console-consumer-
88710 generation 1 (kafka.coordinator.GroupCoordinator)
[2017-02-16 09:08:09,870] INFO [GroupCoordinator 0]: Assignment received from leader fo
r group console-consumer-88710 for generation 1 (kafka.coordinator.GroupCoordinator)
{"id":0,"firstName":"tomcy","lastName":"john","dob":"1985-10-20"}
{"id":1,"firstName":"rahul","lastName":"dev","dob":"1989-08-15"}
{"id":2,"firstName":"pankaj","lastName":"misra","dob":"1982-08-10"}
{"id":3,"firstName":"devi","lastName":"lal","dob":"1990-05-06"}
{"id":4,"firstName":"john","lastName":"doe","dob":"1992-06-25"}
```

Figure 32: Running Kafka consumer (logs revisited)

Example 3: Interceptors

There are multiple interceptors supported by Flume out of the box, and are very useful for specific scenarios. As indicated previously, the interceptors act on source events, to intercept them and add a few more details to the event as needed.

In order to better understand the usage of Interceptors, we will take the example of spooled events being streamed into kafka. We will intercept these spooled events and add 2 more attributes which can be useful for our Data Lake:

1. **Timestamp (timestamp)**: Adding of timestamp to every event will help maintain the time profile of event, such that an event's end to end timing can be tracked.
2. **UUID (eventId)**: Adding UUID to an event will help uniquely identify each event. Since an event is immutable, tracking event via UUID provides traceability.

This will require creating a new configuration file, `${FLUME_HOME}/conf/spool-interceptor-kafka-flume-conf.properties`, having similar configurations as in the spool example, with minor changes in source and sink configuration with additional interceptor configuration as shown next:

1. **Source configuration changes**: As shown, the source configuration is only around defining additional interceptors, namely timestamp and UUID and their respective properties:

```
agent.sources = spool-source
agent.sources.spool-source.type=spooldir
agent.sources.spool-source.spoolDir=/home/centos/flume-data
agent.sources.spool-source.interceptors=ts uuid

#Timestamp Interceptor Definition
agent.sources.spool-source.interceptors.ts.type=timestamp

#UUID Interceptor Definition
agent.sources.spool-
source.interceptors.uuid.type=org.apache.flume.sink.solr.morphline.
UUIDInterceptor$Builder
agent.sources.spool-source.interceptors.uuid.headerName=eventId
```

2. **Channel configuration**: The channel configuration remains the same as in the previous example:

```
agent.channels = memoryChannel
agent.sources.spool-source.channels = memoryChannel
agent.channels.memoryChannel.type = memory
agent.channels.memoryChannel.capacity = 100
```

3. **Sink Configuration Changes**:

```
# Each sink  must be defined
agent.sinks = kafkaSink
agent.sinks.kafkaSink.type=org.apache.flume.sink.kafka.KafkaSink
agent.sinks.kafkaSink.brokerList=localhost:9092
agent.sinks.kafkaSink.topic=spooled-intercepted
agent.sinks.kafkaSink.channel = memoryChannel
agent.sinks.kafkaSink.useFlumeEventFormat=true
```

As we observe the change in sink configuration is addition of the property `useFlumeEventFormat` so that the event headers are also captured while capturing the event body as part of the Kafka message.

In order to rerun the preceding example but with interceptors, do the following:

1. Rename the spool file to be uncompleted and delete the Kafka logs for the spooled topic using the commands provided here:

```
mv ~/flume-data/spool-1.COMPLETED ~/flume-data/spool-1
```

2. Change the directory to <FLUME_HOME> and run the following command to reprocess the spool file:

```
${FLUME_HOME}/bin/flume-ng agent --conf ${FLUME_HOME}/conf/  -f
${FLUME_HOME}/conf/spool-interceptor-kafka-flume-conf.properties  -
n agent -Dflume.root.logger=INFO,console
```

3. The output from the Kafka console consumer can be observed as shown next:

```
${KAFKA_HOME}/bin/kafka-console-consumer.sh
${KAFKA_HOME}/config/consumer.properties --topic spooled-
intercepted -bootstrap-server localhost:9092 --from-beginning
```

```
[centos@localhost kafka_2.11-0.10.1.1]$ bin/kafka-console-consumer.sh ./config/consumer.properties  --topic spooled -bootstrap-server
localhost:9092 --from-beginning
[2017-02-16 10:35:43,946] INFO [GroupCoordinator 0]: Preparing to restabilize group console-consumer-24139 with old generation 0 (kafk
a.coordinator.GroupCoordinator)
[2017-02-16 10:35:43,947] INFO [GroupCoordinator 0]: Stabilized group console-consumer-24139 generation 1 (kafka.coordinator.GroupCoor]
dinator)
[2017-02-16 10:35:43,954] INFO [GroupCoordinator 0]: Assignment received from leader for group console-consumer-24139 for generation 1
 (kafka.coordinator.GroupCoordinator)
eventIdHd8c45b62-1550-4f28-9304-36f4a344e34ftimestamp1487259309006?{"id":0,"firstName":"tomcy","lastName":"john","dob":"1985-10-20"}
eventIdHf44c01dc-0ecb-45a1-8147-a85a766e89e1timestamp1487259309006?{"id":1,"firstName":"rahul","lastName":"dev","dob":"1989-08-15"}
eventIdHa061a57e-862f-44bb-b568-bad63b62f583timestamp1487259309006?{"id":2,"firstName":"pankaj","lastName":"misra","dob":"1982-08-10"}]
eventIdH9f778d11-ce22-4335-b486-b4e67d95c574timestamp1487259309006~{"id":3,"firstName":"devi","lastName":"lal","dob":"1990-05-06"}
eventIdHd14be034-14e3-4c52-9380-5e5eed179757timestamp1487259309006~{"id":4,"firstName":"john","lastName":"doe","dob":"1992-06-25"}
```

Figure 35: Kafka logs revisited again to show consumer details

As shown here, the interceptor headers have been captured as part of the message, however the consumer will need to process the message accordingly for message headers and the message body.

Example 4 - Memory channel, file channel, and Kafka channel

So far, we have seen in all our examples the usage of the memory channel. Flume supports a few more channels, of which File channel and Kafka channel are well-known. Each of these channels is capable of connecting to source and sink in exactly the same way, however there are a few subtle differences in the way they are defined. For example, if we define a File channel, we will need to provide the location of the file and a few other file related attributes, and also ensure that the file location has sufficient permissions to be accessible.

On other hand, if we define a Kafka channel, we will need the Kafka connection URL as well as the topic name, which will act as a channel for further consumption. Hence in this case, the topology can be Source ◉ Kafka Channel ◉ HDFS, as an example.

Let us replay the spool example with the preceding variations and observe how it changes the way our example works:

1. **File Channel**:
    1. Copy the `${FLUME_HOME}/conf/spool-interceptor-kafka-flume-conf.properties` file to `${FLUME_HOME}/conf/spool-fileChannel-kafka-flume-conf.properties` and change the source, channel and sink configurations as shown next:

```
agent.sources = spool-source
agent.sources.spool-source.type=spooldir
agent.sources.spool-source.spoolDir=/home/centos/flume-data
agent.sources.spool-source.interceptors=ts uuid

#Timestamp Interceptor Definition
agent.sources.spool-source.interceptors.ts.type=timestamp

#UUID Interceptor Definition
agent.sources.spool-source.interceptors.uuid.type=org.apache.flume.sink.solr.morphline.UUIDInterceptor$Builder
agent.sources.spool-source.interceptors.uuid.headerName=eventId

# The channel can be defined as follows.
agent.channels = fileChannel
agent.channels.fileChannel.type = file
agent.channels.fileChannel.capacity = 100
agent.channels.fileChannel.transactionCapacity=10
agent.channels.fileChannel.dataDirs=/home/centos/flume-data/flume-channel/data
agent.channels.fileChannel.checkpointDir=/home/centos/flume-data/flume-channel/checkpoint
agent.sources.spool-source.channels = fileChannel

# Each sink  must be defined
agent.sinks = kafkaSink
agent.sinks.kafkaSink.type=org.apache.flume.sink.kafka.KafkaSink
agent.sinks.kafkaSink.brokerList=localhost:9092
agent.sinks.kafkaSink.topic=spooled-fileChannel
agent.sinks.kafkaSink.channel = fileChannel
agent.sinks.kafkaSink.useFlumeEventFormat=true
```

2. Rename the completed spool file to `spool-1` as specified in the earlier example.

3. Create the flume channel's data and checkpoint directories for transactionsal and rollback needs:

```
mkdir  -p ~/flume-data/flume-channel/data
mkdir  -p ~/flume-data/flume-channel/checkpoint
```

4. Ensure that that channel capacity (in configuration, `agent.channels.fileChannel.capacity = 100`) is always greater than the transaction capacity (in configuration, `agent.channels.fileChannel.transactionCapacity=10`)

5. Run the flume process again for spool file with the following command:

```
${FLUME_HOME}/bin/flume-ng agent --conf ${FLUME_HOME}/conf/
-f ${FLUME_HOME}/conf/spool-fileChannel-kafka-flume-
conf.properties  -n agent -Dflume.root.logger=INFO,console
```

6. Verification and Observations:
    - Verify the messages with the same Kafka console consumer command as in the previous example, all the messages must be seen exactly the same way as in the previous example.

    ```
    ${KAFKA_HOME}/bin/kafka-console-consumer.sh
    ${KAFKA_HOME}/config/consumer.properties --topic
    spooled-fileChannel -bootstrap-server localhost:9092 --
    from-beginning
    ```

- Observe the flume channel data directory for the flume log created, and inspect the content of the log (`~/flume-data/flume-channel/data/log-1`) file as shown next:

```
?
/
eventId$53383d9d-1ded-4060-955a-8547ce1a40ae

1487264842472A{"id":0,"firstName":"tomcy","lastName":"john","dob":"1985-10-20"}/5
?
/
eventId$9f79c492-1d05-4008-8acc-7a3974abf28e

1487264842472@{"id":1,"firstName":"rahul","lastName":"dev","dob":"1989-08-15"}?]?
?
/
eventId$71bf0954-f3a9-4499-b86d-a2f2425b939f

1487264842472C{"id":2,"firstName":"pankaj","lastName":"misra","dob":"1982-08-10"}{4?
?
/
eventId$14b3233e-3652-442b-8230-b481d46ef165

1487264842472?{"id":3,"firstName":"devi","lastName":"lal","dob":"1990-05-06"}m?
?
/
eventId$d10611c3-0d00-42c4-b58c-c71b1ab6cbc5

1487264842472?{"id":4,"firstName":"john","lastName":"doe","dob":"1992-06-25"}??
0
/
eventId$ecc94e4f-68c1-46dd-b400-30ebc0c14b74

1487264842472tamp
```

Figure 37: Flume log

2. **Kafka Channel**:
   1. Copy `${FLUME_HOME}/conf/spool-interceptor-kafka-flume-conf.properties` file to `${FLUME_HOME}/conf/spool-kafkaChannel-kafka-flume-conf.properties` and change the source, channel, and sink configurations as shown next:

```
agent.sources = spool-source
agent.sources.spool-source.type=spooldir
agent.sources.spool-source.spoolDir=/home/centos/flume-data
agent.sources.spool-source.interceptors=ts uuid
```

```
#Timestamp Interceptor Definition
agent.sources.spool-source.interceptors.ts.type=timestamp

#UUID Interceptor Definition
agent.sources.spool-
source.interceptors.uuid.type=org.apache.flume.sink.solr.mo
rphline.UUIDInterceptor$Builder
agent.sources.spool-
source.interceptors.uuid.headerName=eventId

# The channel can be defined as follows.
agent.channels = kafkaChannel
agent.channels.kafkaChannel.type
=org.apache.flume.channel.kafka.KafkaChannel
agent.channels.kafkaChannel.kafka.bootstrap.servers=localho
st:9092
agent.channels.kafkaChannel.kafka.topic=datalakeChannel
agent.sources.spool-source.channels = kafkaChannel

# Each sink  must be defined
agent.sinks = kafkaSink
agent.sinks.kafkaSink.type=org.apache.flume.sink.kafka.Kafk
aSink
agent.sinks.kafkaSink.brokerList=localhost:9092
agent.sinks.kafkaSink.topic=spooled
agent.sinks.kafkaSink.channel = kafkaChannel
agent.sinks.kafkaSink.useFlumeEventFormat=true
```

2. Rename the completed spool file to `spool-1.log` and clear the Kafka logs as specified in the earlier example.

3. Run the flume process again for the spool file with the following command:

```
${FLUME_HOME}/bin/flume-ng agent --conf
${FLUME_HOME}/conf/  -f
${FLUME_HOME}/conf/spool-kafkaChannel-kafka-flume-
conf.properties  -n agent -Dflume.root.logger=INFO,console
```

4. Verification and Observation:

- Observe the channel-specific Kafka topic and its queue depth:

```
${KAFKA_HOME}/bin/kafka-run-class.sh
kafka.tools.GetOffsetShell --broker-list localhost:9092
--topic datalakeChannel
```

```
[centos@localhost kafka_2.11-0.10.1.1]$ bin/kafka-run-class.sh kafka.tools.GetOffsetShell
--broker-list localhost:9092 --topic datalakeChannel
datalakeChannel:0:6
```

Figure 38: The channel-specific Kafka topic's queue depth in the log

- Verify the messages with the same Kafka console consumer command as in the previous example; all the messages must be seen exactly the same way as in the previous example:

```
${KAFKA_HOME}/bin/kafka-console-consumer.sh
${KAFKA_HOME}/config/consumer.properties --topic
datalakeChannel -bootstrap-server localhost:9092 --
from-beginning
```

As we observed here, we used Kafka as a channel; and then we again propagated the event back into a Kafka topic. This does not sound right, and for all practical cases, this will not be the case since we will be more interested in putting the events into a processing pipeline from a kafka channel or directly ingesting into the storage layers. This example was taken more as a reference to indicate a very important aspect--that Kafka can be used as a channel rather than a destination sink. This will be a big advantage since most near-real-time processing frameworks and batch frameworks would want to consume the events from Kafka as a channel.

In this chapter, we looked at Flume as an additional acquisition layer component to capture much richer customer information through various sources. Here, we have covered RDBMS as well as spool file as input, both of them aggregating the customer information into the data layer. The overall acquisition layer with Flume being added to already existing sqoop component can be visualized in the following figure:

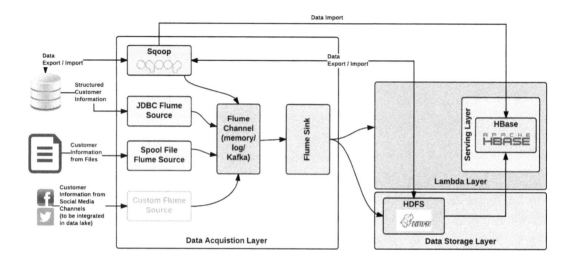

Figure 39: Acquisition Layer with Sqoop and Flume for Single Customer View

When to use Flume

Some of the consideration which you can use when choosing Flume for handling different use cases is as follows - choose Flume when you want:

- To acquire data from a variety of source and store into Hadoop system
- To handle high-velocity and high-volume data into Hadoop system
- Reliable delivery of data to the destination
- A scalable solution that can run quite easily just by adding more machine to it, when the velocity and volume of data increases

- The capability of dynamically configuring the various components in the architecture without incurring any downtime.
- To achieve a single point of contact for all the various configurations based on which the overall architecture is functioning

When not to use Flume

In some scenarios, usage of Flume is not the ideal choice. There are other options out there which can be employed to solve those use case and not Flume. Do not choose Flume when:

- You need more data processing as against transfer of data. They are more suited for other stream processing technologies.
- You need more batch data transfer scenarios (regular batch as against micro-batch).
- You need a more available setup with no data loss.
- You need a durable message with very high scalability requirements (there isn't a scientific quantitative figure for that though).
- You have a huge number of consumers as this has a very high impact on Flume's scalability.

Even through Flume can be dynamically configured in many cases, it does incur downtime in certain configuration changes (topology changes).

Other options

As always, it doesn't mean that Apache Flume is the only option that can be used to solve the use case problem in hand. We chose Flume for its merit and advantages especially considering our use case of SCV. There are other options which can be considered and these are discussed in brief in his section.

Apache Flink

Apache Flume is used mainly for data acquisition capability. We will be using Flume to transfer data from source systems sending stream data to the messaging layer (for further processing) and all the way into HDFS.

For transferring data all the way to HDFS, Apache Flume is best fit for stream data. However for getting stream data and then processing is one of the main use case for **Apache Flink** and it does have additional features suited for this.

This doesn't mean that Apache Flink can be used for transferring data to HDFS, it does have the mechanism but there willn't be so many built-in capabilities. It does have many features as against Flume but they are more on the stream processing aspects. Flink does have a rolling file sink, using which we can write data streams to HDFS but definitely lack many features provided by built-in features in Flume.

Apache Flink is growing in popularity day by day but stream processing is its main capability and Flume will still be around mainly in the space of data acquisition and persisting into Hadoop and related big data storage systems.

Apache NiFi

The **Apache NiFi** website states Apache NiFi as - An easy to use, powerful, and reliable system to process and distribute data.

It definitely is an alternate to Apache Flume and does have a rich set of features and easy to use web user interface. It is highly configurable, security thought and built bottom up and is highly customizable (extensibility principle).

One of the strong features notable is its drag and drop capable web user interface in which most of properties of components dropped can be configured dynamically on the fly. Another notable feature is it capability of ingesting almost any data. If you do have a very particular data, you can write your own ingestion methodologies. Similar to inputting data, it also have a wide range of support for various protocols used to send data out of NiFi. Again, the output aspect is also customizable if the need be by writing some custom implementation class according to your use case requirement.

Summary

First of all, a pat on your back for coming this far. We have completed the technologies that we are going to use in our Data Lake's first layer namely Data Acquisition Layer. Even though we have covered just two technologies (we willn't say we have covered these topic in depth but we have covered these in some breath and in alignment with our use case implementation) we have covered fair distance in our journey to implement Data Lake for your enterprise.

In this chapter, similar to other chapters in this part, we first set our context by seeing where exactly this technology will be placed in the overall Data Lake architecture. We then gave enough details on why we chose Apache Flume as the technology for handling stream data from source systems.

After that we went deep into Apache Flume and start learning main concepts and working of Flume. We then looked at a full-fledged working example of Flume, in line with our use case of SCV. Before wrapping up we did put in bullet points, when and when not to you Flume. We then wrapped up the chapter by introducing you to other technology options which you can consider replacing Flume when you actually implement Data Lake, obviously if it is right suit.

After reading this chapter you should have a fair bit of idea on Flume as a whole and will also have a full-fledged working example ready. You will now have fair bit of idea of handling both stream and batch data acquisition methodologies which can be employed in your enterprise.

7

Messaging Layer using Apache Kafka

Handling streamed data is a very important aspect of a Data Lake. In the Data Lake architecture discussed in this book, the handling of streamed data is the responsibility of the messaging layer. In this chapter, we will go into detail on this layer and will also discuss the technology that we have chosen to be a part of this layer doing the actual work.

We have chosen Apache Kafka as the fitting technology to be used in messaging layer. This chapter delves deep into this technology and it's architecture in regards to Data Lake.

Context in Data Lake - messaging layer

In this chapter, we are dealing with a technology which constitutes one of the core layers of Data Lake namely, the messaging layer. Its crucial to have a fully functional messaging layer for dealing with a real-time data stream flowing in from different applications in an enterprise.

The technology that we have shortlisted to do this very important job of handling such, stream data is Apache Kafka. This chapter will take you through the functioning of messaging layer and then deep dive into the technology, Kafka.

Messaging layer

In Chapter 2, *Comprehensive Concepts of a Data Lake,* you already a high-level view of the messaging layer and how it works, especially in the context of Data Lake.

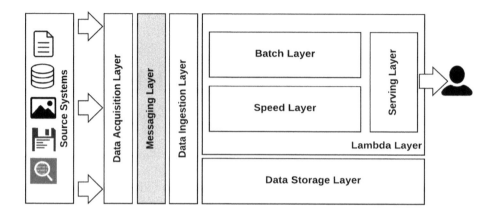

Figure 01: Data Lake: Messaging layer

The messaging layer in Data Lake takes care of as mentioned in the bulleted list has a set of functions/capabilities:

- One of the core capabilities of this layer is it's ability to decouple both the source (producer) and destination (consumer).
- Ability to handle high-velocity messages of the order of hundreds of megabytes per second from each application server node.
- Ability to handle huge volumes of data of the order of terabytes to petabytes.
- Ability to deal with messages with very low latency under extreme throughput requirements.
- Ability to guarantee message delivery (durability) in an ordered fashion.
- Ability to supply the same message to multiple consumers with less hassle of doing so. In our context, supplying messages to **Lambda Speed Layer** (the speed layer within the **Lambda Layer**) and **Data Storage Layer** at the same time to do two different functions.
- Capability of data analysis to derive operational statistics. Ability to aggregate data coming from various sources and to do some analysis.
- Obviously, high performance with less hardware requirements (yes, indeed this is a requirement).
- Ability to perform bare minimum enrichment and transformation capabilities.

Messaging layer - technology mapping

If data is the lifeblood of high technology, Apache Kafka is the circulatory system

- Todd Palino, LinkedIn

To cover our use case and to build our Data Lake, we use Apache Kafka in this layer as the technology.

The following figure brings in the technology aspect to the conceptual architecture that we will be following throughout this book. We will keep explaining each technology and its relevance in terms of overall architecture before bringing all the technologies together in the final part of this book (*Part 3*).

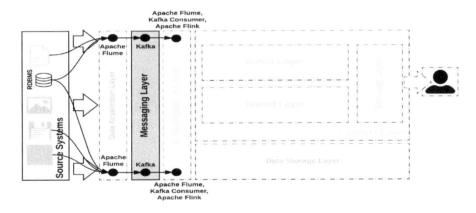

Figure 02: Technology mapping for Messaging Layer

In line with our use case of SCV, the real-time data from various business applications will flow into Flume. From there, using the messaging layer, it will flow to the Hadoop file system for storage as well as the Lambda speed layer. The real-time data from business applications that we are going to handle is customer's, behavioral data coming from user interaction with enterprise's website. For example, data such as page visits, link clicks, location details, browser details and so on, will flow into Flume. Using the publish subscribe capability of Kafka it is then streamed to the **Data Ingestion Layer**. The **Data Ingestion Layer** will handle multi-target ingestion, where one path goes to the **Data Storage Layer** (HDFS) and the other goes to **Data Ingestion Layer** for required processing as needed.

What is Apache Kafka?

Apache Kafka is an open-source stream processing platform developed by the Apache Software Foundation written in Scala and Java. The project aims to provide a unified, high-throughput, low-latency platform for handling real-time data feeds. Its storage layer is essentially a "massively scalable pub/sub message queue architected as a distributed transaction log," making it highly valuable for enterprise infrastructures to process streaming data.

- Wikipedia

The next sections of this chapter will definitely give you more details on what Kafka is in detail. In one sentence, Kafka gives a level of indirection, by which it disconnects the source from the consumer and also gives capability which a messaging layer should process, as detailed in the previous section.

Why Apache Kafka

We are using Apache Kafka as the stream data platform (**MOM: message-oriented middleware**). Core reasons for choosing Kafka is it's high reliability and ability to deal with data with a very low latency.

 Message-oriented middleware (**MOM**) is software or hardware infrastructure supporting the sending and receiving of messages between distributed systems.

- Wikipedia

Apache Kafka has some key attributes attached to it making it an ideal choice for us in achieving the capability that we are looking to implement the Data Lake. They are bulleted below:

- **Scalability**: Capable of handling high-velocity and high-volume data. Hundreds of megabytes per second throughput with terabytes of data.
- **Distributed**: Kafka is distributed by design and handles some of the distributed capabilities as follows:
    - **Replication**: The replication feature is one of the default features which needs to be available for any distributed enabled technology and Kafka has this feature built-in.
    - **Partition capable**: Again, capability to partition is one of the inherent features required for distributed architecture.
- **Faster**: This attribute can be quite relative and subjective. However, for such a capability, in the market, Kafka is considered to be quite fast and performant.
- Capable of supporting a variety of consumers. However, consumers are considered inherently slow because of more work configured to be done by them.
- **Inherent buffering capability**: To cater to a variety of consumers, Kafka has a built-in buffering capability.
- **Publish/subscribe feature**: Asynchronous and capable of a pub/sub integration pattern. This is one of the key features of a messaging based technology.
- **Reliability/guarantee similar to database**: all the data sent to Kafka is ordered and is persistent by default.
- **Fault tolerance**: inherent built-in fault tolerance in Kafka because of distributed nature and replication.

History of Kafka

Kafka was initially developed by an engineering team at LinkedIn and later released as an open source project with the Apache Software Foundation in early 2011. Kafka is LinkedIn's messaging platform. The project went from incubation to top-level Apache project on October 23, 2012.

Jay Kreps, Neha Narkhede and *Jun Rao* are the founders of Kafka while working for LinkedIn's engineering team. Jay Kreps has been a big fan of the famous writer Franz Kafka and found the name Kafka to be apt for this messaging platform, which is optimized for writing purposes (as quoted by Jay Kreps in Quora).

Kafka is primarily developed by keeping in mind some of the important new-generation messaging requirements like high-throughput, low-latency and capability of handling high-velocity and high-volume real-time feeds. It is written in Scala and is one of the top projects in **Apache Software Foundation** (**ASF**) with big community backing. The design of Kafka is heavily borrowed or influenced from how transaction/commit logs work and function.

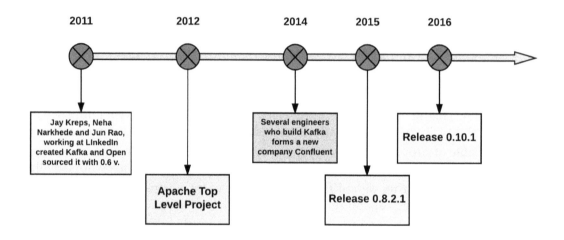

Figure 03: History of Apache Kafka

In 2014, the Kafka founders started their own company, Confluent, which actively develops multiple solutions using Kafka at it's core. The company is also a forerunner which develops multiple connectors for Kafka and maintains it in the industry.

Advantages of Kafka

Apache Kafka is selected for it's strengths in the space of messaging. The following are some of the advantages which Kafka possess, making it ideal for our Data Lake implementation:

- **High-throughput**: Kafka is capable of handling high-velocity and high-volume data using not so large hardware. It is capable of supporting message throughput of thousands of messages per second.
- **Low latency**: Kafka is able to handle these messages with very low latency of the range of milliseconds, demanded by most of new use cases.

- **Fault tolerant**: The inherent capability of Kafka to be resistant to node/machine failure within a cluster.
- **Durability**: The data/messages are persistent on disk, making it durable and messages are also replicated so the messages are never lost.
- **Scalability**: Kafka can be scaled-out without incurring any downtime on the fly by adding additional nodes. The message handling inside the Kafka cluster is fully transparent and these are seamless.
- **Distributed**: Inherently supports distributed architecture making it scalable using capabilities like replication and partitioning.
- Message broker capabilities.
- **High concurrency**: Capable of handling thousands of messages per second and that too in low latency conditions with high throughput. Kafka allows the reading and writing of messages into it at high concurrency.
- **By default persistent**: By default, the messages are persistent making it durable and reliable.
- **Consumer friendly**: Kafka can be integrated with a variety of consumers. Each customer has a different ability to handle these messages coming out of Kafka and because of it's inherent persistence capability, it can behave or act differently according to the consumer that it integrates with. It also integrates well with a variety of consumers written in a variety of languages.
- **Batch handling capable** (ETL like functionality): Since Kafka persists messages, it could also be employed for batch like use cases and can also do the work of a traditional ETL.
- Capable of handling a variety of use cases commonly required for a Data Lake, namely log aggregation, web activity tracking, and so on.
- Designed to work on commodity hardware. For POC's it is fine, but for an enterprise, because of many reasons, selecting a commodity hardware is not recommended, even though it should work just fine.
- Helps decouple the data pipeline bringing a level of indirection.
- Helps handle real-time data pipeline. This is one of the core reasons for our choice, as we need to find a technology piece to handle real-time messages from applications.
- Apache Kafka is open source and has a huge fan following community. Also, there are many companies that are ready to provide commercial support, which can be an important aspect for big enterprises because of their criticality.

- Kafka works well with Apache Spark. For us, Spark is in our technology list and that also makes Kafka a good choice.
- For streaming messages to consumers, it uses system capabilities and because of this, it can perform quite well. It also uses many operation system features for doing many things efficiently, and that is definitely a plus point.

Disadvantages of Kafka

Although Kafka's advantages overshadows its disadvantages, it's good to know it's limitations and consider it only when advantages are too compelling to omit. The following are the disadvantages mostly associated with Kafka and some might be more relevant for a particular use case but not really linked with ours.

- Doesn't possess a full set of management and monitoring tools. This makes enterprise support staff a bit apprehensive about choosing Kafka and supporting it in the long run.
- The broker uses certain system calls to deliver messages to the consumer, but if the message needs some tweaking, doing so reduces Kafka's performance significantly. If the message is unchanged, it can perform quite well, as it uses the capabilities of the system.
- Kafka only matches the exact topic name and does not support wildcard topic selection, making it incapable of addressing certain use cases.
- API's which are needed by other languages are maintained by different individuals and corporates, so these can be a problem because of the lack of pace by which these vendors update the connectors.
- Kafka broker and its approach are often attributed to be really simple and uncomplicated in nature. Because of this, other components are used to cater to certain requirements like **Zookeeper** (state coordination), and MirrorMaker (inter-cluster communication) which makes the deployment and support of the overall architecture a nightmare, especially for support staff.
- Inherently, Kafka doesn't have any problems with the individual message size. But, as the size increases, the brokers and consumers start compressing these messages and because of this, the node memory gets slowly used when decompress and compress happens when the data flows in the pipeline. This could impact throughput and also performance.

- It's often criticized that, as the number for queues in a Kafka cluster increases, it starts behaving a bit clumsy and and slowly. Kafka will say this is as it is by design (as Microsoft will always categorize certain bugs in their software as this is by design).
- Kafka lacks other messaging paradigms like request/reply, point-to-point queues and so on, making it problematic for certain use cases.

Kafka architecture

This section aims to explain ins and outs of Apache Kafka. We will try to dive deep into its architecture and then, later on try expanding each part of it's architecture's components in a bit more detail.

So, let's stream forward.

Core architecture principles of Kafka

The main motivation behind Kafka when developed by LinkedIn's engineering team was

> *To create a unified messaging platform to cater to real-time data from various applications in a big organization.*

- LinkedIn

There are core architecture principles based on which Kafka was conceived and designed. The bulleted points sum up these principles:

- Maximize performance (compression and B-tree usage is an example)
- Wherever possible, core kernel capabilities to offload work to drive optimization and performance (zero-copy and direct use of Linux filesystem cache is an example)
- Distributed architecture
- Fault tolerance
- Durability of messages
- Wherever possible, eliminate redundant work
- Offload responsibility of tasks to consuming application, as the case may be (consumers manage the message state and work on a No ACK approach).

- **Extensibility**: provide as many ways by which applications can plug in and make use of Kafka. Also, provide ways by which to write new connectors as needed.
- High throughput (capable of handling high-volume messages)
- Real-time processing of these messages to derive processed messages in real-time
- Low latency delivery

Data stream life cycle

Apache Kafka is a piece of technology that enables us to handle data streams. Before getting into the working of Kafka, let's see what life cycle events that are when a data stream flow takes place. *Rassul Fazelat,* in one of his LinkedIn blogs, has explained this in detail as shown pictorially in the following figure.

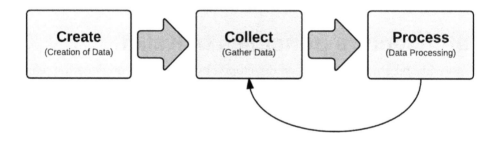

Figure 04: Life cycle of Data Stream

As shown in the preceding figure, the life cycle events of a data stream have three components, each having a definite job to do:

- **Create**: The most important component. It produces the data streams from a variety of internal business applications and external partners as well as other applications. For example, server logs from servers where business applications are hosted, behavioural data collected from various business applications in the form of click stream, page views, social data coming from various social sites, various sensors (IoT) emitting different parameters, and so on.
- **Collect**: This is one of the components that helps in collecting this data and making it available for processing. This capability is achieved by the technology we are diving deep into this chapter, Apache Kafka. Other options that give you this capability do exist, such as **ActiveMQ**, **HornetQ** and so on.

- **Process**: Component which processes the data stream and derives meaningful data stream for various analyses. In our Data Lake architecture, we have this capability requirement and we also have a technology in mind, which will be delved deep into the following chapters. Some of the example technologies in this space are Apache Spark, Apache Flink, and so on.

Working of Kafka

Kafka's architecture in whole is quite simplistic in nature and has some very important components, which are the crux of the whole workings of it.

The following figure shows the workings of Kafka with all components labelled. The main components which constitute Kafka architecture are as follows:

- **Message**: Flows from producer all the way to consumer through topics existing in a broker.
- **Producer**: Producer, as the name suggests produces these stream messages and pumps into the topic.
- **Topic**: The category into which the producer pumps the message. The producer produces messages of a particular category which fall into this topic. Ideally, for each category of messages a new topic is created in Kafka.
- **Broker**: Kafka cluster comprising of multiple servers/nodes. Each node is a Kafka broker and contains multiple partitions holding multiple topics.
- **Partition**: Each of the Kafka topic, is partitioned and each partition contains ordered messages from the producer. Writes to each partition are sequential in nature and this aspect is one of the main reasons for Kafka's high performance. When writing onto the topic partition, each message is given a sequence number referred to as offset and this uniquely identifies a message in a partition. Kafka, being distributed in nature, distributes these topic partitions across multiple brokers for fault tolerance and durability of messages.
- **Consumer**: Again as the name suggests, subscribes to a particular message category (a topic) and consumes messages in that topic. This consumer reads messages from the topic and is entrusted with maintaining the audit of which message has been read and actioned. Kafka does not remove these messages nor take an audit of messages read by various consumers connecting to the topic and reading messages.
- **Consumer Group**: A group of consumers logically grouped in Kafka is known as the consumer group.

So, the producers produce messages and dumps into various categorized topics, from there consumers subscribed to these topic reads the messages and do the necessary. The communication of various components is over the efficient and reliable TCP protocol. This is the overall architecture of Kafka.

We have dedicated the sections here to detailing each of these components:

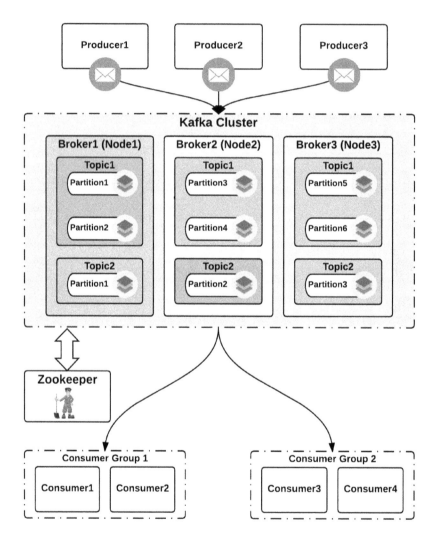

Figure 05: Kafka architecture

Detailed Kafka documentation can be found on Kafka's official site, available at `https://ka fka.apache.org/documentation/`.

Kafka message

As said in Apache Kafka documentation, the message contains a fixed header and an array of variable length key and variable length value. The header contains the following fields:

- CRC32 checksum to detect any corruption (4 bytes)
- A so-called magic identifier, having a value of either 0 or 1 (1 byte)
- Attributes identifier (1 byte):
  - **Bit 0-2**: Compression codec: contains the following values
    - 0: No compression
    - 1: GZIP gives a high compression ratio but low performance on compression and decompression with higher load on the CPU
    - 2: Snappy gives lower compression ratio with high performance in decompression and less burden on the CPU
    - 3: lz4 is a lossless compression algorithm (`http://lz 4.github.io/lz4/`)
  - **Bit 3**: Timestamp type
    - 0: Create time
    - 1: Log append time
  - **Bit 4-7**: Reserved
- Optional timestamp only if magic identifier is greater than 0 (8 bytes)

The body part of the message contains the following fields:

- Key length (4 bytes), say a length of K
- Actual key value (K bytes)
- Payload length (4 bytes), say a length of V
- Actual payload value (V bytes)

It's been documented that the key and value length is kept open as there are a lot of optimizations being done in regards to message format and this design makes Kafka quite easily adaptable.

The following figure shows the message format in Kafka in a pictorial format covering all the aspects we just covered:

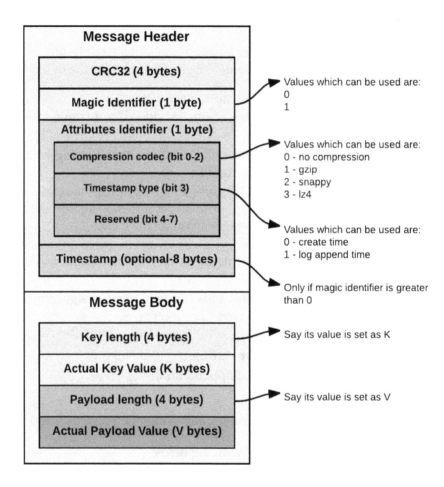

Figure 06: Kafka message format (courtesy: Kafka Apache documentation)

Kafka producer

As the name suggests, this is the client which produces message (stream data) to the Kafka cluster into the designated Kafka topics. There are different types of producers that exist and each have different ways by how they pump these messages. Some produce at a high-velocity with low volume (a message with less payload and high throughput). Some produce low velocity data at a very high-volume (low throughput with the message size being high).

The producer has a choice of sending messages in a synchronous or asynchronous manner. Asynchronous support in Kafka allows producers to send micro-batch messages and can reduce the chattiness between the producer and the cluster. In certain situations, this is quite useful and it is always dependent on the use case being developed. If real-time message processing is required, this micro-catching will be the best choice, as it incurs a lag between message production and actual processing/analysis.

Persistence of data in Kafka using topics

High-level abstraction provided by Kafka where the data pushed by producers is persisted, having a defined name. To cater to replication and fault tolerance each topic is divided into multiple partitions and each partition is distributed in different brokers inside the Kafka cluster.

The topic doesn't keep a note of consumers who have consumed the messages inside the topic, rather the full control of monitoring is offloaded to the consumer and it's their responsibility to keep the track of messages consumed. The consumer comes to a topic and collects a message beginning from a particular message ID and this has to be managed by the consumer.

The following figure shows the inner structure of a topic, how the partitions are created, and how messages get into each message:

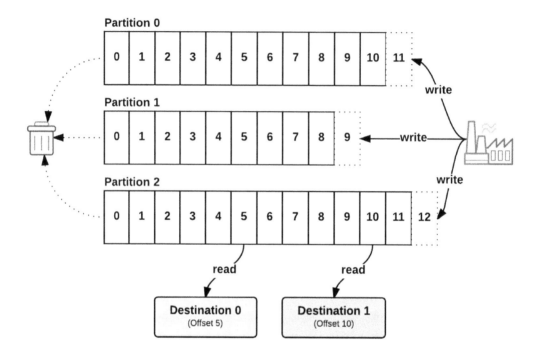

Figure 07: Inner structure of a Kafka topic

Messages pumped to the topic get appended to the partition towards the end, as shown in the preceding figure. Each partition in a topic is logically a log file.

Kafka does keep the messages in the partitions, even though all consumers have consumed them, and follows a different approach of removing these from the partition. Kafka gives the user ways by which these messages should be removed from partitions using well defined properties. The following are the configurations based on which messages are removed:

Description	Configuration property
Number of messages in the partition	`log.flush.interval.messages`
Timestamp	`log.default.flush.interval.ms,` `log.flush.interval.ms`
Size of the all messages in the partition	`log.retention.size`

Table 01: Kafka message removal configurations

Partitions - Kafka topic division

To achieve fault tolerance and replication, Kafka's topic is divided into partitions and also distributed over multiple brokers. Each partition elects one server (broker or node) as the leader (known as leader) and zero or more servers follows the leader (known as followers).

The leader takes care of the read and write activities. The followers keep replicating the leader and always sync with it. As with any distributed system, if the leader fails due to any reason, one of the followers takes charge of the situation automatically and becomes the leader. This allows seamless fault tolerance and message durability in Kafka.

To divide the leader and followers throughout the Kafka cluster, Kafka makes optimal partitions in a server as leader and others as followers. Again, these are seamless to the user and handled internally by Kafka's architecture.

Kafka message broker

One of the important component, which brings the decoupling behaviour of Kafka in action is the all important message broker. The messages produced by the producer is pumped to the topic residing in the broker and the consumer consumes the messages from the topic (the consumer subscribes to topics in the broker and the broker publishes the messages to it). The messages are published to this broker and there could be more than one broker (node) which forms the Kafka cluster. The storage responsibility in Kafka is taken care of by the broker. Finding the message from within the partition and within a broker is the responsibility of the broker. This is required when the consumer requests a message from within a subscribe topic.

The messages are stored in the topic consisting of multiple partitions and these partitions get replicated in multiple brokers with the same cluster. The following figure shows an example replication which a Kafka cluster having 4 brokers could employ (this is just a pictorial representation; internals are completely handled by Kafka).

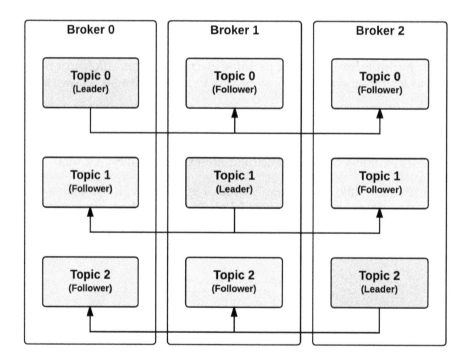

Figure 08: Message replication in topic across broker in Kafka cluster

In the figure, the red block is the leader and the green blocks are the followers. Each topic partition is also replicated into multiple nodes with the cluster. For clarity the partitions within a topic are not shown.

One of the brokers in the Kafka cluster takes the role of controller and manages these partition leaders and the state of these partitions. In addition, it is given the responsibility to do partition reassignment, as the case may be and to deal with replicas as configured.

Kafka consumer

Consumers consume messages from the topic from within the Kafka cluster. It consumes messages in a sequential manner from within a partition of a topic. The consumer is required to make sure that it tracks the messages being taken/read from the topic and when asked for a message it is required to supply a sequential ID and the messages from that ID onwards are read in a sequential manner thereafter. Kafka uses a pull approach from the consumer to consume a message and this is one of the main reason for the high throughput of message consumption in Kafka. Also, the throughput of message consumption is left to individual consumers, and because of this Kafka is ready to integrate with a variety of consumers having different capabilities.

If needed, consumer can always come back and consume old messages if needed (replay) because the messages are kept in the memory of Kafka according to defined configuration properties.

Within a consumer group, it is guaranteed that a message will be consumed at least once.

Consumer groups

Consumer groups allow multiple hosts to form a group (using the same group) to access a particular topic. Consumer groups guarantee that a message is only read by one consumer in the group. As shown in the following figure, partitions are assigned to each consumer in a group and these are entrusted to read the messages in a topic. A consumer may get one or more partitions from which to read the messages, but it's care is taken that one partition is only assigned to a single consumer in a group.

This figure shows the working of a consumer group in action in a Kafka deployment.

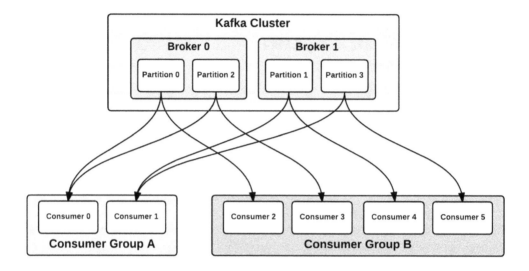

Figure 09: Multiple consumers logically grouped in a consumer group

As shown in the figure, for easy understanding of a consumer group we have just taken two brokers with one topic replicated with the two brokers, and in each broker the topic has two partitions. We have two consumer groups, group A having two consumers and group B having 4 consumers. Group A consumers read messages from two partitions of a topic from broker 0 and two partitions of the same topic from broker 1. Group B consumers read messages from two partitions of a topic from broker 0 and other consumers reads the messages from two partitions of a topic from broker 1.

Other Kafka components

In addition to these components, there are some important components in a Kafka deployment without which the Kafka won't work as intended. These are a couple of the important components that could be used:

- Zookeeper
- MirrorMaker

Zookeeper

Zookeeper is one of the very important hidden component, needed (mandatory) for Kafka to function properly. It is entrusted to do the following jobs:

- Taking care of bringing each broker into the cluster membership.
- Electing the Kafka controller which does some very important functions within the cluster such as managing the state of partitions and their replicas.
- Complete topic configurations like number of partitions, leader partitions election, partition replication location and so on.
- Access control list maintenance and various quotas within each broker.

MirrorMaker

As the name suggests, it helps mirror data cross Kafka clusters. This component can be used to mirror an entire cluster from one data center to another, as shown in the next figure.

Inherently, this component uses both consumer and producer APIs to mirror the cluster. It reads messages from one or more source cluster and then writes to the target cluster.

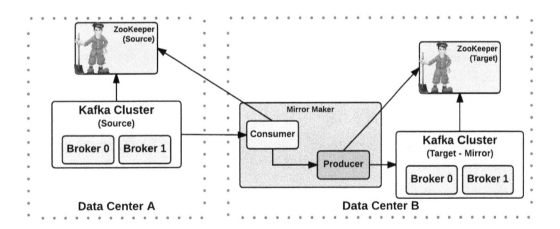

Figure 10: MirrorMaker working in mirroring Kafka cluster from one data center to another

Kafka programming interface

Kafka contains two programming interface mechanisms:

- Low level core API's
- REST API's: REST interface wrapping the core API's for easy access

Kafka core API's

These are the core API's in Apache Kafka, as documented in the Apache Kafka documentation:

- **Producer API**: Contains a set of API's which allows us to publish a stream of data to one or more of the named/categorized Kafka topics in the cluster.
- **Streams API**: Contains relevant API's which acts on the stream of data. They can process this stream data and can transform it from existing form to a designated form according to your use case demands. These are relatively new API's as against existing producer and consumer API's.
- **Connect API**: API's which allows Kafka to be extensible. It contains methods which can be used to build Kafka connectors for the inputting and outputting of data into Kafka.
- **Consumer API**: Contains relevant API's to subscribe to one or more topics in the broker. Since consumer takes care of a message and it's consumption, there are API's using which a message can be consumed precisely from a partition.

Kafka REST interface

The REST interface wrapping the core API's created and maintained by Confluent (company created by ex-LinkedIn engineering team who created Kafka). Using these API's does have performance overhead, as it needs two hops to do a piece of work. It also requires an additional server for hosting these REST API's. In addition, for every call to these API's, additional time is lost in parsing the JSON request and also for creating the JSON response.

Producer and consumer reliability

In distributed systems, components fail. Its a common practice to design your code to take care of these failures in a seamless fashion (fault-tolerant).

One of the ways by which Kafka tolerates failure is by maintaining the replication of messages. Messages are replicated in so called partitions and Kafka automatically elects one partition as leader and other follower partitions just replicate the leader. The leader also maintains a list of replicas which are in sync so as to make sure that ideal replication is maintained to handle failures.

The producer sends message to the topic (Kafka broker in Kafka cluster) and durability can be configured using the producer configuration, `request.required.acks`, which has the following values:

- 0: message written to network/buffer
- 1: message written directly to partition leader
- all: producer gets an acknowledgement when all in-sync replicas (ISR's) get the message

Consumer reads data from topics and in Kafka the state of the message read from topic by a consumer is kept with the consumer itself rather than Kafka. This allows Kafka to take away management of message consumption by each of the consumers. It's the responsibility of each consumer to manage this and they do this using what is called consumer offset (the sequence message ID from where the consumer last read the message). The messages in topic are kept as is and are not deleted soon after consumers have subscribed to a topic read. The messages are deleted from the topic, according to set broker/topic configuration. So, even though the consumer is dead or is not in a position to consume messages, it's still kept in the topic and if the retention period is kept at a reasonable level, when the consumer comes online, using it's offset, it can read all the messages from that offset value, without much of a problem. This is how consumer reliability is achieved in Kafka.

This figure shows the various positions that a consumer uses while traversing a topic partition in a broker.

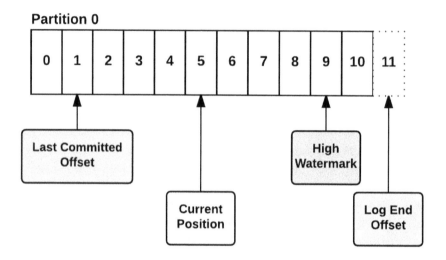

Figure 11: Offsets which consumer uses to track message consumption

This figure shows some of the important positions maintained by a consumer in a log partition as summarized here:

- **Last committed offset**: Offset of the last message written to the log. If a partition fails and the consumer is hooked to a new partition, this offset is used as the starting point.
- **Current position**: offset which is read by the consumer
- **High watermark**: Offset that holds the message which has been successfully copied to all replicas within the cluster. This is a message till a consumer can ideally read other messages after that won't be exposed for consumption till all replicas get the message and then the watermark offset moves forward.
- **Log end offset**: Message which is last written by the producer to a log.

Kafka security

When designed and developed at LinkedIn, security was kept out to a large extent. Security for Kafka was an afterthought after it became a main project at Apache. Later on in the year 2014, various security discussions were considered for Kafka, especially data at rest security and transport layer security.

Kafka broker allows clients to connect to multiple ports and each port supports a different security mechanism, as detailed here:

- No wire encryption and authentication
- **SSL**: wire encryption and authentication
- **SASL**: Kerberos authentication
- SSL + SASL: SSL is for wire encryption and SASL for authentication
- Authorization similar to Unix permissions for read/write by a client

These security features are led by Confluent and more details can be found at `http://docs.confluent.io/2.0.0/kafka/security.html`.

Kafka as message-oriented middleware

Message-oriented middleware (MOM) is software or hardware infrastructure supporting sending and receiving messages between distributed systems. MOM allows application modules to be distributed over heterogeneous platforms and reduces the complexity of developing applications that span multiple operating systems and network protocols. The middleware creates a distributed communications layer that insulates the application developer from the details of the various operating systems and network interfaces.

- Wikipedia

Looking at the definition for MOM above, Kafka fits in the category of an MOM and does cater to all the capabilities needed by it. But, Kafka is not just a simple queue/message management solution and has certain core capabilities making it more marketable than traditional MOM. Some of it's inherent capabilities that are advantages are:

- Approach used is log (distributed commit log) based with zero-copy and messages are always appended
- Uses partitions heavily to distribute messages within a topic in multiple partitions across brokers in a cluster
- Distribution built-in and this helps fault-tolerance and message durability
- Replication built-in
- Scalability built-in. One consumer per partition allocated and for scaling keeps adding partitions.
- It's a queuing mechanism which will work just fine if the subscribed consumer is not available or offline as the message state is managed by the consumer as against the broker/topic.
- **Durable messaging**: since Kafka persists the data on the disk without performance issues, the message durability is guaranteed and this is one of the aspects not seen in traditional messaging systems. This also allows the consumer to consume these messages at their pace rather than according to the producer rate.

As it stands today, Kafka does the job of a MOM plus some more additional core features required for big data platform and for modern messaging requirements as against traditional ones.

With more and more data generated through various social websites and with evolution of IoT, more and more data streams will come into the existence. Kafka with it's inherent capabilities, will be able to take care of these streams of data to do meaningful derivations to solve many business problems for an enterprise.

 Zero-copy describes computer operations in which the CPU does not perform the task of copying data from one memory area to another. This is frequently used to save CPU cycles and memory bandwidth when transmitting a file over a network.

- Wikipedia

Scale-out architecture with Kafka

Main principles on which Kafka works have been covered in this chapter earlier. We won't cover those again here; however below are the main reasons for scale-out architecture in Kafka:

- **Partition**: Splits a topic into multiple partitions and increasing partitions is a mechanism of scaling.
- **Distribution**: Cluster can have one or more brokers and these brokers can be increased to achieve scaling.
- **Replication**: Similar to partitions, multiple replication of a message is there for fault-tolerance and this aspect also brings in scalability in Kafka.
- **Scaling**: Each consumer reads a message from a single partition (of a topic) and to scale out we add more consumers and the newly added consumers read the message from new partition (one consumer cannot read from the same partition; this is a rule) as shown in this figure.

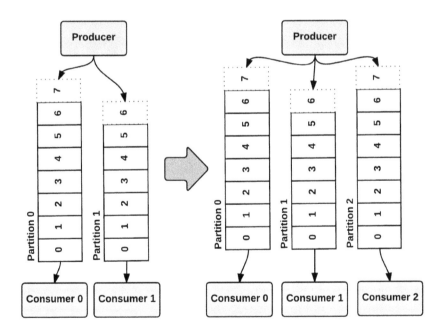

Figure 12: Scale out by adding more consumers

Kafka connect

Extensibility is one of the important design principle followed rigorously by Kafka. The Kafka Connect tool makes Kafka extensible. The tool enables Kafka to connect with external systems and helps bring data into it, and also out from it to other systems. It has a common framework, using which custom connectors can be written. More details on Kafka connect can be found in Kafka documentation in `https://kafka.apache.org/documentation.htm l#connect`.

The following figure shows how Kafka Connect works.

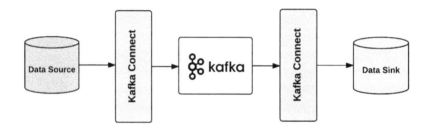

Figure 13: Kafka connect working

The Kafka connectors are categorized into two:

- **Source Connectors**: Connectors which bring data into Kafka topics.
- **Sink Connectors**: Connectors which take data away from topics into other external systems

There are a huge list of connectors available, catering to various external systems, using which Kafka can hook onto them. These existing connectors are again categorized broadly into two:

- **Certified connectors**: Connectors which are written using the Kafka Connect framework and have already passed the best coding practice. They are usually created and managed by vendors. These vendors write these connectors to enable Kafka to connect and integrate into their tool.
- **Other connectors** (non-certified): These are connectors which are not yet certified and are maintained and managed by the community.

A full list of certified and non-certified connectors can be found at the link `https://www.co nfluent.io/product/connectors/`.

Kafka working example

We have briefly discussed a basic setup of Kafka as part of Flume examples. The basic setup of Kafka as listed there remains the same, hence the installation steps will remain the same, however we will also look additionally at usage examples of Kafka as a message broker.

The most natural programming language for Kafka is currently Scala or Java. Hence, to keep things simple, we will be using Java as our choice of language for examples.

Installation

1. Download the Kafka binaries from the following link, using the command:

   ```
   wget http://redrockdigimark.com/apachemirror/kafka/0.10.1.1/kafka_2
   .11-0.10.1.1.tgz
   ```

2. Change the directory to a user directory, where we will want to extract the contents of the Kafka tarball using the following command. Let us refer the extracted KAFKA directory as ${KAFKA_HOME}:

   ```
   tar -xzvf ${DOWNLOAD_DIRECTORY}/kafka_2.11-0.10.1.1.tgz
   ```

3. Set KAFKA_HOME as environment variable using the following commands and add the same into ~/.bashrc:

   ```
   export KAFKA_HOME=<PATH to KAFKA Directory>
   export PATH=$PATH:$KAFKA_HOME/bin
   ```

4. Change the directory into the extracted Kafka folder, that is, ${KAFKA_HOME}, and run the following command to start the Kafka server:

   ```
   ${KAFKA_HOME}/bin/kafka-server-start.sh
   ${KAFKA_HOME}/config/server.properties
   ```

5. This Kafka instance is started based on the default server.properties file, which is bundled within the Kafka binary.

The Kafka installation comes bundled with default configurations for producer, broker (server), as well as consumer. We will have a deeper look at each one of these with working examples.

Producer - putting messages into Kafka

The default producer configuration that comes bundled with Kafka is as given below, located at ${KAFKA_HOME}/config/producer.properties:

```
############################## Producer Basics ##############################

# list of brokers used for bootstrapping knowledge about the rest of the
cluster
# format: host1:port1,host2:port2 ...
bootstrap.servers=localhost:9092

# specify the compression codec for all data generated: none, gzip, snappy,
lz4
compression.type=none

# name of the partitioner class for partitioning events; default partition
spreads data randomly
#partitioner.class=

# the maximum amount of time the client will wait for the response of a
request
#request.timeout.ms=

# how long `KafkaProducer.send` and `KafkaProducer.partitionsFor` will
block for
#max.block.ms=

# the producer will wait for up to the given delay to allow other records
to be sent so that the sends can be batched together
#linger.ms=

# the maximum size of a request in bytes
#max.request.size=

# the default batch size in bytes when batching multiple records sent to a
partition
#batch.size=

# the total bytes of memory the producer can use to buffer records waiting
to be sent to the server
```

Code 01: Console Producer Configuration

This is the basic configuration required for Kafka producer, wherein, the most important and the only required configuration parameters are:

1. `bootstrap.servers`: Refers to the Kafka broker listening ports, which will be comma-separated to specify a cluster of brokers in a multi-broker Kafka cluster.

2. `key.serializer`: Specifies the serializer for serializing the key of the message (value). The value of which is a fully qualified class name of the desired serializer. The default for the console producer is `org.apache.kafka.common.serialization.StringSerializer`.

3. `value.serializer`: A property that specifies the serializer for serializing the message (value). The value of which is a fully qualified class name of the desired serializer. The default for console producer is: `org.apache.kafka.common.serialization.StringSerializer`.

 Serialization is the process of converting an object into a stream of bytes in order to store the object or transmit it to memory, a database, or a file. `htt ps://goo.gl/eDQE5A`(`https://docs.microsoft.com`)

A simple producer can be built easily by using Kafka libraries as follows:

1. Checkout the latest code from the source repository using the following command:

```
git clone
https://github.com/PacktPublishing/Data-Lakes-for-Enterprises
```

If the repository is already cloned, ensure to check out the latest source code with the following command:

```
git pull
```

2. Within the repository, the source code of this chapter is under the folder named, `chapter07`.

3. The following is the maven dependency for a simple producer, declared in `chapter07/pom.xml`.

```
<dependencies>
    <!-- https://mvnrepository.com/artifact/org.apache.kafka
    /kafka-clients -->
    <dependency>
```

```
                <groupId>org.apache.kafka</groupId>
                <artifactId>kafka-clients</artifactId>
                <version>0.10.1.1</version>
        </dependency>
    </dependencies>
```

Code 02: Maven Dependencies for Simple Producer

4. A simple producer Java implementation is as shown in the following code snippet:

```
public class SimpleProducer {

    public static void main(String[] args) throws
    ExecutionException, InterruptedException {
        Properties props = new Properties();

        /*
        Set the list of broker addresses separated by commas.
        This needs to be updated with IP of your VM running Kafka
        broker
        */
        props.setProperty("bootstrap.servers",
        "192.168.0.117:9092");

        //Set the serializer for key of the message(value)
        props.put("key.serializer",

"org.apache.kafka.common.serialization.StringSerializer");

        //Set the serializer for the message (value)
        props.put("value.serializer",

"org.apache.kafka.common.serialization.StringSerializer");

        //Create a producer
        Producer<String, String> producer = new
KafkaProducer<String, String>(props);

        //Create a message to be sent to a topic
        ProducerRecord message = new
        ProducerRecord("customer", "001", "A Sample Message...");

        //send the message
        producer.send(message);

        System.out.println("Message Published");
```

```
        //close the producer connection
        producer.close();
    }
}
```

Code 03: A Simple Producer

Few observations in the preceding examples are:

- The minimum required configuration for a Kafka producer has been put in as a properties object. This could have been provided as a map as well.
- We are using the default serializers for message key and it's value.
- While publishing the message we are also specifying the topic as well as key of the message.
- The topic specified while sending the message will get created if it does not exist already.

5. For the simple producer to publish messages to a remote broker process, it is important to change the following setting in the server.properties, that is, `${KAFKA_HOME}/config/server.properties`, of Kafka server such that the Kafka server binds to the correct external IP, rather than binding to the localhost.

```
######################### Socket Server Settings #########################

# java.net.InetAddress.getCanonicalHostName() if not configured.
#    FORMAT:
#      listeners = security_protocol://host_name:port
#    EXAMPLE:
#      listeners = PLAINTEXT://your.host.name:9092
listeners=PLAINTEXT://192.168.0.165:9092
```

Figure 14: Binding Host (external IP) configuration of Kafka Server

6. The preceding source code can be run by simply executing the main program in an IDE of your choice. The only precondition is that the Kafka must be running. Make sure that the broker IP in the `SimpleProducer` class (line 18) is changed before running the class. The console output will show a message stating `Message Published` once the message is published to the topic.

7. The message published can be verified from the Kafka console by running the following command:

```
${KAFKA_HOME}/bin/kafka-console-consumer.sh --topic customer --bootstrap-server <broker-ip>:9092 --from-beginning
```

```
[centos@localhost kafka_2.11-0.10.1.1]$ bin/kafka-console-consumer.sh --topic
customer --bootstrap-server 192.168.0.117:9092 --from-beginning
A Sample Message...
```

Figure 15: Output of console consumer for Messages published by Simple Producer

Kafka Connect

As discussed earlier, Kafka Connect can be used to copy streaming messages from or to Kafka and is very similar to Flume. However, in order to use Kafka connect there is a dependency to have confluent setup. Provided here are the steps to install Confluent:

1. Download the latest Confluent package from the following link, using the command given below. It's a big download so it may take some time to complete:

```
wget http://packages.confluent.io/archive/3.2/confluent-oss-3.2.0-2
.11.tar.gz
```

2. Change directory to a user directory and extract the contents of the preceding tarball using the following command. We will refer the extracted confluent folder as ${CONFLUENT_HOME}:

```
tar zxvf ${DOWNLOAD_DIRECTORY}/confluent-oss-3.2.0-2.11.tar.gz
```

3. Set CONFLUENT_HOME as an environment variable using the following command and add the same to ~/.bashrc file:

```
export CONFLUENT_HOME=<PATH to CONFLUENT Directory>
```

4. Start the Zookeeper and Kafka server with the following commands if it is not already started:

```
${KAFKA_HOME}/bin/zookeeper-server-start.sh
${KAFKA_HOME}/config/zookeeper.properties ${KAFKA_HOME}/bin/kafka-
server-start.sh -daemon ${KAFKA_HOME}/config/server.properties
```

5. Start the schema registry with the following command:

```
${CONFLUENT_HOME}/bin/schema-registry-start
${CONFLUENT_HOME}./etc/schema-registry/schema-registry.properties
```

Once the schema registry is successfully started, it will display a log message as shown:

```
[2017-05-09 22:10:10,088] INFO Server started, listening for
requests...
(io.confluent.kafka.schemaregistry.rest.SchemaRegistryMain:45)
```

6. Follow the **Quickstart** instructions for the Avro schema example as provided at the following URL (from *Step 5* onwards in the Quickstart guide). All the instructions specified in the Quickstart guide are required to be run from `${CONFLUENT_HOME}` and wherever, localhost is mentioned, it needs to be replaced with the IP to which Kafka is binding to.(`http://docs.confluent.io /2.0.0/quickstart.html#quickstart`).

7. This is a good Quickstart article to make us understand the purpose of Kafka Connect.

8. Once you have run the Avro example, switch back to `${KAFKA_HOME}` and see the results from the test topic by running the following command:

```
${KAFKA_HOME}/bin/kafka-console-consumer.sh --topic test --
bootstrap-server <broker-ip>:9092 --from-beginning
```

9. Here, we ran Zookeeper and Kafka from our existing Kafka install. We also ran schema registry from the confluent platform and were able to push messages in the Avro format and in a parallel fashion consume them with Avro validations.

Consumer - getting messages from Kafka

The default consumer configuration (`$KAFKA_HOME/config/consumer.properties`) that comes bundled with Kafka is as shown:

```
# Zookeeper connection string
# comma separated host:port pairs, each corresponding to a zk
# server. e.g. "127.0.0.1:3000,127.0.0.1:3001,127.0.0.1:3002"
zookeeper.connect=127.0.0.1:2181

# timeout in ms for connecting to zookeeper
zookeeper.connection.timeout.ms=6000
```

```
#consumer group id
group.id=test-consumer-group

#consumer timeout
#consumer.timeout.ms=5000
```

Code 04: Console Consumer Configuration

As seen here, the only configuration required by the console consumer (the consumer that comes by default with Kafka for terminal/ssh based consumption) is the Zookeeper connection (this is an old property but kept for backward compatibility), or bootstrap servers (this is the new property), details and group ID. Other settings are around timeouts and group ID which are optional. The group ID indicates the consumers belonging to a group, such that the group always processes every message only once. The key and value deserializers default to a string deserializer, as explained in the producer section before.

Hence the mandatory settings for a consumer are:

1. `bootstrap.servers`: Refers to the Kafka broker listening addresses (comma separated `ip:port`), which specifies a cluster of brokers in a multi-broker Kafka cluster.
2. `key.deserializer`: Specifies the serializer for serializing the key of the message (value). The value of which is a fully qualified class name of the desired serializer. The default for console producer is `org.apache.kafka.common.serialization.StringSerializer`.
3. `value.deserializer`: Specifies the serializer for serializing the message (value). The value of which is a fully qualified class name of the desired serializer. The default for console producer is `org.apache.kafka.common.serialization.StringSerializer`.
4. `group.id`: defines a group for the consumers.

Now, let us look at how a simple consumer can be built by using Consumer API.

1. The maven dependencies for a simple consumer are the same as for a simple producer and are as follows for reference:

```
<dependencies>
    <!-- https://mvnrepository.com/artifact/org.apache.kafka/
    kafka-clients -->
    <dependency>
        <groupId>org.apache.kafka</groupId>
        <artifactId>kafka-clients</artifactId>
        <version>0.10.1.1</version>
```

```
        </dependency>
    </dependencies>
```

Code 05: Maven Dependencies for Simple Consumer

2. A simple consumer Java implementation is as shown here:

```
public class SimpleConsumer {
    public static void main(String[] args) {
        Properties props = new Properties();

        /*
        Set the list of broker addresses separated by commas.
        This needs to be updated with IP of your VM running
        Kafka broker
        */
        props.setProperty("bootstrap.servers",
        "192.168.0.117:9092");

        //Set the deserializer for the key of the message
        props.put("key.deserializer",

"org.apache.kafka.common.serialization.StringDeserializer");

        //Set the deserializer for the message (value)
        props.put("value.deserializer",

"org.apache.kafka.common.serialization.StringDeserializer");

        //Set the groupId
        props.put("group.id", "1234");

        //Create a consumer from Kafka Consumer
        Consumer<String, String> consumer = new
        KafkaConsumer<String, String>(props);

        //Subscribe the consumer to the topic
        consumer.subscribe(Arrays.asList("customer"));

        try {
            while (true) {
                //Get All records from latest offset
                ConsumerRecords<String, String> records =
                consumer.poll(100);

                //Display all records
```

```
              for (ConsumerRecord<String, String> record :
                records) {
                    System.out.println("key:" + record.key() +
                    "\nvalue:" + record.value());
                }
            }
        } finally {
            consumer.close();
        }

    }
}
```

Code 06: A Simple Consumer

Looking at the code, we can observe and verify the following:

- The minimum required configuration for a Kafka consumer has been put in as a properties object. This could have been provided as a map as well
- The consumer is continuously watching the topic for new messages
- The polling interval is defined as 100 ms for consuming new messages and is a configurable value, as evident from the previous code

3. The preceding source code can be run by simply executing the main program in IDE of your choice. The only precondition is that the Kafka must be running and the producer has published some messages into the topic. Make sure that the broker IP in the SimpleConsumer class (line 22) is changed before running the class. The console output will show all the messages consumed from the topic, as shown in this figure.

```
/Library/Java/JavaVirtualMachines/jdk1.8.0_101.jdk/Contents/Home/bin/java ...
SLF4J: Failed to load class "org.slf4j.impl.StaticLoggerBinder".
SLF4J: Defaulting to no-operation (NOP) logger implementation
SLF4J: See http://www.slf4j.org/codes.html#StaticLoggerBinder for further details.
key:001
value:A Sample Message...
```

Figure 16: Output from Simple Consumer

Setting up multi-broker cluster

While we may be setting up the Kafka server on a single node deployment in our example code, we can always have multiple broker deployment for single node level resiliency. In that case, if one broker fails, the other broker is still available to serve the messages.

Setting up multiple brokers on a single node is very straightforward and involves changing the following settings in `${KAFKA_HOME}/config/server.properties`.

Configuration Parameter	Description
`broker.id`	This should always be unique in a Kafka cluster for each of the broker instances
`port`	The port must be different if multiple brokers are to be set up on the same node
`logs.dir`	The log location for each of the brokers must be defined on different paths for single node deployment

A general recommendation is to have 2 different `server.properties` file for each of the broker instances. An example of this file is as shown next (observe the parameters changed). The broker ID is required to be distinct for both the broker configurations. Accordingly the logs directory need to be configured, so that both broker are writing to different log folders.

```
############################# Server Basics #############################

# The id of the broker. This must be set to a unique integer for each
broker.
broker.id=10

# Switch to enable topic deletion or not, default value is false
delete.topic.enable=true

############################# Socket Server Settings
#############################

# java.net.InetAddress.getCanonicalHostName() if not configured.
#    FORMAT:
#       listeners = security_protocol://host_name:port
#    EXAMPLE:
#       listeners = PLAINTEXT://your.host.name:9092
listeners=PLAINTEXT://192.168.0.117:9092

# Hostname and port the broker will advertise to producers and consumers.
If not set,
# it uses the value for "listeners" if configured.  Otherwise, it will use
```

```
the value
# returned from java.net.InetAddress.getCanonicalHostName().
#advertised.listeners=PLAINTEXT://your.host.name:9092

# The number of threads handling network requests
num.network.threads=3

# The number of threads doing disk I/O
num.io.threads=8

# The send buffer (SO_SNDBUF) used by the socket server
socket.send.buffer.bytes=102400

# The receive buffer (SO_RCVBUF) used by the socket server
socket.receive.buffer.bytes=102400

# The maximum size of a request that the socket server will accept
(protection against OOM)
socket.request.max.bytes=104857600


############################# Log Basics #############################

# A comma seperated list of directories under which to store log files
log.dirs=/tmp/kafka-broker10-logs

# The default number of log partitions per topic. More partitions allow
greater
# parallelism for consumption, but this will also result in more files
across
# the brokers.
num.partitions=1

# The number of threads per data directory to be used for log recovery at
startup and flushing at shutdown.
# This value is recommended to be increased for installations with data
dirs located in RAID array.
num.recovery.threads.per.data.dir=1

############################# Log Flush Policy
#############################

# Messages are immediately written to the filesystem but by default we only
fsync() to sync
# the OS cache lazily. The following configurations control the flush of
data to disk.
# There are a few important trade-offs here:
#    1. Durability: Unflushed data may be lost if you are not using
```

replication.
\#   2. Latency: Very large flush intervals may lead to latency spikes when the flush does occur as there will be a lot of data to flush.
\#   3. Throughput: The flush is generally the most expensive operation, and a small flush interval may lead to exceessive seeks.
\# The settings below allow one to configure the flush policy to flush data after a period of time or
\# every N messages (or both). This can be done globally and overridden on a per-topic basis.

\# The number of messages to accept before forcing a flush of data to disk
\#log.flush.interval.messages=10000

\# The maximum amount of time a message can sit in a log before we force a flush
\#log.flush.interval.ms=1000

\############################## Log Retention Policy ##############################

\# The following configurations control the disposal of log segments. The policy can
\# be set to delete segments after a period of time, or after a given size has accumulated.
\# A segment will be deleted whenever *either* of these criteria are met. Deletion always happens
\# from the end of the log.

\# The minimum age of a log file to be eligible for deletion
log.retention.hours=168

\# A size-based retention policy for logs. Segments are pruned from the log as long as the remaining
\# segments don't drop below log.retention.bytes.
\#log.retention.bytes=1073741824

\# The maximum size of a log segment file. When this size is reached a new log segment will be created.
log.segment.bytes=1073741824

\# The interval at which log segments are checked to see if they can be deleted according
\# to the retention policies
log.retention.check.interval.ms=300000

\############################## Zookeeper ##############################

\# Zookeeper connection string (see zookeeper docs for details).

```
# This is a comma separated host:port pairs, each corresponding to a zk
# server. e.g. "127.0.0.1:3000,127.0.0.1:3001,127.0.0.1:3002".
# You can also append an optional chroot string to the urls to specify the
# root directory for all kafka znodes.
zookeeper.connect=localhost:2181

# Timeout in ms for connecting to zookeeper
zookeeper.connection.timeout.ms=6000
```

Code 07: Multi-Broker Setup

Once the preceding changes are done, we can launch the Kafka server in daemon mode using the following commands:

```
${KAFKA_HOME}/bin/kafka-server-start.sh -daemon
${KAFKA_HOME}/config/server-broker10.properties ${KAFKA_HOME}/bin/kafka-
server-start.sh -daemon ${KAFKA_HOME}/config/server-broker20.properties
```

After the Kafka instances are started, observe the creation of logs in the `tmp` folder: (`/tmp/kafka-logs/`) as shown here:

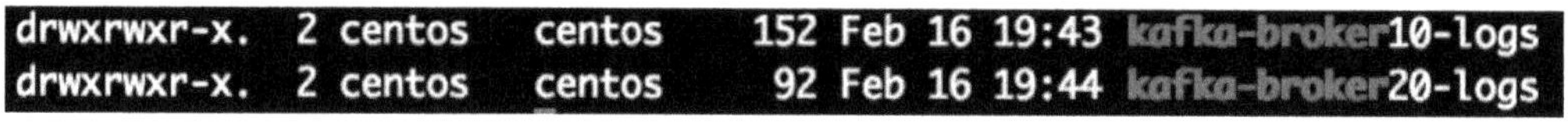

```
drwxrwxr-x. 2 centos   centos   152 Feb 16 19:43 kafka-broker10-logs
drwxrwxr-x. 2 centos   centos    92 Feb 16 19:44 kafka-broker20-logs
```

Figure 17: Multiple Broker Logs

Kafka in the purview of an SCV use case

The usage of this technology (Apache Kafka) in the purview of SCV can be summarized very well by this figure:

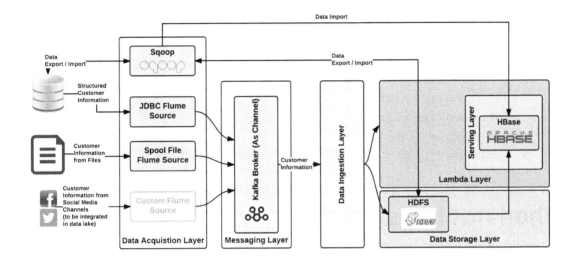

Figure 18: Kafka technology usage in SCV use case

In this chapter, we looked at the publishing, message broker and consuming aspects of information. In the previous chapter, we used Kafka both as a channel as well as a sink. While using Kafka as a channel, it was acting both as a producer as well as a consumer; while using Kafka as a sink it was more of doing a producer function.

What this basically means is that we intend to use Kafka more as a message broker and as a channel so that we can define acquisition and ingestion interfaces around it from a single customer view perspective. This information could be a mix of structured and unstructured information exchanged via messages with standard data formats like XML/JSON. In the previous chapter, we saw how we can acquire both structured as well as unstructured data as a Spool file into Kafka. There could be additional/custom interfaces built with custom serializers/sinks, making Kafka as the central broker of message/events disseminated into target systems via an ingestion layer.

When to use Kafka

Kafka has its core capabilities making it a choice for our use case and these were documented in this chapter when we started of Kafka should be used:

- When you need a highly distributed messaging system
- When you need a messaging system which can scale out exponentially
- When you need high throughput on publishing and subscribing
- When you have varied consumers having varied capabilities by which to subscribe these published messages in the topics
- When you need a fault tolerance operation
- When you need durability in message delivery
- Obviously, all of the preceding without tolerating performance degrade. With all the preceding it should be blazing fast in operation.

When not to use Kafka

For certain scenarios and use cases, you shouldn't use Kafka:

- If you need to have your messages processed in order, you need to have one consumer and one partition. But this is not at all the way Kafka works and we do have multiple consumers and multiple partitions (by design one consumer consumes from one partition) and because of this, it won't serve the use case that we are looking to implement.
- If you need to implement a task queue because of the same reason in the preceding point. It doesn't have all the bells and whistles that you associate with a typical queue service.
- If you need a typical topic capability (first in first out) as the way it functions is quite different.
- If your development and production environment is Windows or Node.js based (subjective point but it's good to know that this aspect is quite true).
- If you need high security with finer controls. The original design of Kafka is not really created with security in mind and this plagues Kafka at times.

Other options

There are sections in this chapter that details advantages of using Kafka. Also in this chapter, there are sections that details disadvantages and when not to use Kafka. That means, Kafka for us is just a choice suited for the topic that we are covering in this book and also for the SCV use case. The main reason for this choice is because of Kafka's clear advantages; especially when dealing with big data and its associated technologies.

There are other options in market which is a full-fledged messaging system (MOM) and possess rich features compared to Kafka. Some of the alternatives that we think you could look into and replace Kafka are briefly summarized in this section. In no way we mean to say that these cannot be used in our use case, just that we thought Kafka is the best fit. If we are to look at other options in place of Kafka these alternatives are our favorites.

All the technology choices have been made after careful technical analysis and with our book we want to give the right steer for you in the right direction.

RabbitMQ

One of the strong alternatives that we see is **RabbitMQ**. It's one of the most powerful and well-known message brokers in the industry. Some of its important features are as follows:

- Written in Erlang programming language
- Very good documentation with lots of resources online
- Developed and maintained by Pivotal
- Open source and commercially supported by many vendors
- Matured
- Rich routing capabilities
- Distributed in nature
- Possess durability and persistence options (optional though)
- Possess order message processing if needed
- Supports clustering if needed
- Licensed under Mozilla Public License

Use/choose RabbitMQ if:

- You need messages to be routed in more complex ways
- Each message needs delivery guarantees
- Don't really care much about ordered message delivery and it is left to the consumer to maintain the order
- Your enterprise demands paid commercial support for production environment
- High-availability requirements in deployment aspect
- You need good routing capabilities
- You are looking to support multiple protocols (AMQP, STOMP, MQTT, and so on.)
- You need better security features
- You need transaction features

The Advanced Message Queuing Protocol (AMQP) is an open standard application layer protocol for message-oriented middleware. The defining features of AMQP are message orientation, queuing, routing (including point-to-point and publish-and-subscribe), reliability and security.

Simple (or Streaming) Text Oriented Message Protocol (STOMP), *formerly known as TTMP, is a simple text-based protocol, designed for working with message-oriented middleware (MOM). It provides an interoperable wire format that allows STOMP clients to talk with any message broker supporting the protocol.*

MQTT (Message Queuing Telemetry Transport) is an ISO standard publish-subscribe-based "lightweight" messaging protocol for use on top of the TCP/IP protocol. It is designed for connections with remote locations where a "small code footprint" is required or the network bandwidth is limited.

- Wikipedia

ZeroMQ

Some of its important features are as follows:

- Lightweight messaging system
- Capable of high throughput with low latency operation
- Capable of handling many messaging scenarios by bringing in various components within ZeroMQ
- Capable of asynchronous programming
- Not very good support for transaction based messaging systems
- Licensed under GPL
- Supports variety/multiple language bindings

Use/choose ZeroMQ if:

- You are looking for the simplest messaging system in regards to implementation
- You are looking for fast message transmission of transient messages
- You need to connect multiple applications using messaging architecture and should have a very low footprint on the nodes
- You need an asynchronous messaging model

Apache ActiveMQ

Some of its important features are as follows:

- Provides different persistence mechanisms
- Horizontally scalable
- Highly flexible in configuration aspect
- Support for a variety of transport protocols
- Many projects internally use Apache ActiveMQ as an enterprise service bus
- Supports many advanced messaging system features
- Easily integrates with many applications, especially Java-based
- Reliable
- Faster
- Supports transaction in messaging system
- Open source with vibrant community
- Has scheduler support

Use/choose ActiveMQ if:

- You are looking for ease by which a product can be configured
- You are looking at messaging system having high performance with no persistence

Summary

The topic covered in this chapter is quite exhaustive. Rest assured that you have covered enough of Apache Kafka to implement a Data Lake.

In this chapter, we started with the relevance of messaging layer in the context of a Data Lake. After that, the chapter deep dived into Kafka and detailed it's architecture and its various components. It then showed you the full working example of Kafka with step-by-step instructions from installation all the way to taking data from a source, to destination using Kafka. Finally, as in other chapters we introduced other choices which can replace Kafka as the technology to achieve the same capability.

After reading this chapter, you should now have a clear idea of the messaging layer and a deep understanding of Apache Kafka and how it works. You should also have a clear idea of how our use case can use this technology and what exactly it accomplishes.

8

Data Processing using Apache Flink

By now, I am sure you have got the approach of each chapter in this part of the book. This chapter follows the same approach. It will introduce the **Data Ingestion Layer** initially and then it will make a technology mapping, in our case, Apache Flink.

Handling both stream and batch data and appropriately processing it is an important feature required for our Data Lake implementation, and Flink is the choice for us. In this chapter, we will give you just enough details that you need to know about Flink to execute the Data Lake use case in hand. Covering Flink in its full aspects is out of the scope of this book and would take a book in itself. We will initially dive into Flink's core strengths and weaknesses, followed by its architecture and important components. We will then delve deep into an actual hand on coding session of Flink and the connection with our SCV use case.

Finally, we will explain some of the alternate technologies that you can think of if Flink is not something you would like to import for your chosen use case in your organization.

Context in a Data Lake - Data Ingestion Layer

In this chapter, we are dealing with a technology that constitutes one of the core layers of Data Lake, namely Data Ingestion Layer. For dealing with processing of data from both streaming and batch data from different applications in an enterprise having the layer is very important.

The technology that we have shortlisted to do this very important job of processing data is Apache Flink. I have to say that this selection was quite difficult as we have another technology in mind, namely Apache Spark, which was really strong in this area and more matured. But we decided to go with Flink in the end considering its pros. However, we have also detailed Spark a bit as opposed to other chapters in which we have just named other options and left it, because of its significance in this space.

This chapter will take you through the Data Ingestion Layer and its working first and then it will dive deep into the technology, Flink.

Data Ingestion Layer

> *Data ingestion is the process of obtaining and importing data for immediate use or storage in a database. To ingest something is to "take something in or absorb something."*

- whatis.com

In Chapter 2, *Comprehensive Concepts of a Data Lake* you will have got a glimpse of the Data Ingestion Layer. This layer's responsibility is to gather both stream and batch data and then apply any processing logic as demanded by your chosen use case. The following figure will refresh your memory and give you a good pictorial view of this layer:

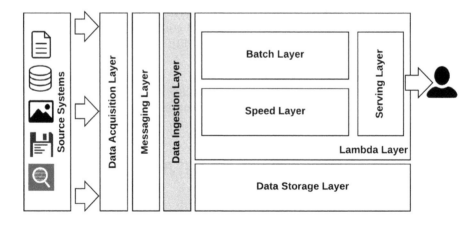

Figure 01: Data Lake - Data Ingestion Layer

In our Data Lake implementation, the Data Ingestion Layer is responsible for consuming the messages from the messaging layer and performing the required transformation for ingesting them into the Lambda Layer (batch and speed layer) such that the transformed output conforms to the expected storage or processing formats. The Data Ingestion Layer must ensure that the rate of message consumption is always better or equal to the message ingestion rates, such that there is no latency to process the messages/events.

Some of the characteristics of Data Ingestion Layer can be summarized as follows:

- Less complex and really fast to cater to data input (in our case, output from the messaging layer)
- Capable of handling different data flows (real-time or batch, continuous or asynchronous)
- Capable of handling various data types (structured, unstructured, and semi-structured)
- Integration with various persistence store mechanisms
- Multiple transport protocol support
- Capable of handling four V's of big data
- Capable of connecting with disparate systems and technologies

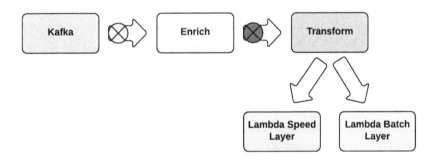

Figure 02: Working of Data Ingestion layer in our Data Lake implementation

As shown in the preceding figure, we will take data from the messaging layer and will enrich and transform it accordingly to pass it to the Lambda Layer (both Speed and Batch Layer).

Data Ingestion Layer - technology mapping

For covering our use case and to build Data Lake we use Apache Flink in this layer as the technology. Other strong technology choices namely Apache Spark will also be explained a bit as we do feel that this is an equally good choice, in this layer. This chapter dives deep into Flink, though.

The following figure brings in the technology aspect to the conceptual architecture that we will be following throughout this book. We will keep explaining each technology and its relevance in the overall architecture before we brings all the technologies together in the final part of this book (*Part 3*):

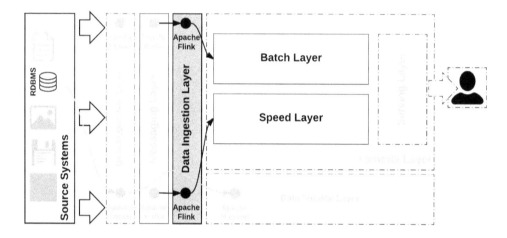

Figure 03: Technology mapping for Data Ingestion Layer

Inline with our use case of SCV, the data from the messaging layer is taken in by this layer and then enriched and transformed accordingly and passed onto the Lambda Layer. We might also pass this data to the Data Storage Layer for persisting as well.

In this layer there might be other technologies such as Kafka Consumer, Flume and so on. to take of certain aspects in the real working example of SCV. *Part 3* will bring these technologies together so that a clear SCV is derived for enterprise use.

What is Apache Flink?

Apache Flink is an open-source stream processing framework for distributed, high-performing, always-available, and accurate data streaming applications.

- flink.apache.org

Apache Flink is a community-driven open source framework for distributed big data analytics, like Hadoop and Spark. The core of Apache Flink is a distributed streaming dataflow engine written in Java and Scala. Flink executes arbitrary dataflow programs in a data-parallel and pipelined manner. Flink's pipelined runtime system enables the execution of bulk/batch and stream processing programs.

- Wikipedia

Apache's definition of Flink is somewhat easy to understand and the second part of Wikipedia's definition is quite hard to understand. For the time being just understand that Flink brings a unified programming model for handling stream and batch data using one technology.

This chapter in no way covers in a comprehensive way the working of Apache Flink. Apache Flink is a topic by itself spanning an entire book.

However, without giving too much details, it tries to cover many aspects of this awesome tool. We will skim through some of the core aspects and we will also give you enough information to actually use Flink in your Data Lake implementation.

For comprehensive coverage of Flink, I suggest going through, latest documentation of Flink in Apache, which can be found at `https://ci.apache.org/projects/flink/flink-docs-release-1.1/`.

Why Apache Flink?

The technology choice in this layer was really tough for us. Apache Spark was initially our choice, but Apache Flink had something in it that made us think over and at the time of writing this book, the industry did have some pointers favoring Flink and this made us do the final choice as Flink. However, we could have implemented this layer using Spark and it would have worked well for sure.

This section tries to give the reader reasons for why Flink was chosen. Obviously we have a subsection that gives detail advantages of Flink and those are these primary reasons for the choice.

But before going to the advantages and disadvantages of Flink, lets see how Flink started its journey and what were the advantages it had when it started. Some aspects is definitely its learning from existing similar technologies and that itself is an advantage. Other aspect is new things get developed when there is such a requirement (necessity is the mother of all inventions as stated by the famous proverb). One of the main differences between the two is to do with how these two are actually implemented (implementation design and details).

The following are some of the reasons for its selection as against its competitors:

- Easier to use application programming interface (API) and also at much higher level
- Lighting fast data processing using many inherent Flink features (in-memory processing)
- Capable of touching each stream data and perform required analysis
- Low latency data processing
- Support for exactly once processing
- High throughput
- Fault tolerant
- Easy configuration
- Open source
- Capable of providing accurate results for late coming data and also out of order data streams
- Stateful in nature

Spark operates in micro-batch and that's one of the core reasons to move to Flink. Going forwards micro-batch can be an issue (bottleneck) to handle real-time data and giving results as required by use cases in a timely manner. Due to this reason only, Spark is not considered as it does impose a latency in analyzing data in real-time and to produce relevant results.

History of Flink

Flink started as a fork from the **Stratosphere** project and in April, 2014 it was incubated in Apache Incubator. In the same year *(December, 2014)*, Flink became Apache's top-level project and the 0.9 version was Flink's first version after becoming top-level Apache project and 1.1 is the latest release of Flink released in December, 2016.

> *In 2010, the research project "Stratosphere: Information Management on the Cloud" (funded by the German Research Foundation (DFG)) was started as a collaboration of Technical University Berlin, Humboldt-Universität zu Berlin, and Hasso-Plattner-Institut Potsdam.*

- Wikipedia

The following figure summarizes Flink's evolution in a pictorial fashion for easy understanding:

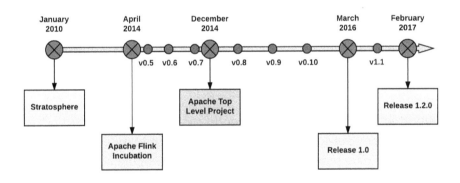

Figure 04: History of Apache Flink

It was a complete rewrite from Stratosphere 0.2 to Flink 0.8. Flink was added on real-time data streams and integration with a variety of frontend and backends making it more acceptable in the industry. It also has been well integrated with many of the open source big data technologies and gels with this ecosystem quite well. The Fink community has been thriving since then and has started challenging more mature frameworks like Spark in due course because of its subtly implementation philosophies of avoiding micro-batch and dealing with stream data as is in real-time.

Advantages of Flink

Apache Flink was chosen for its inherent strengths and new designs. It was also chosen, considering use case that we are dealing with and also how the big data space is going forward. It is also considering how enterprises see data at real-time as a mechanism to make more profit. Dealing with real-time data with less latency as against dealing with micro-batch inherently providing results with some latency is needed in modern industries and Flink does live up to this aspect quite well.

Some of the core advantages offered by Flink are as follows:

- Capable of working with filesystems apart from Hadoop File Systems.
- Easy API's.
- Open source.
- Better testing capability and support.
- Extremely fast data processing.
- Unified programming model for both batch and stream data. This internally helps enterprises to get resources (people) in this technology to handle these disparate types of data into Data Lake.
- Capable of analyzing stream data at extreme velocity as required by use case and transform accordingly.
- Flink has its own **Machine Learning** (**ML**) library, **FlinkML**, for dealing with ML related use cases.
- Support for iterative queries and algorithms natively.
- Supports many new operators along with built-in MapReduce models.
- Low latency data processing using its pipelined engine.
- By design capable of handling higher throughput.
- Fault tolerance support using light-weight methodologies.
- Also support batch processing.
- Built-in storm support allowing reusing of code written for Storm.
- Bult-in memory manager supporting customizations as required by your use case
- Little or no configuration.
- Most of tuning in regards to performance handled internally by the Flink engine.
- Possesses different windowing features for the streamed data required for modern big data technologies (for handling steady data streams, Flink divides the arriving data into slices based on timestamp, count and other criteria, this is called as a window).
- Being stateful is one of the features making it come out of failure.

- Capable of large scale enterprise deployment capable of handling high volume and velocity data from various business applications.
- Decouples APIs from actual execution (what this means is the same program can be ran in many ways and this is hidden from users) making it easy to achieve performance.
- Many required metric for monitoring and management is exposed via REST APIs.
- Easy to use dashboard for rich user interface experience.
- Supports highly-available cluster setup.

For more details, Flink documentation does have a specific section detailing with Flink, which can be found at this link `http://flink.apache.org/introduction.html#features -why-flink`.

Disadvantages of Flink

Being the latest in this space (not really the latest, its origin dates back to 2008), it does try to cover many of the shortcomings its more popular competitors have within them. So in that league it does possess only a very few disadvantages as of now.

Some of the disadvantages associated with Flink can be bulleted as follows:

- Compared to competitors not ahead in popularity and community adoption at the time of writing this book
- Maturity in the industry is less
- Pipelined execution in Flink does have some limitation in regards to memory management (for long running pipelines) and fault tolerance
- Flink uses raw bytes as internal data representation, which if needed, can be hard to program
- Doesn't have matured APIs for querying data (Flink's Table API is not quite there when compared with other competitors)
- Data source integration API's are not the best and are limited in options.
- Only Java and Scala API's available as of now

Working of Flink

An image conveys much more than a paragraph and because of that reason we will start this section with a figure. The functioning of Flink is as shown in the following figure:

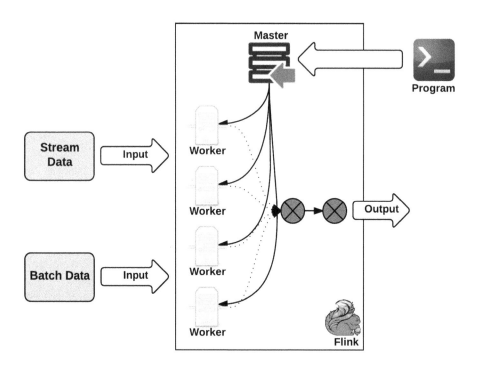

Figure 05: Functioning of Flink

Flink is capable of taking in both batch and stream data. It operates on batch data as if it is another form of stream data and this itself is quite a unique feature of Flink. We have in one of the chapters in *Part 1* explained a bit on **Kappa Architecture** was explained, in which all data is being considered and dealt with stream data and Flink uses that exact principle in its architecture and implementation.

In the preceding figure, both types of data (batch and stream) from various source systems gets into Flink. The Flink program submits the job and using master and worker, deals with these data and produces output.

Flink architecture

The crux of the Flink architecture as shown in the preceding figure are three important components working together namely:

- Client
- Job Manager
- Task Manager

The following figure shows this aspect extracted out for easy understanding:

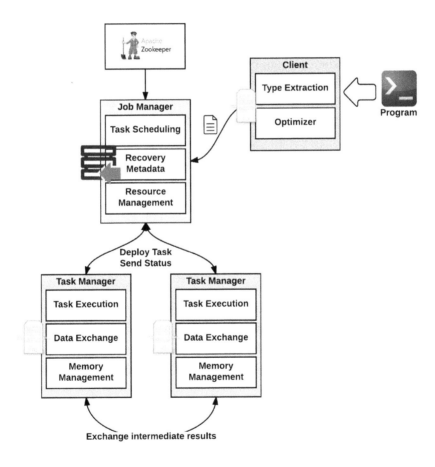

Figure 06: Core components in Flink architecture

The preceding figure clearly shows the interaction between these components pretty well. Now let's get into each component into a bit more detail in following subsections.

Client

The client has the following defined functions to be performed for each Flink program execution:

- Code parsing
- Type extraction
- **Optimizer**: Optimization to select the best since, Flink has a built-in optimizer that optimizes the code before actual execution
- **Graph Builder**: Construction of dataflow graph for every job
- Transfer the constructed dataflow graph to job manager
- Get the job results generated

The following figure gives you anatomy of the Flink client component and also gives the link between another Flink component:

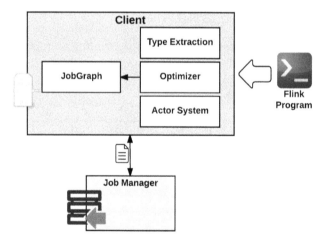

Figure 07: Flink client component

Job Manager

The main functions performed by the Job Manager (master node) are as follows:

- Prepares to parallelize execution of tasks.
- **Task Scheduling**: Schedules the tasks on the task managers. It deploys, stops, and cancels tasks in the task manager.
- Contains the checkpoint coordinator, which is used to trigger checkpoints in the task manager.
- **Execution Tracking**: Tracks the execution of tasks in the task manager and gathers task results.
- Gathers and keeps the metadata associated with the dataflow graph.

The following figure shows the anatomy of Job Manager in detail and also shows its link to the next component:

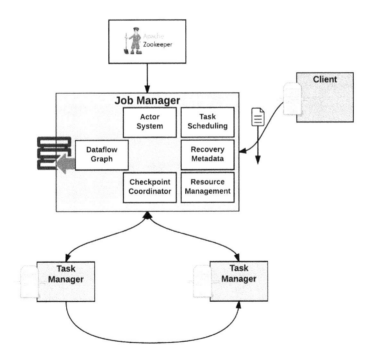

Figure 08: Flink Job Manager component

Task Manager

Task Manager is the worker node where the tasks are finally executed. It contains multiple task slots in which it executes the tasks as specified/demanded by the **Job Manager**.

The following figure shows the anatomy of the **Task Manager**. It shows multiple workers task nodes showing that this component is usually more than one in a typical deployment:

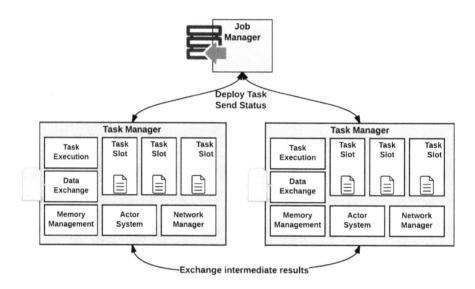

Figure 09: Flink Task Manager component

The following figure shows all these components in the Flink architecture in action, but unlike the previous high-level image, this details each components and its interaction:

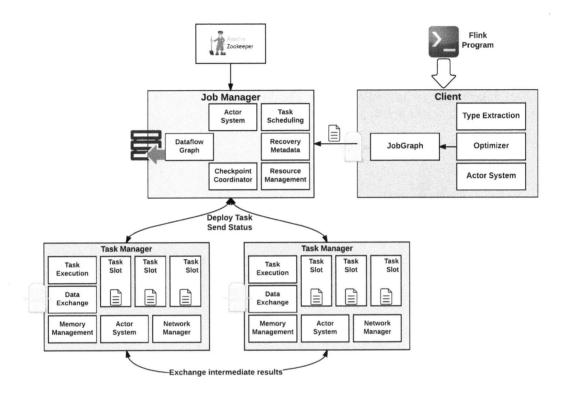

Figure 10: Flink architecture component nitty-gritties (courtesy-Flink documentation)

The preceding figure shows that each component is linked by a coordination system built on the Akka library. Flink has different deployment topology. If Flink is started in local mode, one Job Manager with one or more task manager is started with the same JVM.

As shown in the preceding figure, the client submits a job to the job manager, which in turn controls the task manager, inside which tasks are placed in tasks slots and then executed.

The next section gives us the Flink execution model and the path a job takes to execute it and produce results.

Flink execution model

The following figure shows Flink's execution model. The Flink program written is parsed by the program compiler and then type extracted and then optimized (Flink Optimizer). Each submitted job is then converted to a dataflow graph and then passed onto Job Manager, which then creates an execution plan and the job graph is then passed onto Task Manager where the tasks are finally executed (execution graph).

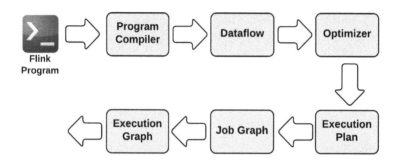

Figure 11: Flink execution model

Core architecture principles of Flink

We have gone through Flink's architecture and its important components in the previous section. Before going deep into Flink internals it's very important to understand the principles on which Flink was conceived and developed. Some of the core architecture principles followed by Flink are as follows:

- Hide internal workings of many aspects away from users (abstract as much as possible so as to become easy for users).
- Decouple API's from actual execution logic (interface-implementation approach). This helps Flink to execute the same program in multiple ways hidden away from the users achieving maximum performance.
- Declarative.
- Little or no tuning.
- Execute everything as stream (even batch data).
- Little or no configuration.
- Support for many filesystems (**BYOS - Bring Your Own Storage**).

- Multiple deployment options **(BYOC - Bring Your Own Cluster)**.
- Work very close with various Hadoop systems and technologies.
- Separation of application logic from fault-tolerance.

Flink Component Stack

The following figure shows Flink's stack in detail. Getting in each component in the stack is out of the scope of this book and we would suggest going through Flink's official documentation (`https://ci.apache.org/projects/flink/flink-docs-release-1.1/`).

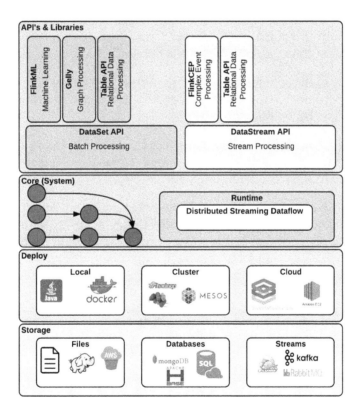

Figure 12: Flink Component Stack (Courtesy Apache Flink doc - `http://flink.apache.org`*)*

The preceding figure shows the various components in Flink stack in a layer fashion (conceptual architecture). As shown, Flink supports variety of storage (BYOS) and that constitutes the bottom later. The next layer is the deployment topology that Flink supports (BYOC) and as shown, it does support a variety of them. The next layer labelled **Runtime** is the core of Flink's execution model and consists of Batch Optimizer for batch operation and Stream Builder for stream handling. On top of that is the layer that is interacted by the developer and it is quite well abstracted away from the developer in the form of well-defined API's and libraries.

Checkpointing in Flink

One aspect of Apache Flink that allows it to handle stateful streaming is checkpointing and this is one of core features that makes it different from others. Other aspect namely *savepoint* (explained in the next section), also enables Flink to handle stateful streaming.

Fault tolerance is one of the core features of Flink. Achieving this feature with high throughput and performance is quite a tricky combination to achieve. But Flink achieves this using the so called checkpointing feature.

As against batch (which has a defined start and end), stream data does not have a clear start and end. Also the stream data coming in has a state that has to be preserved and this poses additional challenges in achieving fault tolerance.

Checkpointing in Flink uses the Distributed Snapshots approach, which is based on a technique by *Chandy* and *Lamport* in the year *1985*. Flink has slightly varied the algorithm by saving the snapshot state periodically (frequency is configurable) in the background of the running data stream to a persistent storage (Flink supports multiple filesystems). This mechanism, however does not put any pressure on other components and is quite lightweight and happens very seamlessly to the developer under the hoods.

Stream barriers is the mechanism by which Flink's checkpointing mechanism works. These barriers are inserted at sources and flow through the stream. These streams as shown in the following figure are part of either current snapshot or the next snapshot. When these barriers pass through operators, it triggers state snapshots and is persistent in the storage. Once the checkpointing is done the barriers flow through and the process continues. When all the sinks receives these checkpoints, the current checkpoint is complete and can be taken away from storage (if needed). In case of failure, the checkpoint stored on storage can be restored and continued from there.

The following figure shows the stream barriers and checkpointing aspects in detail:

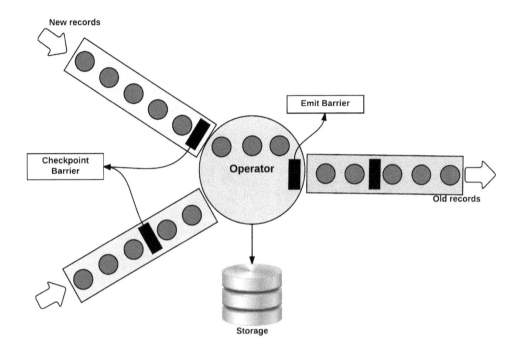

Figure 13: Checkpointing in Apache Flink

Checkpointing is one of the very important technical aspects in Flink and many other design principles such as fault tolerance are fully relying on this.

Savepoints in Flink

Savepoint is another important feature in Flink, which takes it ahead of many of its competitors. Savepoint is a point in time snapshot that keeps track of where exactly we are in the processing of input streams and also holds its associated metadata. It also keeps track of all the pending states or in flight sessions in Flink execution engine. Conceptually its like taking a picture by literally stopping the stream data. By doing so, however, it doesn't actually stop the operation but does this silently in the background.

Internally Flink handles savepoints very much similar to checkpointing, but it does have some notable differences, as follows:

- Triggering can be done manually by relevant configurations
- Is never terminated by Flink until it is explicitly done by the user

The following figure shows the savepoint working in a pictorial fashion for easy understanding:

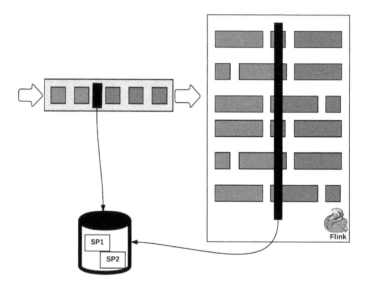

Figure 14: Savepoints (SP) in Flink

Savepoint features allows us to do many operations quite easily and give a versioning mechanism of the snapshots being taken at an internal. Some of those are:

- Can help in applying Flink upgrade/bug fixes quite easily. If due to any reason, issue is seen, it can always use a previous savepoint to restore.
- Can help in doing A/B testing. A savepoint can be used to spin off another Flink execution with variation and tested.
- If you would like to reprocess data streams due to some reason or replay certain scenarios.

For more details, we would suggest going through the following blog http://data-artisa ns.com/how-apache-flink-enables-new-streaming-applications/.

Streaming window options in Flink

Generally speaking, a window defines a finite set of elements on an unbounded stream. This set can be based on time, element counts, a combination of counts and time, or some custom logic to assign elements to windows.

- Flink documentation (`flink.apache.org`*)*

Dealing with infinite data stream demands the need for such window functions. Flink's DataStream API (discussed in following sections) does have some built-in windowing functions that takes care of most use cases. It also allows us to define custom window behavior as required by your use case by letting developers implement its interfaces and implementing appropriate methods.

The following are Flink's built-in windowing options:

- Time window
- Count window

Time window

As the name suggests, it groups the incoming data stream by time. Timestamp which Flink looks are:

- **Processing time**: Uses the system/machine time where Flink executes.
- **Event time**: Uses an existing timestamp on the data stream event.
- **Ingestion time**: A mix of the preceding two. When each event arrives, it attaches the event with the system time and then uses these stamped time on these events for grouping.

Count window

As the name suggests, windows are based on the configured count. If the event count hits the configured value, the data streams are windowed/grouped.

Both time and count windows can be configured in two different ways:

- Tumbling
- Sliding

Tumbling window configuration

As the name suggests, it tumbles over the data stream. Tumbling windows do not overlap with each other and because of which events in a tumbled window do not fall into two windows. Tumbling configuration can be done for both time and count windows by mere configuration.

The following figure shows tumbling window in action:

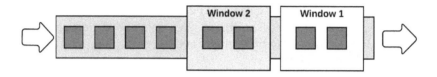

Figure 15: Tumbling window

Sliding window configuration

As the name suggests, the window slides over the data stream. Because of this sliding nature, the windows tend to overlap with other sliding windows. Due to this the data stream events in one windows can belong to other windows as well. Again, this can be configured for both time and count windows by appropriate configuration.

The following figure shows the sliding window in action:

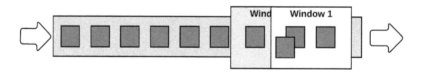

Figure 16: Sliding window

In this section, we just have skimmed through one of the important Flink's capability of windowing, that is a mandatory functionality especially for processing infinite data streams. These become more significant when you need to do an aggregation.

Memory management

Memory management in Flink is often attributed to be innovative and claims to be one of the first big data technology which has implemented custom memory management. To achieve this Flink has its own mechanisms for type extraction and serialization.

The following figure shows the JVM heap that is divided into areas dedicated to do certain defined activities in regards to memory. As shown in the figure, Flink has a managed heap, which is a dedicated memory fraction given to Flink for various Flink related operations such as caching and data processing:

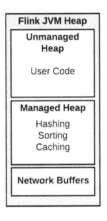

Figure 17: Flink memory management

Some of the core features of Flink's memory management is as follows:

- Non GC (Garbage Collection) based approach
- Serialization is based on individual fields as against the whole object
- Employs C++ style memory management as against Java (based on GC)
- Works on pool of memory pages comprising of bytes and map objects

The preceding listed features give some unique advantages to Flink in regards to memory management as follows:

- Does not throw **Out Of Memory (OOM)** exceptions
- Garbage collection is quite a stress on the hardware and because of these features in Flink GC doesn't put pressure

- Binary representation of storing data is more efficient and uses less memory.
- Limited or no memory tuning required
- Stable performance and more reliable
- Binary representation can be compared and operated with other binary representation easily, making it more performant

 In computer science, **garbage collection** (**GC**) is a form of automatic memory management. The garbage collector, or just collector, attempts to reclaim garbage, or memory occupied by objects that are no longer in use by the program. Garbage collection was invented by John McCarthy around 1959 to abstract away manual memory management in Lisp.

- Wikipedia

Elaboration on this subject is out of scope of this book but more information can be found from the Flink documentation at `https://cwiki.apache.org/confluence/pages/viewpag e.action?pageId=53741525`.

Flink API's

Basic operation of Flink can be explained in very simple terms, as shown in the the following figure:

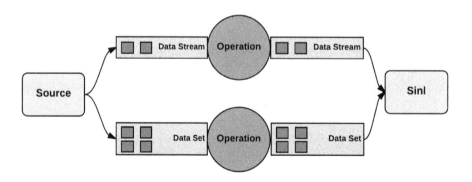

Figure 18: Flink program execution

As shown in the preceding figure, a Flink programs connects to a source, and then applies use case related operations (transformation, calculations and so on) and then finally outputs the results to the sink. Flink is capable of taking in data of two forms, namely, real-time data (DataStream) and batch data (DataSet). To cater to these distinct data types Flink has two main API's namely:

- **DataStream API**: To handle continuous real-time flowing data to cater to real-time stream analytics. API's are available in Java and Scala.
- **DataSet API**: To handle stagnant data in batch format. API's are available in Java, Scala, and Python.

In addition to these main API's, Flink also has domain specific libraries. The following figure shows some of the important ones that we will be discussing in detail in the following subsections:

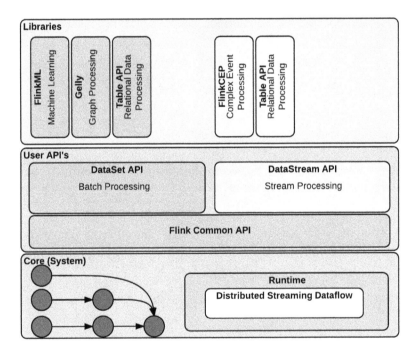

Figure 19: Flink API's

DataStream API

As the name says it all, the DataStream API in Flink can be used to do any operation on the stream of the inflowing data. The operation is one on each element in a stream or stream windows as the case may be. It offers many built-in transformations and also gives a toolbox to create custom ones if needed for your use case. DataStream is the core structure in the DataStream API.

Flink's DataStream API is capable of handling almost any kind of data types (basic types such as string arrays, and so on, and composite types such as tuples, POJO's, and so on).

The following figure shows DataStream program execution in Flink:

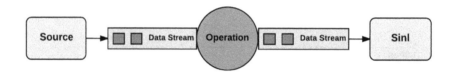

Figure 20: Flink DataStream API program execution

Flink DataStream API example

To handle a stream of incoming data, these numbered steps (as documented in the Flink documentation) have to be done programmatically:

1. Get the `StreamExecutionEnvironment` object.
   `StreamExecutionEnvironment` is the basis for all Flink data stream execution programs. The following code block shows one way to get this object created in Java:

   ```
   final StreamExecutionEnvironment env = StreamExecutionEnvironment
   . getExecutionEnvironment ( );
   ```

2. Load the initial data from the appropriate source.
3. Do the necessary transformation on this loaded data. The full set of transformations available can be found in the Flink documentation at this link: ht tps://goo.gl/YI82xY.

4. Specify the destination where the results after transformation has to be kept.

5. Trigger the program execution.

We wouldn't want to replicate the Flink documentation here; rather we would say that you go to this link to have a deep understanding of the DataStream API in the Flink documentation: `https://goo.gl/NS69SK`.

Streaming connectors

Flink has many connectors for easy integration that can be broadly categorized as follows:

1. Built-in Connectors: Connectors that are already there along with the Flink installation and developed by various providers and are already supported and maintained come under this category:
   - **File**: Reads file from a specified file path. It can monitor a directory and as and when a file is added or changed can read and do the needful
   - **Collection**: Reads from elements and also is capable of reading from Java collections
   - **Socket**: Reads text socket from exposed port
   - Basic:
     - File
     - Socket
     - Standard output
   - Advanced:
     - **Elasticsearch**: Used to store and index JSON documents. We do have a dedicated chapter on this in which we will discuss this technology in a bit more detail. Flink supports both Elasticsearch 1.x and Elasticsearch 2.x
     - Cassandra
     - **HDFS (Hadoop FileSystem)**
   - **RabbitMQ**
   - **Apache Kafka**: Gives provision to convert a Kafka topic to DataStream and also can write to a DataStream. Flink has good integration support with Kafka
   - Apache NiFi
   - Amazon Kinesis Streams
   - **Sources**: Connectors that are configured as source in Flink comes in this.

- **Sinks**: Connectors which are configured as sink in Flink are categorized in this
- **Source and Sink**: Connectors that behave as both source and sink in the Flink ecosystem come into this category

2. **Custom Connectors**: If these built-in connectors suit your chosen use case, Flink does give provision to implement your own connector. Flink has a toolbox using which you could do this with ease. Using the toolbox (specification interfaces), both custom source and sink can be implemented.

DataSet API

Flink handles batch data and processes it using the Flink's built-in DataSet API. The DataSet API also has mechanisms to do necessary transformations necessary for common use cases. After transformation, the DataSet is transformed to DataSet. API's are in Java, Scala, and Python. In Flink batch data and its processing also work on the same aspect as stream data. The following figure shows basic working of the DataSet API on a batch data using the MapReduce paradigm producing DataSet (class of objects created when data is read and processed):

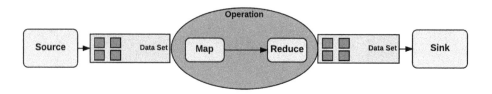

Figure 21: Flink DataSet API program execution

Flink DataSet API example

Apart from the environment, rest of the steps in DataSet API program are identical to that of the DataStream API. The following are the steps you have to perform to actually deal with batch data using the DataSet API in Flink:

1. Before doing anything with the DataSet API, you need to get an environment specific to batch data handling. `ExecutionEnvironment` is the object require to start using the API and its capability as shown in this code snippet (there are many ways and this is just a basic way):

```
final ExecutionEnvironment env =
ExecutionEnvironment.getExecutionEnvironment();
```

2. To do operations on data, the data has to be created or loaded from the source. In this set data is prepared. Data can be loaded/created from file-based, collection-based, socket-based, and so on.

3. Do the necessary transformations on the loaded/created data next. There are various transformations possible on the batch data such as Map, FlatMap, Filter, Reduce and so on. The complete list of transformations can be found in the Flink documentation at this URL https://goo.gl/HLg3bN.

4. In this step specify where the transformed data results are to be put (Sink configuration). For example, write results to file, socket and so on.

5. This is the final step in which the program execution is triggered, which triggers off the actual program execution.

Table API

API's built on top of DataStream and DataSet API's enabling SQL like queries on the data is termed as **Table API**. They are available in the Java and Scala languages. Using these API's you can use SQL-like expressions for specifying the required operations.

The Table API creates this abstraction above DataStream and DataSet, making it easy for coding. Using this, its easy to deal with structured data using the popular SQL expression. Basic data structures that the API deals with is Table.

SQL (Structured Query Language) is a domain-specific language used in programming and designed for managing data held in a **Relational Database Management System (RDBMS)**, or for stream processing in a RDBMS.

- Wikipedia

Similar to the DataStream and DataSet APIs, using the Table API can done by doing the following steps:

1. Get the ExecutionEnvironment as this is the starting point for any API execution in Flink:

```
ExecutionEnvironment env =
ExecutionEnvironment.getExecutionEnvironment();
```

2. After that, you need to get `TableExecutionEnvironment` using `ExecutionEnvironment` as shown next in the code snippet. According to the data type (batch or stream data) to be handled, you need to get either `BatchTableEnvironment` (batch data) and `StreamTableEnvironment` (stream data), as shown in this code snippet:

```
BatchTableEnvironment tableEnv =
TableEnvironment.getTableEnvironment(env);
        OR
StreamTableEnvironment tableEnv =
TableEnvironment.getTableEnvironment(env);
```

3. Now, register the table. This can be from DataStream, DataSet, and so on, shown in this code snippet as an example:

```
tableEnv.registerDataSet("table_name", mytable);
        OR
tableEnv.registerDataStream("table_name", mytable);
```

4. Now, using the TableAPI, perform various operations.

The Flink documentation has all the details with regards to this API at `https://goo.gl/B6F8Ey`.

Flink domain specific libraries

Apart from the core API's (DataStream and DataSet) there are other API's for easy handling of certain operation as shown in the following list. Similar to the Table API most of the libraries are also built on top of core Flink API's:

- **Gelly** (Graph Library)
- **FlinkML** (Machine Learning Library)
- **FlinkCEP** (Complex Event Processing Library)

 Event processing is a method of tracking and analyzing (processing) streams of information (data) about things that happen (events), and deriving a conclusion from them. **Complex event processing** (CEP), is event processing that combines data from multiple sources to infer events or patterns that suggest more complicated circumstances.

- Wikipedia

Gelly - Flink Graph API

Gelly is Flink's Graph API and library. There are various algorithms built-in long with this library to deal with graph capability. Graph management was initially offloaded to another library, namely **Apache Spargel**, to be handled. However a new project namely Gelly was launched by Gelly to deal with graph management, more aligned with other core API's and also using core Flink capabilities.

The Gelly library requires objects inheriting from DataSet, so at the end it caters to addressing graph-related functionality for batch data.

Gelly offers various graph analysis utilities and also allows doing many iterative processes on graphs and has many algorithms to deal with the graph data.

Similar to the core API's in Flink, Gelly offers various functions to transform and modify various types of batch data. A graph representation in Gelly is based on vertices and edges (DataSet - batch data).

This section has just skimmed through the Gelly library and more details can be found in official Flink documentation in the following URL `https://goo.gl/S5plEP`.

Figure 22: Flink Graph API (Gelly)

Flink's Gelly has both Java and Scala APIs.

FlinkML

Flink's answer to the **Machine Learning (ML)** library is FlinkML. It has built-in support for various ML libraries and the list keeps growing. It works on the pipeline mechanism inspired by **scikit-learn** (`http://scikit-learn.org/`).

FlinkML can act on both batch and stream data. Stream data and the ML application is quite significant and one of the use cases can be to deal with payment transactions and detect fraud.

For more details, see Flink documentation at the following URL https://goo.gl/zDL2Cn.

> *Scikit-learn (formerly scikits.learn) is a free software machine learning library for the Python programming language.*
>
> *- Wikipedia*

A project name Apache **SAMOA (Scalable Advanced Massive Online Analysis)**, is a streaming machine language framework that could also be used along with Flink to cater to stream data ML capabilities.

FlinkCEP

Flink has its own **Complex Event Processing** (**CEP**) library called FlinkCEP. The library allows to deal with vent patterns in a stream and accordingly deals with it to cater to use case in hand. It is built on top of the DataStream API and helps defining user patterns and then injecting into a stream and according to the pattern generates new events and deals with those accordingly.

Again we wouldn't want to delve deep into this topic in this book as it would be a book by itself. We strongly suggest going through the official Flink documentation at the following URL https://goo.gl/Tsu6q7.

Flink working example

This section details a full working example using Flink. Towards the end of this section, it also brings a connection of our use case with Flink and how its features are used.

 At the time of authoring this book, we had Flink Release Candidate 3 source code available for download, while official release of Flink 1.3.0 was just about to be released. As we observed Flink Release Candidate 3 (RC3) was versioned as 1.3.0, and its implementation is expected to be very close to the official release of Flink 1.3.0.

Installation

Follow the steps for full installation of Flink:

1. Download the latest source code for release candidate of flink 1.3.0, which was **RC3** (release candidate 3) at the time of authoring this book, using the following command in your download directory, `${DOWNLOAD_DIR}`:

   wget https://github.com/apache/flink/archive/release-1.3.0-rc3.zip

2. Change to a user directory and extract the contents from the zip using the following command. Let us refer to the extracted `Flink` source folder, flink-release-1.3.0-rc3, as `${FLINK_SRC}`:

   unzip ${DOWNLOAD_DIR}/release-1.3.0-rc3.zip

3. Change directory into `${FLINK_SRC}` and use the following command to compile the source code. It may take some time for the build the complete.

   mvn install –DskipTests

4. Once the build completes, copy the generated build-target folder to a separate user folder, `<flink-install-dir>`. This user folder would be our working installation of Flink 1.3.0 RC3. The command below would inherently create the Flink install directory as part of its execution:

   cp –r ${FLINK_SRC}/build-target <flink-install-dir>

5. Configure the `${FLINK_HOME}` environment variable using the following command and add the same into `~/.bashrc`:

   export FLINK_HOME=<flink-install-dir>
   export PATH=$PATH:$FLINK_HOME/bin

6. Change to the user directory of Flink's extracted content and start the Flink server using the following command:

   ${FLINK_HOME}/bin/start-local.sh

7. Navigate to `http://<vm-ip-address>:8081`, and the following screenshot should be visible, confirming a successful setup of Flink on a single node:

Figure 23: Flink Dashboard

If you are planning to run the Flink examples from a development environment, it is advisable to build Flink source on the same machine, since such builds are platform dependent. This is also due to the fact that, we are using the latest Flink version for our examples, i.e. RC3, which is not yet available in most of the public maven repositories at the time of authoring the book.

Example - data processing with Flink

Let us build an example to process some data with Flink. For this purpose, let's try to process the data that we have in our database, stream the data via Flink, and store it in the database.

In order to have substantial data for our examples, it would be good to have a bit larger volume of data. In the following section, we will see how we can generate the required data.

Data generation

In this section, we will go in steps explaining how we can generate the required data to showcase our example/use case:

1. The commands/steps outlined in these examples, can be run either from within an IDE of your choice or directly from within CentOS. If it is done from within CentOS, additional copy/move steps between your IDE and CentOS could be avoided.

2. In your local (cloned) git repository, navigate to the `chapter08` folder which contains the code that will be detailed in this chapter. For data generation, the code is contained in one of the modules of `chapter08`, in the `client-generator` folder.

3. Change the directory into a `client-generator` folder and run the following command to build from source:

   ```
   mvn install
   ```

4. Once the package is built successfully, observe that the tarball is built in the target folder of the `client-generator` project

5. Change the directory to a user folder, we suggest creating a `~/data-generators` directory and extract the contents of the tarball with the following command:

   ```
   tar -zxvf <client-generator project>/target/client-generator-1.0-SNAPSHOT-bin.tar.gz
   ```

6. Once the contents are extracted, change the directory into the extracted folder and configure the properties file (`~/data-generators/client-generator-1.0-SNAPSHOT/config/db.properties`), based on your database configurations:

   ```
   jdbc.url=jdbc:postgresql://<DB_IP_ADDRESS>/sourcedb?schema=public
   user=
   password=
   ```

7. Run the following command from within `~/data-generators/client-generator-1.0-SNAPSHOT` to generate the content. For the purpose of our examples, let us generate 100,000 customer records including their addresses. Please make sure that the PostgreSQL database server is running before executing this command:

```
java -jar client-generator-1.0-SNAPSHOT.jar config/db.properties
100000
```

8. After successful execution, the script will display the status of records generated in the console.

Now that we have about 100,000+ rows in our database for customer profile (customer + address), let us build the example that we intend to in which we will stream all of these rows in PostgreSQL DB into Hadoop storage via Flink.

For now, we will build the examples in such a way that it can be used as an extendable piece for our SCV use case.

The overall example can be divided into multiple steps, as detailed in the following sections.

Step 1 - Preparing streams

This step involves preparing data streams by publishing the data into the Kafka topic, for which we will utilize the simple producer API (explained in Chapter 7, *Messaging Layer with Apache Kafka*). In this step, we will read the data from the database and publish the records into a topic in Kafka:

1. In order to prepare streams, navigate to the `chapter08` folder, which contains the code for this chapter. For preparing the streams, the code is contained in one of the modules of `chapter08`, that is, in the `chapter08/flink-example1` folder.

2. Change the following properties files as per your environment:
   - `chapter08/flink-example1/config/db.properties`: This file contains all the database related properties to access the database
   - `chapter08/flink-example1/config/producer.properties`: This file contains all the configurations required for the producer to publish the customer records read from the database and publish them into a Kafka topic

- chapter08/flink-example1/config/flink.properties: This file contains Flink-related configuration, which currently contains the HDFS path and user account only
- The main class doing the job in this example is DBProducer.java, the complete source code of this class is as shown as follows. The DBProducer class reads the customer records from the database and publishes the customer records as JSON strings into a Kafka topic, named customer. The code is well commented and it's quite straightforward to understand going through it line by line:

```
public class DBProducer {

private static final String CUSTOMER_QUERY = "SELECT * FROM CUSTOMER";

public static void main(String[] args) throws SQLException,
IOException,        ClassNotFoundException {
publishCustomers();
    }

private static void publishCustomers() throws SQLException,
IOException,        ClassNotFoundException {

//Initialize the object mapper for serialization/deserialization
        ObjectMapper mapper = new ObjectMapper();

//Load the producer properties and initialize Kafka producer
        Properties producerProps =
        PropertyLoader.loadProperty("producer.properties");
        Producer kafkaProducer = initializeProducer(producerProps);

//Establish database connection & execute query to retrieve all
customer records
        Connection conn = getConnection();
        System.out.println("Database Connection Established...");
        Statement stmt = conn.createStatement();
        ResultSet result = stmt.executeQuery(CUSTOMER_QUERY);
        System.out.println("Query Executed...");

//Serialize all customer records into JSON string and publish to
Kafka topic
            while(result.next()) {
                Customer cust = new Customer();
                cust.setId(result.getInt("id"));
                cust.setFirstName(result.getString("first_Name"));
                cust.setLastName(result.getString("last_Name"));
```

```
                cust.setDob(result.getDate("dob"));

//Serialize object into a JSON string
                String customerMessage =
mapper.writeValueAsString(cust);

//Publish customer record as JSON message
                ProducerRecord message = new
ProducerRecord(producerProps.getProperty("topicName"),

                String.valueOf(cust.getId()), customerMessage);
                kafkaProducer.send(message);
            }
            System.out.println("Messages Published");

//Close producer and exit
                conn.close();
                kafkaProducer.close();
            }

private static Producer initializeProducer(Properties
producerConfig) throws IOException {
                Producer<String, String> producer = new
KafkaProducer<String, String>(producerConfig);
return  producer;
            }

private static void closeProducer(Producer producer) {
if (producer != null) {
                    producer.close();
                }
            }

private static Connection getConnection() throws
ClassNotFoundException, IOException,        SQLException {
                Class.forName("org.postgresql.Driver");
                Properties props =
PropertyLoader.loadProperty("db.properties");
return DriverManager.getConnection(props.getProperty("jdbc.url"),
props);
            }
        }
```

Code 01: Publish DB Records into Kafka

As shown in the preceding code, we are reading all the customer records from the database and then publishing them into a topic named customer into Kafka.

While doing so, we are also converting the records into objects and serializing those objects into JSON representation by using `ObjectMapper`.

4. From within `chapter08/flink-example1`, run the following command to compile the code:

    ```
    mvn install
    ```

5. Execute the preceding code, which is in `DBProducer.java` from within your IDE or from command line. Before executing the Java class please go through the preceding listed class and understand it's working. This will queue the customer records as messages in the customer Kafka topic:

    • While executing the class from within the IDE, please make sure that the working directory is properly set pointing to the project folder, that is, `flink-example1`, and the module `classpath` in **Run Configuration**. This can be set by navigating to the top-level menu **Run** and under that selecting **Run...** opens these settings. Once this is set, you may simply execute the class from IDE. This is with reference IntelliJ IDEA. Similar setting are available in Eclipse as well.

    • If you are executing the class from Command Prompt/shell, you may run the following command to execute the program from within the project folder, that is, `chapter08/flink-example1`:

    ```
    java -cp target/flink-example1-1.0-SNAPSHOT.jar
    com.laketravels.ch08.db.producer.DBProducer
    ```

Step 2 - Consuming Streams via Flink

Now that we have all 100K records queued into Kafka, the next step is to consume these messages using Flink and start establishing an execution pipeline within Flink.

Flink comes with a lot of inbuilt connectors, and one of the source connectors is the Kafka connector. In order to include the Kafka connector, the following dependency is required to be added into the project's `pom.xml` file (refer to `flink-example1/pom.xml`):

```
<dependency>
    <groupId>org.apache.flink</groupId>
    <artifactId>flink-connector-kafka-0.10_2.10</artifactId>
    <version>1.2.0</version>
</dependency>
```

```
<dependency>
    <groupId>org.apache.flink</groupId>
    <artifactId>flink-streaming-java_2.11</artifactId>
    <version>1.2.0</version>
</dependency>
```

Code 02: Flink Dependencies for Consumption from Kafka

In order to consume the messages from the Kafka topic, the following code can be taken as a reference. This same code is being used in our example in the `com.laketravels.ch08.consumer.FlinkProcessor` class, which contains the main method:

```
final ObjectMapper mapper = new ObjectMapper();
Properties flinkProps = PropertyLoader.loadProperty("flink.properties");
// create execution environment
StreamExecutionEnvironment env =
StreamExecutionEnvironment.getExecutionEnvironment();

env.enableCheckpointing(2000, CheckpointingMode.EXACTLY_ONCE);

// parse user parameters
ParameterTool parameterTool = ParameterTool.fromArgs(args);

DataStream<Tuple2<IntWritable, Text>> messageStream = env.addSource(
new FlinkKafkaConsumer010(
parameterTool.getRequired("topic"),
new Tuple2DeserializerSchema(),
parameterTool.getProperties()));

messageStream.rebalance().print();
```

Code 03: Code to consume Kafka messages from Flink Process

The main method in the `FlinkProcessor` class needs the following arguments for a successful launch of the execution pipeline. The parameters required for this example are:

- `topic` - Contains the name of the topic from where the messages are to be consumed
- `bootstrap.servers` - Contains comma separated list of `ip:port` of Kafka broker processes

- `zookeeper.connect` - Contains the zookeeper connect address, in the form `ip:port`
- `group.id` - Identifies the consumer group for message consumption and group level offset management of the consumer

In our example, we are passing the parameters as command line arguments as follows. Once the arguments are passed, they are decoded/interpreted by `ParameterTool` for substitutions within the code:

```
--topic customer --bootstrap.servers <KAFKA_SERVER_IP>:9092 --
zookeeper.connect <ZOOKEEPER_IP>:2181 --group.id 1 --auto.offset.reset
earliest
```

In the preceding code, the messages are being consumed using the `SimpleStringSchema` deserializer. This deserializer is required by `FlinkKafkaConsumer` to deserialize messages into the data stream.

> In order to replay the messages/re-submit the job, the Flink job can be run with different Group IDs

We have now consumed the messages from Kafka and now we have to use Flink as a channel to persist into HDFS. This is explained in the next step.

Step 3 - Streaming data into HDFS

Flink also provides a number of connectors including HDFS connectors as sinks. All the HDFS connectors have very similar constructs. HDFS connectors can sink messages from Flink DataStreams that have a tuple structure. HDFS also stores data as tuples. The specific class provided for this purpose by Flink is the `Tuple2` class.

> A tuple is a finite ordered list of elements. (`https://en.wikipedia.org/wiki/Tuple`).

Any sink can be added to the Flink environment by making a call to the `env.addSink(...)` method. The specific class that we have used here is `BucketingSink`. The following code can be considered as a reference for understanding our example:

```
System.setProperty("HADOOP_USER_NAME", flinkProps.getProperty("hdfsUser"));
BucketingSink<Tuple2<IntWritable, Text>> hdfsSink = new
```

```
BucketingSink<Tuple2<IntWritable,
Text>>(flinkProps.getProperty("hdfsPath"));
hdfsSink.setBucketer(new DateTimeBucketer("yyyy-MM-dd--HHmm"));
hdfsSink.setWriter(new SequenceFileWriter<IntWritable, Text>());
hdfsSink.setBatchSize(1024 * 1024 * 400);
messageStream.addSink(hdfsSink);
```

Code 04: HDFS Sink in Flink Processor

If we try to connect the code shown in the previous step with the preceding code, we may realize a bit of an issue in terms of source and sink.

The main issue here is that, in the previous step the source is sourcing messages from Kafka as String messages, while Sink requires the messages to be in tuple structure. This creates a gap in what is coming in and what is required to be persisted.

In order to solve this we can implement a custom deserializer schema class at the source, a reference implementation can be seen here:

```
public class Tuple2DeserializerSchema implements DeserializationSchema {
    public Object deserialize(byte[] bytes) throws IOException {
        ObjectMapper mapper = new ObjectMapper();
        Customer cust = (Customer) mapper.readValue(new String(bytes),
            Customer.class);
        Tuple2<IntWritable, Text> tuple = new Tuple2<IntWritable, Text>();
        tuple.setFields( new IntWritable(cust.getId()), new Text(new
            String(bytes)));
        return tuple;
    }

    public boolean isEndOfStream(Object o) {
        return false;
    }

    public TypeInformation<Tuple2<IntWritable, Text>> getProducedType() {
        return new TupleTypeInfo<Tuple2<IntWritable, Text>>
            (TypeExtractor.createTypeInfo(IntWritable.class),
            TypeExtractor.createTypeInfo(Text.class));
    }
}
```

Code 05: Tuple2 Deserializer Schema for Flink Source

During the initialization of DataStream in the `FlinkProcessor` class, we can pass the custom serializer (`Tuple2DeserializerSchema`) instead of the String serializer as shown in the following, with complete code:

```
public class FlinkProcessor {

public static void main(String[] args) throws Exception {

final ObjectMapper mapper = new ObjectMapper();
        Properties flinkProps =
PropertyLoader.loadProperty("flink.properties");
// create execution environment
        StreamExecutionEnvironment env =
StreamExecutionEnvironment.getExecutionEnvironment();

        env.enableCheckpointing(2000, CheckpointingMode.EXACTLY_ONCE);

// parse user parameters
        ParameterTool parameterTool = ParameterTool.fromArgs(args);

        DataStream<Tuple2<IntWritable, Text>> messageStream =
env.addSource(
new FlinkKafkaConsumer010(
parameterTool.getRequired("topic"),
new Tuple2DeserializerSchema(),
parameterTool.getProperties())));

        messageStream.rebalance().print();

        System.setProperty("HADOOP_USER_NAME",
flinkProps.getProperty("hdfsUser"));
        BucketingSink<Tuple2<IntWritable, Text>> hdfsSink = new
BucketingSink<Tuple2<IntWritable,
Text>>(flinkProps.getProperty("hdfsPath"));
        hdfsSink.setBucketer(new DateTimeBucketer("yyyy-MM-dd--HHmm"));
        hdfsSink.setWriter(new SequenceFileWriter<IntWritable, Text>());
        hdfsSink.setBatchSize(1024 * 1024 * 400);
        messageStream.addSink(hdfsSink);

        env.execute();
    }
}
```

Code 06: Flink Processor for Reading Messages from Kafka and writing into HDFS

The preceding example can be run from the IDE as a standalone process or from the command prompt. In case this needs to be run from the command line, the following command may be used, assuming that the working directory is the source directory of this example, that is, `flink-example1`:

```
java -cp target/flink-example1-1.0-SNAPSHOT.jar
com.laketravels.ch08.consumer.FlinkProcessor --topic customer --
bootstrap.servers <kafka-server-ip>:9092 --zookeeper.connect <zookeeper-
ip>:2181 --group.id 1 --auto.offset.reset earliest
```

Please ensure that HDFS services are running and exposed on an accessible IP before executing the `FlinkProcessor`. In case the HDFS is configured to run on localhost, it will need to be changed in core-site.xml. A sample is shown as follows:

```
<property>
  <name>fs.defaultFS</name>
  <value>hdfs://192.168.0.165:9000</value>
</property>
```

The output of this execution is that the customer JSON is stored against the the customer ID in HDFS, as follows:

Figure 24: Messages Sinked into HDFS

Flink in purview of SCV use cases

Now that we have seen an example of Flink based processing, it is time that we apply this to the single customer view use case and continue building the Data Lake landscape. For this purpose, let us consider integrating sources such as customer information stored in relational format and user location logs. For user logs, we will generate them as spool files which can then be consumed by Flume with Kafka channel. This Kafka channel would be eventually consumed and processed by the Flink pipeline into HDFS sink. In this use case Flume acts as the acquisition layer that would acquire data from these sources and store them as messages in Kafka topics. We will define two Flink processing pipelines, that would consume these information from both of these Kafka topics and then process and store these information in the HDFS layer.

User Log Data Generation

In order to generate a sample log of customer location (100,000 records), please follow the following steps, which are very similar to the above mentioned customer generation.

1. Clone/Update the source code for the project (we assume this is already done as you have cloned the whole book's code from git when you started) `chapter08/web-generator`

2. Change into the directory containing the project (web-generator) and run the following command to generate the tarball:

   mvn install

3. Change to a user directory, `~/data-generators` as in previous case, and extract contents with the following command:

   tar -zxvf <web-generator project>/target/web-generator-1.0-SNAPSHOT-bin.tar.gz

4. Change to the user directory containing the extracted content and run the following command to generate the records as a spool file (`location.log`):

   java -jar web-generator-1.0-SNAPSHOT.jar location.log 100000

5. The log thus generated has the following structure of content:

```
"id":100095,"longitude":160.98048,"latitude":-62.541742
"id":100096,"longitude":157.16113,"latitude":68.544508
"id":100097,"longitude":11.078648,"latitude":82.648036
"id":100098,"longitude":-133.38267,"latitude":-10.155658
"id":100099,"longitude":-107.13184,"latitude":-88.434630
"id":100100,"longitude":-58.465704,"latitude":-44.031773
```

Figure 25: Location Log Content

As we can see above, the location log contents are mostly free flowing and these logs may contain additional fields as required. The only correlation here is the customer identifier.

6. Copy the generated location.log to the spool directory which would be configured in Flume configuration. This could be the same directory which was created while running Flume examples

Flume Setup

Flume configuration will be required for us to stream the contents from DB and the log file into Kafka topics. Here we will follow similar steps to configure both the data sources as discussed in earlier chapters:

1. Make a new Flume configuration in ${FLUME_HOME}/conf, let us call it as customer-data-kafkaChannel-flume-conf.properties. As the name suggests, this would contain all the configurations required to capture customer data.

2. Now let us have a look at the source configuration as shown below:

```
agent.sources = sql-source spool-source

agent.sources.spool-source.type=spooldir
agent.sources.spool-source.spoolDir=<directory containing the
spool file>
agent.sources.spool-source.inputCharset=ASCII

agent.sources.sql-source.type=org.keedio.flume.source.SQLSource
agent.sources.sql-
```

```
source.hibernate.connection.url=jdbc:postgresql://<db-ip-
address>/sourcedb?schema=public
agent.sources.sql-source.hibernate.connection.user=postgres
agent.sources.sql-source.hibernate.connection.password=<db-
password>
agent.sources.sql-source.table=customer
agent.sources.sql-source.columns.to.select=*
agent.sources.sql-source.status.file.path=<path-for-status-
file>
agent.sources.sql-source.status.file.name=sql-source.status
```

As seen from the above configuration, we are configuring two sources of data in this Flume configuration, i.e. SQL source and SPOOL source.
Please replace the following with specific values as per your environment.

- `<db-password>` with the database password as in your setup.
- `<directory containing the spool file>` with the complete path of directory, should not include the spool file name
- `<db-ip-address>` with the ip address of the PostgreSQL database
- `<path-for-status-file>` with complete path of a directory where status file can be written

3. The next step would be to configure channel, which in this case is Kafka. With Kafka as a channel all the messages would flow into Kafka before the data is ingested into HDFS. Since we have two sources, we will need to configure two channels as shown below (in the same file namely `customer-data-kafkaChannel-flume-conf.properties`):

```
agent.channels = kafkaCustomerLocationLogChannel
kafkaCustomerDBChannel

agent.channels.kafkaCustomerLocationLogChannel.type
=org.apache.flume.channel.kafka.KafkaChannel
agent.channels.kafkaCustomerLocationLogChannel.kafka.bootstrap.
servers=<kafka-broker-ip>:9092
agent.channels.kafkaCustomerLocationLogChannel.kafka.topic=cust
omerLocation
agent.sources.spool-source.channels =
kafkaCustomerLocationLogChannel
agent.channels.kafkaCustomerLocationLogChannel.parseAsFlumeEven
t = true

agent.channels.kafkaCustomerDBChannel.type
=org.apache.flume.channel.kafka.KafkaChannel
agent.channels.kafkaCustomerDBChannel.kafka.bootstrap.servers=<
```

```
kafka-broker-ip>:9092
agent.channels.kafkaCustomerDBChannel.kafka.topic=customer
agent.sources.sql-source.channels = kafkaCustomerDBChannel
```

In the above configuration, please replace `<kafka-broker-ip>` with the IP address of Kafka broker as per your environment. Here we have defined separate topics for each of the data source.

4. Now let us launch the flume process with the following command:

```
${FLUME_HOME}/bin/flume-ng agent --conf ${FLUME_HOME}/conf/  -f
${FLUME_HOME}/conf/customer-data-kafkaChannel-flume-conf.properties  -n
agent -Dflume.root.logger=INFO,console
```

If the above command runs successfully the Spool file would be renamed by appending COMPLETED by the Flume process.

5. As soon as Flume process starts we would observe that messages from both the sources, i.e. database as well as log are streamed into respective Kafka topics for Flink processes to consume. This can be verified with the following commands, that would display the respective queue depths for the topics namely customer and customerLocation.

```
${KAFKA_HOME}/bin/kafka-run-class.sh kafka.tools.GetOffsetShell --
broker-list <kafka-broker-ip>:9092 --topic customer
```

```
${KAFKA_HOME}/bin/kafka-run-class.sh kafka.tools.GetOffsetShell --
broker-list <kafka-broker-ip>:9092 --topic customerLocation
```

Flink Processors

Since we are working with two types of data sources with different data structures, we have streamed them into two different topics respectively. This will require us to build two execution Flink pipelines in Flume that would be working in parallel.

The fundamental code remains the same as in chapter08/flume-example1 in both the cases since the messages are originating from Kafka topic and are then stored in HDFS. But the message types for both have very different structures, hence we will need to modify the Deserialization schema implementation as shown below. The source for this class can be found in chapter08/flink-customer-db project. The class is well documented for easy understanding of its working.

```
public class Tuple2CustomerProfileMessageDeserializationSchema implements
DeserializationSchema {
```

```
private static final ObjectMapper MAPPER = new ObjectMapper();

public Object deserialize(byte[] bytes) throws IOException {
        String message = new String(bytes);
        message=message.replace("\",\"", ",");
        message=message.substring(message.indexOf("\"")+1,
message.lastIndexOf("\""));
        String[] data = message.split(",");
        Customer cust = new Customer();
        cust.setId(Integer.parseInt(data[0]));
        cust.setFirstName(data[1]);
        cust.setLastName(data[2]);
        DateTimeFormatter formatter = DateTimeFormatter.ofPattern("yyyy-MM-
dd");
        LocalDate date = LocalDate.parse(data[3], formatter);
        cust.setDob(java.sql.Date.valueOf(date));
        String customerMessage = MAPPER.writeValueAsString(cust);
        Tuple2<IntWritable, Text> tuple = new Tuple2<IntWritable, Text>();
        tuple.setFields( new IntWritable(cust.getId()), new
Text(customerMessage));
return tuple;
    }

public boolean isEndOfStream(Object o) {
return false;
    }

public TypeInformation<Tuple2<IntWritable, Text>> getProducedType() {
return new TupleTypeInfo<Tuple2<IntWritable,
Text>>(TypeExtractor.createTypeInfo(IntWritable.class),
TypeExtractor.createTypeInfo(Text.class));
    }
}
```

Code 07: Customer Profile Message Deserialization Schema

As shown in the above code, the `customer` datails captured into the `Customer` Object and then serialized into the `Tuple2` object so that it can be written into HDFS. The following arguments should be passed for running the `CustomerDBMessageProcessor` class. Use the below command to execute the class in command prompt:

```
java -cp target/flink-customer-db-1.0-SNAPSHOT.jar
com.laketravels.ch08.ingestor.customer.CustomerDBMessageProcessor --topic
customer --bootstrap.servers <kafka-server-ip>:9092 --zookeeper.connect
<zookeeper-ip>:2181 --group.id 1 --auto.offset.reset earliest
```

If things go well you should see Flink consuming messages from Kafka topic (customer) and persisting into HDFS which can be viewed in HDFS browser within Hue. Similar to the code snippet shows the deserialisation schema for the customer location:

```
public class Tuple2CustomerLocationMessageDeserializationSchema implements
DeserializationSchema {
    private static final ObjectMapper MAPPER = new ObjectMapper();
    public Object deserialize(byte[] bytes) throws IOException {

        //Spooled messages have 2 bytes of leading unicode chars
        String message = new String(bytes, 2, bytes.length-2);
        if (message.trim().length()>0) {
            String[] locationAttributes = message.split(",");
            ObjectNode locationObject = MAPPER.createObjectNode();
            for (String attribute : locationAttributes) {
                String[] attributeElments = attribute.split(":");
                String attributeName = attributeElments[0].replaceAll("""", "");
                String attributeValue = attributeElments[1].replaceAll("""",
                    "");
                locationObject.put(attributeName, attributeValue);
            }
            Tuple2<IntWritable, Text> tuple = new Tuple2<IntWritable,
Text>();
            tuple.setFields(new
IntWritable(locationObject.get("id").asInt()),
                new Text(locationObject.toString()));
            return tuple;
        } else {
            return null;
        }
    }

    public boolean isEndOfStream(Object o) {
        return false;
    }

    public TypeInformation<Tuple2<IntWritable, Text>> getProducedType() {
        return new TupleTypeInfo<Tuple2<IntWritable, Text>>
            (TypeExtractor.createTypeInfo(IntWritable.class),
            TypeExtractor.createTypeInfo(Text.class));
    }
}
```

Code 08: Customer Location Flink Processor Serialization Schema

As shown in the previous code snippet, for customer location message, the deserialization is flexible and will also work even if there are any additional attributes added in the future.

For processing the customer location data via Flink, please pass the following arguments to the `CustomerLocationMessageProcessor` class from `chapter08/flink-customer-log` project folder. Use the below command to execute the class in Command Prompt:

```
java -cp target/flink-customer-log-1.0-SNAPSHOT.jar
com.laketravels.ch08.ingestor.location.CustomerLocationMessageProcessor --
topic customerLocation --bootstrap.servers <KAFKA_SERVER_IP>:9092 --
zookeeper.connect <ZOOKEEPER_IP>:2181 --group.id 1 --auto.offset.reset
earliest
```

We can observe the data written into HDFS via `Namenode Server UI` as shown in the following figure, which can be accessed by opening the URL `http://<hadoop-server-ip>:50070/` and navigating to `Browse the file system` menu option.

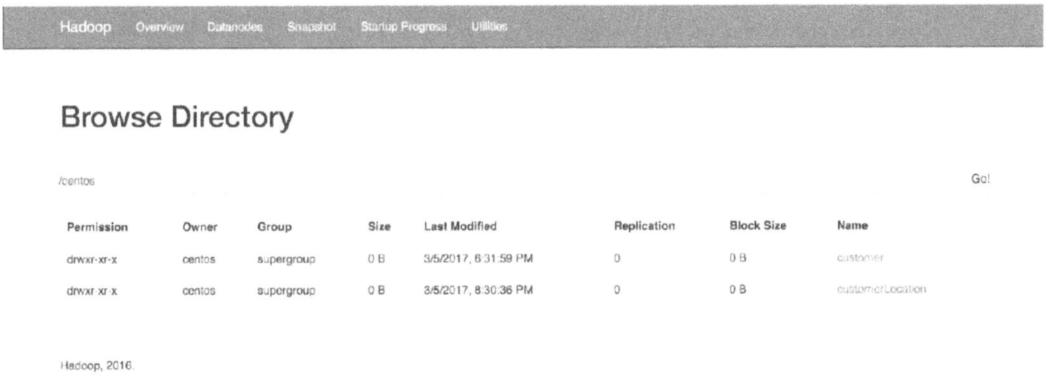

Figure 26: Data From Multiple Sources Stored in HDFS via Flink

The following figure sums up quite well as to how our SCV use case gels with the Flink technology. In our use case, Flink applies appropriate processing of stream data as and when it flows into our Data Lake:

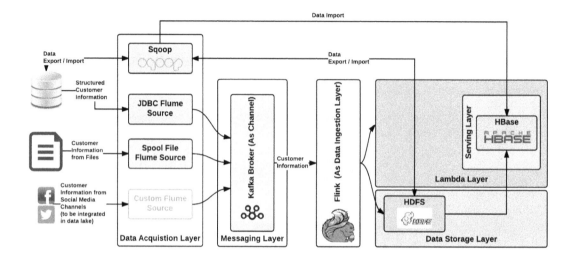

Figure 27: Flink in purview of SCV use case

When to use Flink

Select Flink as your data processing technology when:

- You need high performance. Flink at the moment is one of the best in performance for stream processing.
- Your use case needs machine learning. Flink's native closed loop iterations operators make the processing perform much faster.
- Your use case needs graph processing. Again, because of the preceding same feature, Flink will process data faster.
- You require high throughput rates with guaranteed consistency.
- You need exactly one time processing. This also eliminates duplicate record processing.
- You want to avoid handling memory manually and leave that to the framework. Flink has automatic memory management.

- You need to deal with intermediate results and Flink follows the data flow approach making it easy to do this.
- You need less configuration. Many aspects in Flink are abstracted away from the user and this makes configuration simple.
- You need to deal with both batch and stream data using the same framework. Flink is a hybrid framework capable of dealing with both batch and stream.
- You need different deployment options.

When not to use Flink

Try to avoid using Flink and go for other options when:

- You need a more matured framework compared to other competitors in the same space
- You need more API support apart from the Java and Scala languages

There isn't many disadvantages associated with Apache Flink making it ideal choice for our use case.

Other options

The following figure shows other options which can be considered as alternates to Apache Flink, which is our choice of technology in this space.

Figure 28: Data Processing engine alternates

Apache Spark

If Apache Flink wasn't selected as technology of choice, Apache Spark would have been the most apt choice.

> *Apache Spark is an open-source cluster-computing framework. Originally developed at the University of California, Berkeley's AMPLab, the Spark codebase was later donated to the Apache Software Foundation, which has maintained it since. Spark provides an interface for programming entire clusters with implicit data parallelism and fault-tolerance.*

> *- Wikipedia*

Apache Spark is one of the most well-known data processing technologies in the open source community with a huge user base and contributors. The base working of Apache Spark is based on micro-batching and this is one of the main reasons for choosing Apache Flink as against Spark as this can be one of the problems to cater to many use cases in the future (many use cases require data processing to be in real-time as against micro-batch).

Spark can be deployed and run in multiple topologies and on different technology platforms. It also has integration support with multiple data sources including HDFS, Cassandra, and so on. It's easy to make use of SPark with API's in Java, Scala, Python, and R. This aspect is quite an advantage with Spark as against Flink. It is also highly performant with processing happening with low latency.

Apache Storm

> *Apache Storm is a distributed stream processing computation framework written predominantly in the Clojure programming language. Originally created by Nathan Marz and team at BackType, the project was open sourced after being acquired by Twitter. It uses custom created "spouts" and "bolts" to define information sources and manipulations to allow batch, distributed processing of streaming data. The initial release was on 17 September 2011.*

> *- Wikipedia*

Storm is an open source real-time data processing framework and it can be worked with any programming language. Storm like Spark and Flink is distributed, high-performing, and fault-tolerant and also supports message delivery guarantees. Storm integrates with many technologies with ease, making it apt for implementing many use cases.

Apache Tez

Apache Tez is an extensible framework for building high performance batch and interactive data processing applications, coordinated by YARN in Apache Hadoop. Tez improves the MapReduce paradigm by dramatically improving its speed, while maintaining MapReduce's ability to scale to petabytes of data. Important Hadoop ecosystem projects like Apache Hive and Apache Pig use Apache Tez, as do a growing number of third party data access applications developed for the broader Hadoop ecosystem.

- hortonworks.com (`http://hortonworks.com/apache/tez/`)

Apache Tez is designed for Yarn on top of Hadoop 2. Tez is designed for high performance, functioning at low latency mainly for processing. Tez is developed with extensibility in mind and allows us to plugin many technologies for data transfer use cases quite easily. One of the main reasons for the evolution of this framework is taking away the limitations imposed by native MapReduce. Since Hadoop is still the core at any big data technology, Tez can be quite handy in that case as it natively supports HDFS.

Summary

In this chapter, as with any other chapter in this part of the book, we started with introducing the layer where the technology would fall. Then we introduced the chosen technology in this layer, namely Apache Flink. We slowly went into the details of Apache Flink. Its architecture was elaborated and many core aspects of this all-important framework were covered in brief. We then got our hands dirty with an actual implementation of Apache Flink technology pertaining to our use case--SCV. We finally explained when to use and when not to use Flink, and closed the chapter with alternatives to Apache Flink.

After reading this chapter, you should have a fair idea of the Data Ingestion layer and the full working and functioning of Apache Flink. Now you also know about Flink's architecture along with its core components and working. You should have also got hands-on working experience with Flink and a high-level view of the alternatives to Flink.

9
Data Store Using Apache Hadoop

We acquired data, then we processed data, and now we will have to store this data. This chapter aims at covering this all important aspect of the Data Lake.

One of the core principles that we will follow in our Data Lake implementation is to store all the data as is in the lake as against storing only processed or sanitized data. This is key as data that is not significant today can become significant at a later stage and, during that time, we can make use of this stored raw data.

In this chapter, like other chapters in this part of the book, we will start off by introducing the layer and then go into technology mapping. After that, we will delve deeply into the chosen technology and then ensure that you are introduced to all the important aspects of this technology.

As the title of this chapter says, the chosen technology is Apache Hadoop, for storing non-indexed data in raw format for our Data Lake. We will, as with the other chapters, start with reasons for choosing this technology in this layer and then go in-depth on its architecture. We will then go into its various architecture components and tools then make it our choice. We will then get your hands dirty with a walk through of the actual code and data store layer implementation. Finally, we will cover some other options/alternatives that you can choose instead of Hadoop, and we will also give a final picture of our SCV use case implementation.

Get ready, let's persist data that we have got in hand.

Context for Data Lake - Data Storage and lambda Batch layer

In our Data Lake implementation, we have a dedicated layer where the data permanently resides and this is the Data Storage Layer. The data gathered from various sources is persisted in various stores capable of handling different types and forms of data. In this chapter, we are storing non-indexed raw data in our Data Lake.

We have chosen Apache Hadoop as our technology for this data storage capability. I am sure there was not much debate when we chose this technology in this layer, obviously because of the fantastic features this technology. Also, the level of maturity and support this technology possesses is quite astonishing over the short span of its existence.

The following sections of this chapter aim at covering Hadoop in detail so that you get a clear picture of this technology as well as get to know the data storage layer in detail.

Data Storage and the Lambda Batch Layer

In Chapter 2, *Comprehensive Concepts of a Data Lake,* you got a glimpse into the data storage layer. This layer's responsibility is to persist gathered data into a permanent place in our Data Lake. The Lambda Batch Layer's responsibility is to create batch views for the data stored in the Data Storage layer. The following figure will refresh your memory and give you a good pictorial view of this layer:

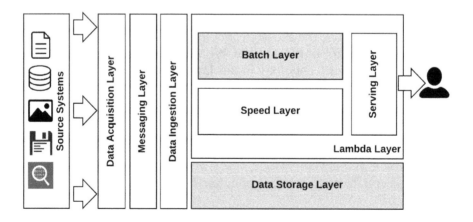

Figure 01: Data Lake - Data Storage and Lambda Batch Layer

The Data Storage Layer is one of the very important layers, which should persist different types of raw data coming from different source systems, and it also should be easy to scale according to need. It's very important for this layer to have a defined **IOPS** (see info) as this can be one of the deciding factors of how much and how frequently the data from the source system can be taken into the data lake. For unstructured data, Hadoop is one of the de-facto technologies used for this purpose. There are other mechanisms, such as NoSQL (see info) and NewSQL (see info).

> **Input/output operations per second** (IOPS, pronounced **eye-ops**) is a performance measurement used to characterize computer storage devices, such as hard disk drives (HDDs), **Solid State Drives** (**SSDs**), and **Storage Area Networks** (**SANs**).

> A NoSQL (originally referring to non-SQL, non relational, or not only SQL) database provides a mechanism for the storage and retrieval of data, which is modeled by means other than the tabular relations used in relational databases.
>
> NewSQL is a class of modern relational database management systems that seek to provide the same scalable performance of NoSQL systems for **online transaction processing** (**OLTP**) read-write workloads while still maintaining the ACID guarantees of a traditional database system.

- Wikipedia

The storage layer should be able to handle the following:

- Support for a wide variety of analytics tool to be bound on top of it for various queries
- Different types of data in different modes (batch and real-time)
- Different formats of data, such as structured, unstructured, and semi-structured data, with ease
- Different scaling requirements
- Various compression methodologies for efficient persistence and efficiency
- Different data velocities (KB per second, MB per second, and so on)
- Different querying mechanism and language capabilities for extracting relevant data out of the lake for various analysis, as the case may be

Data Storage and Lambda Batch Layer - technology mapping

To cover our use case and to build the Data Lake, we use multiple stores. This chapter aims at covering storage mechanism for non-indexed raw data. This chapter delve deeply into Hadoop, which is our choice for this capability.

The following figure brings in the technology aspects of the conceptual architecture that we will be following throughout this book. We will keep explaining each technology and its relevance in the overall architecture before we bring all the technologies together in the final part of this book (*part 3*):

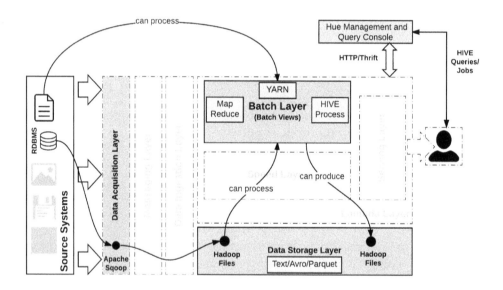

Figure 02: Technology mapping for Data Storage and Lambda Batch Layer

For our use case, SCV, we have already gathered data from various source system data stores, and we will just be persisting these raw data in Hadoop, as shown in the preceding figure.

The subsequent sections of this chapter give more details on Hadoop and will make you conversant with many important components of the Hadoop architecture.

What is Apache Hadoop?

Before going into Hadoop in detail, let's give you a high-level idea of what Hadoop is. This is the approach we have followed, and let's stick to that pattern for consistency.

Apache Hadoop is a framework capable of using a cluster of computers (need not be a server range but can be normal computers that you use in day-to-day life) to do distributed computing and also to store large amount of varied formats of data. Yes, you read it correctly, it can also be used for computing and this aspect is one of the fundamental aspects of Hadoop. We will be using Hadoop's computing aspect, but a more important aspect of Hadoop that we will use is its capability for distributed data storage.

Due to its sheer capabilities and popularity, Hadoop has embedded itself in the technology stack of almost all organizations, and we are sure your organization will already have this, making it easy for the Data Lake implementation using this as a store.

Why Hadoop?

For me, the question *Why Hadoop?* is not really a question. In the industry as of now, for big data Apache Hadoop is indispensable. There are alternatives, but most of them work in conjunction with Hadoop. Listed here are some of the prominent reasons why Hadoop is technology of choice for the technical capability that we are looking for in a Data Lake implementation:

- It can handle high volumes of structured, semi-structured, and unstructured data with ease.
- It is less costly to implement as it can start off using commodity hardware and scale according to organization all requirement.
- It has the ever growing Apache community to support it with frequent releases, releasing bug fixes and enhancements alike. Hadoop, as you know, has two core layers, namely the compute and data (HDFS) layers. The compute layer adds new frameworks and libraries, such as Pig and Hive, on top of the Hadoop ecosystem, making Hadoop all the more relevant for many use cases.
- The library of Hadoop itself is built with availability in mind and is not reliant on underlying hardware to do this capability. This is quite useful for organizations starting to build a Hadoop-based data lake from commodity hardwares as a start.
- It's flexible to handle a wide variety of data, and this is because of Hadoop's inherent schema-less capability of handling data.
- Recently, with the ever-growing Hadoop ecosystem, Hadoop is becoming more real-time as against its conventional batch data operation.

- Hadoop is inherently cloud capable, so hosting a full-fledged Hadoop in cloud is simple to implement and more cost-effective for organizations taking baby steps in the direction of big data and Data Lake.
- It has built-in robust and fault-tolerance.
- It has a very good compute layer, making it ideal for intensive computations required for deriving meaningful analytic requirements.
- It has a high speed of execution. It can handle complex computational logic quite easily.
- It runs on the majority of operating systems, such as Linux, Mac, Windows, and Solaris.

History of Hadoop

Doug Cutting, after getting inspiration from Google's MapReduce (published in 2004, where an application is broken down into multiple blocks/fragments and then run on multiple nodes belonging to the same cluster), created this framework and named it Hadoop (in 2006), after his child's stuffed yellow elephant toy. According to him, the name was short, unique, and relatively easy to spell and pronounce. In the same year (2006), Doug joined Yahoo and in the year 2008, he created a Hadoop cluster comprising of 4,000 nodes in Yahoo, using which Yahoo breaks the TeraByte sort benchmark (http://sortbenc hmark.org/). The following figure explains Hadoop's history in a more readable and pictorial fashion:

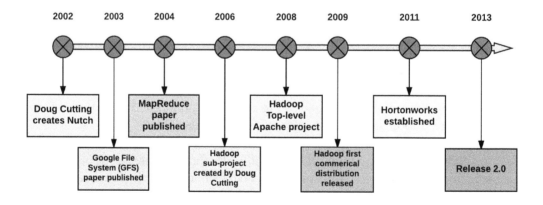

Figure 03: Apache Hadoop's brief history

Let's decipher the preceding figure in more detail. *Doug* Cutting (creator of Hadoop), in the year 2002, created **Nutch**, which is a crawl and search system. In the year 2003, *Sanjay Ghemawat*, *Howard Gobioff*, and *Shun Tak Leung* published the **Google File System** (**GFS**) paper. Following that publication, *Sanjay Ghemawat* and *Jeffrey Dean* published another paper (MapReduce: Simplified Data Processing on Large Cluster) in the year 2004. Doug rearchitected the Nutch project inspired by MapReduce paper and, in the year 2006, created the Hadoop sub-project. *Owen O'Malley* was the first committer added to the Hadoop project in 2006. Hadoop 0.1.0 was released in April 2006. In 2008, Hadoop became a top-level project in **Apache Software Foundation (ASF)** and in 2009, Hadoop's first commercial distribution was released. In 2011, Hortonworks was established by Rob Bearden partnering with Yahoo, including key Hadoop team members, namely *Arun Murthy*, *Devaraj Das*, *Sanjay Radia*, *Suresh Srinivas*, *Alan Gates*, and all-important *Owen O'Malley*.

Advantages of Hadoop

The *Why Hadoop?* section covered some of the reasons we chose Hadoop, which are in turn the core advantages. The following list reiterates those points with much more in-depth details and coverage in a crisp and easy-to-read manner:

- **Scalability:** It is capable of handling a huge volume and variety of data. You can add more nodes to keep handling more data (linearly scalable).
- **Flexibility:** There is no structured schema (schema-less). It is capable of handling different types of data (big data *V*, namely Variety).
- **High performance:** It is capable of high performance for these huge volumes of data.
- **Low cost:** It is capable of running on commodity hardware, making it a less costly prospect for implementation. It's open source with a vibrant community, so things keep moving, and it is never stagnant.
- **Advanced analytics:** It is capable of the high computing output needed for producing advanced analytics.
- **Large ecosystem:** Hadoop ecosystem, especially its computing layer, is growing at a rapid pace with the introduction of new open source projects in an ongoing manner.
- **Data warehouse:** It a good alternative to a data warehouse for an organization with lots of flexibility built in.
- **Capablility:** It is capable of handling or catering to a wide variety of organizational and important use cases, such as sentiment analysis, click stream behavioral data analysis, and fraud detection.

Disadvantages of Hadoop

Hadoop's advantages outweigh its disadvantages; it does suffer from disadvantages, which are listed here:

- Hadoop stores data in chunks and, because of this, reading data will have to be done by querying the whole file. This can make random data access problematic with Hadoop as the data store.
- If your data is small (in our case, it isn't), usage of Hadoop can be troublesome or will not reap the benefits envisaged.
- Execution of advanced algorithms, which demands more specific hardware requirements, can be problematic using Hadoop.
- Getting niche/skilled people was a problem early on, but this skill is increasing in the market day by day. However, this is still an issue rolling out the Hadoop ecosystem in an organization.
- Security issues/concerns exist as Hadoop was not thought through with enterprise-grade security in mind. So, this tends to be when Hadoop is used to store enterprise-grade customer information (**PII** - see the following information box).
- Deficiency in tooling is again improving, but this is still a problem as many aspects have to be still handcoded (skills come into play here as well).
- Hadoop runs on commodity hardware, but to make it enterprise-grade, the organization invests in costly hardware. So, even though it is less costly theoretically, it is considered costly for enterprises.

 Personally identifiable information (PII), or **sensitive personal information** (**SPI**), as used in information security and privacy laws, is information that can be used on its own or with other information to identify, contact, or locate a single person, or to identify an individual in context.

- Wikipedia

Working of Hadoop

Let's now see the internals of Hadoop and its components, it's architecture, and how it works in this section. We will start off by understanding some of Hadoop's core architecture principles, and then we will explain its architecture and important components in detail.

Hadoop core architecture principles

Hadoop was built and conceived with well-defined architecture goals and principles, as listed here, (the following are in no way authoritative as we can't find one; rather we gathered this from `https://goo.gl/3nvER1`):

- **Linear scalability** (Scale-Out rather than Scale-Up): Add more nodes for scalability to increase data storage and computing power.
- **Bring code to data rather than data to code**: In big data, data is usually huge and code working on data is small. So, this principle states that bring or distribute code to the nodes/machines where it can act on data and not distribute or move data. In essence, it means minimize data transfer and distribute code instead.
- **Deal with failures as they are common**: Bring reliability and fault-tolerance by actually anticipating and dealing with these situations.
- **Simple computational model**: Reliability and fault-tolerance demands distribution and concurrency; hide these details from the user and give an abstracted layer to deal with it. This is one of the main reasons for the high adoption of Hadoop.
- **Sequential data processing**: Avoid random access reads.
- **Auto managing**: Manage many aspects common to distributed applications/framework automatically, rather than depending on manual intervention.
- **Parallel processing**: By default, embrace parallel processing in an automated fashion.

Scale-Out (Horizontal Scaling) refers to adding more nodes/machines having less memory and processing power. Considered less costly and cheaper option, it is a more practical option.

Scale-Up (Vertical Scaling) refers to adding more memory and processing power to the existing node/server. This, in general, is considered costly as against the scale-out option. It is a less practical option over a period of time and can cause a maintenance havoc.

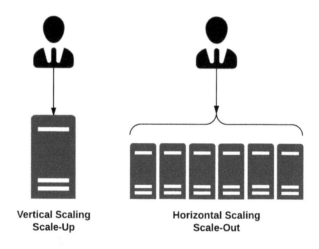

Vertical Scaling
Scale-Up

Horizontal Scaling
Scale-Out

Figure 04: Scale-Up and Scale-Out architectures

Hadoop architecture

Let's get into Hadoop's architecture. We are covering both the Hadoop 1.x and Hadoop 2.x versions to give you in context and evolution of this wonderful framework. In our use case implementation and example, we are using the Hadoop 2.x version.

Hadoop architecture 1.x

It's important to know that there was Hadoop first generation, many aspects were bundled and performed by the MapReduce component, such as resource management, job scheduling, and job processing. To address this aspect, Hadoop second generation was envisaged and is used widely now. To understand the Hadoop 2.x architecture, it's good to know the basics of the Hadoop 1.x architecture and that's what we will do in a very brief fashion in this section.

The following figure shows the conceptual architecture of the Hadoop 1.x framework:

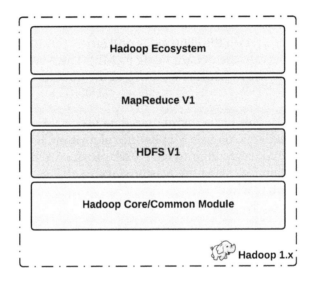

Figure 05: High-level Hadoop 1.x conceptual architecture

Let's delve deeply into each of the components in the preceding figure from the bottom up:

- **Hadoop Core/Common Module**: It contains the base Hadoop API used by all the preceding components. Hadoop is written in Java, so these are packaged along with Hadoop as a JAR file (see the following information box). This is a mandatory component required for other components to work and contains reusable code and utilities.

- **HDFS** (V1): This is short for Hadoop Distributed File System. It's important to note that in Hadoop 1.x, V1 of HDFS is being used. It's also referred to as HDFS V1, and we will be using this name further in this book. This is the core component responsible for giving Hadoop the distributed storage functionality. It has a default block size of 64 MB, which can be flexibly changed according to your use case. HDFS V1 is divided into two sub-components:
  - NameNode
  - DataNode

It's important to know that being distributed in nature, it does have the concept of Master-Slave. In HDFS V1, the NameNode exists in the master node and is responsible for storing metadata for the successful working of Hadoop.

The DataNode resides on the slave node and stores the application's data in blocks defined by size (the default being 64 MB). The NameNode stores metadata such as how many slave nodes there are and the number of blocks in each data node.

- **MapReduce** (V1): This is the distributed data processing system in the Hadoop framework. Based on Google's MapReduce algorithm, it is also known as **MRV1** or Classic MapReduce. Similar to HDFS, MapReduce also has two sub-components, again following the master-slave model, as follows:
  - **JobTracker**
  - **TaskTracker**

Very much similar to the HDFS component, **JobTracker** resides in the Master node and **TaskTracker** in the Slave node. JobTracker, as the name suggests, assigns tasks to the TaskTracker and also records and maintains the status of each of the TaskTrackers. TaskTracker, on the other hand, executes the assigned tasks and sends the status back to JobTracker after execution.

- **Hadoop Ecosystem**: All the various Hadoop external tools and libraries work on top of these core components: HDFS V1 and MapReduce V1.

 A JAR file is a **Java archive (JAR)** file used by the **Java Runtime Environment (JRE)**, a framework used for executing Java programs. JAR files may serve as program libraries or as standalone programs that run if the JRE is installed on the computer or mobile device.

- https://fileinfo.com

The following figure shows a more detailed Hadoop 1.x conceptual architecture inline with the detailed explanation given earlier:

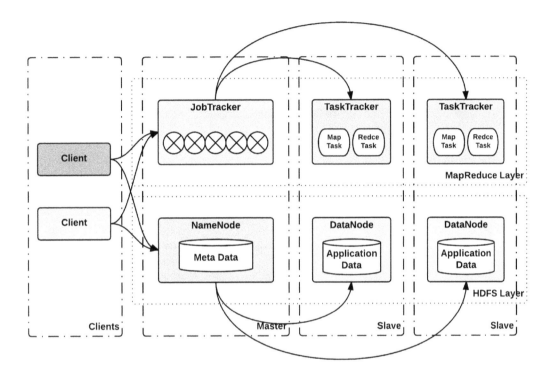

Figure 06: Low-level Hadoop 1.x conceptual architecture

The preceding figure is quite self-explanatory. As you would have already understood, both the master and slave nodes have two core components: HDFS V1 and MapReduce V1. According to the master and slave node, various sub-components within these core components become active and take effect for the full functioning of Hadoop. The slave node's HDFS sub-component, TaskTracker, contains two tasks, namely **Map Task** and **Reduce Task**, inline with the MapReduce algorithm.

Hadoop architecture 2.x

We hope that by now you understand the Hadoop 1.x architecture; let's dive into the version that we will be using in our book, which is Hadoop 2.7.3 (2.x).

The following figure shows the various components of the Hadoop 2.x architecture at a high level:

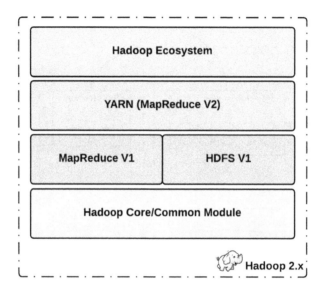

Figure 07: High-level Hadoop 2.x conceptual architecture

The core aspects of the Hadoop 2.x architecture are very much similar to the Hadoop 1.x architecture. As shown in the preceding figure, the main components in the Hadoop architecture are as follows:

- **Hadoop Core/Common Module**: As detailed earlier, it refers to the core modules in the form of a JAR file that all the other modules depend on and make use of to accomplish their core functionality.
- **HDFS** (V2): HDFS V1 with some enhanced features constitutes HDFS V2.
- **YARN** (MR V2): This stands for **Yet Another Resource Negotiator** and forms one of the core components, which is a differentiator from its predecessor.
- **MapReduce** (V1): The same component used in Hadoop 1.x is taken along in Hadoop 2.x architecture as well. However, in Hadoop 2.x, it does the job of data processing and all the rest is offloaded into the mighty hands of YARN.
- **Hadoop Ecosystem**: The Hadoop ecosystem works on top of these explained core components.

Having got an initial high-level explanation for each of the components, it's time to delve deeply into each of the components and to arrive at the Hadoop Architecture in detail. From now on, we will only discuss Hadoop 2.x, so we will not explicitly mention the version; rather it will be termed as Hadoop.

For comparison purposes, the following figure lays both the Hadoop 1.x and Hadoop 2.x architecture components side by side:

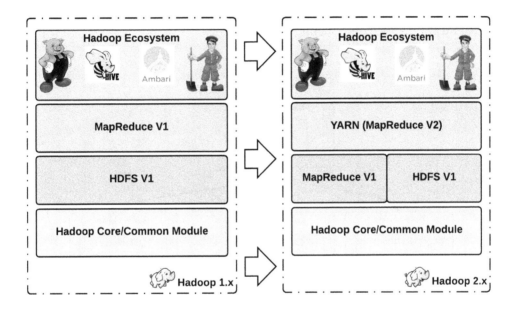

Figure 08: Hadoop 1.x and 2.x side by side

Let's now detail each of the core components of Hadoop 2.x. At the end, we will explain the Hadoop 2.x architecture in detail similarly to what we have for Hadoop 1.x.

Hadoop architecture components

Let's delve into each component of Hadoop in this section.

HDFS

As detailed earlier, Hadoop follows the Master-Slave architecture pattern for both data storage and computing. For data storage, it uses HDFS as the main component. Two sub-components, namely NameNode and DataNode, are present in master and slave nodes respectively. The DataNode stores the application data and NameNode stores the filesystem metadata. The communication between NameNode and DataNode is through TCP-based protocols and is quite reliable and high-performant.

The following figure shows the Master-Slave architecture used in HDFS, with the NameNode and DataNode components:

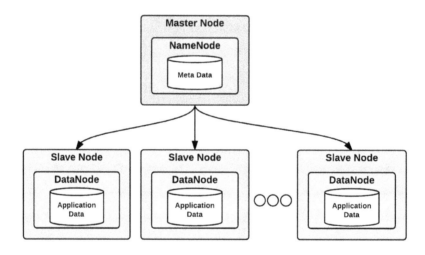

Figure 09: Master-Slave architecture of HDFS showing NameNode and DataNode

HDFS, in working, is a distributed filesystem similar to the **Google File System** (**GFS**). The application data is split into multiple blocks of a fixed size (64 MB by default, but can be configured according to requirement) and then distributed to multiple nodes in the Hadoop cluster, making adequate data replication according to the replication factor setup in the cluster. This replication makes Hadoop fault-tolerant and reliable.

The HDFS filesystem allows you to write once, and random writes are forbidden. Also, HDFS is not good for random data access inherently, but is highly optimized for streaming reads of files.

YARN

A handy addition to Hadoop (as against Hadoop 1.x) is the resource negotiator YARN, enabling Hadoop to utilize resources in a dynamic fashion, allowing applications to do the job rather than figuring out their impact on the resources. It allows Hadoop to effectively and efficiently use each of the nodes in a cluster. YARN in Hadoop 2.x is also called MR V2 (MapReduce V2).

The following figure shows YARN's architecture and its components in detail along with how it works:

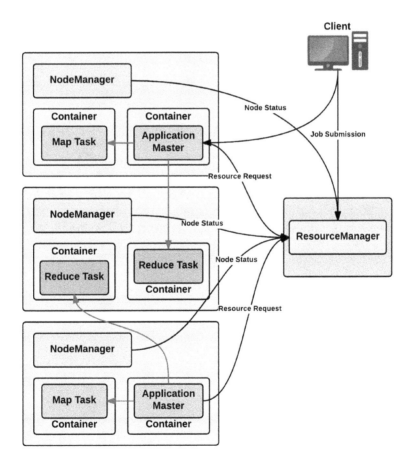

Figure 10: YARN (MR V2) architecture showing off its components

These are the important components constituting the YARN architecture:

- **ResourceManager** (**RM**): This is the main agent that manages resources from within the cluster nodes and them allocates accordingly. It is entrusted with managing cluster resources efficiently and is the Master node of YARN and the real negotiator. ResourceManager has two sub-components, namely the following:
  - Application Manager
  - Scheduler caters to scheduler requirements for applications, monitors them, and then tracks them
- **NodeManager** (**NM**): Each node has one NodeManager and resources within a node are allocated and handled. It's considered as the Slave node of YARN. It accepts requests from Resource Manager and reports back on the health and resources of the nodes.
- **ApplicationMaster** (**AM**): ApplicationMaster exists for each application, and is entrusted with the application life cycle, and it's task allocation and execution.

MapReduce

One of the important paradelvems on which the Hadoop framework processes large datasets is using the MapReduce programming model. Again, MapReduce also uses the master-slave concept, in which the input file is first broken into smaller ones and then each piece is fed to worker nodes, which process (map task) the data and then the master collects it (reduce task) and sends it back. This is depicted in a pictorial fashion in the following figure:

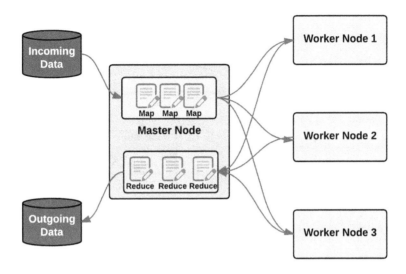

Figure 11: Working of MapReduce programming model in Hadoop

As shown in the preceding figure, **Map** sends the queries (code to data) to the nodes and then reduce collects the results and collates and sends them back. YARN does the parallel processing job here, and MapReduce gives a framework by which to distribute the code (query) across multiple nodes for execution/processing. MapReduce is a Java-based programming model inspired from Google.

Hadoop ecosystem

Hadoop ecosystem has a section by itself as there is so much to cover under that heading. The next main heading covers on this subject.

Hadoop architecture in detail

We have now detailed each of the components in Hadoop in detail in the previous section. Now, it's time to discuss the Hadoop 2.x architecture in detail, looking at each of its components and sub-components.

The next figure delves into each component and sub-component in the Hadoop 2.x architecture in detail:

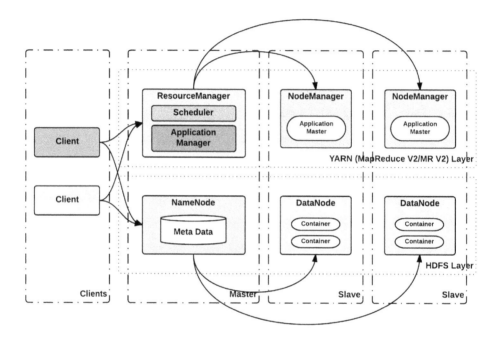

Figure 12: Low-level Hadoop 2.x conceptual architecture

The primary challenge that Hadoop 2.x solved over the Hadoop1 framework was around removing a single point of failure, which was the **NameNode** in Hadoop 1.x.

This has been achieved by the inclusion of the YARN framework as part of Hadoop 2.x. As seen from the preceding architecture, the ResourceManager manages the applications and also contains a scheduler for job management. The resource manager works in coordination with **NodeManager** (which is per machine agent). **NodeManager** is responsible for containers, resource monitoring, and reporting for the specific machine. This information is used by **ResourceManager** to allocate and distribute resources across all the applications. The Application Master is a per-application process that negotiates resources with **ResourceManager** and works with NodeManager to execute and monitor tasks. The scheduler is responsible for the allocation of resources to various applications based on their resource requirements. A scheduler does not perform any role for status tracking or monitoring of the applications. The **ApplicationManager** manages job submissions and failure recovery in coordination with Application Master.

With this architecture in place, the single point of failure is completely eliminated with critical dependency on NameNode of job management taken up by the YARN framework in Hadoop 2.x.

Hadoop ecosystem

Apart from the core components, Hadoop contains many tools and libraries existing on top of the core, collectively called the Hadoop ecosystem.

The following figure just lists a few commonly-used frameworks constituting the Hadoop ecosystem:

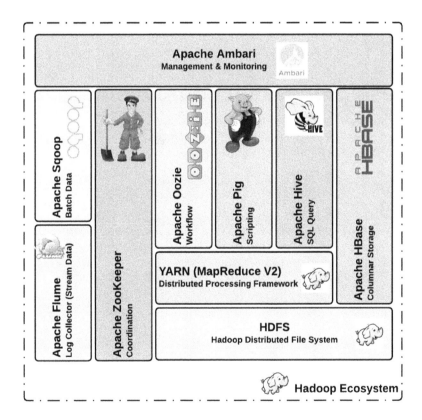

Figure 13: Hadoop Ecosystem (a few important components shown)

The following section tries to categorize these frameworks on top of Hadoop according to its core capability and briefly explains them. Getting into the details of each one is not possible and the section is intended for a skim knowledge so that you are well aware of Hadoop's capabilities and choices.

The following section covers various frameworks in the Hadoop ecosystem, categorizing each into a capability. The various capabilities are these:

- Data access/processing components
- Data storage components
- Monitoring, management, and orchestration components
- Data integration components

Apart from the components discussed, there are many components created and managed by the open source community, but the ones discussed are the more prominent and widely known ones.

Data access/processing components

Components in Hadoop ecosystem, which allow us to access and process data stored in HDFS by having a component on top of HDFS, fall into this category. Let's discuss some of the very well-known components and see how they works.

Apache Pig

Apache Pig is a platform developed by Yahoo for data access and processing, which works on top of HDFS dealing with large datasets. Pig has two components, namely these:

- A high-level data flow language, called **Pig Latin**, which has a SQL-like command structure
- Pig runtime, where the Pig Latin language gets executed

A Pig job abstracts the MapReduce complexity, fires the MapReduce job in the background and executes it in a sequential manner. Apart from MapReduce, Pig's Hadoop job can be executed with **Apache Tez** and Apache Spark. Pig gives Hadoop Ecosystem a data flow capability abstracting ETL-like functionality away from the user. It allows us to extract a large dataset from HDFS, then allows it to do necessary functions (such as grouping and filtering), and then either persists the results back to HDFS or dumps the results back, as demanded by your use case. Pig's data flow language provides extensibility by allowing its users to write a **User Defined Function** (**UDF**), using which the user can write the required functionality in a variety of languages, namely Groovy, Python, Java, JavaScript, and Ruby.

The following figure shows the basic working of Apache Pig:

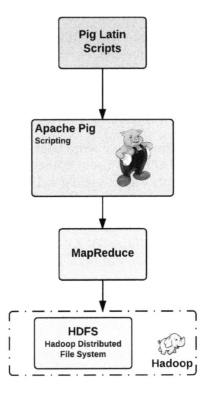

Figure 14: Working of Apache Pig

One of the more common use-cases that can be performed using Apache Pig is to search and mask confidential data in a large dataset stored in HDFS.

For more details, refer to the **Apache Pig** documentation at `http://pig.apache.org/docs/r0.16.0/`.

Apache Hive

Apache Hive was created by Facebook, and provides data warehouse capability on top of Hadoop. Its main capability is data summarization and ad-hoc query execution on Hadoop.

Hive contains two components, namely these:

- **Hive Command Line**: An interface used to execute HiveQL
- **JDBC (Java DataBase Connectivity)/ODBC (Object DataBase Connectivity)** driver: This is to establish connectivity to the data storage

Query execution is done through uses of **Hive Query Language (HQL or HiveQL)**, very much similar to SQL. Query results produced are performant and real time using various indexing capabilities. Apache Hive is capable of batch and real-time data processing alike.

Similar to Apache Pig, Hive also allows you to write **User Defined Function (UDF), User Defined Aggregate Functions (UDAF)**, and **User Defined Table Functions (UDTF)** to cater to your specific use-case requirements. Again, similar to Pig, query execution can use MapReduce, Apache Spark, and Apache Tez, as required by the user.

Apache Hive is not a suitable candidate for **OnLine Transaction Processing (OLTP)**, rather it is more suited for warehousing capabilities (**OLAP--OnLine Analytical Processing**). It is, however, capable of handling huge datasets of the scale of petabytes quite easily.

The main use case that Hive supports lies in ad-hoc data analysis and reporting. It does have very good support for well-known BI tools, such as **MicroSTRategy (MSTR)**, **Tableau and BO (Business Objects)**.

For more details, refer to the **Apache Hive** documentation at `http://hive.apache.org/`.

Data storage components

Components in Hadoop ecosystem that allow us to store data and to execute a query by giving an abstraction fall into this category. Let's discuss some very well-known components and see how they work.

Apache HBase

Apache HBase is the Data storage component on top of Hadoop using HDFS as the storage. HBase is non-relational (NoSQL) and distributed in nature and belongs to column family oriented database. It is good for random reads and batch operations. HBase is capable of handling large datasets with millions of rows and columns.

Apache HBase is modeled after **Google's Bigtable** and is considered one of the best implementations of it in the industry and internally, it is a sorted map in implementation.

HBase has multiple APIs, the main one being the Java API. In addition to this, it also has the REST (for HTTP access) and Thrift (for other language programming access) APIs.

HBase is quite useful for handling use cases dealing with real-time data analysis; also, it is very good for real-time data monitoring. In our examples, we are using the 1.1.8 version of HBase.

For more details, refer to the Apache HBase documentation at `http://hbase.apache.org/`.

Monitoring, management and orchestration components

Components in Hadoop ecosystem that allows us to monitor, manage, and orchestrate many moving parts in Hadoop fall into this category. Let's discuss some very well-known components and see how they work.

Apache ZooKeeper

Apache ZooKeeper is a popular open source Distributed Coordination service. It can work as a centralized service capable of doing many operations such as configuration management and other common coordination services required for a distributed systems.

ZooKeeper works with a group of servers (an odd number ideally), commonly known as an ensemble. When the ensemble is started, one of the servers is elected as leader and the others automatically become followers. The data residing in each server (so-called state) is broadcasted, because of which each server has an up-to-date state with it. After leader election, all the write requests are routed to the leader and all the followers get the data from the chosen leader server. If due to any reason a leader perishes, a new leader is elected and continues its operation. A client connects to only one server in the ensemble. The client establishes a connection with the ZooKeeper service and all requests are sent through this session connected via the TCP protocol. The ZooKeeper session orders the incoming requests and follows **FIFO** (**First In First Out**) pattern (Queue). The following figure shows the basic working of ZooKeeper:

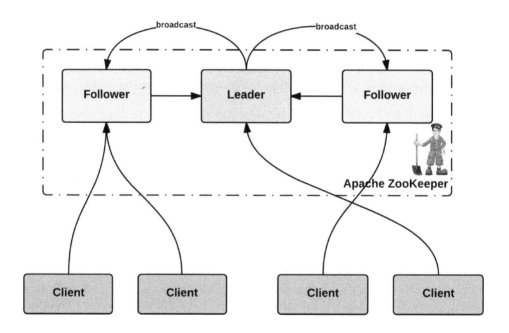

Figure 15: Working of Apache ZooKeeper

Many well-known projects use ZooKeeper for the distributed coordination service capability. Some of them are as follows:

- Apache YARN
- Apache HBase

- Apache Kafka
- Neo4j

For more details, refer to the **Apache ZooKeeper** documentation at `https://zookeeper.ap ache.org/`.

Apache Oozie

Apache Oozie is an open source Java-based web application used for pipeline creation, and it is well integrated with the Hadoop stack.

Oozie can be used to schedule and run Oozie jobs in a Hadoop cluster. It can combine small jobs into more complex ones and can do this according to the pipeline configured to achieve the required use case. Oozie triggers the configured workflow and leverages the Hadoop engine to execute the individual jobs in the workflow.

Job completion of Oozie tasks is detected by two mechanisms, namely, callback and polling. When a job is configured, a callback URL can be configured, which is invoked when the job is completed.

This figure shows the basic working of Oozie:

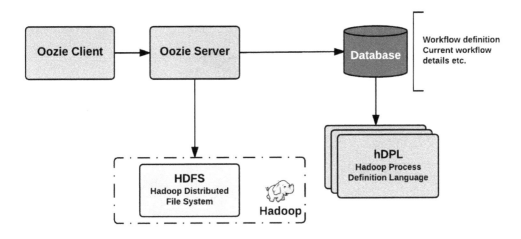

Figure 16: Basic working of Oozie

The Oozie client invokes the server that stores the workflow definitions and job execution details in a database along with the execution details of a triggered Oozie task. The database also holds the status and URL callbacks for all the jobs in the workflow. The Oozie server then uses the Hadoop engine for actual execution of the jobs and receives callback triggers when the jobs are completed and when the whole workflow is completed.

For more details, refer to Apache Oozie documentation at `http://oozie.apache.org/`.

Apache Ambari

Apache Ambari is a software project of the Apache Software Foundation. Ambari enables system administrators to provision, manage, and monitor a Hadoop cluster, and also to integrate Hadoop with the existing enterprise infrastructure. Ambari was a sub-project of Hadoop, but it is now a top-level project in its own right.

- Wikipedia

The following figure shows the basic working of Apache Ambari:

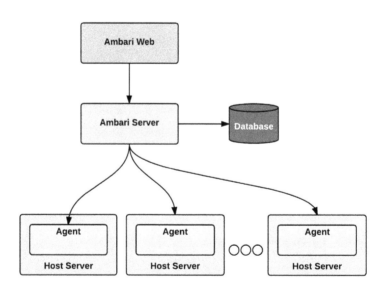

Figure 17: Apache Ambari architecture

It operates on the client-server model in which the Ambari server exposes various RESTful endpoints that are consumed and used for various pages in the Ambari web application. Users interact with Ambari using this Web UI. Each node in the Hadoop cluster is installed with Ambari Agent, which sends and stores data in the Ambari server. Monitoring in Ambari leverages two open source technologies, namely Ganglia and Nagios.

For more details, refer to Apache Ambari documentation at `https://ambari.apache.org/`.

Data integration components

Components in Hadoop ecosystem that allow us to integrate Hadoop with other data stores in other technologies (legacy) fall into this category. Let's discuss some very well-known components and see how they work.

Apache Sqoop

We have already covered Apache Sqoop in detail in `Chapter 5`, *Data Acquisition of Batch Data with Apache Sqoop*, so we don't want to repeat ourselves here in any manner.

For more details, you can also refer to Apache Sqoop documentation at `http://sqoop.apache.org/`.

Apache Flume

Again, Apache Flume has already been covered quite extensively in `Chapter 6`, *Data Acquisition of Stream Data with Apache Flume*. Again, we really don't want any sort of repetition.

For more details, refer to the Apache Flume documentation at `http://flume.apache.org/`.

Hadoop distributions

One of the first technologies in the open source world to deal with big data for use cases apart from the mining and searching was Hadoop. Hadoop put big data into the hands of enterprises to deal with the so called data existing within the organization.

Being open source, there is a huge community base and backing from big enterprises. The same is the case with Apache Hadoop and earlier, Hadoop distribution was released by Cloudera in 2008. Every distributor adds on many features and also enriches or enhances existing features, making it more attractive for people to adopt and use.

Cloudera is still the most widely used distribution of Hadoop. MapR soon followed by releasing its Hadoop distribution in 2009 and in 2011, Hortonworks released its own distribution. These three players control by far the largest part of the market share at this time.

These distributions not only enhance the existing features; they also try to and integrate many open source products to produce a whole bundle ideal for any enterprise to purchase and use along with enterprise-grade support. Also, these distributions hide the complexities of various versions and upgrade the process, making it easy for implementation.

Some of the features for enterprises from these distributions are as listed:

- Easy upgrade of versions
- Ensuring that each of the distinct projects works well in tandem
- Various operating system-compliant distributions
- Enterprise-grade support contract
- Good abstraction avoiding complexities in the form of additional scripts for execution and various Hadoop commands
- On-time critical bug fix and application
- Rich enhancements often needed by enterprises
- Deployment and other infrastructure consultancy and support

As discussed earlier, here are some of the main Hadoop distributions and their details:

- **Cloudera Distribution for Hadoop (CDH)**
  - Leader in industry
  - Popular Hadoop distribution
  - The first to enrich and enhance Hadoop features in the industry
  - Offers support for enterprises under Cloudera Enterprise subscription service
  - Two options, free and premium (based on cluster size), available
- **Hortonworks Data Platform (HDP)**
  - Completely open source
  - Amazon and IBM offer this distribution as a service

- Looks for standardization and, because of this, will be the most supported distribution over a period of time

- **MapR Distribution**
  - Similar to Cloudera and Hortonworks
  - Integrates its own database system--MapR DB
  - High speed and quite powerful
  - Own filesystem as against HDFS, supported
  - Two versions, free and premium, available

- **Altiscale**
  - Hadoop-as-a-Service
  - Acquired by SAP

- **Amazon Elastic MapReduce**
  - Hadoop on cloud (on-demand Hadoop)
  - Amazon's slightly different varient of Apache Hadoop as well as MapR distribution available

In this section, you would have clearly understood the various Hadoop distribution options available in the market. According to your organization and its requirements, choose wisely or you can very well choose the community maintained Hadoop.

HDFS and formats

Hadoop stores data in blocks of 64/128/256 MB. Hadoop also detects many of the common file formats and deals accordingly when stored. It supports compression, but the compression methodology can support splitting and random seeks, but in a non-splittable format. Hadoop has a number of default codecs for compression. They are as follows:

- **File-based**: It is similar to how you compress various files on your desktop. Some formats support splitting while some don't, but most of these be persisted in Hadoop. This codec compresses the whole file as is, that too, any file format coming its way.
- **Block-based**: As we know, data in Hadoop is stored in blocks, and this codec compresses each block.

However, compression increases CPU utilization and also degrades performance. Hadoop supports a variety of traditional file formats to be stored. However, Hadoop does very specific filesystem for data, as shown:

- **Text storage** (**CSV--Comma Separated Values**, **TSV--Tab Separated Values**, **JSON--JavaScript Object Notation**, and so on): Text files where data is stored in a line with some delimiter at the end to demarcate each record. You can also use well-defined JSON as a record and store it in Hadoop. When using this, it's common to use compression as these formats inherently support this.
- **Avro**: It's a file format with some built-in serialization and deserialization capability. It allows storing simple and complex objects and abstracts many of the complexities away from you and also has many tools at your disposal to be used for easy management of this data. It also supports block-level compression and is one of the favorite Hadoop file formats.
- **Sequence File**: It is designed by MapReduce, so the support by Hadoop is quite extensive. Each record is an encoded key and value that supports block-level compression.
- **Columnar File format**: As the name suggests, it partitions data in horizontal (row) and vertical (column) fashion in the Hadoop system for easy access of subsets of data (data stored for all records in a column, for example). If you plan to query data and want to do slide and dice, this format can be quite handy as against row-only kind of data:
    - **Parquet**: It is most widely used in columnar file format
    - **RCFile** (Record Columnar File): It is the first columnar file format in Hadoop created by Doug Cutting (founder of Hadoop), and has good compression and performance.
    - **ORC File** (Optimized RC File): This is a compressed and optimized RCFile; it compresses and performs better than RCFile

Choose the right format suiting your use case and its requirements. Ensure that when selection is made, some important aspects, such as how you want to read the data and how fast you want it (performance), are to be considered.

Hadoop for near real-time applications

Hadoop has been popular for its capability for fast and performant batch processing of large amounts of varied data with considerable variance and high velocity. However, there was always an inherent need for handling data for near real-time applications as well.

While Flume did provide some level of stream based processing in the Hadoop ecosystem, it required considerable amount of implementation for custom processing. Most of the source and sink implementations of flume are performing data ETL roles. For any flume processing requirement, it required implementation of custom sinks.

A more mature implementation for near real-time processing of data came with Spark Streaming, which works with HDFS, based on micro-batches as discussed earlier, and provided greater capabilities compared to flume, as pipeline-based processing in near real time.

However, even if the data was processed in near real time and stored in the Hadoop File System, there was an even greater challenge of how to access data randomly from HDFS, it being primarily a sequential filesystem.

In order to solve the problem of random access of data, HBase was implemented based on Google's Bigtable architecture. Though it allows random access of data, it is key value oriented. The data can be directly looked up only if the key of the data is available. For any partial match scenarios, this is not appropriate as it can potentially cause file scans within HDFS.

Hadoop deployment modes

Hadoop supports three deployment modes, which are briefly (don't want to deviate too far from the crux of this chapter) detailed here:

- **Standalone (Local) Mode**
  - Default mode
  - Single Java (JVM) process
  - Non-distributed or non-clustered architecture
  - The easiest setup of the three
  - Mostly used for learning and running examples and for development
  - Very useful for debugging purposes
- **Pseudo Distributed Mode (single node cluster)**
  - Single-node installation
  - Each daemon runs in its own Java (JVM) process
  - Can be used for simulating multi-node installation/support issues in a single node itself (mini cluster setup on single node)

- Much easier to setup than fully distributed Hadoop installation
- Similar to the first mode, it is non-distributed installation

- **Fully Distributed Mode (multi-node cluster)**
  - Fully distributed clustered architecture
  - Mostly used for production deployment
  - Can be set using a few to thousands of nodes, as the requirement demands
  - On each node, Hadoop installation and then clustering configuration has to be done
  - Uses YARN and its capabilities bring in true distribution and clustering capabilities internally
  - Highly configurable and supports high availability and security
  - Good support for monitoring and manageability (does offer various web UI for visual depiction of Hadoop components)

Choose the deployment you want to go with wisely. The code done remains the same for any of these deployment modes and can be changed from one to another, as required at any point.

Hadoop working examples

This section covers the full working example using Apache Hadoop as the data storage in conjunction with our SCV use case.

Installation

We have already covered the pseudo-distributed deployment of Hadoop in the earlier chapters. We will continue with the same setup for understanding the examples in this chapter.

Data preparation

For Hadoop examples, we will expand the data generation utility of customer profile even further. For batch processes it is generally expected that the volume of data is quite substantial.

Hence we will try and generate about 2 million customer records and their related information for batch processing.

We shall use the same data generation utility as before for populating the data in the database, the only difference being that we will be generating 2 million customer records in the DB. Generating these many rows in relational database may take some time depending on the machine configuration.

If you would like to cleanup the PostgreSQL database before running the data generation utilities, please run the following queries, in the order specified.

```
DELETE from address;
DELETE from customer;
```

Execute the following command from the directory containing data generation libraries as covered in Chapter 8, *Data Processing using Apache Flink.*

```
java -jar client-generator-1.0-SNAPSHOT.jar config/db.properties  2000000
```

Now that we have created 2 million records in our database, let us generate 2 million records for customer contact information as well, the only difference being that, we will be creating this information as a text file, with comma delimited data. Execute the following command from the directory containing data generation libraries as covered in Chapter 8, *Data Processing using Apache Flink*:

```
java -jar web-generator-1.0-SNAPSHOT.jar contacts.log 2000000 contact
```

A rough schema of the text file generated executing the previous command is as:

cust_id:int	cell_number:string	work_phone:string	email_address:string

In these examples we would also want to visualize data as Hive tables, hence we would also need to install and configure Hive service. As part of Hadoop ecosystem we have covered Apache Hive in high-level which can be referred.

Hive installation

1. Download the latest stable release of Hive from the following location, using the command:

   ```
   wget
   http://www-us.apache.org/dist/hive/hive-2.1.1/apache-hive-2.1.1-bin
   .tar.gz
   ```

2. Change to a user directory and extract the contents of the tar using the following command:

```
tar -xzvf ${DOWNLOAD_DIR}/apache-hive-2.1.1-bin.tar.gz
```

3. Configure and export the environment variable ${HIVE_HOME} pointing to the extracted directory and append its binaries to the path. Append the same to ~/.bashrc file

```
export HIVE_HOME=<Hive directory>
export PATH=$PATH:$HIVE_HOME/bin
```

4. Install latest SASL (Simple Authentication and Security Layer) packages for your operating system as Hive has dependency on this. For CentOS, these can be installed with following command:

```
sudo yum install *sasl*
```

5. Hive provides services which needs a metadata store for managing metadata information. Let us configure PostgreSQL server as the metadata server using the following commands using psql (interactive terminal for working with PostgreSQL) client in shell/Command Prompt.:

   - Create postgresql user as hiveuser and the database as metastore with the following commands:

     ```
     sudo -u postgres psql
     ```

     The previous command initializes and starts the psql client (the shell would show postgres=#) for running queries. Now let us create the user and database for Hive metastore with following queries:

     ```
     postgres=# CREATE USER hiveuser WITH PASSWORD
     'mypassword';
     postgres=# CREATE DATABASE metastore;
     ```

   - Configure permissions on the metastore for hiveuser with the following commands:

     ```
     postgres=# \c metastore
     metastore=# \pset tuples_only on
     metastore=# \o /tmp/grant-privs
     metastore=#   SELECT 'GRANT SELECT,INSERT,UPDATE,DELETE ON
     "'  || schemaname || '". "' ||tablename ||'" TO hiveuser ;'
     ```

```
metastore-#    FROM pg_tables
metastore-#    WHERE tableowner = CURRENT_USER and
schemaname = 'public';
metastore=# \o
metastore=# \pset tuples_only off
metastore=# \i /tmp/grant-privs
```

- Copy the ${HIVE_HOME}/conf/hive-default.xml.template to ${HIVE_HOME}/conf/hive-site.xml file with following command:

  ```
  cp ${HIVE_HOME}/conf/hive-default.xml.template
  ${HIVE_HOME}/conf/hive-site.xml
  ```

- Configure the following properties in ${HIVE_HOME}/conf/hive-site.xml:

HIVE Property	Suggested Value
hive.exec.scratchdir	/tmp/hive
hive.exec.local.scratchdir	/tmp/hive/centos Here, centos is the user account under which the hive queries will be executed
hive.downloaded.resources.dir	/tmp/hive/${hive.session.id}_resources
javax.jdo.option.ConnectionPassword	hivepass The password created in PSQL client.
javax.jdo.option.ConnectionURL	jdbc:postgresql://<POSTGRESQL_SERVER_IP:PORT>/metastore
javax.jdo.option.ConnectionDriverName	org.postgresql.Driver
javax.jdo.option.ConnectionUserName	hiveuser
hive.server2.enable.doAs	false

- Copy the PostgreSQL driver JAR in Hive lib directory, i.e. in ${HIVE_HOME}/lib, in the same way as was done for Sqoop setup. The PostgreSQL driver can be downloaded from the following location with the command. As part of Sqoop setup this should be already existing in the download folder.

  ```
  wget
  https://jdbc.postgresql.org/download/postgresql-9.4.1212.jre6.jar
  ```

6. Configure the `${HADOOP_HOME}/etc/hadoop/core-site.xml` with the following entries. Change hadoop.proxyuser.centos to your user account, instead of centos, in the following sample configurations:

```
<property>
    <name>hadoop.proxyuser.centos.hosts</name>
    <value>*</value>
</property>
<property>
    <name>hadoop.proxyuser.centos.groups</name>
    <value>*</value>
</property>
```

7. Restart the DFS service using the following commands:

```
stop-dfs.sh
start-dfs.sh
```

8. Configure `${HUE_HOME}/desktop/conf/hue.ini` to make Hue work with the Hive service with following properties. Search for this property in `hue.ini` and change the CentOS to your user account name:

```
hive_conf_dir=/home/centos/apache-hive-2.1.1-bin/conf
```

9. Restart the hue service by gracefully stopping (find the supervisor process and then kill it) and starting it with following command:

```
${HUE_HOME}/build/env/bin/supervisor -d
```

10. Use the `schematool` to generate schema with the following command:

```
${HIVE_HOME}/bin/schematool -dbType postgres -initSchema --verbose
```

Go to **pgAdmin** and you should see a new database namely `metastore` containing the various tables generated by the `schematool`

11. Verify the install by following steps:
    1. Check for hive shell by running the given command:

```
${HIVE_HOME}/bin/hive
```

If things go well you should see the hive shell. You can run various Hive queries using this shell if needed.

2. Launch the `hiveserver2` service with the following command. Hiveserver2 is the remoting process which enables Hue integration with Hive and enable Hue to run queries in Hue UI.:

```
${HIVE_HOME}/bin/hive --service hiveserver2 -hiveconf
hive.root.logging=console
```

3. After successful start of `hiveserver2`, open Hue and navigate to **Query Editor|HIVE**, which should open without any errors being reported.

Now that we have all the required components installed and working, we will look at a few examples. The initial example would cover loading aspect of the data and as we proceed through these examples we will also see the processing aspects of Hadoop layer.

Example - Bulk Data Load

Now, let us look at how we can load data in bulk into the Hadoop layer and see the support provided by Hadoop ecosystem in achieving this.

File Data Load

1. Files from a linux machine can be easily copied into HDFS cluster by using fs put command. This command is part of Hadoop client which can be installed on any Linux machine. In our case, Hadoop client is available as part of Hadoop pseudo-distributed setup.

   A general syntax of this command is as given:

   ```
   hdfs dfs -put /local/path/test.file
   hdfs://namenode:9000/user/stage
   ```

2. For this example, let us create a raw area of data in HDFS (a folder in HDFS). This area would contain the data in its most natural form as acquired from the source using the command:

   ```
   hdfs dfs -mkdir -p /<any-path>/raw/txt
   ```

   Once the previous command is executed, it will create the folder structure (`<any-path>/raw/txt`) in HDFS which can be viewed using the NameNode UI.

3. Now change the directory into where the generated file of contacts exists and run the following command:

```
hdfs dfs -put  contacts.log hdfs://<hadoop-namenode-ip-
address>:9000/<any-path>/raw/txt/contact.log
```

4. The content of this file can now be viewed in Hue as shown in the following screenshot:

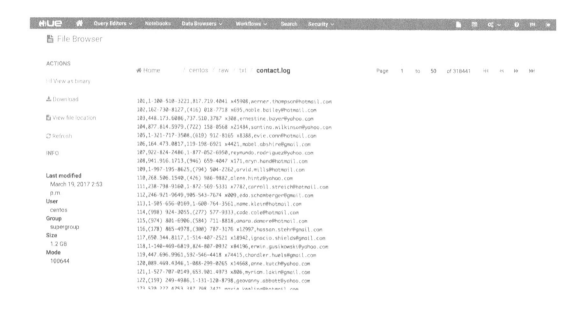

Figure 18: Text file loaded in HDFS via dfs put

RDBMS Data Load

As discussed earlier in `Chapter 5`, *Data Acquisition of Batch Data using Apache Sqoop* the bulk load from RDBMS can be done by using Sqoop. The same command that we discussed in Sqoop chapter can be used to achieve this.

Example - MapReduce processing

Now let us load this data using a MapReduce process from the same file, `contacts.log`. A very simple MapReduce program can be used for doing this, which is shown in the following code snippet. The source code for all the code in this chapter can be found in `chapter09` folder on GitHub repository which we have cloned earlier. The following code block can be found in `chapter09/contacts-loader-mr` project:

```java
import org.apache.hadoop.conf.Configuration;
import org.apache.hadoop.fs.Path;
import org.apache.hadoop.io.LongWritable;
import org.apache.hadoop.io.Text;
import org.apache.hadoop.mapreduce.Job;
import org.apache.hadoop.mapreduce.Mapper;
import org.apache.hadoop.mapreduce.lib.input.FileInputFormat;
import org.apache.hadoop.mapreduce.lib.output.FileOutputFormat;
import java.io.IOException;
import java.util.Random;

public class ContactsLoader  {
    public static void main(String[] args) throws Exception {
        //Define Job Configurations
        Configuration conf = new Configuration();
        Job job = Job.getInstance(conf, "Contacts Loader - Simple Mapper");
        job.setJarByClass(ContactsLoader.class);
        job.setMapperClass(LoadMapper.class);
        //Included support for file:// and hdfs:// file schemes
        conf.set("fs.hdfs.impl",
            org.apache.hadoop.hdfs.DistributedFileSystem.class.getName()
        );
        conf.set("fs.file.impl",
            org.apache.hadoop.fs.LocalFileSystem.class.getName()
        );
        //Set Input and Output Paths
        FileInputFormat.addInputPath(job, new Path(args[0]));
        FileOutputFormat.setOutputPath(job, new Path(args[1]));

        System.exit(job.waitForCompletion(true) ? 0 : 1);
    }
    private static class LoadMapper extends Mapper<Object, Text,
        LongWritable, Text> {
        @Override
        protected void setup(Context context) throws IOException,
            InterruptedException {
            super.setup(context);
        }
        @Override
```

```
       protected void map(Object key, Text value, Context context) throws
           IOException, InterruptedException {
           String line = value.toString();
           try {
             context.write(new LongWritable(Long.parseLong(line.substring(0,
                 line.indexOf(",")))), value);
           } catch (Exception e) {
             e.printStackTrace();
           }
       }
   }
}
```

Code 01: Simple Mapper Code for loading contacts from external file

In order to compile this code, go to the folder `chapter09/contacts-loader-mr` and run the following command:

mvn install

Once compiled, it creates a self executable JAR with all the dependencies included such that MapReduce job can be launched. This is achieved by using the following maven POM file configuration, including shaded plugin (used to create self-executable JAR). In this POM file, we have included few Hadoop dependencies and shaded plugin configuration (in build section) with `ManifestResourceTransformer` for main class declaration and `ServiceResourceTransformer` to omit unwanted files from dependent JARs.

```xml
<?xml version="1.0" encoding="UTF-8"?>
<project xmlns="http://maven.apache.org/POM/4.0.0"
         xmlns:xsi="http://www.w3.org/2001/XMLSchema-instance"
         xsi:schemaLocation="http://maven.apache.org/POM/4.0.0
http://maven.apache.org/xsd/maven-4.0.0.xsd">
<modelVersion>4.0.0</modelVersion>

<parent>
<groupId>com.laketravels</groupId>
<artifactId>chapter09</artifactId>
<version>1.0-SNAPSHOT</version>
</parent>

<groupId>com.laketravels.batch</groupId>
<artifactId>contacts-loader-mr</artifactId>
<packaging>jar</packaging>

<dependencies>
<dependency>
```

```
<groupId>org.apache.hadoop</groupId>
<artifactId>hadoop-client</artifactId>
<version>2.7.3</version>
</dependency>

<dependency>
<groupId>org.apache.hadoop</groupId>
<artifactId>hadoop-hdfs</artifactId>
<version>2.7.3</version>
</dependency>
</dependencies>
<build>
<plugins>
<plugin>
<groupId>org.apache.maven.plugins</groupId>
<artifactId>maven-shade-plugin</artifactId>
<version>3.0.0</version>
<executions>
<execution>
<phase>package</phase>
<goals>
<goal>shade</goal>
</goals>
<configuration>
<transformers>
<transformer
implementation="org.apache.maven.plugins.shade.resource.ManifestResourceTra
nsformer">
<mainClass>com.laketravels.ch09.batch.mr.loader.ContactsLoader</mainClass>
</transformer>
<transformer
implementation="org.apache.maven.plugins.shade.resource.ServicesResourceTra
nsformer"/>
</transformers>
</configuration>
</execution>
</executions>
</plugin>
</plugins>
</build>
</project>
```

Code 02: POM Configuration for MapReduce

Navigate to contacts-loader-mr project where the JAR is generated and run it by using the following command:

```
java -jar target/contacts-loader-mr-1.0-SNAPSHOT.jar file:///<any-
path>/contacts.log hdfs://<hadoop-namenode-ip-address>:9000/<any-
path>/raw/contact/mr
```

For visualizing and querying capabilities, we can also create Hive tables on the underlying data. Hive has a concept of EXTERNAL table which helps linking files to the Hive tables. This is extremely helpful in a Data Lake implementation as we can keep writing files and the the Hive tables keeps reflecting the newly added/updated data. We will see examples of Hive support for Avro data and Parquet storage using in-built **Serializer-Deserializer(SerDe)** provided by Hive in later examples in this book.

Text Data as Hive Tables

In this section we will visualize the output from bulk data upload and MapReduce examples explained in previous sections in Hive tables. In order to achieve this, let us follow given steps:

1. Open Hue and navigate to **Query Editor | HIVE**.
2. In the **Query** box, lets run a DDL command to create a Hive table over the contacts file uploaded earlier:

Text File Visualization with Hive Table	MapReduce Output with Hive Table

<pre>CREATE EXTERNAL TABLE IF NOT EXISTS
ContactsText(
     id STRING,
     cell STRING,
     phone STRING,
     email STRING)
  ROW FORMAT DELIMITED
  FIELDS TERMINATED BY ','
  STORED AS TEXTFILE
  location '<hdfs-path-to-txt-file>';</pre>
	<pre>CREATE EXTERNAL TABLE IF NOT EXISTS ContactsMR(
	     id STRING,
	     cell STRING,
	     phone STRING,
	     email STRING)
	  ROW FORMAT DELIMITED
	  FIELDS TERMINATED BY ','
	  STORED AS TEXTFILE
	  location '<hdfs-path-to-mr-upload-data>';</pre>

3. Once Hive returns with a success message, run a select query to verify the data as shown the following command:

Figure 19: *Hive External Table view of text file*

As observed from the previous result set, the data has been correctly represented in the Hive table. The following figure shows the uploaded content from MapReduce process from **contactsMR** table as visible in Hive UI:

Figure 20: *Text file loaded in HDFS via MapReduce*

As we see here, the id column of contacts does not look right, since the Hadoop file is a sequential file written with tuples of keys and values. The ID is seen twice because it is for the tuple (example record is: `101 101,1-796-079-4366,1-596-679-6710 x481,` `elna.nienow@yahoo.com`) containing the complete contact record as value which contains the id as well.

Avro Data as HIVE Table

In order to create Avro data from the contacts text file, we will make use of INTERNAL Hive table. They come with in-built mechanisms to convert text data to Avro data. However, having an EXTERNAL table for Avro data would be more practical as discussed before from integration perspective with Sqoop, Flume and Flink.

In order to see this in action we will need to execute the following steps:

1. Avro schema for contacts namely contact.ascv (schema file) could be represented as shown the following command:

```
{
    "namespace": "example.avro",
    "type": "record",
    "name": "Contact",
    "fields": [
        {"name": "id", "type": "string"},
        {"name": "cell",  "type": "string"},
        {"name": "phone", "type": "string"},
        {"name": "email", "type": "string"}
    ]
}
```

All Avro objects are dependent on schema definition and at the storage layer these Avro objects are serialized into Avro data files. The Avro serializers need to have reference to this schema to perform serialization. Avro serializations should be incremental in nature so that external tables can be created over Avro data files. When a Sqoop job is run to load the data as Avro data files, a default schema is generated by Ssqoop to serialize data into Avro data files.

As seen previously, Avro schema definition is similar to JSON schema draft specification. But, there are differences in data type support and the structure of the Avro schema declaration.

2. In the Hive editor run the following command to create another Hive table, but this time with Avro data format with inline schema definition

```
CREATE TABLE contactsAvro
ROW FORMAT SERDE 'org.apache.hadoop.hive.serde2.avro.AvroSerDe'
STORED AS INPUTFORMAT
'org.apache.hadoop.hive.ql.io.avro.AvroContainerInputFormat'
OUTPUTFORMAT
'org.apache.hadoop.hive.ql.io.avro.AvroContainerOutputFormat'
TBLPROPERTIES (
    'avro.schema.literal'='{"namespace": "example.avro",
    "type": "record",
    "name": "Contact",
    "fields": [
        {"name": "id", "type": "string"},
        {"name": "cell",  "type": "string"},
        {"name": "phone", "type": "string"},
        {"name": "email", "type": "string"}
```

```
        ]
      }
  ');
```

3. Now let us load the data into this Hive table using `INSERT OVERWRITE` query in the Hive Query Builder. This may take some time as internally it triggers MapReduce jobs for this data load:

   ```
   INSERT OVERWRITE TABLE contactsAvro SELECT id, cell, phone, email
   FROM contactsText;
   ```

4. Querying from the newly created table (contactsAvro) gives us the same output as we saw before, but if we look into the Hive warehouse we see Avro data files created from the data load operation as shown the following command:

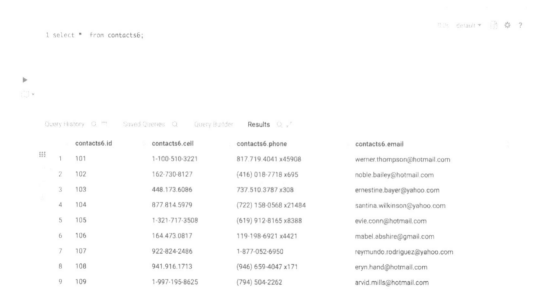

Figure 21: Avro Data Backed HIVE Table - Data Loaded with INSERT OVERWRITE

The following figure shows Avro data files shown in the Hive warehouse folder:

Figure 22: Generated Avro Data Files

The following screenshot shows the content of one of the Avro data files :

Figure 23: View of Avro Data file

Similarly, even for Parquet storage Hive tables can be defined and the data would be stored in Parquet format. The only difference would be in the way table is created, with a different SERDE.

Hadoop in purview of SCV use case

From the perspective of SCV use case, we can load the data from DB as well as generated contact file to provide complete view of customer and enable query execution across all these tables. Let us now see how we can build this step by step.

As discussed earlier, we had loaded 2 million records in database and generated 2 million contacts in text file format. We consider this as raw data existing in the source system, let us define the RAW storage area for our Data Lake.

Initial directory setup

Create the following directories in HDFS by running the following command:

```
hdfs dfs —mkdir -p /datalake/raw/customer
hdfs dfs —mkdir -p /datalake/raw/address
hdfs dfs —mkdir -p /datalake/raw/contacts
```

Data loads

Now, let's load data from our database, one table at a time, so that we can store it in different RAW areas:

1. Loading of Customer Data:
    1. Run a Sqoop Job for importing customer profile from DB with the following command:

    ```
    ${SQOOP_HOME}/bin/sqoop import --connect
    jdbc:postgresql://<DB-SERVER-
    ADDRESS>/sourcedb?schema=public --table customer --m 10 --
    username postgres --password <DB-PASSWORD> --as-
    avrodatafile --append --target-dir /datalake/raw/customer
    ```

2. Once the Sqoop MapReduce jobs are complete, the customer directory can be seen populated with a number of Avro data files as shown in the following figure:

Figure 24: Avro Data loaded in RAW Storage via Sqoop for Customer Profile

2. Loading of Customer Address Data:

1. Run a Sqoop Job for importing customer address with following command:

```
${SQOOP_HOME}/bin/sqoop import --connect
jdbc:postgresql://<DB-SERVERADDRESS>/sourcedb?schema=public
--table address --m 10 --username postgres --password <DB-
PASSWORD> --as-avrodatafile --append --target-dir
/datalake/raw/address
```

2. Once the Sqoop MapReduce jobs are complete, the address directory can be seen populated with a number of Avro data files as shown the following command:

Figure 25: Avro data loaded in RAW Storage via Sqoop for customer address

3. Loading of Contacts Data from Log File:

   1. Let us consider running a more complete MapReduce program (as against the sample that we ran earlier in this chapter) to load data from the log file stored in an external file system into the Hadoop directory with YARN job monitoring capability.

   2. The following code which can be found in `chapter09/contacts-loader-mr-avro` project is a MapReduce code that will help us load the data into Hadoop. Change the configurations `fs.defaultFS`, `mapreduce.jobtracker.address` and `yarn.resourcemanager.address` as needed in the code before compiling and running it:

```
package com.laketravels.ch09.batch.mr.loader;

import org.apache.avro.Schema;
import org.apache.avro.generic.GenericData;
import org.apache.avro.generic.GenericRecord;
import org.apache.avro.mapred.AvroKey;
```

```
import org.apache.avro.mapreduce.AvroJob;
import org.apache.avro.mapreduce.AvroKeyOutputFormat;
import org.apache.hadoop.conf.Configuration;
import org.apache.hadoop.conf.Configured;
import org.apache.hadoop.fs.Path;
import org.apache.hadoop.io.LongWritable;
import org.apache.hadoop.io.NullWritable;
import org.apache.hadoop.io.Text;
import org.apache.hadoop.mapreduce.Job;
import org.apache.hadoop.mapreduce.Mapper;
import org.apache.hadoop.mapreduce.Reducer;
import
org.apache.hadoop.mapreduce.lib.input.FileInputFormat;
import
org.apache.hadoop.mapreduce.lib.input.TextInputFormat;
import
org.apache.hadoop.mapreduce.lib.output.FileOutputFormat;
import org.apache.hadoop.util.Tool;
import org.apache.hadoop.util.ToolRunner;

import java.io.IOException;


public class ContactsLoader extends Configured implements
Tool{

public static void main(String[] args) throws Exception {
int exitCode= ToolRunner.run(new ContactsLoader(),args );
        System.out.println("Exit code "+exitCode);
    }

public int run(String[] args) throws Exception {
        Configuration conf = new Configuration();

//Integrate with YARN endpoints for Job Control and
Monitoring
        conf.set("fs.defaultFS",
"hdfs://192.168.0.117:9000");
        conf.set("mapreduce.jobtracker.address",
"192.168.0.117:54311");
        conf.set("mapreduce.framework.name", "yarn");
        conf.set("yarn.resourcemanager.address",
"192.168.0.117:8032");

//Included support for file:// and hdfs:// file schemes
        conf.set("fs.hdfs.impl",
org.apache.hadoop.hdfs.DistributedFileSystem.class.getName(
)
```

```
        );
        conf.set("fs.file.impl",
org.apache.hadoop.fs.LocalFileSystem.class.getName()
        );

        Job job= Job.getInstance(conf,"Contacts Loader");
        job.setJarByClass(ContactsLoader.class);

//Set Input and Output Paths
        FileInputFormat.setInputPaths(job, new
Path(args[0]));
        FileOutputFormat.setOutputPath(job, new
Path(args[1]));

//Configure Schema for avro data load
        Schema.Parser parser = new Schema.Parser();
        Schema
schema=parser.parse(Thread.currentThread().getContextClassL
oader()
.getResourceAsStream("contacts.avsc"));

//Overide default class loading policy to load application
specific libraries first
        job.getConfiguration().setBoolean(
                Job.MAPREDUCE_JOB_USER_CLASSPATH_FIRST,
true);

//Configure Job Mapper and Reducer classes
        job.setMapperClass(LoadMapper.class);
        job.setReducerClass(LoadReducer.class);


//Set Map Output Value Format, Input Format and final
Output Format Class
        job.setMapOutputValueClass(NullWritable.class);
        job.setInputFormatClass(TextInputFormat.class);
job.setOutputFormatClass(AvroKeyOutputFormat.class);

//Set Avro Job schema parameters for Map Output and Reducer
Output
        AvroJob.setMapOutputKeySchema(job, schema);
        AvroJob.setOutputKeySchema(job, schema);

int status = job.waitForCompletion(true) ? 0 : 1;
return status;
    }

private static class LoadMapper extends
```

```
Mapper<LongWritable, Text, AvroKey<GenericRecord>,
NullWritable> {
        Schema schema;

@Override
        protected void setup(Context context) throws
IOException, InterruptedException {
super.setup(context);
//Setup initializes the contacts schema
            Schema.Parser parser = new Schema.Parser();
schema=parser.parse(Thread.currentThread().getContextClassL
oader()
                    .getResourceAsStream("contacts.avsc"));
        }


@Override
        protected void map(LongWritable key, Text value,
Context context) throws IOException, InterruptedException {
try {
//Schema and Data used for Record population
                GenericRecord record = new
GenericData.Record(schema);
                String inputRecord=value.toString();
                String[] values = inputRecord.split(",");
                record.put("id", values[0]);
                record.put("cell", values[1]);
                record.put("phone", values[2]);
                record.put("email", values[3]);

                context.write(new AvroKey(record),
NullWritable.get());
            } catch (Exception e) {
                e.printStackTrace();
            }
        }


    }

private static class LoadReducer extends
Reducer<AvroKey<GenericRecord>,NullWritable,AvroKey<Generic
Record>,NullWritable> {

@Override
        public void reduce(AvroKey<GenericRecord> key,
Iterable<NullWritable> value, Context context) throws
IOException, InterruptedException{
```

```
try {
            context.write(key, NullWritable.get());
        } catch (Exception e) {
            e.printStackTrace();
        }
    }
}
```

The code has inline comments to explain the code segments.

3. The code has inline comments to explain the code segments. After doing relevant configuration changes in the source code, navigate to `chapter09/contacts-loader-mr-avro` folder and execute the following command to compile the source:

   mvn install

4. Please ensure YARN is properly setup. In order to configure yarn, please add the following configurations in `${HADOOP_HOME}/etc/hadoop/yarn-site.xml`:

```
<property>
  <name>yarn.nodemanager.aux-services</name>
  <value>mapreduce_shuffle</value>
</property>
<property>
  <name>yarn.nodemanager.aux-
services.mapreduce_shuffle.class</name>
  <value>org.apache.hadoop.mapred.ShuffleHandler</value>
</property>
```

5. In order to launch YARN process run following command:

   ${HADOOP_HOME}/sbin/start-yarn.sh

   Executing the jps command should show NodeManager and ResourceManager processes.

6. The preceding code can be run with this command to be run with YARN:

   yarn -jar target/contacts-loader-mr-avro-1.0-SNAPSHOT.jar
   file:///<any-path>/contacts.log hdfs://<hadoop-namenode-ip-
   address>:9000/datalake/raw/contacts/load1

7. Monitor the job at the following YARN URL:

`http://<YARN_BINDING_ADDRESS>:8088`

The following figure shows **RUNNING Applications** screen in YARN UI:

Figure 26: YARN view of applications in running state

The following figure shows the **Scheduler** screen in the YARN UI:

Figure 27: YARN view of scheduler state

8. Once the job is completed, the Avro data file is generated as shown in the Hue UI (HDFS Browser).

Figure 28: Avro data load via MapReduce in Hue UI

Data visualization with HIVE tables

Now let us visualize the loaded data by creating Hive tables over the binary Avro data by executing the following Hive table scripts (using Hive Query Editor):

1. Create a `customer` Hive table by executing the following script:

```
CREATE EXTERNAL TABLE customer
ROW FORMAT SERDE 'org.apache.hadoop.hive.serde2.avro.AvroSerDe'
STORED AS INPUTFORMAT
'org.apache.hadoop.hive.ql.io.avro.AvroContainerInputFormat'
OUTPUTFORMAT
'org.apache.hadoop.hive.ql.io.avro.AvroContainerOutputFormat'
LOCATION '/datalake/raw/customer'
TBLPROPERTIES (
  'avro.schema.literal'='{"namespace": "example.avro",
    "type": "record",
    "name": "Customer",
    "fields": [
       {"name": "id", "type": "int"},
       {"name": "first_name",  "type": "string"},
       {"name": "last_name", "type": "string"},
       {"name": "dob", "type": "long"}
    ]}'
);
```

2. Create `address` Hive table by executing the following script:

```
CREATE EXTERNAL TABLE address
ROW FORMAT SERDE 'org.apache.hadoop.hive.serde2.avro.AvroSerDe'
STORED AS INPUTFORMAT
'org.apache.hadoop.hive.ql.io.avro.AvroContainerInputFormat'
OUTPUTFORMAT
'org.apache.hadoop.hive.ql.io.avro.AvroContainerOutputFormat'
LOCATION '/datalake/raw/address'
TBLPROPERTIES (
  'avro.schema.literal'='{"namespace": "example.avro",
    "type": "record",
    "name": "Address",
      "fields": [
        {"name": "id", "type": "int"},
        {"name": "street1",  "type": "string"},
        {"name": "street2", "type": "string"},
        {"name": "city", "type": "string"},
        {"name": "state", "type": "string"},
        {"name": "country", "type": "string"},
        {"name": "zip_pin_postal_code", "type": "string"}
    ]}'
);
```

3. Create `contacts` Hive table by executing the following script:

```
CREATE EXTERNAL TABLE contacts
ROW FORMAT SERDE 'org.apache.hadoop.hive.serde2.avro.AvroSerDe'
STORED AS INPUTFORMAT
'org.apache.hadoop.hive.ql.io.avro.AvroContainerInputFormat'
OUTPUTFORMAT
'org.apache.hadoop.hive.ql.io.avro.AvroContainerOutputFormat'
LOCATION '/datalake/raw/contacts/load1'
TBLPROPERTIES (
  'avro.schema.literal'='{"namespace": "example.avro",
    "type": "record",
    "name": "Contact",
    "fields": [
      {"name": "id", "type": "string"},
      {"name": "cell",  "type": "string"},
      {"name": "phone", "type": "string"},
      {"name": "email", "type": "string"}
    ]}'
);
```

Now we have all the data ingested into Hadoop represented as external Hive tables, which have been actually sourced differently, but are all now coming together into the Data Lake in a way that enables querying and further processing. With the mechanisms explained in this chapter the whole Data Lake is coming together as shown in the figure (*Figure 29*) from coverage perspective.:

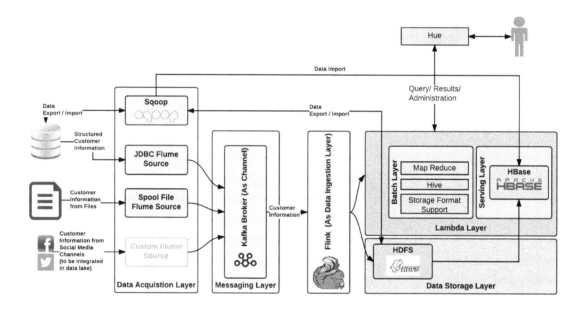

Figure 29: Single Customer View Coverage

When not to use Hadoop

Not all use cases require Hadoop, and when used in a use case that doesn't require Hadoop, it can be a maintenance havoc.

Hadoop should not be used if you need the following things:

- To do graph-based data processing. You might have to bring another Hadoop ecosystem product (say, Apache Tez) to do this.
- To process real-time data processing. However, using many products in Hadoop ecosystem, this can also be done, but it has to be analysed and then decided. Apache Flink or Spark on top of HDFS can be an option that can be considered.

- To process data stored in relational databases. Using Hive over HDFS can be an option though which could be considered.
- Access to shared state for processing data. Hadoop works by splitting data across multiple nodes in a cluster and tends to do jobs in parallel fashion, which is stateless in nature.
- To process small datasets.

Other Hadoop Processing Options

Apache Hadoop is something that will always pop up whenever a big data term is used. It has almost become a mandatory piece when dealing with Big Data. There is no doubt that Hadoop is an excellent choice, but it does have some inherent aspects that put a doubt in developers' minds when the choice has to be made, especially when big data and its processing is ever increasing in any enterprise, obviously due to changing business dynamics. Some of its pointed disadvantages are Hadoop's complexity and the way it actually does execution. Due to these reasons, there have been some recent innovations to simplify Hadoop processing further, and some of these simplifications have been brought in by the advent of Pig scripts and Apache Spark.

Pig scripts provide a good alternate to simplify MapReduce activity with pig Latin language, while still enabling non-Java developers to perform MapReduce via a simpler programming style.

Apache Spark streaming, on the other hand, has simplified the querying mechanism via programming languages, such as Scala, Java, and Python. If we might have observed in the examples covered, HIVE is good at querying HDFS data, but when it comes to joining one table with another, it kicks into more complex MapReduce jobs with high probability of failure. Hence, the HIVE MapReduce has been deprecated as the same action can be performed in a very optimized way with Apache Spark and Apache Tez.

Summary

In this chapter, similar to the other chapters in this part of the book, we started with the layer where Apache Hadoop was discussed in detail. We then mapped the technology, namely Hadoop, to this layer. Once we named the technology, we went into detail on the Hadoop technology.

First of all, we gave reasons for choosing this technology and then got into its history, advantages, and disadvantages. Soon, we delved into Hadoop's working by explaining both Hadoop 1.x and Hadoop 2.x architecture. Since we are using Hadoop 2.x, we explained Hadoop's architecture components. We then looked at some of the very important components in Hadoop Ecosystem, and we will be using some of these in implementing our SVC use case.

We then delved into some of the other aspects of Hadoop, namely its distributions, HDFS, and its various formats and finally, various deployment modes. We then dived deep into hands on coding using Hadoop and also saw how SCV use case is using the Hadoop technology. Finally, we wrapped up with two sections where we explained when to and when not to use Hadoop. As always, we finally discussed some of the alternatives that can be considered in place of Hadoop.

After reading this chapter, you would have a clear idea of the Data Storage layer and Hadoop technology. Full coverage of Hadoop technology is out of scope of this book, so we briefly discussed the core aspects of Hadoop that are key to implementing our use case.

Hadoop is one of the core technologies in our Data Lake implementation, and we are sure you have another technology under your kitty after going through this chapter.

Well done! You are one step close to knowing the full technology stack of our Data Lake.

10

Indexed Data Store using Elasticsearch

In the previous chapter on Hadoop, we persisted the data in hand onto Hadoop (HDFS). Reading/querying data from Hadoop at a fast pace is an issue, and that's when an indexed data store such as Elasticsearch and its significance come forth in our Data Lake implementation.

As in other chapters in this part of the book, we will start off the chapter by explaining the layer where this technology will be used. We will then explain the reason for choosing this technology for this capability and start diving deep into Elasticsearch and its working. We will cover enough details on Elasticsearch so that you have adequate details to understand this technology. As always we will only give enough details and full deep dive is beyond the scope of this book.

We would then take you through a hands-on coding session, where you will first learn to install this technology and then see it in action. We will also make sure to connect you to the SCV use case that we are trying to implement using Data Lake.

Finally we will see scenarios where we should and should not use this indexed data store. We will wrap the chapter by looking into other technology options that could be used in place of Elasticsearch.

Let's dig into it!

Context in Data Lake: data storage and lambda speed layer

The Data Storage Layer is where data is persisted. Our core persistent store is HDFS but because of its inherent slowness in querying, we need to have a technology on top of it for fast reading/querying. After indexing, the appropriate speed views are created and kept in the Lambda Speed Layer. The Lambda Speed Layer is entrusted with indexing the data stored in HDFS for high performance and scalable querying of required data.

Elasticsearch is our choice of technology capable of doing this effectively. Elasticsearch is one of the de-facto choices for such a capability, and with not much deliberation this technology choice was made.

The following sections of this chapter aim at covering Elasticsearch in detail so that you get a clear picture of this technology as well as get to know the data storage layer in detail.

Data Storage and Lambda Speed Layer

In Chapter 2, *Comprehensive Concepts of a Data Lake,* you would have got a glimpse of Data Storage and Lambda Speed layer. The Data Storage layer's responsibility is to persist the gathered data into a permanent place in our data lake. The Lambda Speed Layer's responsibility is to index the data stored in Data Storage layer and create appropriate speed views. The following figure would refresh your memory and give you a good pictorial view of this layer:

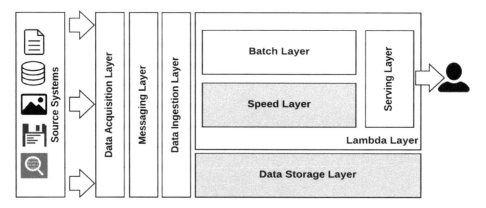

Figure 01: Data Lake: Data Storage and Lambda Speed Layer

We have given enough details in a previous chapter on the Data Storage Layer so we don't want to repeat ourselves. The Lambda Speed layer stores the various speed views created from the data storage layer. Since it was just the previous chapter, your memory would also be quite fresh.

Data Storage and Lambda Speed Layer: technology mapping

This chapter aims at covering the storage mechanism for an indexed data store. This chapter dives deep into Elasticsearch, which is our choice for this capability.

The following figure (*Figure 02*), brings in the technology aspect to the conceptual architecture that we will be the following throughout this book. We will keep explaining each technology and its relevance in the overall architecture before we bring all the technologies together in the final part of this book (*Part 3*).

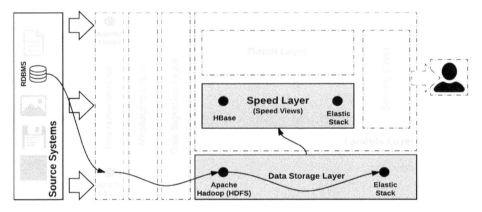

Figure 02: Technology mapping for Data Storage and Lambda Speed Layer

For our use case, SCV, we have already gathered data from various source system data stores and persisted in HDFS. Elasticsearch is a layer on top of HDFS, which does data indexing and makes sure that querying required data is very fast.

The next sections of this chapter give more details on Elasticsearch and will make you conversant with many important aspects and working of this technology.

What is Elasticsearch?

The *Wikipedia* description of Elasticsearch is as follows:

> *Elasticsearch is a search engine based on Lucene. It provides a distributed, multitenant-capable full-text search engine with an HTTP web interface and schema-free JSON documents. Elasticsearch is developed in Java and is released as open source under the terms of the Apache License. Official clients are available in Java, .NET (C#), Python, Groovy and many other languages.*

The given description does cover every aspect of what Elasticsearch is and also gives some details on how exactly it works and its core capabilities. It is distributed, scalable, enterprise-grade, and offers high performance querying and it does this by indexing the data available in HDFS. It also has rich API's and also supports a variety of languages. Let's keep this section crisp as we have this entire chapter explaining Elasticsearch and its working.

Why Elasticsearch

For the capability that we are looking for, Elasticsearch is the leading technology and that's the main reason for this choice.

Some of the prominent reasons why Elasticsearch has been chosen as the technology of choice for the technical capability that we are looking for in our Data Lake implementation:

- Compatibility with Hadoop (as this is our persistent store)
- Distributed
- Scalable
- Capability of indexing data
- Highly performant (fast query and search)
- Battle hardened technology (enterprise-grade having all the capabilities required by an enterprise)
- Capability of handling a huge volume and variety of data
- Failover and data redundancy capability

History of Elasticsearch

Compared to other technologies in the Big Data arena, Elasticsearch is more recent with a short history. This doesn't mean that the technology is immature; rather, it is one of the mature (70+ Million product downloads) and well adopted technologies with a vibrant community (70,000+ community members) backing.

In March 2015, the company Elasticsearch changed their name to Elastic.

A brief history of Elasticsearch in a pictorial manner, similar to how we have been covering this section for other technologies, is given in the following figure:

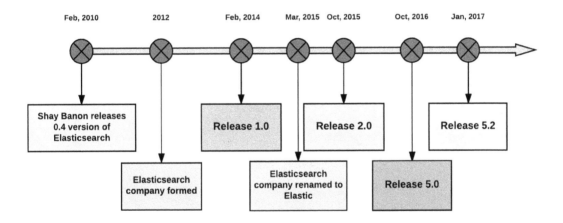

Figure 03: History of Elasticsearch

Elasticsearch is where it is because of some of the other products in the industry, and the following figure shows Elasticsearch and its evolution with other products; knowing this is quite significant to know the history of Elasticsearch in a holistic fashion.

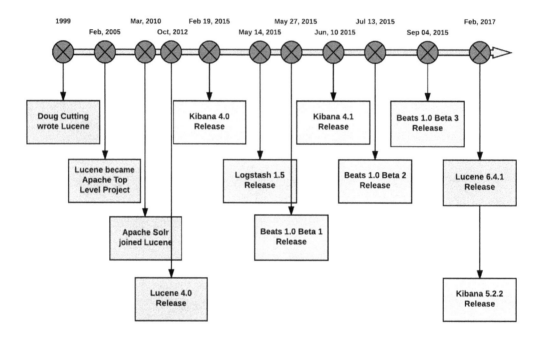

Figure 04: Other products and their rise along with Elasticsearch

The previous figure is a bit cluttered but shows the various Elasticsearch assisting products and its history side by side.

Advantages of Elasticsearch

Some of the advantages of Elasticsearch are:

- Open source (Apache 2 License) with strong community backup
- Distributed by birth
- RESTful (JSON over HTTP) in nature
- Really fast in operation
- Feature-rich search capabilities: capable of supporting a variety of search related use cases

- Faceted (see info) search/analysis capability
- Full-featured and powerful query DSL (Domain Specific Language)
- Can be extended via use of plugins available in industry or by creating new ones
- Very good visualization support (use of Kibana built-in)
- Multiple deployment topology support out of the box
- Multi-tenancy capability
- Cloud-ready
- Developer friendly. Familiar syntax to work with
- Built-in efficient cache mechanism to make queries fast
- Highly scalable: single node to hundreds of nodes. It scales horizontally. Handles petabytes of data with ease by scaling as needed.
- High availability and resiliency built in
- Built-in management and monitoring capability giving adequate details to help maintain the product for an enterprise (formerly known as Marvel, now packaged as x-pack)
- Highly reliable and predictable in nature
- Multi-language support to interact and deal with Elasticsearch
- Security is well thought through, and this makes it enterprise ready as against many big data products in the market
- Has good integration capability with other products, especially many of the Big Data products, Hadoop being one of the very important ones

The term "software multitenancy" refers to a software architecture in which a single instance of software runs on a server and serves multiple tenants. A tenant is a group of users who share a common access with specific privileges to the software instance. With a multitenant architecture, a software application is designed to provide every tenant a dedicated share of the instance: including its data, configuration, user management, tenant individual functionality and non-functional properties.

Faceted search, also called faceted navigation or faceted browsing, is a technique for accessing information organized according to a faceted classification system, allowing users to explore a collection of information by applying multiple filters. A faceted classification system classifies each information element along multiple explicit dimensions, called facets, enabling the classifications to be accessed and ordered in multiple ways rather than in a single, pre-determined, taxonomic order.

- Wikipedia

Disadvantages of Elasticsearch

Elasticsearch should be used for its strengths as there are core principles based on which it is created. However, it does end up being used for other capabilities where it shouldn't be. When used in certain use cases, it will backfire, and those aspects are listed as disadvantages:

- Should not be used as a primary persistence store. So, apart from Elasticsearch, we need to have another store for actual persistence.
- Elasticsearch is not ACID-compliant out of the box.
- Even though Hadoop in a production environment is not run on commodity hardware, theoretically it does support this. In the production state, Elasticsearch inherently doesn't run on commodity hardware.
- Elasticsearch has **Garbage Collection (GC)** issues.
- Product updates can be troublesome at times. Index rebuild, data merge and so on can be quite tedious in production environments.
- For effective management in production, Elasticsearch is often said to have a steep learning curve. This point is quite subjective and we acknowledge that.
- Minimal supports for achieving use cases requiring transaction.
- Not really a choice when it comes to searching large data scans and advanced computations on data retrieved.

Working of Elasticsearch

In this section, we will get more into the working of Elasticsearch, its architecture, its main components, various terminologies and important concepts. This is the most interesting aspect of this chapter, which is aimed at making you understand this technology before getting your hands dirty with the actual coding session.

Elasticsearch core architecture principles

The core Elasticsearch architecture principles are as mentioned here:

- Elasticsearch is largely memory driven, with the index and data being served from memory, while being stored on storage devices for persistence.
- Elasticsearch is based on **Apache Lucene** engine at the core, with the core indexing capabilities still driven by Lucene engine, while index distribution, scalability and other features are managed by Elasticsearch.

- Elasticsearch has been built for distribution from the ground up with scalability in mind; hence it has a scale-out architecture at its core.
- Elasticsearch is fundamentally built as a more available system, and less consistent system, with eventual consistency.
- Supports replication of indexes and data that can be altered dynamically for read and write availability.
- With its highly distributed architecture, it can easily scale to petabytes of data for both structured as well as unstructured data.
- Use of analyzers and tokenizers must be carefully considered. Wherever possible use analyzers and tokenizers that produce the optimal number of tokens for better search efficiency.
- Have partitioning a schema for indexes such that the indexes are partitioned by key attributes and can be independently dropped.
- Use a separate master cluster for large cluster deployments (>10 nodes). Small clusters may have both the roles of master as well as data.
- All the Elastic nodes must be of same type of infrastructure for a balanced cluster
- All the elastic nodes must be within the same network, so that the distance to each node can be accurately determined and avoid split brain scenarios.
- Single clusters may not span across data centers. A cross data center cluster would be possible only if the end to end network latency is less than 10 ms. A cross-data-center deployment may also limit cluster extensibility.

Elasticsearch terminologies

The Elasticsearch architecture is quite simple to understand and it is important for you to understand its various terminology in detail before we explain its simple working. This section aims at explaining its terminologies. It's quite hard to go through these terminologies in order as these terminologies get used when we talk about a term interchangeably. Rest assured, keep reading and at the end of these sections, you will have a clear grasp of all terms and this is quite important for understanding the rest of the chapter.

Document in Elasticsearch

Data in Elasticsearch is stored in the form of documents. These documents are addressable and have identifiable attributes that can be queried from the store. A sample document (JSON format) is shown in the figure:

```
{
    "first_name": "John",
    "last_name": "Doe",
    "dob": "01-01-2017,
    "communication": {
        "email": "xx@xx.com",
        "mobile": "0097112345678"
    },
    "other_attributes":{
        "field1": "field_value",
        "field2": "field_value"
    }
}
```

Figure 05: Sample document in Elasticsearch

Similar to String objects in Java, documents in Elasticsearch are immutable, so once created, you cannot update them. If you would want to update one, you have to either reindex or replace it.

Apart from the real data, a document does have additional information about the document itself, called document metadata. The most important metadata for a document are as follows:

- _index: Logical grouping where documents having a common reason to exist in Elasticsearch are grouped together. For example, all the customer index in an organization could be saved in customer index and so on. The _index value cannot start with an underscore nor can it contain commas and should be in lowercase.
- _type: Class of object which the document belongs to or represents. This allows Elasticsearch to logically partition data inside an index. These are usually subcategories existing inside an index in Elasticsearch. The _type cannot start with an underscore or a period but can be either lowercase or uppercase; similar to _index, they cannot contain commas and are limited to 256 character length.

- _id: Uniquely identifies a document when this string (_id) is combined with _index and _type. It can either be explicitly provided or Elasticsearch would automatically put a value for this.

In object-oriented and functional programming, an immutable object (unchangeable object) is an object whose state cannot be modified after it is created.

- Wikipedia

ID	Document
1	data lake for enterprises
2	data enterprises for lake
3	enterprises lake
4	data lake
5	lake data
6	enterprises

Figure 06: Multiple documents (string format) in Elasticsearch

Index in Elasticsearch

Elasticsearch stores the data in a logical grouping called an index. In an index you store documents sharing similar characteristics. One of the very important terms that you will use with Elasticsearch as defining this has huge impact on how you work with Elasticsearch, doing searching, updating and so on. In a cluster, you can define any number of indexes according to your requirement, but it does look into how the node and cluster is configured for Elasticsearch. An index can store a large amount of data (billions of documents) amounting to 1TB in an index. But storing this much data on a single index could affect its performance when searching or selecting data. When an index is being created you can specify the numbers of shards and replicas it need to have.

What is Inverted Index?

There is a very important concept called as *Inverted Index* in Elasticsearch. The Lucene text processing library is used in Elasticsearch for breaking down raw text into a series of terms. Once terms are broken these are stored in what is known as Inverted Index. The figure (*Figure 07*) shows an Inverted Index, which is in turn is a map data structure with key as term and value as list of document ID's where this term exists in the document. Now you know why it is called Inverted Index, because in this data structure we have term as key and value as ID:

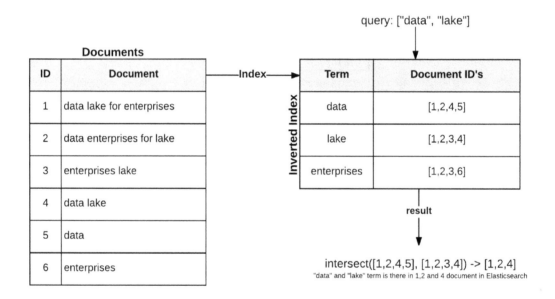

Figure 07: Document and Index (Inverted Index)

Shard in Elasticsearch

The data in Elasticsearch is stored and indexed in so-called Shards and the index brings in a logical grouping of one or more shards containing data stored having a common sense. Shard is something quite internal to Elasticsearch and index is something that we have to know of in Elasticsearch. The shard is the self-contained part in Elasticsearch, which can be distributed across multiple nodes in an Elasticsearch cluster. Shard allows Elasticsearch's ability to scale horizontally (Scale out).

An index can be replicated into one or more shards as needed. Once replicated, an index has:

- **Primary shards**: Shard from which the replicated shards were created
- **Replicated shards**: Copy from the original (primary) shard

An index can define the number of shards and replicas that it needs to have when the index is created.

Nodes in Elasticsearch

A node is a server in an Elasticsearch cluster which can consist of one or more nodes (servers). A node in an Elasticsearch cluster is unique and assigned a UUID when the cluster is started by default but can also be given any unique name as needed. This name is an important aspect and is used for various administration purposes. A node joins by default to a cluster named Elasticsearch but can also be configured to join a particular cluster name if needed. Even if only one node is there in a cluster, Elasticsearch forms a cluster with this only node when started.

> *A universally unique identifier (UUID) is a 128-bit number used to identify information in computer systems. When generated according to the standard methods, UUIDs are for practical purposes unique, without depending for their uniqueness on a central registration authority or coordination between the parties generating them, unlike most other numbering schemes. While the probability that a UUID will be duplicated is not zero, it is so close to zero as to be negligible.*
>
> *- Wikipedia*

Cluster in Elasticsearch

As detailed in the previous section, a cluster consists of one or more nodes (servers) and act as an Elasticsearch instance participating in various Elasticsearch query options. This figure brings in cluster, node and shards (primary and replica) together in a working scenario:

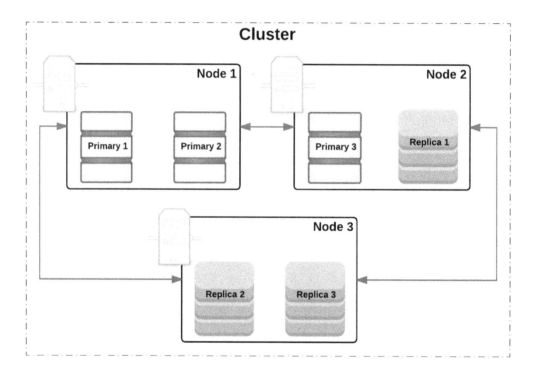

Figure 08: A typical Elasticsearch cluster showing nodes and shards (primary and replicas)

Elastic Stack

With Elasticsearch 1.x and Elasticsearch 2.x, the various products which work together have to be chosen and dealt with individually. Many aspects are purely decided based on prior Elastic Stack experience. With **Elastic Stack** (5.x), these products (Elasticsearch, Logstash, Kibana, Beats and X-Pack) have all come together and now really form a stack (platform) with minimal trial and error on various versions. This aspect has made implementing Elasticsearch very easier as compared to earlier versions.

This figure shows the Elastic Stack with harmonized working of all components:

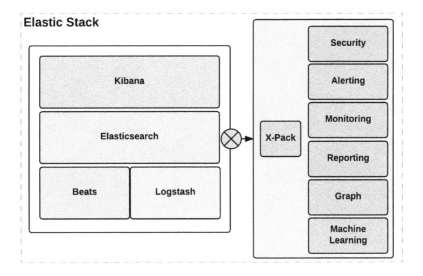

Figure 09: Elastic Stack 5.x (all icons courtesy of https://www.elastic.co/v5)

In the next subsections, we will discuss each of the components forming Elastic Stack in adequate detail for your understanding. Again, these wouldn't delve too deep into each component, but would give adequate details for playing with the examples in this chapter.

Elastic Stack - Kibana

Your Window into the Elastic Stack.

Kibana gives shape to your data and is the extensible user interface for configuring and managing all aspects of the Elastic Stack.

`- elastic.co/v5`

Kibana give eye to the data residing in Elastic Stack. It has a wide range of visualization capabilities which can be used to make the data residing in Elastic a visual insight. Kibana has visualizations ranging from classic line graph, bar graph, histograms and so on to more complex visualizations such as Time series visualization, graph data visualization and geospatial (map) data visualization.

The following figures (*Figure 10A* and *Figure 10B*) show the Kibana dashboard representing data in classic pie and bar graphs:

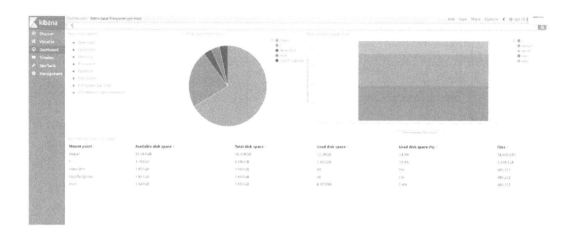

Figure 10A: Sample visualization in Kibana

Similar to the preceding figure, *Figure 10B* shows the Kibana dashboard with more graph choices for easy visualization:

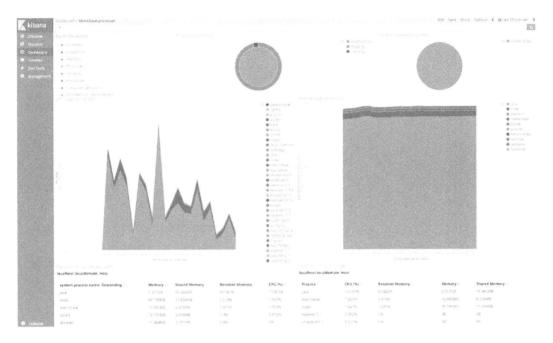

Figure 10B: Sample visualization in Kibana

Kibana also gives a visual representation of the Elastic Stack itself by helping administrators manage and monitor the Elastic Stack more efficiently. One such example of the management screen in Kibana is shown in the following figure:

Figure 11: Kibana Elastic Stack Management screen

Kibana also offers developer tools (console, for example), using which you could query elastic data. It also gives features such as auto-completion, which is quite useful for the developer community.

Elastic Stack - Elasticsearch

Search, analyze and store your data. The heart of Elastic Stack

Elasticsearch is a distributed, JSON-based search and analytics engine designed for horizontal scalability, maximum reliability, and easy management.

-elastic.co

Elasticsearch is called the heart of Elastic Stack. It stores data which could be discovered and analyzed for a number of modern day enterprise use cases. It also has RESTful APIs, using which data residing could be indexed and searched.

The Elasticsearch aggregation methodology helps in searching huge volumes of log data originating from source systems to make useful deductions. Above all, Elasticsearch gives these a full-text search capability on data with high performance. Not only is Elasticsearch distributed but is also highly scalable and is able to run on commodity hardware or enterprise grade servers alike, from one server to a series of server (hundreds of nodes) as demanded by the use case.

Elasticsearch is also highly available and fault-tolerant. It also has API's exposed, using which it can be monitored and managed quite easily by administrators.

Elasticsearch also allows the client to be written in a variety of languages such as Java, Python and so on and deals with JSON and RESTful API's.

Elastic Stack - Logstash

Centralize, Transform & Stash Your Data.

Logstash is a dynamic data collection pipeline with an extensible plugin ecosystem and strong Elasticsearch synergy.

Logstash is an open source, server-side data processing pipeline that ingests data from a multitude of sources simultaneously, transforms it, and then sends it to your favorite "stash." (Ours is Elasticsearch, naturally.)

- elastic.co

The main features of **Logstash** (from the original elastic website at `https://www.elastic.c o/products/logstash`) are as follows:

- Logstash allows data to be ingested of different types (variety) and sizes (volume) from a variety of source systems existing in an enterprise.

- Logstash has the concept of filters, using which the ingested data (stream of data) could be parsed, transformed (using filter) and converted into a single format for easy and fast analysis of data as dictated by the use case. There are rich logstash filters available in the market, maintained and managed by open-source contributors, which can be found at this link: `https://www.elastic.co/guide/en/logstash/current/filter-plugins.html`.

- Once the data is ingested and transformed, Logstash allows us to stash the output into a variety of stores (in our case, we will storing the indexed data in Elasticsearch itself). The full list of supported output stores can be found at `https://www.elastic.co/guide/en/logstash/current/output-plugins.html`.

- Logstash is built with extensibility in mind and this can be utilized by writing so-called plugins. Using these plugins judiciously, any required data pipeline can be formed and dealt with. There is already a rich ecosystem of plugins and it is ever growing with support from open source contributors.

Figure 12: Working on Logstash in Elastic Stack (image taken from `https://www.elastic.co/products/logstash`*)*

Elastic Stack - Beats

Lightweight Data Shippers.

Beats is a platform for lightweight shippers that send data from edge machines to Logstash and Elasticsearch.

Beats is the platform for single-purpose data shippers. They install as lightweight agents and send data from hundreds or thousands of machines to Logstash or Elasticsearch.

- elastic.co

Beats sits on the server and according to the type of data employs so-called shippers to collect data. The data collected by these shippers can be directly sent to Elasticsearch or can be passed to Logstash for appropriate transformation as needed and then sent to Elasticsearch (or in fact any output stores as detailed in a previous section).

Some built-in shippers in Beats are listed here, but if needed, they can also be extended. There are many shippers maintained and managed by contributors; the complete list is at `ht tps://www.elastic.co/guide/en/beats/libbeat/current/community-beats.html`:

- **Filebeat**: Lightweight shipper for collecting logs generated in a server. It does this by forwarding log lines to either Logstash or Elasticsearch.
- **Metricbeat**: Lightweight shipper for collecting metrics. Metricbeat is used to collect a variety of metric information of the server (memory, CPU and so on) and also other technologies (**Nginx**, **Redis** and so on) and forward it to either Logstash or Elasticsearch. These metrics when logged can be visualized in a very decent manner using Kibana. A variety of modules allow collection of these metric data from various technologies and as always it is extensible, so anything newly required could be easily built.
- **Packetbeat**: Shipper for network data collection and visualization. It supports a variety of protocols and again allows extensibility by allowing to write our own and plugging it in.
- **Winlogbeat**: Shipper for windows event logs.
- **Heartbeat**: Shipper which can be used for uptime monitoring of applications hosted on the server.

The following figure shows the working of Beats:

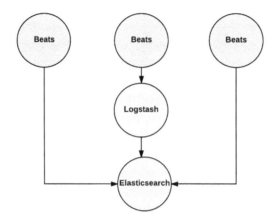

Figure 13: Working of Beats

Elastic Stack - X-Pack

One Pack. Loads of Possibilities.

Built and maintained by Elastic engineers, X-Pack is a single extension that integrates handy features you can trust across the Elastic Stack.

- elastic.co

The overarching component spans across all the components that we've discussed in Elastic Stack so far. Prior to Elastic 5.x, all these were separate and had to be brought together for getting a fully functional enterprise ready Elasticsearch instance. With Elastic Stack, this is no more the case and we have a fully functional, fully integrated stack with all the versions of these components working in harmony with each other. These are features built and maintained by the Elastic engineers and from now on will make sure that each one works with the other without any issues when Elastic Stack undergoes regular upgrades.

Most of the non-functional aspects of Elastic Stack are taken care of by this component. Some of the key ones are as follows:

- **Security**: Can be used to enable security to your cluster. It also has built-in authorization in the form of roles and permissions for easy administration. Capable of integrating with **Active Directory (AD)** and **Lightweight Directory Access Protocol (LDAP)**, it is also capable of integrating with custom **Identity and Access Management (IDAM)** systems within your organization. Security can be enforced even at the data level using X-Pack's security capability. It also allows securing the infrastructure by enabling SSL communication between nodes and the ability to secure and mask data as demanded by specific use cases. X-Pack's security feature also audits various system and user activity as part of its auditing capability.

- **Alerting**: Helps to configure various alerts. One example can be triggering alerts by looking into various cluster health-related indicators. It helps look into various system level parameters and can trigger configured alerts as needed. It also has the ability to look for changes in data residing in Elasticsearch and can trigger configured alerts. There are many existing integrations in X-Pack, using which the alerting mechanism can be chosen. There are built-in mechanisms such as E-mail, Slack, **PagerDuty**, and **HipChat** to choose from for the alerting mechanism. It also has the concept of **WebHook**, using which any URL can be configured and when necessary rules are met, this URL is called and this can act as a mechanism for dealing with such alerts.

- **Monitoring**: Gives you a view of how Elastic Stack is running. It monitors cluster, nodes forming the cluster, various indices in Elasticsearch, Kibana, and Logstash and visualizes this data for easy analysis. It also stores the variously collected data for a period as necessary, which can be used for historical analysis as well as contemporary analysis.

- **Reporting**: Allows creating various reports. These reports can be scheduled, triggered based on various rules set up, and then sent in various formats using different mechanisms.

- **Graph**: Helps in analyzing the relationships of data stored in Elasticsearch. This aspect gives a new way of looking at the data and can provide deep and new insights.

A WebHook in web development is a method of augmenting or altering the behavior of a web page, or web application, with custom callbacks. These callbacks may be maintained, modified, and managed by third-party users and developers who may not necessarily be affiliated with the originating website or application.

- Wikipedia

Elastic Cloud

Official Elasticsearch-as-a-Service managed by the Elastic folks, fully loaded and ready for enterprises. Easy to scale, Elastic Stack is always kept updated. For more details on this, visit `https://www.elastic.co/cloud/enterprise`.

Apache Lucene

The Elasticsearch component in Elastic Stack is based on Apache Lucene. Elasticsearch uses the main concept of Inverted Indexes and this aspect is the base on which Apache Lucene indexes documents.

> *Apache Lucene is a high-performance, full-featured text search engine library written entirely in Java. It is a technology suitable for nearly any application that requires full-text search, especially cross-platform.*

> *- Apache Lucene*

Doug Cutting, the creator of Hadoop, is the creator of Lucene. Apache Lucene is a high-performance search engine library capable of providing advanced search options, utilizing the inverted index methodology in which the terms in a document are extracted and stored as keys. Each term has a value containing the document IDs (Elasticsearch is a document-oriented store). Each document has many indexes and each index has multiple documents. Each document contains multiple fields and each field has multiple attributes.

Some of the important aspects Elasticsearch brings are:

- Provides a convenient abstraction layer on top of core Lucene, and this makes the use of Elasticsearch more easy and convenient
- Is based on shards, and each shard is a separate Lucene instance
- Brings distributed computing on top of Lucene with different API's available on top of it to interact with the core Lucene
- Also brings many features on top of Lucene and has extensive monitoring and management features

How Lucene works

The primary role played by Lucene is to support search requirements in an application. While an application may implement an end-to-end use case, searching may need some very specialized capability, which can be provided by Lucene.

The basic unit of operation for Lucene is information stored as a document. While the information may be captured by external mechanisms, the information is stored as a Lucene Document. The primary motive to keep information/content in a document is to keep the information/content in a format that can be easily interpreted by the Lucene engine.

Once the document is created and stored, the document is analyzed based on the schema/mapping provided, wherein the Lucene engine determines what is to be indexed and what is not to be indexed. After the document analysis is complete, the specific areas/attributes of the document undergo the indexing process, which includes applying the required tokenizers on the content of the document to produce tokens. These are mapped to the document identifier to create, which are actually inverted indexes. At this stage, we have terms that are ready to be searched.

Optionally, the tokenizer can also include multiple token filters, such that a certain token generations could be customized. One can also program a custom token filter and use it with a tokenizer, and we can also have a chain of such token filters defined.

The Lucene engine also provides us with a query interface that can be used for performing queries on the documents stored. Lucene provides its own query language, which is also referred to as Lucene Query language. Once a query is executed, the query terms are used to match against the inverted index of tokens, which refers to the document identifier, and can also return the document source if the document source was stored along with the document indexes.

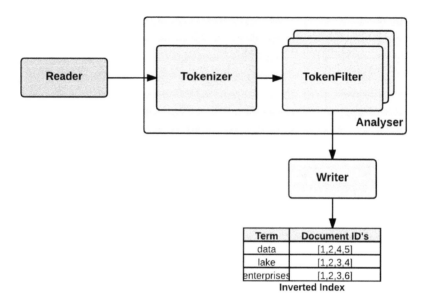

Figure 14: Inverted Indexing operation in Lucene

The previous figure shows the working of an inverted index in the context of Apache Lucene and the following figure shows the same Lucene inverted index in the context of Elasticsearch:

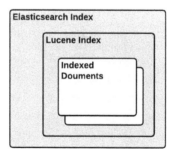

Figure 15: Elasticsearch and Lucene Index

Elasticsearch DSL (Query DSL)

Elasticsearch DSL is a library abstracted on top of Elasticsearch, using which you can write and run queries against the data stored. It in turn wraps Lucene's query syntax and makes these interactions easy by allowing a query to be composed using a JSON syntax.

A sample query of customer data in Elasticsearch is shown here:

```
Curl -XPOST 'http://localhost:9200/customer/_search?pretty=true' -H
'Content-Type: application/json' -d '
{ "from" : 0,
"Size": 20,
"query": <QUERY_JSON>,
<FILTER_JSON>,
<SORT_JSON>
}'
```

In the previous code <QUERY_JSON> can be { "match_all": {} } and <SORT_JSON> can be "sort": { "name": { "order": "desc" } }.

Code 01: Sample Elasticsearch DSL query

Important queries in Query DSL

The following are some of the important queries showing off Query DSL:

- match_all: Matches all the documents. The default query that runs when nothing is specified. This can be used in conjunction with filter and returns all the documents satisfying the filter condition.

  ```
  {
      "match_all": {}
  }
  ```

- match: Used when you need full text or exact match on any of the fields in the document:

  ```
  {
      "match": {
          "field_name": "phrase_which_has_to_be_searched"
      }
  }
  ```

- `multi_match`: Can be used to match multiple fields in a document. It is like executing multiple match queries:

```
{
    "multi_match" : {
        "query" : "phrase_which_has_to_be_searched",
        "fields" : [ "field1", "field2" ]
    }
}
```

- `range`: Used for numbers or date fields that fall in between a particular specified value:

```
{
    "range": {
        "field_name": {
            "<gt or gte>":   5,
            "<lt or lte>":    50
        }
    }
}
```

- `term`: Used for an exact value search:

```
{
    "term" : {
        "field_name" : "search_text"
    }
}
```

- `terms`: The same as a term query but allows us to enter multiple search texts, which can be searched on:

```
{
    "terms" : {
        "field_name" : [ "search_text1", "search_text2",
"search_text3" ]
    }
}
```

Nodes in Elasticsearch

As detailed earlier, a node in Elasticsearch is one of the servers forming the cluster. A node in a cluster can be configured to work as different node types as follows:

- Master node
- Data node
- Client node

Elasticsearch - master node

Any node in a cluster is eligible to become the master node if the node.master property is set to true in the `elasticsearch.yml` file. Once the master node is elected automatically by the cluster, this node is entrusted with some key responsibilities, as follows:

- Allocate of shards across various nodes within the cluster.
- Create and delete indexes.
- Broadcast the cluster state to all the nodes in the cluster and in turn receives confirmations from each of those nodes back.
- Take necessary actions when a node joins or leaves the cluster.
- Ping all the nodes periodically and all nodes ping back the master periodically. If the master fails due to any reason, one of the other master-eligible nodes is elected as master by the cluster.

Elasticsearch - data node

Any node in the cluster is eligible to become the data node. For big clusters, it is de-facto to have a master dedicated to do that job and not store data (don't be data node along with being master by setting `node.data` property to false). The main responsibilities are as follows:

- The node that stores data in the form of shards
- Performs indexing, aggregating, and searching data

By setting the property `node.master` as false, you can make sure that a node will become a data node within the cluster. For an enterprise setup, this is how the cluster in general is set up, and it's more reliable and predictable.

Elasticsearch - client node

Any node which is neither a master (`node.master` is set to false) nor data (`node.data` is set to false) becomes the client node. Being the client node, it behaves as a load balancer that routes the requests and search to the right nodes. In general, this type of node existing in a cluster is not really required because Data Node would be able to do these themselves. However, a big installation having dedicated nodes would reduce the additional work being done by other important nodes within the cluster.

The following figure shows all the types of nodes within an Elasticsearch cluster:

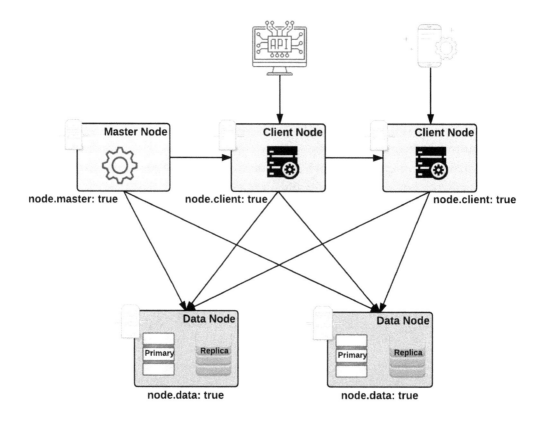

Figure 16: Different types of nodes within an Elasticsearch cluster

Elasticsearch and relational database

We did cover Elasticsearch terminologies in detail in the section. However, Elasticsearch and its terminologies are not that different from a database, which is known common to many in the industry now as well. So let's see a comparison, so that whenever these terminologies are used in Elasticsearch, you could relate these to more RDBMS terminologies:

Elasticsearch Terminology	RDBMS Terminology
Node	DB Instance
Cluster	DB Cluster
Index	Database
Type	Table
Mapping	Schema
Shard	Physical Partition
Route	Logical Partition
Document	Row
Field	Column
Elasticsearch DSL (Query DSL)	SQL

Table 02: Elasticsearch and RDBMS terminologies

Elasticsearch ecosystem

The Elasticsearch ecosystem does have some very important components and some of the important ones, especially for us are as detailed in this section.

Elasticsearch analyzers

Elasticsearch stores data in a very systematic and easily accessible and searchable fashion. To make data analysis easy and data more searchable, when the data is inducted into Elasticsearch, the following steps are done:

1. Initial tidying of the string received (sanitizing). This is done by a character filter in Elasticsearch. This filter can sanitize the string before actual tokenization. It can also take out unnecessary characters or can even transform certain characters as needed.
2. Tokenize the string into terms for creating an Inverted Index. This is done by Tokenizers in Elasticsearch. Various types of tokenizers exist that can do the job of actually splitting the string to terms/tokens.
3. Normalize the data and search terms to make the search easier and relevant (further filtering and sanitizing). This is done by Token Filter in Elasticsearch. These filters can either take out certain tokens that are not so relevant for the search (a, the, and so on) or can change the token as needed.

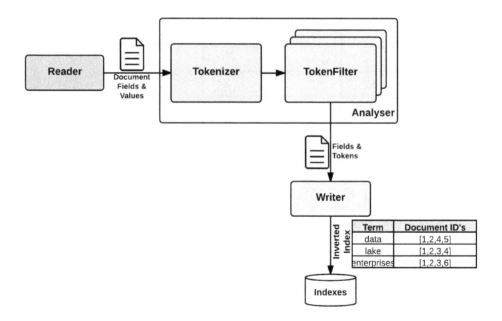

Figure 17: Working of Analyzer

Elasticsearch provides many built-in character filters, tokenizers, and token filters. These components can be combined in any way as needed and this forms the so-called Analyzer.

There are two kinds of Analyzers, as follows:

- Built-in Analyzers
- Custom Analyzers

Built-in analyzers

Elasticsearch does have built-in analyzers packaged and shipped with it. These analyzers would be good enough for many use cases that are commonly needed. Some of the most used built-in analyzers are detailed briefly:

- **Whitespace analyzer**: Uses whitespace to split the string and then generate the terms and put them in Elasticsearch.
- **Standard analyzer**: An analyzer used by default if not specified explicitly. Should be enough for most common use cases. It could be used for text in any language and it converts to lowercase after everything is done.
- **Simple analyzer**: Splits the letter when encountered with anything that isn't a letter and then finally converts it to lowercase.
- **Language analyzer**: As the name suggests, these are for particular languages to understand language-specific characteristics and deal with them. There are many language analyzers built in and shipped with Elasticsearch.

Custom analyzers

As detailed before, if these built-in analyzers are not what you are looking for, you could very well mix these various components to form your own custom analyzers for your use case.

Elasticsearch plugins

Elastic Stack has useful plugins already packaged as part of the **X-Pack** component. However, other plugins are available in the industry and could be used to get more insight into Elasticsearch. Some of those external plugins are as follows:

- **Head plugin**: Classic monitoring and health plugin for Elasticsearch clusters. Not available with X-Pack in favor of the Kopf plugin
- **Kopf plugin**: Monitoring and health plugin that is included as part of X-Pack along with Elastic Stack
- **BigDesk plugin**: Packed with X-Pack and is capable of generating live charts and statistics for the Elasticsearch cluster
- **Elasticsearch-SQL plugin**: Not available as part of X-Pack but could be used for querying Elasticsearch similar to RDBMS
- **Paramedic**: Packed with X-Pack by default

Elasticsearch deployment options

Elasticsearch supports a scale-out deployment architecture, with the main priority on availability. The Elasticsearch cluster is composed of nodes playing master and data node roles. Quorum based availability drives cluster availability in general.

While the most common deployment is that of single data center deployment, which can comprise dedicated master nodes and dedicated data nodes, for larger clusters, multiple data center deployments are also required for very high availability of critical applications.

It is generally not a very good idea to deploy Elasticsearch clusters across data centers, since the Elasticsearch leader election algorithm and data node selection are based on network distance, which assumes that all the nodes are identical in terms of all resources; it is expected that in a cluster all nodes are equidistant. This can go wrong in cross data center clusters at times, and is not worth the risk.

Hence it is generally recommended to have independent clusters in each of the data centers, and there are patterns available to support data availability in terms of ingestions at both the data centers, which are primarily around, either doing a dual drop of a message at both cluster at all times, or having a cross data center mirroring mechanism of data with capabilities such as Kafka Mirror.

Clients for Elasticsearch

Using the Java programming language the following are the ways by which Elasticsearch can be communicated.

- **Transport Client**: Used by REST clients internally. Full support from Elasticsearch as these are used by Elasticsearch internally to achieve various tasks. The most efficient methodology for communication and is quite fast. It uses a binary protocol for communication, the same protocol Elasticsearch uses internally. The following code shows how can you acquire the transport client to communicate with the Elasticsearch. More details on this can be found in elastic's official blog here `https://goo.gl/0ZKZIk`:

  ```
  TransportAddress address = new
  InetSocketTransportAddress(InetAddress.getByName("localhost"),
  9200);
  Settings settings = Settings.builder().put("cluster.name",
  "dataLakeCluster").build();
  Client client = new
  PreBuiltTransportClient(settings).addTransportAddress(address);
  ```

- **Java REST Client**: Communicates with Elasticsearch using HTTP. Compatible with most Elasticsearch versions. Uses Apache HTTP Async Client internally for sending HTTP requests. More detail on this can be found in the official elastic blog here `https://goo.gl/IKui5X`:

  ```
  RestClient restClient = RestClient.builder(new
  HttpHost("localhost", 9200, "http")).build();
  Response response = restClient.performRequest("GET", "/",
          Collections.singletonMap("pretty", "true"));
  ```

- **Jest**: Apart from the default REST client by Elasticsearch, this is an alternative HTTP-based Elasticsearch client. The following Java code shows how you can obtain a Jest client:

  ```
  Client JestClientFactory factory = new JestClientFactory();
  factory.setHttpClientConfig( new
  HttpClientConfig.Builder("http://localhost:9200").multiThreaded(tru
  e) .build());
  JestClient client = factory.getObject();
  ```

- **Spring Data Elasticsearch**: Spring is a very popular framework in Java. It has abstracted many low-level details for many data stores using a module called Spring Data. Spring has a specific module to abstract Elasticsearch from its low-level details in the Spring Data Elasticsearch module.

Elasticsearch for fast streaming layer

Analyzing real-time data is demanded by all enterprises in this digital age where data is at its core. Elasticsearch can play a very important role in dealing with such real-time data along with other stream processors (in our case, it is Apache Flink). The following figure shows a typical setup used for such data handling and is quite relevant with regard to our technology choice and use case implementation. In place of Flink, any other stream processors could be used, say Spark Streaming, to achieve the architecture mentioned here:

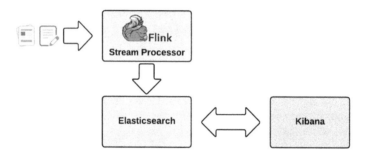

Figure 18: Elasticsearch setup in real-time data handling in conjunction with Flink

This architecture is quite relevant and useful because Flink can do analysis and transformation of data and after that Elastic Stack can be used in the serving layer for fast queries on that data. The built-in component, namely Kibana, in Elastic Stack is an eye into the data in Elasticsearch and is quite complete in many aspects. This makes it easy for visualizations and building a new UI is not required at all.

In the case of Lambda or Kappa architectures, the Elasticsearch technology component plays a very important role in the speed and serving layer. The serving layer can get the real-time views from Elasticsearch and batch views from Hadoop (or other data stores such as Cassandra) to merge and build a consolidated view needed for enterprise applications.

Elasticsearch as a data source

In general, Elasticsearch shouldn't (subjective, yes we do acknowledge this) be used as a primary data store. However, this question is more use case-driven and for some use cases it could very well be used as a data store. Elasticsearch does fall into the NoSQL type of database and doesn't support the ACID property of a typical relational data store, mostly used for transaction-oriented use cases. But it does have features such as optimistic locking and eventual consistency making it apt for certain pointed use cases. For a data lake implementation, it could very well act as a data store because the real data store (system of record) is with the source systems. In the case of any failure, the data could very well be warmed into Elasticsearch (in practical scenarios this is not that straight forward.. smiley) from these source system or even from our Hadoop and back to working condition (obviously depending on the volume of data in your data lake... smiley).

Because of its NoSQL nature it does offer capabilities such as distributed, robustness, and schema-less (schema flexibility) making it definitely a good choice for a data store, but one size doesn't fit all and we would recommend evaluating it use case by use case.

Elasticsearch for content indexing

A typical problem attributed to many **Content Management Systems** (**CMS**) is their lack of scalability and performance because of their tight coupling with some data stores, mostly traditional RDBMS. This could be avoided by keeping the CMS disconnected by publishing the content to a more robust NoSQL data store, and definitely Elasticsearch is one of the strong contenders. The core feature of Elasticsearch is its full-text indexing and searching capability and for a CMS; this capability is required, and the inherently strong capabilities of Elasticsearch as a store could be utilized. Elasticsearch is also supported by many of the CMSes available in the market, making it a more apt technology choice. Because of this reason and more, many platforms in CMS and **Digital Asset Management** (**DAM**) use Elasticsearch as one of the components internally.

A full explanation of this pattern is beyond the scope of this chapter and would take us into a different world of content management and websites. However, we wanted you to understand this capability of Elasticsearch.

Elasticsearch and Hadoop

In big data, Hadoop is a core component/technology that cannot be ignored. Elasticsearch has very good support for Hadoop and Elastic Stack has a product for achieving this integration called **ES-Hadoop**. We will discuss that in some detail in this section. For more details, we urge you to go to the elastic official page here: `https://www.elastic.co/produ cts/hadoop`.

Hadoop is considered to be good for batch analytics but, for modern applications as well as enterprises dealing with batch and real-time data, performing meaningful analysis is crucial. For dealing with real-time data, this integration of Elasticsearch and Hadoop is apt. Elasticsearch brings the real-time analytics capability on top of Hadoop. ES-Hadoop is a connector shipped as a product by elastic along with the Elastic Stack.

This connector works with Hadoop 1.x and 2.x versions and works like a charm with a variety of other big data technologies by enabling data to flow to and fro between Hadoop and Elasticsearch.

This figure shows the exact working of the ES-Hadoop connector:

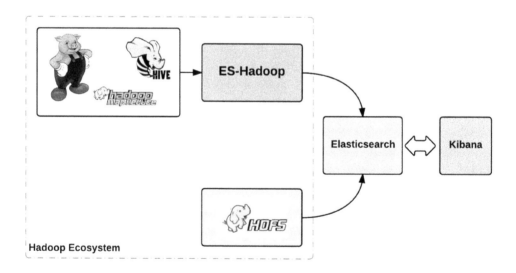

Figure 19: ES-Hadoop connector in action (image inferred from www.elastic.co)

As shown in this figure, ES-Hadoop has native support for many of the big data technologies, allowing data to be read/queried from Elasticsearch. ES-Hadoop has a variety of security options, using which security considerations can also be met.

The full details on this library are beyond the scope of this section, so we urge you to read the elastic documentation at `https://goo.gl/NSwCVE` for more in-depth details on this integration, which is a must for our Data Lake.

Elasticsearch working example

As we have gone through the various capabilities of Elasticsearch in this chapter, we will now try to look at some of the main capabilities via working examples. Let's start by installing Elastic Stack.

Installation

1. Download the Elastic Stack 5.x binary from the following location using the following command:

   ```
   wget
   https://artifacts.elastic.co/downloads/elasticsearch/elasticsearch-
   5.3.0.tar.gz
   ```

2. Change the directory to a user location and extract the contents of the Elastic Stack 5.x binary using the following command:

   ```
   tar -zxvf ${DOWNLOAD_DIR}/elasticsearch-5.3.0.tar.gz
   ```

3. Let's refer to the extracted Elasticsearch folder as `${ES_HOME}` and set it as environment variable as shown here. Append the same into the `~/.bashrc` file:

   ```
   export ES_HOME=<path-to-elasticsearch-folder>
   export PATH=$PATH:$ES_HOME/bin
   ```

4. Edit the `${ES_HOME}/config/elasticsearch.yml` file with the following:

   ```
   network.host : 0.0.0.0
   ```

5. Make sure that the following limits are configured in
   `/etc/security/limits.conf`. If these limits are not configured, then configure
   it by editing the file with `sudo` user. A sample `sudo` command with VI editor can
   be used as given here, followed by the limits configurations:

   sudo vi /etc/security/limits.conf

   ```
   *     softnproc65536
   *     hard nproc 65536
   *     soft nofile 65536
   *     hard nofile 65536
   ```

6. Change the system parameter `vm.max_map_count` by editing the
   `/etc/sysctl.conf` file as a root user (**su - root**). Add the following
   configuration at the end of the file:

   vm.max_map_count = 262144

   The preceding configurations are required to increase the resources availability
   for any of the processes running in Linux environment. From **Elasticsearch 5.x**
   onwards these changes have been mandated for successful start of Elasticsearch
   process.

7. Restart the machine for the preceding changes to apply and launch the Elastic
   process via the following command. Ensure that before restart, all critical
   processes are gracefully shut down:

   ${ES_HOME}/bin/elasticsearch

The preceding steps would launch Elasticsearch in default configuration with Master and
Data node roles. These steps are common and consistent across multiple versions of
Elasticsearch.

In order to work through most of the examples outlined in this chapter, we would be using
the Sense plugin, which works over Kibana. Hence the next step would be to run Kibana
with the Sense plugin.

The Kibana installation package is specific to target operating system (OS). For Linux platforms, they are available as tarballs as well as RPMs with 32-bit and 64-bit variants. For the purpose of our examples, we would be installing tarball for 64-bit Linux. Follow these steps:

1. Download the tarball from the following location, using the following command:

```
wget
https://artifacts.elastic.co/downloads/kibana/kibana-5.3.0-linux-x8
6_64.tar.gz
```

2. Change to a user directory and extract the contents of the tarball using the following command:

```
tar -xzvf ${DOWNLOAD_DIR}/kibana-5.3.0-linux-x86_64.tar.gz
```

3. Set the environment variable ${KIBANA_HOME} pointing to the extracted Kibana folder, using the following commands. Add the same to ~/.bashrc file.

```
export KIBANA_HOME=<path-to-kibana-directory>
export PATH=$PATH:$KIBANA_HOME/bin
```

3. Edit ${KIBANA_HOME}/config/kibana.yml with the following setting for remote connectivity:

```
# To allow connections from remote users, set this parameter to a
non-loopback address.
server.host: 0.0.0.0
```

4. Launch Kibana with the following command:

```
${KIBANA_HOME}/bin/kibana
```

This would launch Kibana and the landing page can be seen by navigating to http://localhost:5601 as shown as follows (localhost can be substituted with IP/machine name if accessing remotely). The Dev Tools (left-hand side menu) shows a console to work with Elasticsearch server. This was known as the Sense plugin till Elasticsearch 2.x and had to be installed separately for those versions.

The reason we have briefly mentioned Elastic 2.x here is that some of the frameworks such as Flink are yet to support Elastic 5.x completely. We may need to switch to Elastic 2.x for Flink-specific integrations, however, the examples outlined here do not change whether we use Elastic 5.x or Elastic 2.x. The only thing that changes is its installation and setup.

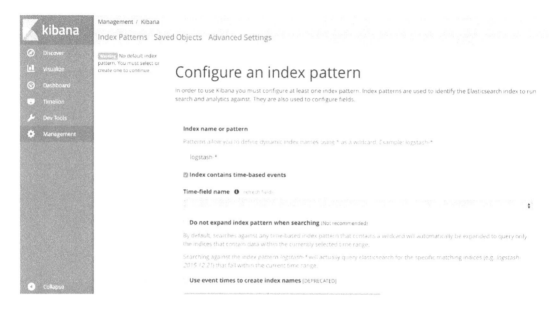

Figure 20: Kibana Landing Page

Kibana 5.x includes Dev Tools console, which we will leverage across all our examples, as shown here. The small Play button beside the command `GET _search` is used to execute the query and the results are shown in the right-hand split of the window:

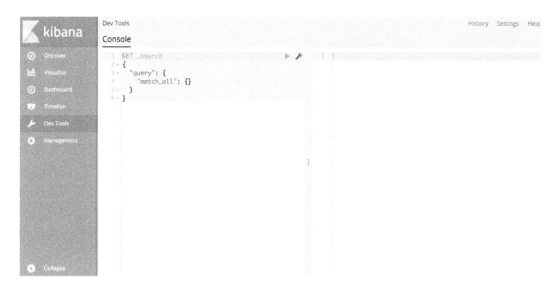

Figure 21: *Kibana Console for Query Execution*

We have now installed both Elasticsearch and Kibana. This completes our toolset to run our examples. Let's see Elasticsearch in action now in the following sections.

Creating and Deleting Indexes

An Index in Elasticsearch cluster can be created by following command (curl), that can be run in Linux's ssh console:

1. **Request:**

   ```
   curl -XPUT http://<es-server-ip>:9200/datalake -d
   '{"settings":{"number_of_shards": 2, "number_of_replicas": 2}}'
   ```

2. **Response:**

   ```
   {"acknowledged":true,"shards_acknowledged":true}
   ```

The reason that we installed Kibana was to simplify such query executions. We can also run the same query using Kibana as shown here. This approach is a much more convenient and user-friendly (REST UI). We would be using this UI for the remaining examples in this chapter; however, the preceding indicates that simple curl commands can also be used from machines that do not have Kibana installed.

With Kibana Dev Tools UI

Before we use the Kibana Dev Tools UI to create the index, we will have to remove the existing one because the index names are unique in an Elasticsearch data repository:

```
DELETE datalake
```

Figure 22: Index removal via the Console

Now let's create the same index again using the following query:

```
PUT datalake { "settings" :{"number_of_shards": 2,
"number_of_replicas": 2 } }
```

Figure 23: Index Creation Query

Indexing Documents

Now that we have the index created, we can indexed a document into the index. The only requirement for a document to be indexed is that it should be a JSON document as Elasticsearch is schema-less and derives the storage schema based on the document structure indexed.

As shown in the following figure, the command to index a document is `PUT {index-name}/{type}/{id}`:

```
PUT datalake/contacts/101
{
  "id":101,
  "cell":"(478) 531-2026",
  "work":"1-906-774-1226",
  "email":"vincenzo.hickle@yahoo.com"
}
```

Figure 24: Document Creation Query

As the document is indexed, Elasticsearch internally creates document mapping based on the data in the initial document. This mapping can be accessed as shown here:

```
GET datalake/_mapping/contacts
```

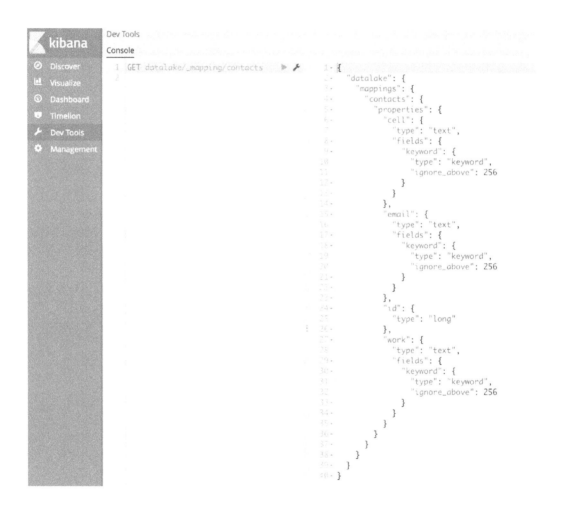

Figure 25: Retrieving Document Mapping via Query

A few observations from the preceding screenshot:

- Keyword analyzer is the default analyzer used for schema-less indexing
- Based on the input type, the type information in the schema has been derived
- Certain default validations have been put in place for text fields

These are very powerful features for a flexible indexing capability of a semi-structured or unstructured information.

Getting Indexed Document

Now that we have document indexed, let's access it and observe how it looks after getting stored in Elasticsearch.

In order to perform this, we would access the document by Id. Getting document by Id is a very important way to access the document from Elasticsearch as it is always real-time, and does not depend on refresh cycles.

A general syntax to access the document by Id is GET {index-name}/{type}/{id}, as shown here:

```
GET datalake/contacts/101
```

Figure 26: Query to Get Document By Id

As we see in the preceding snapshot:

1. The document is created with the same _id attribute as provided while indexing the document.
2. The attribute id, on the other hand, is like any other attribute and is not the _id attribute that Elasticsearch uses for lookup.
3. The version is 1, indicating that the document is just created and has not been updated. With every update, this version will increment.

4. The index name is `datalake` and type is `contacts`.

5. The `_source` contains the entire document provided for indexing. This is optional but is enabled by default. This is useful to keep the entire document along with the indexed fields.

Searching Documents

The documents has to be indexed for it to be searched in Elasticsearch. The document that we have indexed can be searched via the `_search` url with any of the following queries (each query has a different purpose):

```
GET {index-name}/_search
```

Searches for all the documents in an index are as shown here:

```
GET datalake/_search
```

Figure 27: Query to Get All Documents In an Index via Search URI

```
GET {index-name}/{type}/_search
```

Searches for all the documents belonging to a type in an index are as shown here:

```
GET datalake/contacts/_search
```

Figure 28: Query to Get All Documents of a Type in an Index

```
POST {index-name}/{type}/_search
```

Searches for all the documents belonging to a type in an index searched by the parameters specified in the POST are as shown here:

```
POST datalake/contacts/_search
{
  "query": {
    "term": { "email" : "vincenzo.hickle"}
  }
}
```

```
POST datalake/contacts/_search
{
  "query": {
    "term": { "email" : "yahoo.com"}
  }
}
```

```
POST datalake/contacts/_search
{
  "query": {
```

```
    "term": { "email" : "vincenzo.hickle@yahoo.com"}
  }
}
```

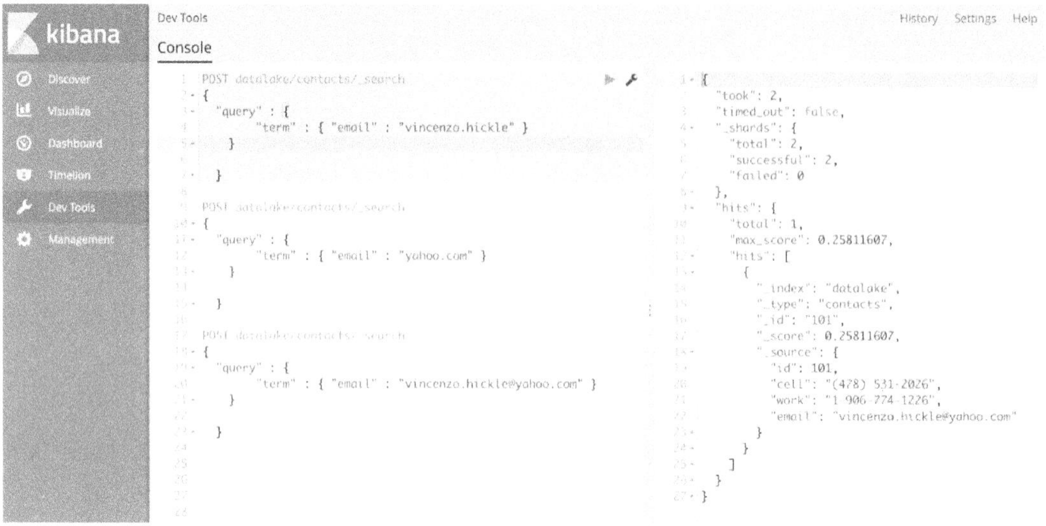

Figure 29: Different variations of search patterns by terms

As you see, there are 3 different types of POST queries and the observations are as given here:

- The first query tries to find matches for the email address, which it gets and responds with a hit with a partial e-mail address
- The second query also tries to find matches for the email address and gets it with the other part of the email address
- The third query, which has a complete email address, does not respond with any successful match since such a token does not exist

The main reason for the third query not to respond with any matching records is due to the keyword analyzer applied on the email field. If we want the email field to also match with the complete email address then we will need to multi-index (a field indexed using multiple analyzers) the email field.

Apart from the multiple patterns of matching, the _search URL supports a large number of additional functions including pagination, sort, aggregations, and multiple match functions.

Updating Documents

Now let's try and update the same document with a change in the email address. The update command has a form of POST {index-name}/{type}/{id} and the request body as shown here:

```
POST datalake/contacts/101
{
    "id":101,
    "cell":"(478) 531-2026",
    "work":"1-906-774-1226",
    "email":"vincenzo2.hickle@yahoo.com"
}
```

Figure 30: Document Update Query

Few observations here in the preceding response are:

- The version is updated to 2.
- The flag created is set to false and the result indicates a successful update.
- Total shards affected are 3 since our index was configured to have 2 replicas and 4 shards. That means there are 3 shards having the affected data; one is the primary and the other two are replica shards.

Deleting a document

Deleting a document can be performed by a command of the form `DELETE {index-name}/{type}/{id}`, as shown here:

```
DELETE datalake/contacts/101
```

Figure 31: Query to Delete a Document

As seen earlier the result indicates a deleted document. The `DELETE` in Elasticsearch is generally performed by id; however, deletion by query is also supported but it is a costlier operation. Again, the number of shards affected is 3 due to the same reason as stated earlier.

A point to remember here is that deletion does not reclaim the space immediately, till the deleted documents are expunged by the internal optimization/compaction processes.

Elasticsearch in purview of SCV use case

We have seen a high-level working of Elasticsearch via some basic examples. Let's put Elasticsearch to work with other components for our single customer view use case in the following sub-sections. This time we will be storing the data in PARQUET format and since this is one of our last examples with all components working together, we will try to build the Data Lake from scratch to understand the sequence of integrations involved starting with data preparation. We will only cover main commands as you can always refer to the previous chapter for more details if needed.

Data preparation

We will be using the same set of data as used before, that is, 2 million customer records, addresses, and contacts.

But before we proceed, let's clean the data created in previous chapters by following the steps explained here. Ensure the required processes are up and running for the cleanup, i.e. Hue, DFS, **hiveserver2**, Zookeeper and Kafka.

Initial Cleanup

Drop the tables from the Hive metadata with commands as shown here in Hue UI. Drop any other additional tables if present:

```
drop table customer;
drop table address;
drop table contacts;
```

Stop the dfs service (stop-dfs.sh) and clean up the Hadoop storage by formatting the Hadoop NameNode with the following command:

```
${HADOOP_HOME}/bin/hdfs namenode -format
```

Create new Hadoop directories with the following commands:

```
hdfs dfs -mkdir -p /datalake/raw/customer
hdfs dfs -mkdir -p /datalake/raw/address
hdfs dfs -mkdir -p /datalake/raw/contact
```

Remove the topics from Kafka servers to ensure we start clean, by using the following commands:

1. Get a list of all the topics:

   ```
   ${KAFKA_HOME}/bin/kafka-topics.sh --list --zookeeper 0.0.0.0:2181
   ```

2. For every topic, issue the following delete command (except for topic names prefixed with _):

   ```
   ${KAFKA_HOME}/bin/kafka-topics.sh --delete --topic <topic-name> --
   zookeeper 0.0.0.0:2181
   ```

Data Generation

Generate the data using the following commands as done in earlier chapters. For this example, we will target to generate 1 million rows for each of the entities:

Populate database

We will be reusing the database tables of customer and address for this example. In case the database tables are empty due to any reasons, the database can be re-populated using the same utility as before. The related command is again specified here briefly for quick reference. This command needs to be run from the location where we had extracted these utilities from the tar files:

```
java -jar client-generator-1.0-SNAPSHOT.jar config/db.properties  2000000
```

Generate Spool File

We can reuse the contacts.log file generated earlier. In case the file does not exist, it can be generated again as explained in the earlier chapter containing customer contacts. The following command is given for quick reference and needs to be run from the same location where these generators were extracted from their tar file:

```
java -jar web-generator-1.0-SNAPSHOT.jar contact.log 200000 contact
```

Once the spool file is available, move the spool file to the ${FLUME_DATA} folders for Flume processing.

Customer data import into Hive using Sqoop

The following configuration may be required to be added in ${HADOOP_HOME}/etc/hadoop/core-site.xml so that hue can impersonate the user creating the Parquet file:

```
<property>
  <name>hadoop.proxyuser.hue.hosts</name>
  <value>*</value>
</property>
<property>
  <name>hadoop.proxyuser.hue.groups</name>
  <value>*</value>
</property>
```

Once the preceding configurations are added, we will need to restart the dfs service with the following command:

```
${HADOOP_HOME}/sbin/stop-dfs.sh && ${HADOOP_HOME}/sbin/start-dfs.sh
```

Import the customer records from database to Hadoop RAW storage using Sqoop job which would write the data in Parquet format, using the following command:

```
${SQOOP_HOME}/bin/sqoop import --connect
jdbc:postgresql://<DB_SERVER_ADDRESS>/sourcedb?schema=public --table
customer --m 1 --username postgres --password <DB_PASSWORD> --as-
parquetfile --append --target-dir /datalake/raw/customer/$(date +%Y-%m-%d--
%H-%M)
```

A few observations from the preceding command:

- We are using Parquet file to store customer information.
- We have used 1 mapper (--m 1)
- We are partitioning the customer data by minute ($(date +%Y-%m-%d--%H-%M))

The Parquet file output can be compressed by snappy codec by specifying additional parameter --compression-codec. Further in this example, we will be partitioning data in HDFS by minute for consistency:

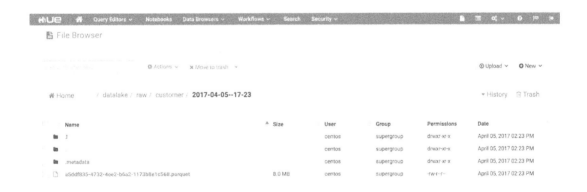

Figure 32: Customer Data Sqooped into HDFS as Parquet Files

Data acquisition via Flume into Kafka channel

Now let's use Flume to acquire the address data as well as contacts data from the database and spool file, respectively (same as we did in the previous chapter). In order to achieve this, we will define a single Flume configuration file, `${FLUME_HOME}/conf/customer-address-contact-conf.properties`, with dedicated Kafka channels to convert the data of both the sources into events.

The complete Flume configuration is as shown here:

```
agent.sources = sql-source spool-source

agent.sources.spool-source.type=spooldir
agent.sources.spool-source.spoolDir=<spool-file-data-dir>
agent.sources.spool-source.inputCharset=ASCII

agent.sources.sql-source.type=org.keedio.flume.source.SQLSource
agent.sources.sql-
source.hibernate.connection.url=jdbc:postgresql://localhost/sourcedb?schema
=public
agent.sources.sql-source.hibernate.connection.user=postgres
agent.sources.sql-source.hibernate.connection.password=<db-password>
agent.sources.sql-
source.hibernate.dialect=org.hibernate.dialect.PostgreSQLDialect
agent.sources.sql-
source.hibernate.connection.driver_class=org.postgresql.Driver
agent.sources.sql-source.custom.query= SELECT id, customer_id, street1,
street2, city, state, country, zip_pin_postal_code from address WHERE id >
$@$ ORDER BY id ASC
agent.sources.sql-source.status.file.path=/data1/var/lib/flume/customer-db
agent.sources.sql-source.status.file.name=<path-of-status-file>
agent.sources.sql-source.batch.size = 5000
agent.sources.sql-source.max.rows = 5000
agent.sources.sql-source.read.only=true
agent.sources.sql-source.hibernate.c3p0.min_size=10
agent.sources.sql-source.hibernate.c3p0.max_size=10
agent.sources.sql-source.hibernate.connection.provider_class =
org.hibernate.connection.C3P0ConnectionProvider

# The channel can be defined as follows.
agent.channels = contactChannel addressChannel

agent.channels.contactChannel.type
=org.apache.flume.channel.kafka.KafkaChannel
agent.channels.contactChannel.kafka.bootstrap.servers=<kafka-broker-ip-
addr>:9092
agent.channels.contactChannel.kafka.topic=contacts
```

```
agent.sources.spool-source.channels = contactChannel

agent.channels.addressChannel.type
=org.apache.flume.channel.kafka.KafkaChannel
agent.channels.addressChannel.kafka.bootstrap.servers=<kafka-broker-ip-
addr>:9092
agent.channels.addressChannel.kafka.topic=address
agent.sources.sql-source.channels = addressChannel
```

Code 02: Flume Configuration

As shown in the preceding configuration, the address data is streamed as events into the address topic and the contacts spool file data is streamed as events into contacts topic. The previous configuration is slightly different from other configuration we have seen so far for sql-source, since the sql-source has a tendency to repeat/duplicate records at large volumes. Here, for sql-source we are specifying custom query with a special string $@$, which acts as a tracker and helps prevent duplication of records.

Launch the Flume agent with the preceding configuration as shown in the following command:

```
${FLUME_HOME}/bin/flume-ng agent --conf ${FLUME_HOME}/conf/  -f
${FLUME_HOME}/conf/customer-address-contact-conf.properties -n agent -
Dflume.root.logger=INFO,console
```

Address data from the database and contacts data from the Spool file would be converted into events and pushed into the respective Kafka topics.

The progress may be checked by looking into the topic offsets with following commands

```
${KAFKA_HOME}/bin/kafka-run-class.sh kafka.tools.GetOffsetShell --broker-
list <broker-ip-address>:9092 --topic address
```

```
${KAFKA_HOME}/bin/kafka-run-class.sh kafka.tools.GetOffsetShell --broker-
list <broker-ip-address>:9092 --topic contacts
```

Data ingestion via Flink to HDFS and Elasticsearch

As the events are queued into the respective Kafka topics, the Flink processing pipeline gets triggered and starts consuming Kafka events from these topics.

Taking as a reference the Flink example covered in an earlier chapter, we build two pipelines here, one for address and the other for contacts. Both of these pipelines would stream the events into two sinks, HDFS and Elasticsearch, respectively so that both of these ingestions are part of the same transaction.

Building over the earlier Flink example, which we ran from IDE, we would now package it in such a way that we can also deploy the code in the Flink container. This aspect of Flink deployment is new and not covered in the earlier chapters.

In order to achieve this, let's start looking at some of the key elements of the Flink pipeline project. The complete source code for this project can be found in `chapter10/speed-address-flink-ingestor` (address Flink pipeline) and `chapter10/speed-contacts-flink-ingestor` (contacts Flink pipeline). In order to simplify, we will be discussing the entire code section by section.

Packaging via POM file

The POM file structure, as shown here includes all the required dependency. Also, it has both Shade and Avro plugin configured, which helps in packaging all the dependencies into a self-executable JAR. The Avro plugin generates the Avro classes based on Avro schema as part of the maven build:

```
<project xmlns="http://maven.apache.org/POM/4.0.0"
xmlns:xsi="http://www.w3.org/2001/XMLSchema-instance"
         xsi:schemaLocation="http://maven.apache.org/POM/4.0.0
http://maven.apache.org/xsd/maven-4.0.0.xsd">
<modelVersion>4.0.0</modelVersion>
<parent>
…..PARENT POM LINKAGE…..
</parent>
<groupId>com.laketravels</groupId>
<artifactId>speed-address-flink-ingestor</artifactId>
<dependencies>
<dependency>
<groupId>org.apache.kafka</groupId>
<artifactId>kafka-clients</artifactId>
<version>0.10.1.1</version>
</dependency>
 …..OTHER DEPENDENCIES…..
</dependencies>
<build>
<plugins>
<plugin>
<groupId>org.apache.maven.plugins</groupId>
<artifactId>maven-shade-plugin</artifactId>
```

```
<version>3.0.0</version>
<executions>
<execution>
<phase>package</phase>
<goals>
<goal>shade</goal>
</goals>
<configuration>
<artifactSet>
<excludes>
<exclude>org.apache.flink:flink-shaded-*</exclude>
<exclude>org.apache.flink:flink-core</exclude>
 …..OTHER EXCLUDES THAT ARE PROVIDED BY FLINK CONTAINER…..
</excludes>
</artifactSet>
<filters>
<filter>
<artifact>org.apache.flink:*</artifact>
<excludes>
 …..FOLDER EXCLUDES FOR FLINK SHADED AND WEB-DOCS…..
</excludes>
</filter>
<filter>
<!- EXCLUDE SIGNATURES -->
<artifact>*:*</artifact>
<excludes>
<exclude>META-INF/*.SF</exclude>
 …..OTHER SIGNATURE EXCLUDES…..
</excludes>
</filter>
</filters>
<transformers>
 …...TRANSFORMERS TO INCLUDE MAIN CLASS AND RESOURCE TRANSFORMER…..
<createDependencyReducedPom>false</createDependencyReducedPom>
</configuration>
</execution>
</executions>
</plugin>
<plugin>
<groupId>org.apache.avro</groupId>
<artifactId>avro-maven-plugin</artifactId>
<version>1.7.7</version>
<executions>
<execution>
 …..AVRO PLUGIN CONFIGURATION FOR GENERATE SOURCE PHASE WITH TARGET CLASS
GENERATION FOLDERS…..
</execution>
</executions>
```

```
</plugin>
</plugins>
</build>
</project>
```

Avro schema definitions

The parquet file format uses Avro schema for object definition. These Avro schemas are placed in the `src/main/resources` folder in both the projects. A typical Avro schema for address is as shown here:

```
{
    "namespace": "example.avro",
    "type": "record",
    "name": "Contact",
    "fields": [
        {"name": "id", "type": "string"},
        {"name": "customerId",  "type": "string"},
        {"name": "street1", "type": "string"},
        {"name": "street2", "type": "string"},
        {"name": "city", "type": "string"},
        {"name": "state", "type": "string"},
        {"name": "country", "type": "string"},
        {"name": "zipCode", "type": "string"}
    ]
}
```

Code 03: Avro Schema

Schema deserialization class

As discussed in the earlier chapter, this class is used for converting a Kafka event into Tuple2 so that they can be written to HDFS. Once the event is converted into Tuple2, it can also be used to write/put into Elasticsearch (ES). Since we want to have both HDFS and ES sinks as part of the same transaction, such a conversion would help.

This deserialization is slightly different for address and contacts, since both are being streamed via different sources. As seen from the Flume configuration, address is sourced from database using sql-source which adds a timestamp and are comma separated elements, while contacts is sourced from spool file, which add the 2 byte character before every Flume event and contains a spool line having comma separated values. Because of this, there is slight difference in deserialization as shown here.

The following is the Deserialization Schema for Address objects:

```java
public class Tuple2CustomerAddressDeserializationSchema implements
DeserializationSchema {

    private static final ObjectMapper MAPPER = new ObjectMapper();
    private static final int KAFKA_TIMESTAMP_LENGTH = 28;

    public Object deserialize(byte[] bytes) throws IOException {
        String message = new String(bytes,KAFKA_TIMESTAMP_LENGTH,
                                    bytes.length-(KAFKA_TIMESTAMP_LENGTH));
        if (message.trim().length()>0) {
            Address address = new Address();
            String[] fields = message.replaceAll("\"","").split(",");
            address.setId(Integer.parseInt(fields[0].trim()));
            address.setCustomerId(Integer.parseInt(fields[1].trim()));
            address.setStreet1(fields[2]);
            address.setStreet2(fields[3]);
            address.setCity(fields[4]);
            address.setState(fields[5]);
            address.setCountry(fields[6]);
            address.setZipCode(fields[7]);
            Tuple2<IntWritable, Text> tuple = new Tuple2<IntWritable,
Text>();
            tuple.setFields(new IntWritable(address.getId()),
                    new Text(MAPPER.writeValueAsString(address)));
            return tuple;
        } else {
            return null;
        }
    }

    public boolean isEndOfStream(Object o) {
        return false;
    }

    public TypeInformation<Tuple2<IntWritable, Text>> getProducedType() {
        return new TupleTypeInfo<Tuple2<IntWritable, Text>>
            (TypeExtractor.createTypeInfo(IntWritable.class),
            TypeExtractor.createTypeInfo(Text.class));
    }
}
```

Code 04: Address Event Deserialization Schema

Shown is the Deserialization Schema for Contact objects:

```
public class Tuple2CustomerContactDeserializationSchema implements
DeserializationSchema {

  private static final ObjectMapper MAPPER = new ObjectMapper();

  public Object deserialize(byte[] bytes) throws IOException {
      //Spooled messages have 2 bytes of leading unicode chars
      String message = new String(bytes, 2, bytes.length-2);
      if (message.trim().length()>0) {
          String[] contactFields = message.split(",");
          Contact contact = new Contact();
          contact.setId(Integer.parseInt(contactFields[0].trim()));
          contact.setCell(contactFields[1]);
          contact.setWork(contactFields[2]);
          contact.setEmail(contactFields[3]);
          Tuple2<IntWritable, Text> tuple = new Tuple2<IntWritable,
Text>();
          tuple.setFields(new IntWritable(contact.getId()),
                  new Text(MAPPER.writeValueAsString(contact)));
          return tuple;
      } else {
        return null;
      }
  }

  public boolean isEndOfStream(Object o) {
      return false;
  }

  public TypeInformation<Tuple2<IntWritable, Text>> getProducedType() {
      return new TupleTypeInfo<Tuple2<IntWritable, Text>>
        (TypeExtractor.createTypeInfo(IntWritable.class),
        TypeExtractor.createTypeInfo(Text.class));
  }
}
```

Code 05: Contacts Deserialization Schema

Writing to HDFS as parquet files

Since we want to write Parquet files into HDFS, we would be using the same BucketSink as used before but with a custom Parquet Writer and a DateTimeBucketer with a minute-based partition, as shown as follows. The Bucket sink path is passed as a command line argument, hdfsPath, which we will discuss later. Update the HADOOP_USER_NAME system property in the code to your user account name in CentOS:

```
System.setProperty("HADOOP_USER_NAME", "centos");

//HDFS Sink
BucketingSink<Tuple2<IntWritable, Text>> hdfsSink = new
BucketingSink<Tuple2<IntWritable,
Text>>(parameterTool.getRequired("hdfsPath"));
hdfsSink.setBucketer(new DateTimeBucketer("yyyy-MM-dd--HH-mm"));
hdfsSink.setWriter(new SinkParquetWriter<Tuple2<IntWritable,
Text>>("address.avsc"));
hdfsSink.setBatchSize(1024 * 1024 * 1);
messageStream.addSink(hdfsSink);
```

Code 06: HDFS Bucket Sink

The custom Parquet writer writes a specific data object as an Avro Record to HDFS. It is then converted to Parquet format using the AvroParquet class with SNAPPY compression enabled as shown here for the address data object:

```
private static class SinkParquetWriter<T> implements Writer<T> {

transient ParquetWriter writer = null;
    String schema = null;
transient Schema schemaInstance = null;
final ObjectMapper MAPPER = new ObjectMapper();

public SinkParquetWriter(String schema) {
this.writer = writer;
this.schema = schema;
try {
this.schemaInstance = new Schema.Parser().parse(getClass().getClassLoader()
                  .getResourceAsStream(schema));
        } catch (IOException e) {
throw new RuntimeException(e);
        }
    }

public void open(FileSystem fileSystem, Path path) throws IOException {
```

```
writer = AvroParquetWriter.builder(path)
                .withSchema(this.schemaInstance)
                .withCompressionCodec(CompressionCodecName.SNAPPY)
                .build();
    }

public long flush() throws IOException {
return writer.getDataSize();
    }

public long getPos() throws IOException {
return writer.getDataSize();
    }

public void close() throws IOException {
writer.close();
    }


public void write(T t) throws IOException {
final Tuple2<IntWritable, Text> tuple = (Tuple2<IntWritable, Text>) t;
final List values = new ArrayList();
        GenericRecord record = new GenericData.Record(schemaInstance);
        String inputRecord=tuple.f1.toString();
        Address address = MAPPER.readValue(inputRecord,
                                                        Address.class);
        record.put("id", String.valueOf(address.getId()));
        record.put("customerId", address.getCustomerId());
        record.put("street1", address.getStreet1());
        record.put("street2", address.getStreet2());
        record.put("city", address.getCity());
        record.put("state", address.getState());
        record.put("country", address.getCountry());
        record.put("zipCode", address.getZipCode());

writer.write(record);
    }

public Writer<T> duplicate() {
return new SinkParquetWriter<T>(schema);
    }
}
```

Code 07: Custom Parquet Writer

Writing into Elasticsearch

Flink supports various connectors which are included as part of the Flink distribution. There is also a connector available for Elasticsearch as part of the Flink distribution. As we see here, we are also writing the documents with the same id as contained in the document, instead of depending on randomly generated document id. Additionally, we are specifying the bulk size and bulk flush interval for optimum throughput with Elasticsearch connector.

The next code snippet uses Elasticsearch ink for Address. A similar code is used for contacts as well. Certain properties such as `esHost` and `esPort` are passed as command line arguments. As we see here, we are also writing the documents with the same id as contained in the document, instead of depending on randomly generated document id. Additionally, we are specifying the bulk size and bulk flush interval for optimum throughput with elasticsearch connector:

```
//Elasticsearch Sink
Map<String, String> config = Maps.newHashMap();
config.put("bulk.flush.max.actions", "1000");
config.put("bulk.flush.interval.ms", "250");
config.put("cluster.name", "elasticsearch");

List<InetSocketAddress> transports = new ArrayList<InetSocketAddress>();
transports.add(new
InetSocketAddress(InetAddress.getByName(parameterTool.getRequired("esHost")
),
Integer.parseInt(parameterTool.getRequired("esPort"))
));

messageStream.addSink(new ElasticsearchSink<Tuple2<IntWritable,
Text>>(config, transports,
new ElasticsearchSinkFunction<Tuple2<IntWritable,Text>>() {
public IndexRequest createIndexRequest(Tuple2<IntWritable, Text> element) {
return Requests.indexRequest()
                    .index("address")
                    .type("address")
                    .id(element.f0.toString())
                    .source(((Text) element.getField(1)).toString());
        }

public void process(Tuple2<IntWritable, Text> intWritableTextTuple2,
RuntimeContext runtimeContext, RequestIndexer requestIndexer) {
requestIndexer.add(createIndexRequest(intWritableTextTuple2));
        }
    }));
```

Code 08: Elasticsearch Sink

Command line arguments

In order to run the Flink ingestors, we need to compile the code into a standalone executable JAR, using the following command within the project `chapter10` folder.

```
mvn install
```

This will generate two JAR files for deployment within Flink, one as `speed-address-flink-ingestor-SNAPSHOT-1.0.jar` and the other as `speed-contacts-flink-ingestor-SNAPSHOT-1.0.jar` in their respective project folders.

Once the JAR is generated, we will need to deploy it within Flink and pass command line arguments in the following pattern as shown here, so that code has all the required details for execution. The same approach is used while running the Flink pipeline from within the Flink container. The arguments are as shownhereow for address and contacts processing, respectively:

```
--topic address --bootstrap.servers <kafka-ip-address>:9092 --
zookeeper.connect <zk-ip-address>:2181 --group.id 1 --hdfsPath
hdfs://<hadoop-namenode-ip-address>:9000/datalake/raw/address --esHost <es-
ip-address>  --esPort 9300 --auto.offset.reset earliest

--topic contacts --bootstrap.servers <kafka-ip-address>:9092 --
zookeeper.connect <zk-ip-address>:2181 --group.id 1 --hdfsPath
hdfs://<hadoop-namenode-ip-address>:9000/datalake/raw/contact --esHost <es-
ip-address>  --esPort 9300 --auto.offset.reset earliest
```

In the next section, we will see how we can deploy these JARS inside the Flink container as Flink jobs.

Flink deployment

Deployment of the Flink pipeline is a simple process. However, it can pose challenges in terms of version mismatch between various libraries. As a rule of thumb, it would be better to reuse the Flink libraries that are available as part of the distribution and then add other libraries which are not available as part of the Flink distribution.

While submitting the JAR as a Flink job, Flink looks for dependencies in its classpath, and if it is not able to find any libraries, it is not able to run the job.

In order to provision all the dependencies in the Flink classpath, it is helpful to copy the shaded jar into `${FLINK_HOME}/lib` folder before submitting the JAR as a job for execution. This takes care of all Hadoop and Avro related dependencies.

However, there would be few libraries which needs to be added additionally to the Flink classpath. With respect to this example, we need to copy `flink-hadoop-compatibility` jar using the following commands (assuming that flink-hadoop-compatibility jar was installed while building from source):

```
cp ~/.m2/repository/org/apache/flink/flink-hadoop-
compatibility_2.10/1.3.0/flink-hadoop-compatibility_2.10-1.3.0.jar
${FLINK_HOME}/lib
```

For Flink to get the other dependencies to the class, we suggest also copying on the jars (`speed-address-flink-ingestor-1.0-SNAPSHOT.jar` or `speed-contacts-flink-ingestor-1.0-SNAPSHOT.jar`) into `${FLINK_HOME}/lib`. You can use the following command if you have build the JAR files in your local machine:

```
scp <source-file-jar> <centos_user>@<ip-of-vm>:~/
```

Additionally, we need to ensure that all the required systems are running that would be required by the Flink pipeline. These include HDFS, KAFKA, ZOOKEEPER and ELASTICSEARCH.

Once these prerequisites are in place, we can build the example and deploy them as Flink pipeline into the Flink container by following these steps:

1. Launch the local Flink Container using the following command:

   ```
   ${FLINK_HOME}/bin/start-local.sh
   ```

2. Navigate to the Flink URL (`http://ip-of-vm:8081`) to submit the job by providing the same command line arguments as discussed earlier and upload the Flink ingestor JARS as shown here. Ensure that the command line arguments are provided to the respective jobs being submitted. The difference would be the topic name and the HDFS path. The complete set of arguments is specified here for reference:

   ```
   --topic address --bootstrap.servers <kafka-ip-address>:9092 --
   zookeeper.connect <zk-ip-address>:2181 --group.id 1 --hdfsPath
   hdfs://<hadoop-namenode-ip-address>:9000/datalake/raw/address --
   esHost <es-ip-address>  --esPort 9300 --auto.offset.reset earliest
   ```

Figure 33: Flink Job Deployment

To check whether Elasticsearch is receiving the messages from Kafka, run the following command and you should see document count in Elasticsearch increasing:

```
curl -XGET <ip-of-VM>:9200/_cat/indices?v
```

If the count is not getting shown, we would say running the Flume command as detailed earlier to start pumping messages into the Kafka queue. This would definitely trigger Flink processing of messages.

3. Once the job is submitted, the Flink UI navigates to a job status and management page, as shown in the following figure:

Figure 34: Job Status Page

4. Similarly, the address job can also be deployed to the Flink pipelines in parallel. You can see that events from the respective topics are consumed and then written to both HDFS and Elasticsearch.

Parquet data visualization as Hive tables

Parquet data files, once ingested, can be easily viewed using Hive tables by creating Hive external tables using the scripts given here. This can be executed via the Hue UI (Hive Query Builder) as detailed in earlier chapters:

```
SET mapred.input.dir.recursive=true;

CREATE EXTERNAL TABLE customer(id int, first_name string, last_name string,
dob BIGINT)
STORED AS PARQUET LOCATION '/datalake/raw/customer';

CREATE EXTERNAL TABLE address(  id string,
                                customerId string,
                                street1 string,
```

```
                        street2 string,
                        city string,
                        state string,
                        country string,
                        zipCode string
                        )
STORED AS PARQUET LOCATION '/datalake/raw/address';

CREATE EXTERNAL TABLE contact(id string, cell string, phone string, email
string)
STORED AS PARQUET LOCATION '/datalake/raw/contact';
```

Code 09: Parquet File Backed HIVE Table Creation Scripts

The tables created using the preceding scripts are as shown in the following figure. The data shown is being sourced from the Parquet files:

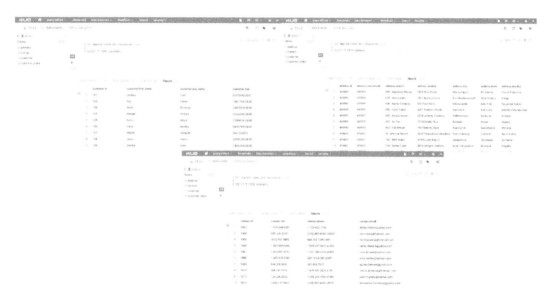

Figure 35: Parquet Backed Hive Tables

Data indexing from Hive

Now that we can visualize all the data loaded into Hadoop via Hive tables, we have complete customer data in Hadoop. The address and contacts data is there in both Elasticsearch and Hadoop, using Flink pipeline. Also, customer profile data is available in Hadoop, using Sqoop job. But, we don't have customer profile data in Elasticsearch.

For this, we can export the Hive data as Elasticsearch indices. This can be achieved by using ES-Hadoop framework, which is part of Elastic Stack.

For ES-Hadoop framework to work with Hive, a quick setup and configuration are required, as summarized here:

1. Download the ES-Hadoop binaries from the following location using the following command

    wget
    http://download.elastic.co/hadoop/elasticsearch-hadoop-5.4.0.zip

2. Change to a user directory and unzip the binaries using the following command:

    unzip ${DOWNLOAD_DIR}/elasticsearch-hadoop-5.4.0.zip

3. Let's refer to the extracted folder as ${ES_HADOOP_HOME}.

4. Configure ${HIVE_HOME}/conf/hive-site.xml with following configuration (the property placeholder would already be available in the file). Replace ${ES_HADOOP_HOME} with the complete path:

    ```
    <property>
        <name>hive.reloadable.aux.jars.path</name>
        <value>
    ${ES_HADOOP_HOME}/dist/elasticsearch-hadoop-hive-5.4.0.jar
        </value>
        <description>
            Jars can be renewed by executing reload command. And these
            jars can be used as the auxiliary classes like creating a
    UDF or
            SerDe.
        </description>
    </property>
    ```

5. Launch or restart the Hive server after stopping with the following command:

```
${HIVE_HOME}/bin/hive --service hiveserver2 -hiveconf
hive.root.logging=info
```

Now let's put ES-Hadoop to action by creating an external Hive table with the Elasticsearch storage by executing the following script in the Hue UI (Hive Query Builder):

```
CREATE EXTERNAL TABLE customer_index (
    id              string,
    firstName       string,
    lastname        string,
    dob             bigint
    )
STORED BY 'org.elasticsearch.hadoop.hive.EsStorageHandler'
TBLPROPERTIES( 'es.resource' = 'customer/customer',
               'es.url' = '<es-server-ip-addr>:9200',
'es.mapping.id' = 'id'
            );
```

Code 10: Hive Index Table Definition Backed by Elasticsearch

Once the external table is created, run the following query to load the external table with data. This would get indexed into the Elasticsearch server with index name as customer and _type as customer as per the preceding table definition:

```
SET mapred.input.dir.recursive=true;

INSERT OVERWRITE TABLE customer_index select id, first_name, last_name, dob
from customer;
```

Code 11: Data Loading from Hive into Elasticsearch

We have now created a Hive view over an Elasticsearch storage using ES-Hadoop framework. The customer mapping is inferred from the data, since elasticsearch supports schema-less indexing:

```
GET customer/_count
GET _mapping/customer
```

Figure 36: Customer Index Document Count and Type Mapping

Query data from ES (customer, address, and contacts)

We now have all the data in Elasticsearch including the customer profile data merged from the Hadoop layer. We can query them by taking advantage of the Lambda architecture, as shown here:

```
POST customer/_search
{
  "query" : {
    "term":{"id" : "18000"}
  }
}
```

Console

```
 1  POST customer/_search
 2      {
 3          "query" : {
 4              "term":{"id" : "18000"}
 5          }
 6      }
 7
 8  POST address/_search
 9      {
10          "query" : {
11              "term":{"id" : "18000"}
12          }
13      }
14
15  POST contacts/_search
16      {
17          "query" : {
18              "term":{"id" : "18000"}
19          }
20      }
```

Figure 37: Queries retrieving indexed records

The query shown in the previous figure when executed, shows the result in the **Sense Chrome** plugin as shown in the following screenshot:

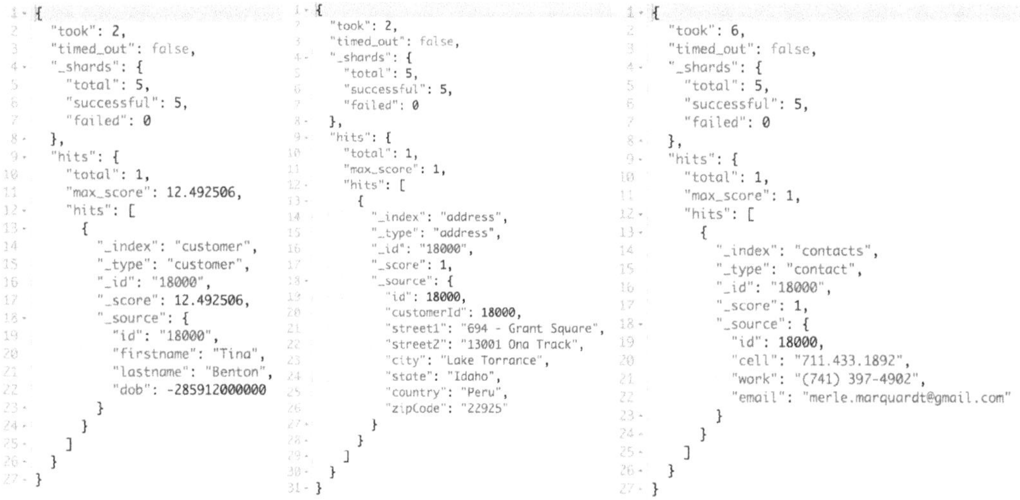

```
{
  "took": 2,
  "timed_out": false,
  "_shards": {
    "total": 5,
    "successful": 5,
    "failed": 0
  },
  "hits": {
    "total": 1,
    "max_score": 12.492506,
    "hits": [
      {
        "_index": "customer",
        "_type": "customer",
        "_id": "18000",
        "_score": 12.492506,
        "_source": {
          "id": "18000",
          "firstname": "Tina",
          "lastname": "Benton",
          "dob": -285912000000
        }
      }
    ]
  }
}
```

```
{
  "took": 2,
  "timed_out": false,
  "_shards": {
    "total": 5,
    "successful": 5,
    "failed": 0
  },
  "hits": {
    "total": 1,
    "max_score": 1,
    "hits": [
      {
        "_index": "address",
        "_type": "address",
        "_id": "18000",
        "_score": 1,
        "_source": {
          "id": 18000,
          "customerId": 18000,
          "street1": "694 - Grant Square",
          "street2": "13001 Ona Track",
          "city": "Lake Torrance",
          "state": "Idaho",
          "country": "Peru",
          "zipCode": "22925"
        }
      }
    ]
  }
}
```

```
{
  "took": 6,
  "timed_out": false,
  "_shards": {
    "total": 5,
    "successful": 5,
    "failed": 0
  },
  "hits": {
    "total": 1,
    "max_score": 1,
    "hits": [
      {
        "_index": "contacts",
        "_type": "contact",
        "_id": "18000",
        "_score": 1,
        "_source": {
          "id": 18000,
          "cell": "711.433.1892",
          "work": "(741) 397-4902",
          "email": "merle.marquardt@gmail.com"
        }
      }
    ]
  }
}
```


Figure 38: Response of Queries from Elasticsearch

As shown in the previous figure, we are performing a search operation on the id field. However, a better approach could have been by performing a lookup using id from a performance perspective for light-weight and absolute real time access.

Getting the document by `_id` (internal id of every document in Elasticsearch) can also be done here, however, we wanted to show lookup by search as another possibility. If we had not specified explicit mapping of id during indexing processes, Elasticsearch would have auto generated an internal id for the documents before ingesting. This would limit us from doing a lookup by id.

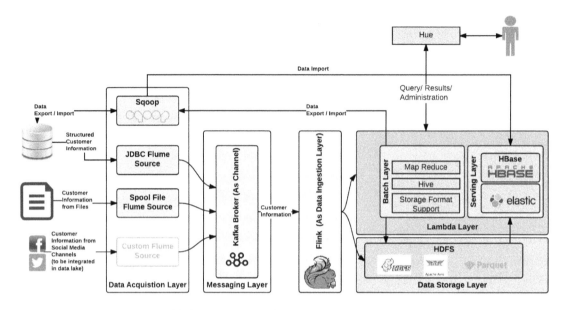

Figure 39: SCV use case with Elasticsearch technical component

When to use Elasticsearch

Use Elasticsearch when:

- You want to do a lot of text based searches.
- You want to analyse huge amounts of data which are non-relational. For example, analyse varied logs from applications which are non-relational and require text based searching to make sense of it.
- You are looking for lightning fast query results, especially if you are looking for text based search for dealing with autocompletion in your application.
- You are looking for a schema-less data store (explicitly it is really good to store JSON documents).

When not to use Elasticsearch

Don't use Elasticsearch or use it with caution if:

- You are looking for catering to transaction handling.
- You are planning to do a highly intensive computational job in the data store layer.
- You are looking to use this as a primary data store. If this is a requirement, when data is inserted, Elasticsearch has to re-index and this would take some time and wouldn't be available as and when the data was inserted and updated.
- You are looking for an ACID compliant data store.
- You are looking for a durable data store.

Other options

We have chosen Elastic Stack as our indexed data store. Even though this is a strong technology choice in this space, we do have options which could be considered and chosen as the case may be. One main contender in this space is Apache Solr and we will discuss that in brief here.

Apache Solr

Apache Solr is the popular, blazing-fast, open source enterprise search platform built on Apache Lucene. Solr is a standalone enterprise search server with a REST-like API. You put documents in it (called "indexing") via JSON, XML, CSV or binary over HTTP. You query it via HTTP GET and receive JSON, XML, CSV or binary results.

`-http://lucene.apache.org/solr/`

The features at `http://lucene.apache.org/solr/features.html`are listed here, making it an ideal choice for the capability that we are looking for in our Data Lake implementation:

- **Advanced and optimized full-text search**: Powered by Lucene's advanced matching and searching capability
- **Capable of handling high-volume traffic**
- **Standards based open interfaces**: XML, JSON and HTTP: because of the following standards, easy to code applications and also easy to maintain
- **Comprehensive administration interfaces**: Built-in responsive administrative user interface
- **Easy monitoring**: Publishes various metrics via **Java Management eXtensions (JMX)**
- **Highly scalable and fault-tolerant**: Uses Apache ZooKeeper internally for scaling out easily and also distributable
- **Flexible with adaptable configuration**
- **Near real-time indexing**: Uses Lucene's real-time indexing capability to achieve this.
- Extensible with plugin architecture: built-in packaged plugins/extensions and easy creation of custom ones as needed.
- **Support for both schema and schema-less documents**
- **Faceted search and filtering capability**
- **Capable of geospatial search**: Location based search features built-in
- **Highly configurable text analysis**: Built-in support for many languages and also has other text analysis tools built-in
- **Configurable and extensible caching**
- **Built-in security**: SSL, authentication and role-based authorization
- **Diverse and advanced storage options**
- **Capable of rich document parsing**: Apache Tika built-in, is making it easy to index rich content in the form of PDF, Word, and so on

These are some of the features that could be looked upon if this technology has to be chosen for your specific use cases.

Summary

As with other chapters in this part of the book, we covered the layer and its technology. We gave the reason this technology was chosen and then soon delved deep into the working of this technology, its architecture, its components and so on.

We then explained some of the important aspects of this technology and delved deep into an actual working example. We brought the SCV use case in conjunction with this technology; we closed off this chapter with sections detailing when and when not to use Elasticsearch and closing with other options that could be used in place of the chosen Elasticsearch.

This technology aspect in our Data Lake is significant, and we are sure it is one of the handy technology additions. With this technology detailed, we are almost done with this part of book. With this chapter, we have indeed covered almost all the technologies in our Data Lake; also we have now connected some links between the technologies in our Data Lake. We have seen part of the SCV use case already implemented, and in our next part we will start making final touches and connections so that other layers in our Data Lake (namely Lambda Batch Layer, Lambda Speed Layer, and Lambda Serving Layer) become alive and kicking.

After going through this chapter, you should have a good understanding of Elasticsearch as a data indexing framework and various data analyzers provided by the framework for efficient searches. You'd also know how Elasticsearch can be leveraged for data lakes and data at scale with efficient sharding and distribution mechanisms for consistent performance. Your understanding on how Elasticsearch can be used for fast streaming and how it can used for high-performance applications should be much better now.

11

Data Lake Components Working Together

Pat on your back for reaching this far! Fabulous!

By this time, if you have followed chapter by chapter and also done your coding side by side, you would have unknowingly implemented almost the complete Data Lake.

Here in this chapter, we are tying some of the loose ends in the Data Lake implemented so far and also making some recommendations and considerations that you can think of while implementing the Data Lake for your organization.

We will start of this chapter with the SCV use case, see where we have reached, and then try closing the gaps. We will then give some aspects of the Data Lake implementation that we haven't covered in detail when we were going through the previous chapters.

We will also give some advice that you could take when going through the Data Lake implementation.

The approach of this book has been that while going through previous part, you would have almost done with the implementation of Data Lake but not really gotten the full picture. Hopefully in this chapter, we can show you that full picture and then close off some of the leftover portions.

Where we stand with Data Lake

This figure shows where we have reached with our Data Lake after covering *part 2* of this book:

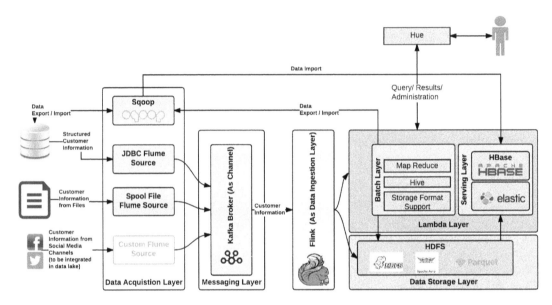

Figure 01: Data Lake implemented so far in this book

HDFS	Distributed File Storage
MapReduce	Batch Processing Engine
YARN	Resource Negotiator
HBase	Columnar and Key Value NoSQL database that runs on HDFS
Hive	Query engine that provides SQL like access to HDFS
Impala	Fast Query Engine for analytical queries on HDFS
Sqoop	Data Acquisition and Ingestion
Flume	Data Acquisition and Ingestion via streamed flume events
Kafka	Highly Scalable Distributed Messaging Engine
Flink	All purpose Real Time data processing and ingestion with Batch Support

| Spark | All purpose Fast Batch Processing and ingestion with support for real time processing via micro-batches |
| Elasticsearch | Fast Distributed Indexing Engine built on Lucene, also used as a Document based NoSQL data store. |

By this time, in your Data Lake data would have flown from various source systems, through various Data Lake components and persisted. You also would have some mechanisms by that you could view the data in the Data Lake and do some analysis.

This is not the end of Data Lake implementation as we have so many additional capabilities that can be build on top of this base Data Lake to make the best use of it for your organization.

In the following sections we will cover those capabilities and also will try and give our recommendation on technology choice to achieve that capabilities.

We will also give some considerations and recommendation that we feel important while implementing such a Data Lake. These are just some thoughts and it is not to be considered as authoritative, rather, some areas that you could think off now and in future in regards to Data Lake.

In some scenarios we will cover some new technologies but, we will cover these in a very high-level as delving deep into each is not in scope of this chapter.

Core architecture principles of Data Lake

We did cover some of the core principles that we have followed when we were actually implementing the Data Lake. But, explicitly we haven't mentioned these because bringing these points upfront can be a daunting and might not enlighten your brain as you are just stepping into a Data Lake implementation. Since you now have a base Data Lake working, it's good time to bring these core principles together and we feel these has to be always remembered when bringing in new capabilities and technologies into your Data Lake ecosystem. This again in no way authoritative, rather, it's just some guiding principles that we thought quite useful.

- Accept any data in raw format (immutable data) into the Data Lake. All data in an enterprise has value attached to it. Don't try getting the value in the first go, rather just ingest and try deriving its value going forward.
- During time of data ingestion don't look for value out of the data getting ingested.

- Be ready to accept any type of data (structured and unstructured).
- Be ready to accept any quantity of data.
- Don't restrain data storage, the way by that you can query the data from Data Lake. Bring in varied technologies according to requirement, for various analysis.
- Give easy way for enterprise applications to ingest data. Initially these data could not make much sense but over period of time, these data could be collaborated with other data elements in Data Lake and could result in value propositions for enterprise.
- Don't worry about data normalization while storing.
- Adding data source should be quick, easy and cheap (highly scalable).
- Should be able to serve Enterprise data in various formats as required by consuming applications.
- Should help in supporting required data intelligence requirements with data aggregations and processing at scale.
- Should be able to de-dup and cleanse the data, either in motion or at rest.
- Should be able to support various security mechanisms for inflight as well as data at rest.
- Must be highly available as it serves critical Enterprise data.
- Don't force the incoming data to change it's format according to your data format, rather accept the data in the form that is required by the incoming data.
- Try as many ways as possible to reduce the data size and network/bandwidth requirement. Use different methodologies like compression to achieve this.

Challenges faced by enterprise Data Lake

It's good to be aware of challenges that you could face while building and managing an enterprise Data Lake. Here we are only discussing the various technical challenges, adoption and business buy-in for a Data Lake and support for this initiative from higher management and so on is not discussed here. Some of those challenges along with our suggested mitigation are as given:

Challenge #1: If you are using open source freely available technologies for building your Data Lake, keeping up with the pace with that these technologies grow can be quite challenging and daunting task.
Mitigation #1: Going with commercial products like Cloudera, Hortonworks and so on can be an option if the Data Lake is adopted in a positive manner by the business.

Challenge #2: If you Data Lake incorporate good amount of technologies to achieve the desired results, keeping with the pace of technology and it's dependencies with other technologies in the Data Lake landscape can again be quite challenging.
Mitigation #2: Similar to the preceding mitigation, going with a commercially supported platforms can be option to mitigate this problem.

Challenge #3: Getting skilled people in Big Data space was quite a challenge sometime back. But, that has improved now, but it's quite hard to get really skilled hands-on people to maintain and manage this diverse technology landscape Data Lake.
Mitigation #3: Building a **Centre of Excellence** (CoE) with the enterprise with programs to keep rejuvenating this team with more resources in a timely manner can be considered.

Challenge #4: Integration challenges within and external to Data Lake with components evolving independently can be challenging.
Mitigation #4: Bringing in a layer of indirection dealing with integration challenge with both internal and external applications can be considered. This layer hides the details and gives a consistent way in that data flows into the Data Lake.

Challenge #5: Because of diverse application in enterprise, ingesting data into Data Lake can be big challenge. The issue becomes more problematic if the applications existing in an enterprise is a mix of in-house and vendor applications, written in a variety of programming languages having varied data ingestion capabilities.
Mitigation #5: If applications can be given a very easy way of ingesting data, say for Java applications (especially built in-house), given then a Java annotation to be put on models, which automagically ingests the data to the Data Lake can be quite tempting for data ingestion of their application data into the Data Lake.

Challenge #6: Being a common data store, departments pose a problem, stating authorization (security and privacy) of data as a big issue.
Mitigation #6: Bring in adequate security for data and all of the Data Lake components with strict control on who does what and how. This can be limiting for disruptive data analysis, but again, it depends on what data is in the Data Lake and who wants to access these.

Challenge #7: Even if data ingestion is fine with regards to a data source, often data quality can be a concern. Data governance can be a challenge. Need domain knowledge to make sure data falling into Data Lake is of highest quality.
Mitigation #7: Implementing a proper data governance framework during data ingestion and keep checking on the data quality in a timely manner as a process. Imbibe this as a culture in the organization over a period of time.

Challenge #8: Usually big organizations lack information/business architecture spanning all departments. Because of this it's quite hard to build a proper data model on top of the raw data. This creates undue dependency to IT departments to create these changing data models for various analysis by business users.
Mitigation #8: Use Data Lake to start building an information/business architecture and start modelling data in the Data Lake using this newly agreed data model.

Challenge #9: Quite hard to achieve full automation and this poses maintenance challenges. This can lead to high maintenance cost often not exceeding advantages derived out of it.
Mitigation #9: aim for small automation and keep pushing it for full automation over a period of time.

Expectations from Data Lake

Data lake does cost money to build and manage. So, the expectation from various parties from Data Lake is quite demanding and varied in nature. Let's divide these expectation into two based on parties involved.

Expectation from business users:

- Analysis is always running on right data with good quality attributes.
- Capability to easily manage data governance.
- Setup security measures whereby the data visibility can be controlled in more fine grained fashion. Easy data masking capability, when needed by employing appropriate transformations controlled by authorizations mechanisms.
- Self service capability with minimal technical knowledge for a broad spectrum of people.
- More easy representation of data lineage and traceability
- Should be able to support metadata management

Data lineage is defined as a data life cycle that includes the data's origins and where it moves over time. It describes what happens to data as it goes through diverse processes. It helps provide visibility into the data analytics pipeline and simplifies tracing errors back to their sources.

- Wikipedia

Expectation from technical department:

- Easy ingestion of data from varied kinds of application. For example, cloud application, in-house built applications, applications written in varied technologies and so on.
- Cost effective and easy/simple management and maintenance of Data Lake.
- Easy to bring in people (skills) capable of maintaining Data Lake as needed from the industry.
- Should be able perform required data processing at scale and derive data intelligence
- Should be able to manage requirements around machine learning and other data algorithms
- Fail-safety and availability mechanisms must be in place for easy recovery and continued availability without business interruptions

Data Lake for other activities

With Data Lake and its huge and expensive infrastructure (in production deployment, ideally we use high-end machines and not commodity hardware), there are potential other uses for which it could be used. The main challenge with high end infrastructure is its effective utilization. While a high end infrastructure may be required for solving a problem, it may not be effectively utilized at all times. This is where we need to think of mechanisms that can help us extract required utilization of the infrastructure.

One of the most practical ways to do this is via multi-tenancy of the Hadoop infrastructure. If we look at Hadoop or any storage systems, there are two fundamental actions performed at the storage layer; one is to read and the other is to write the data for the purpose of data storage and processing.

This can be achieved at a basic level by leveraging security mechanisms supported by various components in the entire infrastructure such that security realms and groups can provide required isolation on shared infrastructure. The security permissions must be provisioned to allow for intended use by various groups and users. This would also help prevent the issue of Data Lake silos within an organization.

These capabilities can be used as a way to attract applications and groups with the organization to come and ingest data into Data Lake. Two fundamentals areas are:

- **Store data (HDFS: Distributed File System)**: At the core of Data Lake is the great Apache Hadoop, capable of storing huge amounts of data in a variety of formats. The Data Lake could be a potential candidate to store huge amount of application data (data such as auditing and logging, for example), and this can also be exploited by an application to store a huge amount of data in a very cheap and easily accessible fashion. This also could be used as an archival solution for an enterprise (a more centralized one with easy data retrieval capability).
- **Processing data (MapReduce programming model)**: Hadoop has huge potential for performing huge data processing capabilities. For various use cases internal and external to Data Lake, this capability could be exploited and used. For many use cases, huge processing is deemed necessary. Using Hadoop's MapReduce, this could be offloaded to Data Lake infrastructure, and processed data could then be taken to the application data store for further needs.

Knowing more about data storage

Storage is one of the most critical parts of a Data Lake. Apache Hadoop (HDFS) is the core of data storage for our Data Lake. The following figure sums up this aspect quite clearly, showing batch and stream data storage components in our Data Lake, along with other technologies within Hadoop Ecosystem with regards to various aspects dealing with the storage:

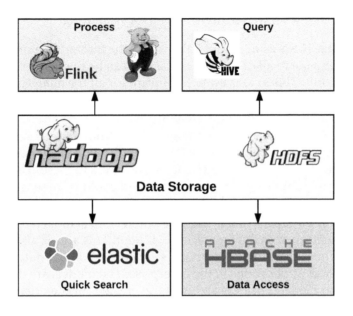

Figure 02: Apache Hadoop (HDFS) as data storage

We will now understand some important concepts in data storage area. We will also concentrate explicitly on batch and speed data and how these gets stored in the Data Lake and also see some specific details in regards to these data types.

Zones in Data Storage

Even though the data in the storage need not follow a certain pattern, but for an organization while going with a Data Lake, it's good to have some clear directions and principles on how the data need to be put in the Data Lake. These are just some of our recommendations that could be considered or kept in mind while structure the data in the storage.

These data can be organized in a multitude of ways, which depends on organization and its structure. On a very high-level we see division of data as follows:

- **Master data**: The area in a Data Lake where the master data resides. Usually this data is accessible to all of the enterprise and can be made over time as single source of truth. This data is quite significant for all the analysis as transaction data is merged with this master data to show meaningful visualization to the data analysts or to the business for that matter.

- **Raw data**: Area in the storage where raw data from various source systems flow in and get persisted. This is an area that is fully controlled and only the Data Lake core technical people and data scientists get access to these. The data here would contain almost anything in the enterprise and could have sensitive information held very close to certain departments within the organization.

- **Enhanced or enterprise data**: The area where data is modeled from raw data and is more generic across the organization is kept. This area is also quite well controlled but according to the models created out of raw data, these can be used by a variety of applications in the enterprise. The models are derived from information model (business architecture) created for the organization. The models in here would be well understood by both business and IT departments alike. At the time of creating these models, there could still be many attributes in the raw data that is not really picked or understood well enough to be included in these models.

- **Application/curated specific data**: The area where more commonly used or so called curated models reside in the storage. Usually Data Lake is for enterprises, so application specific models are not encouraged but this is again more generic but could have been created initially for a requirement very specific for a business application. This is one of the reasons some business applications are ready to ingest data to get the power of Data Lake and it's processing power. This is a more pragmatic approach when we start off Data Lake within an enterprise and have a give and take policy for business applications to pump data into Data Lake.

These zones could also be used to segregate the data residing in the storage into different storage classes having different requirements (low cost storage, highly available storage and so on). the following figure does show this high-level divisions/zones in the storage area that could be considered.

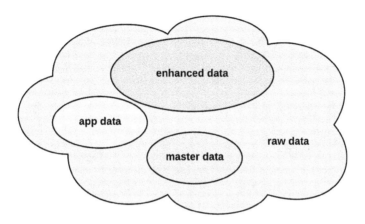

Figure 03: Zones in data storage layer

High-level division in the storage is fine, but in practical scenarios the following are some of the aspects by which this high-level division can be further divided (more subjective, just our thoughts, these changes significantly according to organization where Data Lake is implemented):

- **Data asset classification (business impact)**: Security classification of data asset or business deemed asset classification.
  - High
  - Medium
  - Low
- **Data Archival policy**: According to the retention of data in the Data Lake.
  - Short
  - Medium
  - Long
- **Business domain**: Based on business domain, where the data comes from into the Data Lake.
  - Customer
  - Sales and so on
- **Source**: Source from where the data arrived in Data Lake.
- **Internal or External**

All in all, these divisions are kept in the storage so as to give good visibility to the data scientists to deduce useful insights into the data for deriving meaningful business decisions.

In the next sessions, we will delve a bit more into batch and speed data storage and some of it's nuances that has to be kept in mind.

Data Schema and Model

The raw data when ingested may not have the schema in desired structure, and may get stored in its native format in Data Lake. Data must exist in a target schema structure when the data is being queried from the storage. In order to convert/res-structure the data from its native schema to the target schema, the data needs to be processed. In our case, the final batch views when created will have a defined schema against that the views are build and exposed.

Storage options

We have come across multiple ways of storing data in previous chapters. In order to appreciate different storage options it would be good to understand these options to some extent.

Hadoop enables us to load data in its natural form using basic HDFS commands, and this can be used for visualizing this data into HIVE or Impala views. We saw this in action in earlier chapters. In addition to these we also used certain **Serialization Deserialization** (**SerDe**) adaptors to tell the views how to handle the data.

While handling the RAW files, containing data in its most natural form, the files and data is loaded in Hadoop for further processing. If the data in these RAW files is in a standard format like a CSV file or TAB delimited file it is easier to visualize this data by simply creating a view over it. However we may have data in non standard format as well in these RAW files that necessitates further processing and hence needs additional storage formats to be defines. The natively supported formats at Hadoop layer have been Plain text files (CSV/TAB Delimited Files), sequence files, Avro files and Parquet files as some of the major formats.

The choice of a format needs to be driven by the purpose of data to be stored. A quick comparison of purpose and option analysis can be considered as given here:

Text Format	Sequence File Format	Avro Format	Parquet Format
The text format for instance would provide ease of data loads at an expense of lesser compression and query overheads	Sequence Files are generally used to pack small files that can be used to transfer data between map-reduce jobs	Avro format is a binary format that provides schema based data storage and supports block compression and provides IO gains for faster and more efficient queries	The Parquet storage is another binary format storage that stores data column oriented and is generally useful for queries on specific columns

These formats are the formats supported by HDFS in general, however depending on where the data is stored, there would be variation in patterns of storage as well. In order to better understand this statement, let us consider the two NoSQL data stores that we came across in this book, that is, HBase and Elasticsearch. While both of them belong to NoSQL data store families, each of them employs different ways to store and handle data. HBase is natively non-indexed data store running over HDFS, and stores data as column families, while Elasticsearch is an indexed data stores, which stored data as JSON documents and needs a direct storage mechanism for efficient queries.

Apache HCatalog (Hive Metastore)

If Apache Hive is there in your Data Lake as a technology, including **HCatalog** would be quite handy to deal with the diverse technology ecosystem (especially data processing tools) with a wide variety of storage formats.

> *HCatalog is a table and storage management layer for Hadoop that enables users with different data processing tools — Pig, MapReduce — to more easily read and write data on the grid. HCatalog's table abstraction presents users with a relational view of data in the* **Hadoop distributed file system (HDFS)** *and ensures that users need not worry about where or in what format their data is stored — RCFile format, text files, SequenceFiles, or ORC files.*

HCatalog supports reading and writing files in any format for that a SerDe (serializer-deserializer) can be written. By default, HCatalog supports RCFile, CSV, JSON, and SequenceFile, and ORC file formats. To use a custom format, you must provide the InputFormat, OutputFormat, and SerDe.

- https://cwiki.apache.org/confluence/display/Hive/HCatalog+UsingHCat

The preceding excerpt from the HCatalog confluence page quite well describes what the exact function of HCatalog (also known as HCat) is and we don't feel we need to expand it anymore, nor we have scope to cover this in more detail as part of this chapter.

The following figure (again as detailed in HCatalog confluence page) is quite self explanatory:

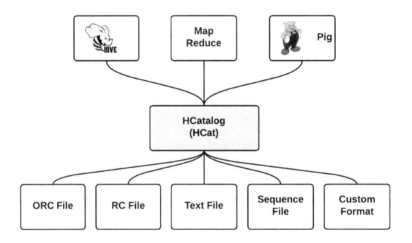

Figure 04: Working of Apache HCatalog

Compression methodologies

In previous part of the book, we did touch this aspect of compression in brief. Since this is an important aspect for Data Lake, this is revisited in a bit more detail here.

While storing data, to optimize storage (reduce space) and to utilize network bandwidth, often compression methodologies are employed. Data lake deals with massive amount of data and data compression is quite significant. This aspect definitely makes the Data Lake more scalable and brings in lot of flexibility.

In many scenarios existing in an enterprise, the data commonly ingested into Data Lake are in different text formats (CSV, TSV, XML, JSON and so on). These are human readable but occupies huge amount of storage space. In Data Lake, however the data is read by machines and as long as that is possible, it's fine. Compression technologies, using serialization, compresses these human readable into machine readable and in the due course makes sure that the space needed for storage is drastically reduced. The following are some of the well-known and commonly used compression formats (called codecs that allows data compression/serialization and decompression/deserialization):

- **Gzip (file extension .gz)**: **GNU Zip (GZip)**, well-known compression format and is used quite heavily in the web/internet world. The request and response can be compressed used this format for efficient usage of bandwidth of a website/web application.

- **Snappy (file extension .snappy)**: **Codec** developed by Google (previously known as **Zippy**). Supposed to be the fastest (serialization/deserialization) with a moderate compression ratio. Speed is more relevant aspect for this format as against the compression ratio. One of the formats, most widely used, obviously because of it's performance.

- **LZO (file extension .lzo)**: licensed under **GNU Public License** (**GPL**), it is very much similar to snappy having fast compression and decompression with moderate compression ratio.

- **Bzip2 (file extension .bz2)**: More or less similar to GZip, with more compression ratio than GZip. The speed by that the data deserializes is slower than GZip as expected. One of the important aspect of this is that, it supports splitting and this is quite important when used HDFS is used as the storage. If data has to be just stored and not queries (which is not our case), this compression can be quite a good choice.

Lempel–Ziv–Oberhumer (LZO) is a lossless data compression algorithm that is focused on decompression speed.

- Wikipedia

Each of the preceding compression algorithms has advantages and disadvantages associated with it. If the compression ratio is high (after compression the space is reduced to a larger extend), the decompression usually takes time and is slow and vice versa. There is no magic pill using that we could choose a method and go with it. It depends on the data coming in and has to be selected on a case-by-case basis.

When you are in a situation to select a compression algorithm, these are some of the options:

- Divide the files into chunks (piece) and then compress using any algorithm as deemed suitable. Since Hadoop (HDFS) is our persistence mechanism, make sure that these chunks and after compression fits into these desired memory slots (configured in HDFS).
- Select a compression format that allows splitting and then compressing.
- Select a container file format that allows splitting and compressing such as Avro and Parquet. These can again be mixed with various compression formats to arrive at right speed and compression ration demanded by your use case. Of the two container file format, Avro is matured and used widely in the industry. Let's discuss these two container file formats in brief:
  - **Avro**: Uses self-describing (creates schema in the background) binary format to serialize data. When data is serialized, a schema is stored along with it fully describing the data being serialized. Because of this very reason many programming languages can read these file formats quite easily. Many of the technologies in the Hadoop Ecosystem like Spark, Pig and so on; therefore it can read these file format and deal with it quite easily. Avro is quite an efficient format for sending data across network in a compressed format. It can also use compression formats like Snappy for higher order compression, if required.
  - **Parquet**: Licensed under Apache License, it's an open source columnar storage format built from the ground up. It gets its name from patterns in Parquet flooring. Parquet have a very efficient compression and encoding schemes. Similar to Avro many Hadoop ecosystem technologies is actively supporting Parquet because of it's advantages and also Parquet is under heavy developments adding new capabilities in every release.

Choose the right option according to your use case requirement. Using container file format with a suitable compression algorithm, having a right balance between speed and compression ration would be our recommendation.

Data partitioning

Data partitioning is a very common technique by that data stored in a persistent store is segregated into sections for faster queries and easy management and monitoring (being segregated, the data to be managed becomes small and more manageable). This is a technique used in RDBMS and it's the same that could be employed in HDFS. HDFS, being a file system, partitioning is achieved using file partitioning. For an enterprise wide Data Lake, data partitioning is a needed aspect that needs serious thought and consideration. In previous section we did see different zones in data storage, this section expands on that aspect by bringing in the implementation aspect using data partitioning.

A table stored in HDFS has a number of rows (each record is a row) consisting of a number of columns (attributes in a record). Partitioning can be achieved in two ways:

- Horizontal partitioning: partitioning based on row/record. In this partitioning technique you divide the rows in a table in different partitions.
- Vertical partitioning: it partitions data based on column values. This is one of the more common way of partitioning and if the queries that are going to be executed is known (especially the parameters), this approach is quite useful and aids in performance gains. The next figure shows sample data stored in HDFS (folder structure) being partitioned into different levels using a particular column value. In the first folder structure division, the data is partitioned based on year and in subsequent partitioning it is divided according to the month.

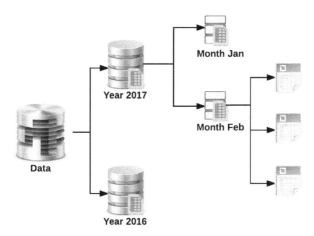

Figure 05: Vertical partitioning using a column value (multiple level partitioning)

Knowing more about Data processing

Data processing is one of the important capabilities in a Data Lake implementation. Our Data Lake is no exception and does participate in data processing, both in batch and speed layer. In this section we will cover some important topics that needs to be looked upon with respect to Data Lake dealing with data processing. With Hadoop 1.x, MapReduce was one of the main processing done in Hadoop. With Hadoop 2.x and with more data ingestion methodologies, more options in the real time/streaming area have also come in and these two aspects with some important considerations are detailed here.

Data validation and cleansing

Validating data before it gets into the persistence layer of Data Lake is a very important step. Validation in the context of Data Lake means two aspects as follows:

- **Origin of data**: Making sure right data from right source is ingested into the Data Lake. The source from where data originates should be known and also the data coming in also should be authorized by Data Lake to be ingested.
- **Quality of data**: Making sure that certain data that are ingested into Data Lake has some initial checks done on its attributes to make sure that the data coming in and it's format qualifies to the format it states. For example data attribute in a record stating it as an email could be checked/validated for a proper email format.

Validation and appropriate cleansing of data is quite a significant aspect in modern day Data Lake as in modern age there are so many source systems capable of pumping huge volume of data into the Data Lake. If you don't do this soon your Data Lake can be quite dirty and turn into a swarm, hard to get data and also see what is in it to do various analysis. Creating zones in Hadoop can be a good step to achieve some control and quality control on the data that lives in the lake. When the data move from one zone to another, various pre-configured rules could be executed to make sure that the data is of utmost quality and meets the common data rules for a particular attribute (mostly these are different for different organizations and rules are to be build according to this requirement in mind).

There should also be rules to make sure that certified sources can only ingest data into the lake and each data from these source need to be verified. One of the mechanisms to enforce the validations is to have schema based storage in place so that any data in ingested into the Data Lake is validated, and any invalid data is separately bucketed to be processed differently as exceptions. For such use cases, using a schema based storage mechanisms like Avro are very helpful.

Cleansing is as important as validation of data. By doing validation, in turn you are doing a bit of cleaning. But, you lake needs periodic cleaning to make sure it doesn't grow out of proportion, so that most valuable and needful insights can be performed quite easily without trouble. You need to have a process by that to identify data that have over time exhausted itself or become irrelevant for the organization and take necessary approach by that to remove it from so called production-grade data in the Data Lake. Data cleansing can be achieved in a number of ways, some of the basic mechanism includes usage of HIVE/Impala queries to process the data and cleanse it as the data moves from one table to another, however such operations via query engines can be very heavy and resource intensive. Instead, cleaning such data with map-reduce based processing can be very efficient and can also integrate with standard libraries that can further simplify the cleansing process.

There is no science on this as this is fully reliant on the enterprise and there isn't a one size fits all solution. However, it is a very important aspect and needs consideration and implementation. For both batch and speed data, validation as well as cleansing is an important aspect that need attention and consideration.

Machine learning

Machine learning is the data science behind building adaptive and continuous learning systems for drawing valuable insights from data. These are at the base level set of algorithms that can help us derive more meaning from the data. These algorithms generally work on the inputs, correlation with historic data, probabilities of various related events and the training data to provide an enhanced experience as an output in form of recommendations or decisions.

Machine learning algorithms are broadly classified into following categories

1. **Supervised Algorithms**: These types of algorithms need supervision in form of training data to get tuned and provide outcomes with expected accuracies. While this can be applied for neural network programing, however the most common implementation of these algorithms has been Naive Bayes, which can classify the incoming events based on training data and pre-defined categories. This is also used in sentiment analysis based on the positive and negative words used in conversations.

2. **Unsupervised Algorithms**: These algorithms are capable of deriving meaning from the data without any training data by continuously analyzing patterns and trends in datasets. These are mostly used for solving problems that require self clustering of data and events into logical groups. Most common algorithm in this space has been K-means, as this algorithm can be directly applied on a wide variety of data to continuously derive data groups.

While the data resides in batch layers, it gives good opportunity to run such algorithms to produce high quality insights from the data. Many of these algorithms can also be leveraged for near real time processing that would continuously provide data insights with fair amount of accuracy. One such framework that has been extremely useful in Hadoop landscape has been Apache Mahout, which has pre-configured routines and algorithms to apply on Hadoop data readily. Application of such algorithms easily extend into Fraud detection, biometrics, facial recognition, digital signal processing of machine data and many others. Most popular example in this space has been the recommendation engine of Amazon, which is very responsive in recommending the possible buying options for a customer based on customer's behaviours and past buying patterns

Scheduler/Workflow

Data lake ingests data in raw format. However, for meaningful analytics on the data, this raw data needs to undergo a certain level of processing. As we have seen in previous section, there are certain zones in the storage and data processing that make sure to convert the raw data to something more useful for various analytics. While this can be done with a series of map-reduce jobs, the main challenge is orchestrating these jobs across these zones and at a scheduled interval or at triggers. Also, since the Hadoop landscape comprises multiple technologies and frameworks, there could be different types of tasks to be executed from one data zone to another. We will cover the mechanisms to achieve this using oozie framework that it achieves via two of its components, that is, workflows and coordinators.

Apache Oozie

Oozie source code is available for download and it needs to be built from source for installation. Oozie installation can be performed with the following steps.

Database setup and configuration

Oozie requires a metastore to store information for Oozie jobs, workflows and coordinators, hence we will need to create a metastore database. As done earlier for other technologies in regards to metastore,we will create and configure this metastore in PostgreSQL Follow the steps below to configure PostgreSQL as our metastore database:

1. Login into PostgreSQL prompt in ssh/command line within CentOS VM:

```
psql -U postgres
```

2. Create the Oozie user by running the following query:

```
CREATE ROLE oozie LOGIN ENCRYPTED PASSWORD 'oozie' NOSUPERUSER
INHERIT CREATEDB NOCREATEROLE;
```

3. Create the Oozie database by running the below query:

```
CREATE DATABASE "oozie" WITH OWNER = oozie
ENCODING = 'UTF8'
TABLESPACE = pg_default
LC_COLLATE = 'en_US.UTF-8'
LC_CTYPE = 'en_US.UTF-8'
CONNECTION LIMIT = -1;
```

We have now created and configured a metastore database with the name oozie, having a user role as Oozie for storing and managing Oozie metadata and job information.

Build from Source

In the next step we will build the Oozie from source and start using it.

1. Download the Oozie source tarball from the following location, using the following command:

```
wget http://www-eu.apache.org/dist/oozie/4.3.0/oozie-4.3.0.tar.gz
```

2. Change to the user directory and extract the contents of tar ball using the following command:

```
tar -zxvf ${DOWNLOAD_DIR}/oozie-4.3.0.tar.gz
```

3. Change into the Oozie source directory, let us refer to it as ${OOZIE_SRC_HOME}, and run the following command to create the build:

```
${OOZIE_SRC_HOME}/bin/mkdistro.sh -Phadoop-2 -DskipTests
```

4. Once the build is complete, the binary tarball can be extracted from ${OOZIE_SRC_HOME}/distro/target into a user directory, lets us refer this directory as ${OOZIE_HOME}. In order to do this, change into the ${OOZIE_HOME} directory and run the following command:

```
tar -zxvf ${OOZIE_SRC_HOME}/distro/target/oozie-4.3.0-distro.tar.gz
```

5. Configure the environment variable ${OOZIE_HOME} to point to the Oozie directory using the following commands. Also, append these commands to the ~/.bashrc file:

```
export OOZIE_HOME=<directory-containing-oozie-install>
export PATH=$PATH:${OOZIE_HOME}/bin
```

6. Once the contents are extracted, configure the ${OOZIE_HOME}/conf/oozie-site.xml with proxy users and database settings by using the below properties as shown below. All the paths mentioned should be complete paths, since the environment variables do not get resolved. The environment variables have been mentioned for reference only:

```
<configuration>
<property>
        <name>oozie.service.ProxyUserService.proxyuser.centos.hosts<
/name>
        <value>*</value>
</property>
<property>
        <name>oozie.service.ProxyUserService.proxyuser.centos.groups
</name>
        <value>*</value>
</property>
<property>
        <name>oozie.service.ProxyUserService.proxyuser.hue.hosts</na
me>
        <value>*</value>
</property>
<property>
        <name>oozie.service.ProxyUserService.proxyuser.hue.groups</n
ame>
        <value>*</value>
</property>
```

```
<property>
      <name>oozie.service.ProxyUserService.proxyuser.oozie.hosts</
name>
      <value>*</value>
</property>
<property>
      <name>oozie.service.ProxyUserService.proxyuser.oozie.groups<
/name>
      <value>*</value>
</property>
<property>
      <name>oozie.service.JPAService.jdbc.driver</name>
      <value>org.postgresql.Driver</value>
</property>
<property>
      <name>oozie.service.JPAService.jdbc.url</name>
      <value>jdbc:postgresql://localhost:5432/oozie</value>
</property>
<property>
      <name>oozie.service.JPAService.jdbc.username</name>
      <value>oozie</value>
</property>
<property>
      <name>oozie.service.JPAService.jdbc.password</name>
      <value>oozie</value>
</property>
<property>
      <name>oozie.service.WorkflowAppService.system.libpath</name>
      <value>/user/centos/share/lib</value>
</property>
<property>
<name>oozie.service.HadoopAccessorService.hadoop.configurations</na
me>
  <value>*=${HADOOP_HOME}/etc/hadoop</value>
</property>
<property>
<name>oozie.service.HadoopAccessorService.action.configurations</na
me>
  <value>*=${HADOOP_HOME}/etc/hadoop</value>
</property>
</configuration>
```

Code 01: Oozie-site.xml configuration

7. Configure the `${HADOOP_HOME}/etc/hadoop/core-site.xml` with the following additional settings:

```
<property>
 <name>hadoop.proxyuser.oozie.hosts</name>
 <value>*</value>
</property>
<property>
 <name>hadoop.proxyuser.oozie.groups</name>
 <value>*</value>
</property>
```

Code 02: core-site.xml configuration

8. Restart the `dfs` service by using the following command

```
stop-dfs.sh && start-dfs.sh
```

9. Configure `${HADOOP_CONF_DIR}` environment variable using the following command and add it to `~/.bashrc` file:

```
export ${HADOOP_CONF_DIR}=${HADOOP_HOME}/etc/hadoop
```

10. Create a folder `libext` under `${OOZIE_HOME}`. We are doing this to copy the Hadoop JARS in this folder for Oozie shared lib configuration and execute various jobs

```
mkdir ${OOZIE_HOME}/libext
```

11. Copy all the Hadoop JARS from `${HADOOP_HOME}` into `${OOZIE_HOME}/libext`. Execute the following commands:

```
cp ${HADOOP_HOME}/share/hadoop/common/lib/* ${OOZIE_HOME}/libext
cp ${HADOOP_HOME}/share/hadoop/common/*.jar ${OOZIE_HOME}/libext

cp ${HADOOP_HOME}/share/hadoop/hdfs/lib/* ${OOZIE_HOME}/libext
cp ${HADOOP_HOME}/share/hadoop/hdfs/*.jar ${OOZIE_HOME}/libext

cp ${HADOOP_HOME}/share/hadoop/mapreduce/lib/* ${OOZIE_HOME}/libext
cp ${HADOOP_HOME}/share/hadoop/mapreduce/*.jar ${OOZIE_HOME}/libext
```

12. Configure Oozie in HDFS for shared library path with following commands:

- Create Oozie folder in HDFS

```
hdfs  dfs -mkdir /user/oozie
```

- Assign the ownership of the folder to the Oozie user

```
hdfs  dfs -chown oozie:oozie /user/oozie
```

- Import the Oozie shared libs into HDFS

```
${OOZIE_HOME}/bin/oozie-setup.sh sharelib create -fs
hdfs://<hadoop-namenode-ip>:9000 -locallib
${OOZIE_HOME}/oozie-sharelib-4.3.0.tar.gz
```

13. Start the Oozie server with following command:

```
${OOZIE_HOME}/bin/oozie-run.sh
```

If Oozie starts without problem, the console should print `INFO: Server startup in xx ms`.

Now launch the Hue console and login to see the Oozie landing page (can be accesses by clicking **Workflows | Editors | Workflows** menu) as shown in the following screenshot:

Figure 06: Oozie landing page in Hue

Oozie Workflows

Oozie provides workflow capability to define the flow of processing from one point to another and supports a variety of Hadoop frameworks. An Oozie workflow defines what components would participate in a defined flow of execution as a single job. In the Oozie workflow editor click on **Create** (in right hand side of the page), which will allows us to visually create workflows. A sample workflow is as shown in the following screenshot:

Figure 07: Oozie workflow designer in Hue

In this example, we are creating a directory and then renaming it in the next step. This is done by dragging and dropping the HDFS component from the Documents toolbar and provide the required commands as shown in previous screenshot.

When we execute this workflow by manually submitting it, the execution status or outcome is indicated in the UI as shown in the screenshot:

Figure 08: Oozie workflow execution in Hue

In production systems, it may not be possible to manually submit the workflow in a system which has continuous incoming data, hence in such situation we may want to schedule such submissions. This can be achieved by using Oozie coordinator, which is explained in next section.

Oozie coordinator

In order to wrap workflows into a coordinator configuration, we need to create a coordinator configuration and add workflow to it. In doing so, we can also define the schedule/interval for the coordinator to run the configured workflows as shown in the following screenshot:

Figure 09: Coordinator scheduling in Hue

Hue UI also exposes the dashboard to summarize the execution outcomes which gives a single view status snapshots of the running/completed jobs. This can help drill down into logs of individual oozie jobs, if required. A snapshot of the dashboard is as shown in the following screenshot:

Figure 10: Oozie dashboards in Hue

Complex event processing

During our discussion of Flink framework, we came across various mechanisms by that Flink can perform in stream analysis since it supports exactly once processing of events and also enables windowing functions. One of the main components of CEP engine is accurate data aggregation that would be possible only if the events are processed only once. These are some of the building blocks of full fledged CEP engine and with these capabilities specific CEP capabilities can be built from ground up.

However in order to build a complete CEP engine, it may need considerable efforts and some use cases may demand use of a complete CEP engine right away. For such scenarios there are embeddable CEP engines like Esper that can be embedded in such real-time processing channels and provide the required analysis capabilities on streaming data.

Complex Event Processing includes rules execution, event correlations, statistical analysis of event and pattern based analysis of multiple input events for enabling automated recommendations and decisions in near real time.

Thoughts on data security

One of the very important capabilities required for a Data Lake implementation in an enterprise is security. In a Data Lake we are bringing in data from around the enterprise into one place. You have convinced all the departments who has agreed to ingest data into the Data Lake that the data in the lake is secured and only authenticated and authorized users have access to the data. So, this aspect needs some serious thought so that data is secured and these departments are quite happy with the access rules for their all important data. In addition to security setup, proper governance through adequate processes also should be setup to make security quite sturdy but quite easy for users having access to it to do their deep analysis work.

By data security, it refers to in-flight transaction data (stream), date at rest (batch), both authentication and authorization (attributes).

Data lake does pose a different risk as it is entrusted to bring data from various silos into one and this create even more data security problem as it allows combining data from disparate systems making it easy for more diverse analytics and if not secured can have adverse effect for your business.

There are number of open source projects that could be integrated with Data Lake helping with various security capabilities, some of that are as detailed in the followingsub-sections.

the following figure clearly and easy to decipher fashion (courtesy Hortonworks) shows security rings around Hadoop, which could be build according to security requirement demanded by your Data Lake in your enterprise. The figure shows various security capability along with technology mapping.

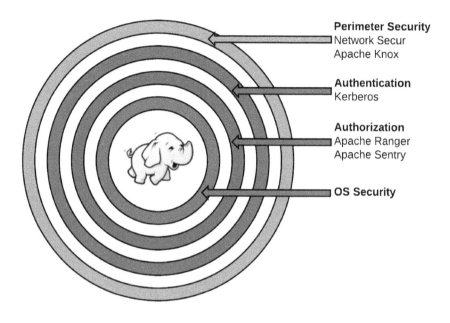

Figure 11: Security rings around Hadoop

Apache Knox

The Apache Knox Gateway is a REST API Gateway for interacting with Apache Hadoop clusters. The Knox Gateway provides a single access point for all REST interactions with Apache Hadoop clusters. In this capacity, the Knox Gateway is able to provide valuable functionality to aid in the control, integration, monitoring and automation of critical administrative and analytical needs of the enterprise.

- https://knox.apache.org/

Hadoop inherently supports Kerberos authentication and authorization can be implemented using its default UNIX based file and directory permissions. In this Hadoop setup, where Hadoop is secured, Apache Knox can complement and add value. Knox can also work with Hadoop clusters that doesn't implement any security.

The following figure shows the working of Apache Knox:

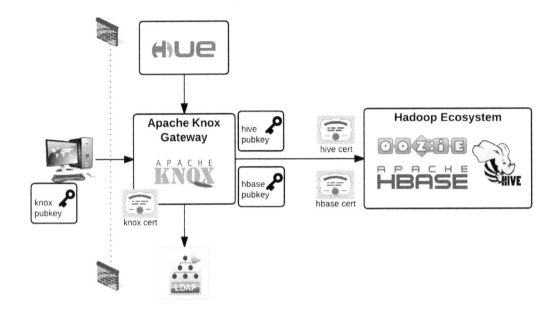

Figure 12: Working of Apache Knox

As detailed in **Knox** documentation (`https://knox.apache.org/`), it functions as a reverse proxy providing perimeter security with possibility of extension (for various security policy compliance checks) in the form of plugin's. It supports various security policy enforcement like authentication, authorization, host mapping and so on by chaining these extensions one after the other (in required order) as specified in topology deployment descriptor. Knox has support for many of the products/technologies in the Hadoop ecosystem like Ambari, Oozie, Hive and so on, which is added advantage.

Apache Ranger

Ranger is a framework to enable, monitor and manage comprehensive data security across the Hadoop platform. The vision with Ranger is to provide comprehensive security across the Apache Hadoop ecosystem.

- http://ranger.apache.org/

The following figure shows the working of Apache Ranger. Ranger provides authorization capabilities for a wide range of products and technologies in the Hadoop ecosystem.

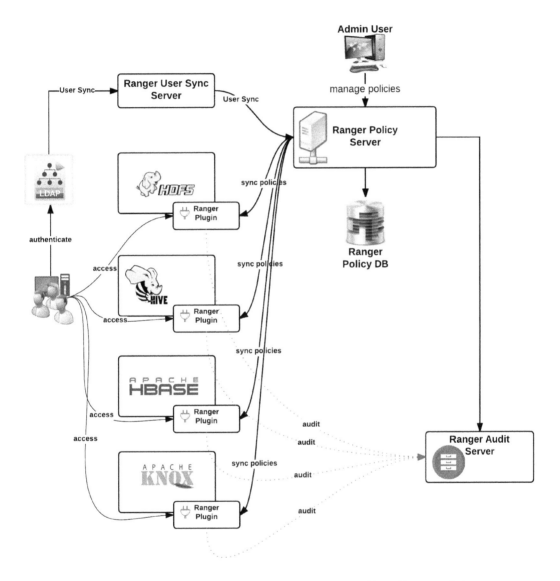

Figure 13: Working of Apache Ranger (figure inferred from Hortonworks)

Ranger's authorization methodology is based on **Attribute Based Access Control (ABAC)**. ABAC is based on four attributes namely subject, action, resource and environment.

As shown in the preceding figure, the Ranger plugin is installed along with the product for that authorization needs to be enforced. Ranger synchronizes user data with the enterprise directory (where user credential are stored) and uses that to set up appropriate security policies by security administrators. These security policies are set by the administrators and is persisted. When a user tries to access data in the products where Ranger plugin is installed, it retrieves the policies stored and does appropriate checks before user getting access to the data that they require. Apache Ranger supports HDFS, Hive, HBase, Storm, Solr, Kafka and Knox in the Hadoop ecosystem.

In addition to authorization (it's core capability), it also captures and persists various audit activities. These captured data can be quite useful when track and trace of a particular activity has to be conducted.

Apache Ranger is started and owned by Hortonworks and because of this it has good compatibility with the Hortonworks Hadoop distribution.

Apache Ranger work in conjunction with Apache Knox and in fact complements each other in many ways to achieve the objective of security.

Apache Sentry

> *Apache Sentry is a system for enforcing fine grained role based authorization to data and metadata stored on a Hadoop cluster.*

> *- https://sentry.apache.org/*

The working of Apache Sentry is very much similar to Apache Ranger. This figure shows the working of Sentry:

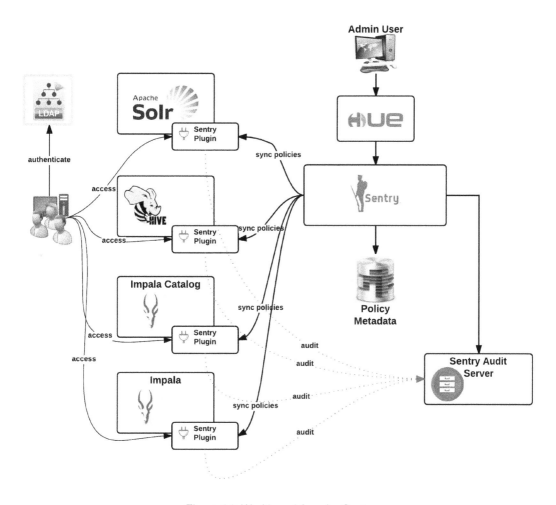

Figure 14: Working of Apache Sentry

Sentry plugin needs to be installed on any of the data processing technologies (Hive, Impala and so on). Any access to data in these technology is first intercepted by the plugin and if it meets all the security policies defined in the policy metadata clubbed with Sentry Server, it allows access. The Sentry server is entrusted to manage all the authorization metadata and is in constant touch with plugin's installed with the data processing technology. This is security project started by Cloudera and this makes it more compatible with Cloudera Hadoop distribution. Sentry supports HDFS, Hive, Impala and Solr in the Hadoop ecosystem.

Both Ranger and Sentry are good choices to implement security for your Data Lake. If you have decided to go with Cloudera, choosing Sentry is a natural choice. If you have chosen Hortonworks as the Hadoop distribution, choosing Ranger is apt.

Thoughts on data encryption

Data in a Data Lake is highly critical for the organization and it has to be secured at all times. In addition, to meet various regulatory and security policies standards within an organization, encryption of data is a must along with authentication and authorization. Encryption should be done to:

- Data at rest and
- Data in transit

The following figure shows both the data in rest and in transit and how encryption enables securing the data:

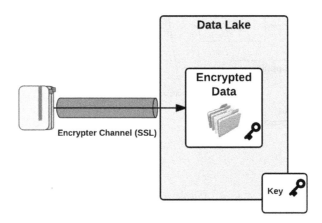

Figure 15: Data Encryption

Before we enable authentication and authorization, it's important to secure the channel through that the credentials would pass through. For this the channel should be secured paving way for data in transit to be transferred in an encrypted fashion. Various technologies in the Hadoop ecosystem communicated with one another using a variety of protocols such as RPC, TCP/IP, HTTP(S) and so on According to the protocol, the channel securing methodologies differ and would have to be dealt with accordingly.

Hadoop key management server

Apache Hadoop now include an in built **Key Management Server (KMS)** that secures the transport protocol over HTTP. It provides both client and server REST APIs for securing the communication channel.

The Hadoop Key Management Server is basically a Jetty application that includes support for java key store that can hold multiple keys and also includes API to access and manage key metadata. From functional security perspective, it includes **Access Control List** (**ACL**) based access as well as support for multiple authentication and authorization protocols like **Kerberos**, Active Directory and LDAP coupled with SSL based channel security. Hadoop KMS include end to end data encryptions that covers both data at rest and data in motion. As soon as data is written into HDFS, it is encrypted using specific algorithm and assigned to a security zone.

- SSL Support
- Server Side Encryption
- Client side encryption
- Mutiple protocol support - Kerberos, AD, LDAP
- ACL Support

Figure 16: Hadoop Key Management Server

Metadata management and governance

These are two areas, metadata management and governance, in that many technologies in big data space needs to innovate and evolve a lot. Some technologies does provide some limited functionality in these areas but isn't sufficient enough to be called as a solution suited for enterprises. However, recently there are some serious work being undertaken by various players in this area to address these two areas. We will discuss a bit of these in this section. Before going further, let's first understand these two terminologies in detail along with some other making more sense in this area.

Metadata

Metadata is structured information that describes, explains, locates, or otherwise makes it easier to retrieve, use, or manage an information resource. Metadata is often called data about data or information about information.

- National Information Standards Organization (`http://www.niso.org/publications/press/Unde`
`rstandingMetadata.pdf`*)*

As detailed in Wikipedia (`https://en.wikipedia.org/wiki/Metadata`), metadata is classified into three:

- **Descriptive metadata**: information/data for a resource making it possible for discovery and identification falls under this category of metadata
- **Structural metadata**: information/data of a container that describes how compound objects inside is composed or build or put together
- **Administrative metadata**: information/data that helps in managing a resource and contains data attributes like, when the object was created, it's filetype and other technical information

Metadata management is really a crucial capability when you deal with data. When the data becomes big (volume) and of different types (variety), this capability becomes even more important. Our Data Lake is based on many Hadoop ecosystem technologies and is diverse and surely requires such a management. Also, our Data Lake doesn't keep data in a normalized fashion and this makes replicas of data with a variety of models to cater to consuming applications.For a Data Lake, this is very important as it allows enterprises to ensure some of the important non functional requirement, important ones are as follows:

- **Discovery of data**: Allows to discover data and its various properties
- **Quality of data**: From where it arrives into the Data Lake and how reliable these data is?
- **Availability of data**: Availability of these data

It has many advantages, but for it to deliver these values, these metadata need to be managed well and time has to be invested to make sure that their quality (correctness and completeness) and availability is also met time and again.

Data governance

Data governance is a control that ensures that the data entry by an operations team member or by automated processes meets precise standards, such as a business rule, a data definition and data integrity constraints in the data model.

Data governance is a set of processes that ensures that important data assets are formally managed throughout the enterprise. Data governance ensures that data can be trusted and that people can be made accountable for any adverse event that happens because of low data quality.

- Wikipedia

Data governance gives the right control and trust in the data present inside the Data Lake. This gives the confidence to the business performing analytics against the Data Lake to make important business decisions and process changes as suggested by the Data Lake.

The importance of data governance have even prompted enterprises to create a new role in the organization know as **Chief Data Officer (CDO)** to govern and control the data in the enterprise.

Data lineage

Data lineage is defined as a data life cycle that includes the data's origins and where it moves over time. It describes what happens to data as it goes through diverse processes. It helps provide visibility into the data analytics pipeline and simplifies tracing errors back to their sources.

- Wikipedia

Data lineage in a visual representation tracks data flow from origin to destination. Metadata is a key aspect to have such a visual representation. Data lineage also represents various processes and transformation in the data flow and also tracks various dependencies in the flow.

Data lineage also identifies the right source within an enterprise having multiple systems for a particular data element. It helps in avoiding data redundancy and establishes data quality and it's completeness.

How can we achieve?

Some of the options by that this can be achieved are detailed briefly. This is just our opinion and in no way authoritative information. We hope we have been able to convey the importance of metadata management and governance.

Apache Atlas

Atlas is a scalable and extensible set of core foundational governance services – enabling enterprises to effectively and efficiently meet their compliance requirements within Hadoop and allows integration with the whole enterprise data ecosystem.

`- http://atlas.apache.org/`

As of writing this book, **Apache Atlas** is an incubating project in the **Apache Software Foundation**, by **Hortonworks**. The project is aimed at solving data governance issue in Apache Hadoop and also helps integrating well with other enterprise data applications in the organization.

High-level Atlas architecture as detailed in `http://atlas.apache.org/Architecture.htm` `l` is as given in the following figure:

There are few other existing commercial offerings in this space like **Informatica** with Big Data adaptors that can track lineage of information across the information lifecycle. Similar capabilities are being developed by various Big Data technology providers like Cloudera, Hortonworks and MapR. This capability enables effective governance around information architecture and handling.

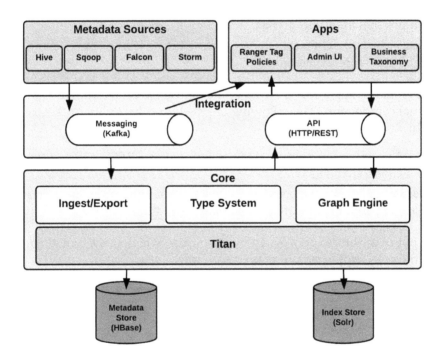

Figure 17: High level architecture of Apache Atlas

Let's quickly run through the working (layers) of Atlas from bottom up. The Atlas core has four blocks:

- **Ingest/Export**: as the name suggest it's the component that ingests and exports the metadata. As shown in the previous figure these are stored in the metadata store
- **Type System**: Atlas allows to define the model of how metadata need to be stored. It uses so called type to do that and this block allows doing exactly this functionality.
- **Graph Engine**: metadata in Atlas is stored in the graph model in Atlas and this is the block that allows to do this.
- **Titan**: Atlas uses **Titan** (http://titan.thinkaurelius.com/) as the graph database to store the metadata.

The next layer namely Integration is the layer that allows so called integration between Atlas and eternal components. The following are the two ways by that Atlas can be contacted with:

- **API**: Most of the functions in Atlas is exposed as a REST API and this component allows this to happen
- **Messaging**: Atlas can also be contacted or rather integrated using classic messaging and it uses Kafka as the topic to do this

Apache Atlas out of the box supports variety of sources to collect the metadata. The following are the ones supported out of box as of now:

- **Hive**: http://atlas.apache.org/Bridge-Hive.html
- **Sqoop**: http://atlas.apache.org/Bridge-Sqoop.html
- **Falcon**: http://atlas.apache.org/Bridge-Falcon.html
- **Storm**: http://atlas.apache.org/StormAtlasHook.html

There are applications that serve as window to Atlas. They are:

- **Admin UI**: Web application using that Atlas can be administered
- **Ranger Tag based Policies**: Ranger can be integrated with Atlas for security policy governance
- **Business Taxonomy**: Component that allows connecting business objects with the metadata stored in Atlas

WhereHows

WhereHows is a metadata management tool used within LinkedIn, open source under Apache License recently, which we feel can be used to achieve metadata management and governance. Usage of WhereHows is an opinion that we might consider in our Data Lake implementation to achieve this very important capability.

> *WhereHows is a data discovery and lineage tool built at LinkedIn. It integrates with all the major data processing systems and collects both catalog and operational metadata from them.*

- WhereHows Github project

More detail on this project could be found in their Github project (`https://github.com/linkedin/WhereHows`).

Thoughts on Data Auditing

In perspective of Data Lake, auditing is quite an important feature needed. The data comes from various sources, various departments, various asset classification (secret, public and so on) and just because of these variations, some data requires special security requirements and handling. Certain data in the lake need tracking of changes that it undergo as well as who accesses that for various legal and contractual aspects.

In the source system, data is kept for time it is really necessary to carry day to day activity (production period). After that, the data is usually categorized as non-production in nature and archived or taken offline. For a Data Lake, there isn't really a concept of archived data and because of this the data needs access control and auditing (changes that it undergoes like various transformation and so on) at all times. Not all data in the lake might require this, but some data does require it and have to be dealt with.

Doing this is a big ask but it will benefit in long run, especially for data that is categorised as highly secure. Auditing requires capturing of old data and the changed (new) data, along with some metadata such as who has done the change, when was it done and so on.

The Data Lake as detailed earlier could be zoned according to data asset classification (high, medium, low) and then auditing can be enabled for data that demands it. Once the auditing is enabled, according to certain rules configured, the lake should be capable of triggering appropriate alerts to admins and also produce reports showing risks and compliance as the case may be.

Having all the preceding capabilities completes the auditing requirement. To recap, these are the ones:

- Appropriate controls to access data
- Tracking data change
- The capability to trigger risks based on configured rules

Configuring Apache Atlas (we briefly discussed this technology earlier) along with Apache Ranger (again in security section we discussed this technology in brief) could give us the data auditing capability that we are looking for.

Atlas does the necessary auditing function and Ranger can do the authorization aspect for the data in the Data Lake.

Thoughts on data traceability

Traceability is the ability to verify the history, location, or application of an item by means of documented recorded identification.

- Wikipedia

Data traceability means the path followed by data in moving from one location (origin) to another (destination), various processes and transformation it undergoes while doing so before reaching its intended destination. We have already seen what data lineage is, so what is the difference between lineage and traceability?

Data lineage is often associated with metadata management and governance and has a difference to what data traceability means.

Data lineage is more technical in nature and shows each and every important step the data undergoes when going from origin to destination. This is a very important capability/resource for a technical team but doesn't give much sense to a non-technical business or other users in the enterprise.

Data traceability brings a non-technical layer on top of this to bring enough details in a non-technical manner to a variety of users in the enterprise.

There isn't a tool that we can suggest to do this automatically but this has to be maintained and managed as a holistic diagram and shared with different users in different departments, so that when they have to take any decisions for the enterprise, they are well aware of its repercussions to data and other department dependencies.

Knowing more about Serving Layer

The layer in our Data Lake that interacts with the outside world is the serving layer. The layer where data in the lake is served to varied number for people according to the requirement. We will discuss in brief some of the important aspects that needs to be considered in regards to this layer. This layer does employ a number of technologies to help serve data to the end users. Most of the technologie fall in the category of persistent store apt for the data it serves. It can have relational databases, NoSQL databases, document stores, Key-Value stores, Column databases and so on.

Principles of Serving Layer

We have delved a bit deep into the serving layer in part 1 of this book. This is just a recap as these principles drive choice of various technologies in this layer.

- **Fast access/high performance**: capability of serving data at high pace to the end users
- **Low latency reads and updates**: Reading and updating data with lowest latency possible enabling faster results to the end users
- **Capability of random reads**: Indexing capability allowing random reads and also serving small portion of the huge data set quite fast
- **High scalability**: Serving layer is window to the Data Lake and because of this it has to be highly scalable to serve a variety of use cases to a variety of customers
- **Fault tolerant**: Over the period the dependency on Data Lake for an enterprise can grow and because of this, it has to be fault tolerant to keep serving people and their use case
- **Capable of serving multiple models (same data different models)**: Denormalized data model, helping in serving the apt data to the end users by doing appropriate pre-computation and storing

Service Types

In serving layer one of the ways by that you can expose data for analysis is by exposing **Representational State Transfer (REST)** endpoints over HTTP(S). You could very well expose web services based on **Simple Object Access Protocol** (**SOAP**). that option is better, REST or SOAP, is not the question to be answered here. We are using REST over SOAP because of some advantages as follows:

- REST is easy compared to SOAP
- REST can exposed services in various data formats, JSON being one of them and is considered lightweight and easy on network and easier/faster to parse
- Works quite well with the internet protocol (HTTP)
- Using **RESTful** services over HTTP brings in all advantages of inherent HTTP protocol like:
  - Understood by many technologies
  - Can be cached (many technology support this by default)
  - Security over wire using SSL/TLS
  - Can use HTTP default methods like `PUT`, `PATCH`, `POST`, `GET` and `DELETE` to deal with resources
  - Various encryption methodologies can be used, which are well established

Various services could be exposed from the serving layer. We are categorising services exposed from this layer into two, data services and business services.

GraphQL

Since we have already covered why we have chosen REST over SOAP, we thought we have to definitely bring **GraphQL** as well into a brief discussion.

One of the main requirements from a Data Lake is to cater to a variety of consumers. Each consumer has different requirements on what are the attributes that they want and in what format. Usually according to requirement of the consumer more endpoints have to be created. Over the period of time this can grow and can soon become a maintenance problem.

GraphQL takes out some aspects of this but not having to write different services according to attribute requirements for a model catering to a consumer.

> *GraphQL is a query language for APIs and a runtime for fulfilling those queries with your existing data. GraphQL provides a complete and understandable description of the data in your API, gives clients the power to ask for exactly what they need and nothing more, makes it easier to evolve APIs over time, and enables powerful developer tools.*

> `- http://graphql.org/`

GraphQL can be indeed considered providing a layer on top of existing REST endpoints to deal with diverse requirements for a model catering to consumer requirements (especially filtering attributes from a model).

Data Lake with REST API

Various data models in the Data Lake could be exposed in the form of RESTful endpoints over HTTP(S) serving data in the form of JSON. This is the main way by that we are exposing our services for the end users.

Documenting web services is quite a tedious job. If these exposed web services are not documented, the lake can soon become like a black box and wouldn't be useful as no one know what exactly is in there.

Swagger is a very powerful and open source framework using that documenting REST endpoints can be really painless.

> *Swagger is a powerful open source framework backed by a large ecosystem of tools that helps you design, build, document, and consume your RESTful APIs.*

> *- http://swagger.io/*

Each API can be quite easily documented using Swagger. If you enterprise has an API gateway, you could very well expose the API's in API gateway and again can use the documentation done in Swagger as most of these gateways support Swagger inherently.

Business services

Data lake is never used as a store (persistence mechanism) for transactional systems. However, many business services exposed in the Data Lake can be used by OLTP systems to cater many use case requirements. Business services typically consume multiple data services to provide a business capability, while data services operate at data level, ensuring that the data is exposed in the its most natural form from the data platform, without any influence of business logic or business processing. Business logic and business processing should happen at Business services level so that we can achieve a loosely coupled services ecosystem while keeping data services at its purest forms.

One of the examples that we could think of around Business Service is as follows:

Consider you have an OLTP application used for selling a product. You have already pumped good amount of data in your Data Lake and have analytic logic build in for finding recommended products for a customer. This product recommendation could be exposed as a business endpoint (REST over HTTP) and could be sued by your OLTP application to show product recommendation when customer is in your website. This recommendation analysis in Data Lake can make use of really old customer behaviour data (this data being old would have already gone away from production datastore, stored in our Lambda Batch Layer) and new data (present transaction data, in our Lambda Speed Layer, flown in real-time from the OLTP application).

Serving Layer components

In the Data Lake both real-time transaction data as well as historic transaction data exists in unison. Most of the analytics that needs to be done in a Data Lake require both these data to arrive at meaningful and useful business insights.

From Data Lake you could ask for specific services against present OLTP data (real-time data services) as well as from old historic OLTP data (batch data service). In our Lambda Architecture, this is achieved through Speed and Batch layer respectively.

Data Services

As discussed before, data services provide a mechanism to deliver data based on a contract to a consuming application over light weight protocols. This component exists in the serving layer of a Data Lake and serves as a pull based mechanism from the consumer applications. While the data may reflect into the underlying data stores in near real time, it also depends on when the consuming applications pull the data via services. Theses services being light-weight can satisfy near real time requirements from the Data Lake serving layer that may be populated via speed layer.

Elasticsearch is one of the data stores that can be considered for quick lookup and near real time queries for searches, and can form a part of the serving layer as well. What we mean by real time here is that document is available for retrieval as soon as it is ingested. Elasticsearch supports key based document lookup in absolute real-time as well as supports near real-time searches as needed for data service and its contract. This storage layer should be ideally placed behind the data services as the data store fulfilling data requirements of the data services. It is an eventually consistent system that does not support ACID transactions but does support lightweight optimistic locking for minimum level of transactional consistency. This option is good for scenarios that require partial matches and searches and need complete document representation of data.

Other options may include NoSQL stores like HBase and Cassandra that are proven for very fast key based lookup and can also be invoked using Java based drivers. Both HBase and Cassandra provide column family based storage that can facilitate access pattern based key design for real-time lookup scenarios. The key advantage here with HBase is that it works over HDFS storage and does not require direct attached storage like Elasticsearch.

While we have seen Apache HIVE more as a Data Lake storage and query component, this can as well play a role into the serving layer, if the data exposed via HIVE views is a modelled data and meant for consumption by other applications. Both types of paradigms may exist here, that is, push and pull. Since HIVE supports access via JDBC driver, other application can pull the processed information over JDBC channel. Also, since it is a part of Hadoop storage layer required ETL mechanisms can be put in place for pushing the data out of the HIVE views containing modelled data.

Apache Impala is general purpose SQL query engine (also known as interactive SQL for Hadoop), quite an apt addition to our Data Lake implementation. It has inherent support to a variety of Hadoop file formats like Avro, Parquet and so on It's quite fast in it's operation and that's the main reason for it's inclusion.

It was developed by Cloudera (based on Google's 2010 published Dremel paper) and then open sourced into ASF and is now incubating with a version of 2.7.0. It has support and integration with a wide range of products in the Hadoop ecosystem. More details on this can be found in `http://impala.apache.org/` and `https://github.com/apache/incubato r-impala`. It's highly performant (in-memory query execution and directly accesses data), flexible and horizontally scalable by adding more nodes as needed. It is shipped or packaged with most of the commercial Hadoop distributions, because of these benefits.

You should definitely consider this technology as a good addition to your Data Lake implementation for performing fast analytical queries on large sets of Hadoop data. Impala utilizes the same HIVE metastore and can perform parallel queries on underlying Hadoop storage via Impala tables. Impala tables can also be accessed using JDBC drivers, which make them viable for data access from consuming applications. All this combined with optimized IO usage helps queries to run faster and avoid investments into costly ETL tools. Impala provides comparatively a more real time query execution when compared to HIVE while utilizing the same shared resource as HIVE for shorter running jobs.

Depending on whether the data process resulting into processed data is a long running job or a short running job, choice of HIVE or Impala view can be made however both have very similar data serving mechanisms.

RDBMS

Mention of an RDBMS as a potential serving layer component may seem to be unexpected, but any layer that can serve a consumer application can be considered as a serving layer component. Many times the consumer may want the data access using relational model. Such relational model can only be persisted in a relational database. A Data Lake may as well need to store processed and modelled data into a relational database as well and expose data views to the consuming application. The primary consideration here should be that, traditionally relational databases have not been built for Big Data scenarios, hence the data in such serving layer components should be as concise as possible and limited to what is required operationally to be accessed by consumer applications.

Data exports

Exposing data using RESTful endpoints (web service) is quite useful and functional for many use cases, but there are use cases that requires data from the lake in a more scheduled manner, and that too, quite huge amount of data. In that case you could even bring in Apache Sqoop as a way by that to expose or transfer data from the lake to other consuming application's data store. Other mechanisms may include scheduling jobs to extract transform and load data out of Hadoop using Map-Reduce jobs that are scheduled to be triggered and push the data to ftp locations using scripts or ETL tools that support HDFS integration like Talend and Pentaho's Data Integration.

Such exports are best to be done from batch storage since batch storage is design for such large batch processes. Running such jobs on data stores meant for near real time scenarios, would impact the responsiveness of such systems and their purpose.

Polyglot data access

Polyglot is a very common word in computing, which means, multiple.

In the serving layer there will be multiple data stores (persistence mechanism) being used to store the same data in a variety of models as dictated by the use cases. We really don't know whether there is a term like Polyglot data access in the industry. By polyglot data access, we mean, existence of multiple data stores in the serving layer, which are being used by serving layer to churn various data services to the end users.

In our Data Lake we already have polyglot data access in action by using Elasticsearch, Hive and HBase as the data access stores.

The concept of Polyglot access can be further extended into persisting parts of information held by an object into multiple target data stores and access them as well. There are frameworks today support such mechanisms for Big Data technologies as well.

One of the very prominent use cases of polyglot access has been to to store the indexes and the data separately, such that the indexing technologies are primarily used for indexing and data technologies are primarily used for efficient storage. There a number of options for polyglot persistence frameworks in context of Big Data, with Hibernate like JPA interface to enable developers to define objects using standard persistence configurations and annotations.

Example: serving layer

Let us see an example of serving layer with data devices in action, as we have discussed in this chapter. Data Services are expected to deliver the data from data repositories of the serving layer. Such repositories should support fast and random access of data; Elasticsearch could be one such repository.

Let us build data services over and above the data that we have ingested into Elasticsearch server in the previous chapter, wherein we had ingested customer, address and contact data. For this example, we will build a Spring Boot based JAX-RS 2.0 REST data services with Swagger UI that would provide the service definitions.

This example has been covered in the project named `chapter11` in the source repository and reuses the the same data model which we have been using throughout the book. Some of the important aspects of this example are; the JAX-RS 2.0 annotations which we can have a quick look and the main service implementation with Swagger annotations as shown below.

A data service implementation like this gives complete freedom as to how we can combine the data for the single customer view. Here, we can see that the customer service is combining the customer address and customer contact with customer profile data and then sending the response back.

The below code shows how such services can be realized by using spring boot with springmvc-jersey bridge dependency, so that we can leverage standard JAX-RS 2.0 annotation. If you are new to Spring framework based application, we would suggest just running this example to see the services in action. The more important parts we would suggest for your focus would be, data services as REST endpoint and how such services should be described/documented using swagger UI. This code can be found in the file `chapter11/src/main/java/com/laketravels/ch11/service/endpoint/CustomerEndpoint.java`.

```
@Controller
@EnableAutoConfiguration
@Api(value = "customer", description = "This is the customer resource that provides"
        + " customer information ")
@Path("customer")
public class CustomerEndpoint {

private ObjectMapper MAPPER  = new ObjectMapper();

public CustomerEndpoint() {
MAPPER.setSerializationInclusion(JsonInclude.Include.NON_NULL);
```

```
MAPPER.configure(MapperFeature.ACCEPT_CASE_INSENSITIVE_PROPERTIES, true);
MAPPER.configure(DeserializationFeature.FAIL_ON_UNKNOWN_PROPERTIES, false);
MAPPER.setDateFormat(new SimpleDateFormat("yyyy-MM-dd"));
    }

@Autowired
    private ESUtil esUtil;


private Logger logger = LoggerFactory.getLogger(CustomerEndpoint.class);


@Path("{customerId}")
@GET
    @ApiOperation(value = "profile", consumes = MediaType.TEXT_PLAIN,
produces = MediaType.APPLICATION_JSON,
            response = Customer.class,
            notes = "This endpoint is used to get customer profile")
public Customer getCustomer(@PathParam("customerId") String customerId)
throws IOException, ParseException {
return getCustomerProfile(customerId);
    }

@Path("{customerId}/address")
@GET
    @ApiOperation(value = "address", consumes = MediaType.TEXT_PLAIN,
produces = MediaType.APPLICATION_JSON,
            response = Address.class,
            notes = "This endpoint is used to get customer address")
public Address getAddress(@ApiParam(
            name = "customerId",
            required = true,
            value = "Contains customer Id"
    ) @PathParam("customerId") String customerId) throws IOException {
return getCustomerAddress(customerId);
    }

@Path("{customerId}/contact")
@GET
    @ApiModelProperty(required = true, dataType =
"org.joda.time.LocalDate")
@ApiOperation(value = "contact", consumes = MediaType.TEXT_PLAIN, produces
= MediaType.APPLICATION_JSON,
            response = Contact.class,
            notes = "This endpoint is used to get customer contact")
public Contact getContact(@ApiParam(
            name = "customerId",
            required = true,
```

```
                        value = "Contains customer Id"
      ) @PathParam("customerId") String customerId) throws IOException {
return getCustomerContact(customerId);
      }

private Customer getCustomerProfile(String customerId) throws IOException {
        SearchRequestBuilder reqBuilder =
esUtil.getConnection().prepareSearch();
        reqBuilder.setIndices("customer").setTypes("customer");
        TermQueryBuilder termQueryBuilder = QueryBuilders.termQuery("id",
customerId);
        reqBuilder.setQuery(termQueryBuilder);
        SearchHits hits = reqBuilder.get().getHits();
long numHits = hits.totalHits();
        Customer customer = null;
if (numHits > 0) {
          customer = MAPPER.readValue(hits.getAt(0).getSourceAsString(),
              Customer.class);
          customer.setAddress(getCustomerAddress(customerId));
          customer.setContact(getCustomerContact(customerId));
        }
return customer;
      }

private Address getCustomerAddress(String customerId) throws IOException {
        SearchRequestBuilder reqBuilder =
esUtil.getConnection().prepareSearch();
        reqBuilder.setIndices("address").setTypes("address");
        TermQueryBuilder termQueryBuilder = QueryBuilders.termQuery("id",
customerId);
        reqBuilder.setQuery(termQueryBuilder);
        SearchHits hits = reqBuilder.get().getHits();
long numHits = hits.totalHits();
        Address address = null;
if (numHits > 0) {
          address = MAPPER.readValue(hits.getAt(0).getSourceAsString(),
              Address.class);
        }
return address;
      }

private Contact getCustomerContact(String customerId) throws IOException {
        SearchRequestBuilder reqBuilder =
esUtil.getConnection().prepareSearch();
        reqBuilder.setIndices("contacts").setTypes("contact");
        TermQueryBuilder termQueryBuilder = QueryBuilders.termQuery("id",
customerId);
        reqBuilder.setQuery(termQueryBuilder);
```

```
        SearchHits hits = reqBuilder.get().getHits();
long numHits = hits.totalHits();
        Contact contact = null;
if (numHits > 0) {
            contact = MAPPER.readValue(hits.getAt(0).getSourceAsString(),
                    Contact.class);
        }
return contact;
    }
}
```

Code 03: Spring Boot Service Implementation

Please run the following command to compile the project, if not already done from the root in source repository. Please make sure that the `chapter08/data-model` project folder is already compiled before compiling this project.

mvn install

Once the compilation is done, please configure `chapter11/config/dev.yml` as per your environment. We can run the example by using the following command from within the `chapter11` project folder:

java -jar target/chapter11-1.0-SNAPSHOT.jar -DconfigFile=config/dev.yml -Dspring.logging.config=config/logback.xml

Once the spring boot server is initialized, navigate to the following URL to open the swagger UI: `http://localhost:8080/swagger/index.html`.

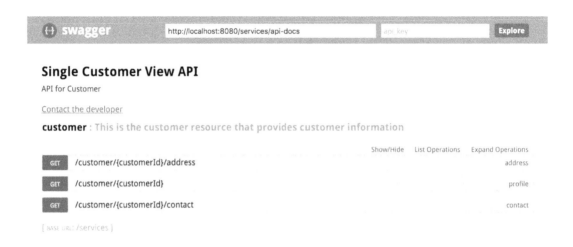

Figure 18: Swagger UI Landing Page

In the swagger UI, try invoking the customer endpoint as shown next with a customer Id and you will see a similar figure as follows: Swagger UI is the eye through that we could see the data residing in the Data Lake. For a non-technical person, this is a very important component and should be considered in a Data Lake implementation:

Figure 19: Customer Service Response in Swagger UI

The complete response as provided by the service is as shown next:

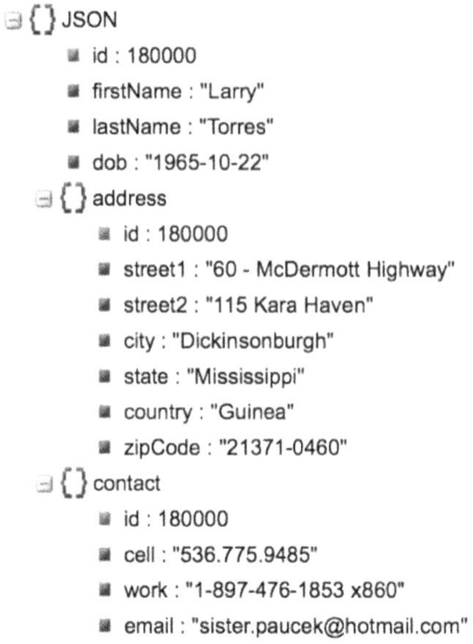

```
⊟ {} JSON
    ▪ id : 180000
    ▪ firstName : "Larry"
    ▪ lastName : "Torres"
    ▪ dob : "1965-10-22"
    ⊟ {} address
        ▪ id : 180000
        ▪ street1 : "60 - McDermott Highway"
        ▪ street2 : "115 Kara Haven"
        ▪ city : "Dickinsonburgh"
        ▪ state : "Mississippi"
        ▪ country : "Guinea"
        ▪ zipCode : "21371-0460"
    ⊟ {} contact
        ▪ id : 180000
        ▪ cell : "536.775.9485"
        ▪ work : "1-897-476-1853 x860"
        ▪ email : "sister.paucek@hotmail.com"
```

Figure 20: Response from the Customer Service

In this example, we have covered the following:

- We have built REST service endpoints to access customer data and all the related entities.
- All the endpoints are leveraging GET HTTP verb which in a way signifies that all of them are read- only services. Service endpoints could also be POST endpoints for submitting request body, which is useful if we have a large number of input parameters.
- The Swagger UI deduces the model and model schema via the annotations and service interface in the endpoint class namely com.laketravels.ch11.service.endpoint.CustomerEndpoint.
- All the endpoints are in context of a particular customer which aligns to some of the basic REST endpoints.

Summary

In this chapter, we brought together all the technologies and capabilities that we have discussed throughout *Part 2* of this book. We tried to explain some important aspects with the whole Data Lake in mind. We introduced you to certain more capabilities like metadata management, governance, auditing, traceability and so on, which are very important one for a typical implementation within an enterprise. We managed to give our technology opinions for each of these capabilities but kept delving deep into it away. We were not able to get deep into some of the technologies discussed in this chapter intentionally to keep the book concise and to the point on main technologies/capabilities in a Data Lake.

After reading this chapter, you would now have a full picture of an operational Data Lake. You would also have brief idea of some other capabilities needed for an enterprise Data Lake, which are usually omitted when a Data Lake is first implemented in an enterprise.

These additional capabilities are required for a true Data Lake, but to cover the scope of the book and to stay within the limit we have to let it go by giving just the right amount of details. We haven't covered much of code in this chapter. Some of the choices of technology are just our opinions. Please take these with a grain of salt. Having said that, we encourage you to build these capabilities in your Data Lake implementation and not omit these.

This chapter was quite an ask as we covered many diverse aspects in brief and can be quite exhausting at this moment. Take a break, and let's come back and complete next two chapter quite quickly.

12

Data Lake Use Case Suggestions

It's quite exhausting to write a book spanning nearly 500 pages, and its quite a big challenge going through these pages to understand what the author has been trying t o explain. In doing so, you would also have to do the hands-on coding so that everything read can be put into action. Indeed, you need a great appreciation for coming this far, going through the pages and also getting your hands dirty in actually implementing a Data Lake, which is considered quite a challenge as it involves myriad technologies. Hats off! Thanks for staying with us through out the book! I hope you have enjoyed reading every page, as we enjoyed writing each one.

This chapter aims at introducing some of the well-known data lake uses in an enterprise. Many companies have this already in some form or other and some are in the process of creating one.

These use cases can be considered as a way by which we prove the capability of a data lake in an organization and then use those success stories to keep building new use cases.

These suggestions are in no way exhaustive in nature, but we do feel that if you have read parts 1 and 2 of this book, you are very well capable of executing these use cases without much trouble. The area that changes is the source data, plus the analytics your enterprise is keen on implementing in each of the use case. However, depending on the business domains, there could be different processing requirements from a business perspective.

Establishing cybersecurity practices in an enterprise

Data is growing day by day. People are becoming tech savvy. Worms and viruses are being created more often and getting stronger than ever. In such a digital environment, enterprises need to be more vigilant with the data they hold and also the applications that are the core of their operations/businesses.

A siloed security team is now turning itself into a full-fledged operations centre. This team is entrusted with the role of looking at data and all applications within an enterprise.

With such a growing scenario of data and application usage, having a platform to monitor various security-related concerns is a must. It is this requirement that makes construction of a data lake for security-related aspects inevitable.

Data is ingested from a variety of sources into the data lake, and then analysts carry out various analyses to create meaningful visualizations and act on certain discrepancies proactively.

Having a central-lake-only security aspect monitoring can aid in identifying breaches quite early and can be proactively acted upon. Data can be collected for network analysis to assess security compliance and various operational activity (more inline with security), and be dealt with according to the security policies defined by an enterprise.

A security analyst can look at various data, visualize it in a more meaningful manner, and then take the necessary action to deal with these threats in a more proactive rather than reactive manner. Integrating a security lake with other pieces of software can trigger various alerting mechanisms according to the set rules configured within the lake. Various complex event processing techniques and machine learning techniques could also be employed on the arriving data to derive additional analytics, which can again be proactively looked upon and actioned.

Apache Metron is an incubating project in ASF, sponsored by Hortonworks, which makes use of the data lake technologies that we have discussed before, particularly in the security landscape. The approach of building a data lake for security is very much similar to ours, but security does require data collection from a variety of sources which can be dealt with quite easily using various tools and Apache Metron can then do security related threat detection on data. Internally, Apache Metron uses many of the technologies that we have already detailed in part 2 of this book and would be quite familiar for you to understand. For more details on Apache Metron, we suggest you go through the Apache official site at `http://metron.apache.org/` and also the official Apache wiki at `https://cwiki.apache.org/confluence/display/METRON/Metron+Wiki`. You could also get some details on Hortonworks site in `https://hortonworks.com/apache/metron/`.

Cybersecurity as an enterprise capability may broadly involve business functions like intrusion/anomaly detection, identification of threat levels, response to the threat with alerts/notifications, performing critical protection activities, and recovering from the threat either by eliminating it or by introducing quarantine mechanisms.

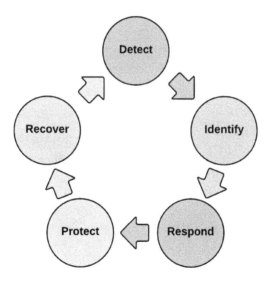

Figure 01: Cybersecurity Lifecycle

Know the customers dealing with your enterprise

In the age of digital transformation and digital disruption, getting to know each customer and their preferences is key. Also, using these preferences and choices, customizing products and offering personalized versions suitable for a specific customer is a necessary function.

Quite often in enterprises, customer data lives in discrete business applications and they don't necessarily exchange data with each other. Our single customer view is one way of bringing customer data from various sources into one and creating this so called single customer view. But that isn't enough in this digital world as customers tend to expect more and this demands enriching the customer data with more personalized data so as to analyse those details and start offering products and services quite targeted and personalized in nature. This makes products and services that are relevant and irresistible for a customer and they also feel taken care off as these are individually targeted as against a generic offer for a group of customers falling into a segment.

A data lake capable of knowing a lot about the customer and their needs can be a great asset for any business and transactional applications could seek the help of a data lake serving layer to get customer insights and start personalizing their whole offering.

Having a data lake capable of knowing a customer and their needs can give the customer true omni-channel experience throughout the day whether they are using a web application on a desktop, a mobile web application on a mobile or a mobile app on a smartphone. This centralized lake gives that consistency and also avoids duplicate campaigns and advertising targets. What we mean by this is, if the customer has indicated through your web application that they don't want a particular type of campaign, they expect that it is also reflected in other customer interaction channels where business connects with the customer and the centralize lake knowing these nitty-gritties of customer choices and their preferences enables organizations to achieve this.

The huge amount of data footprint left by the customer in various digital platforms is quite massive to tackle in normal transaction systems, and this is the time that a data lake as a capability for an enterprise becomes quite significant.

In addition to data from transaction systems, there is tonnes of data that is getting collected, like behavioral data (mostly client-side scripts) and also data flowing in from various social media channels. In addition to behavioral data, certain devices can capture location and gestures, which can be further processed to support the Internet of Things (IOT) use cases with derived recommendations and suggestions.

There is also a requirement to look for content posted in social media for a company to analyze (sentiment analysis for that matter) and deal with them according to a defined set of rules.

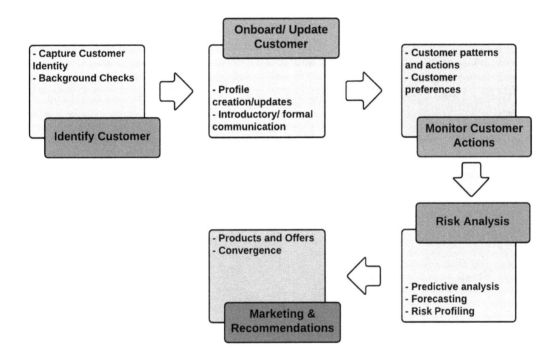

Figure 02: A typical Know Your Customer (KYC) process

Bring efficiency in warehouse management

This is a more business-specific use case where a data lake can come in really handy in many decision making scenarios. If your company has a production line or is dealing with cargo and logistics, this use case can be quite relevant and apt for data lake implementation.

In modern day warehouse, the **Internet of Things** (**IoT**) comes in all forms and sizes. These devices could be used in various movable devices in the warehouse, can be held in each product for tracking and monitoring and so on. Tagging these devices is fine, but to make use of the huge amount of data flowing from these devices, data lake is a perfect solution to collect these and start making sense of them using a defined set of rules. This can add huge operational efficiency in the warehouse operation, in turn increase revenue and profit.

If this data flows in from various transactional application linked with these IoT devices, proactively using past data analytics for new orders placed can make sure that the warehouse is performing at optimal level. Again, if people management system data is also integrated it can also try effectively distributing work and putting their valuable time to good use.

Having a data lake, and properly analyzing data in it, can aid business in redefining their business and can also help take business decisions more confidently and promptly. These recommendations and decisions can play a vital role for achieving a cost and time optimized services delivery. One such indicative example is shown here:

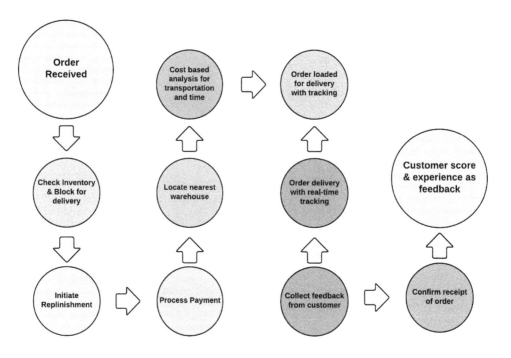

Figure 03: Warehouse management

Developing a brand and marketing of the enterprise

Business has changed a lot, especially in the last decade or so, and has become more of a customer driven society. Customers want to be known well and taken care of accordingly. Many customers are willing to share their details just so that businesses can understand them more, start giving more targeted offers, and also customize their services to cater to their preferences over a variety of channels available in this digital age.

The buyer is king and you have to keep him/her happy at all times. Data analysis in the Data Lake can help you understand customers better. It can be used as a way to develop your brand value and used in a very good way to engage, target and market your products.

Data analysis can help your business keep up with trends in the market in a proactive way, helping your business make better decisions and also proactively take new directions.

Whether you like it or not, you will have to gather data from a variety of sources, especially publicly available data, to shape your business decisions and analyses. This can only be possible if we have a Data Lake type setup with huge and varied analyses possible at your fingertips. Usually, publicly available data is of huge volume, and analysis is only possible using big data technologies.

Bringing in new products will bring in new trends into to business and analysis can help you do this. Analysis can help promote your company as a brand that consumers can trust.

All of these stated things require a huge amount of research, marketing, and advertising. A Data Lake can be one of the capabilities that could be exploited to do exactly this. Various analyses can be used to find new markets where you could start selling your products and expand your marketing and brand value.

Personalization is very big these days and a data lake can help you gather good amount of knowledge of your customer and can learn from these analysis and start selling and targeting right products to the consumers.

Nowadays getting to know a customer's sentiments by going through his/her interaction with social media and listening to them in a timely manner is quite key. Your Data Lake can be the listener and can do a bit of initial filtering to make sure that the most important customer is handled in a priority fashion, using the latest and greatest technologies in the space of **Artificial Intelligence** (**AI**) and Machine Learning. Handling these emotions will be the distinctive feature, will make your brand well-known and also makes it more valuable.

Data Lake cannot only be used to analyze your business data but also to analyze your competitors' publicly available data; using these analyses, your business processes and decisions could be tweaked accordingly for the benefit of your business.

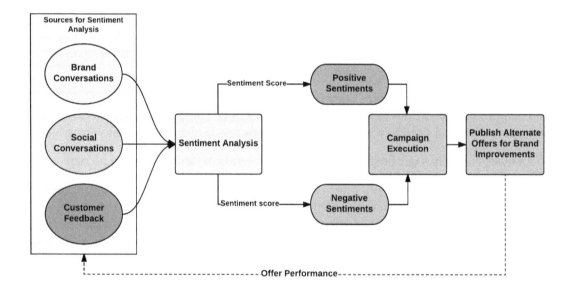

Figure 04: Brand Marketing and Offers via Sentiment Analysis

Achieve a higher degree of personalization with customers

As detailed before in various use cases, personalization is one of the very important aspects in the digital world.

> *Personalization, sometimes known as customization, consists of tailoring a service or a product to accommodate specific individuals, sometimes tied to groups or segments of individuals. A wide variety of organizations use personalization to improve customer satisfaction, digital sales conversion, marketing results, branding, and improved website metrics as well as for advertising. Personalization is a key element in social media and recommender systems.*

> *-Wikipedia*

This definition clearly defines what is meant by personalization. In the modern day, customers expect them to be known by the business through a variety of channels and in a consistent way. They need the business to understand when they are browsing on a browser on a desktop or on mobile phone, and when they actually come into your store or organization, through various IoT mechanisms.

Web personalization can be considered as looking at behavior data (collected from the user's browsing history and other client-side aspects) and real transaction data (actual transaction data that the users have done with your business application such as customer details, order details, payment details and so on) from the Data Lake. Usually this transaction data is not owned by the Data Lake; rather it is flown in from various transactional source systems and consolidated in a holistic fashion. When browsing online, this data is used to actually personalize the site itself or the recommendations. These transactional applications are usually quite limited in various analyses and are always in silos (don't really talk with other business applications and don't know whether the other applications would have already interacted with the customer in the past) and because of this it doesn't clearly don't have a holistic notion of each customer. It is this aspect that a Data Lake can help and can be used to avoid sending in a second recommendation of a product if the customer has already declined an offer of the same nature in one of the other channels. Say, for example, if in mobile app your business would have pushed a campaign for a particular product via a mobile app, and the customer has declined or not interacted. This can be used as a means to avoid sending in same offer when the customer interacts with the business using their website. Rather they could push another offer and see the interaction level of the customer. This can only be possible if there is a holistic view of all the data in one place for various analysis purpose, which then can be used in various transaction systems.

With more channels expected to come up in the near future, with a huge digital footprint for each customer, this is a must and the only distinguishing factor for any business; it should not be delayed in any way.

Bringing IoT data analysis at your fingertips

The Internet of things (IoT) is the inter-networking of physical devices, vehicles (also referred to as "connected devices" and "smart devices"), buildings, and other items—embedded with electronics, software, sensors, actuators, and network connectivity that enable these objects to collect and exchange data.

-Wikipedia

The world of IoT is evolving at a very rapid pace. Every business has to invest time and money in this space for various aspects to be successful or to be on par with their competitors. The IoT churns huge amounts of data, and a Data Lake is the only way by which you can analyze this huge volume of data from these devices and then make sense of it for the business.

The devices would be used in various parts of business, both internal and external and according to various set rules you could use the data from them to carry out many useful business scenarios. For example, you could use IoT to manage your warehouse, maintain and manage various assets in your warehouse, track various products in your warehouse and so on. However, this can only be possible if you have a way by which to get this frequently flowing data from these devices and then run various rules against it to derive meaningful insights for the business to take necessary actions.

In customer-facing stores, this devices can be installed at various parts of the store and when they are near or in vicinity, use the customer data to start the personalization. For example, if your customer has installed your mobile app and has already enabled Bluetooth on their device, when they walk into your store, the mobile device starts communicating using Bluetooth with another Bluetooth-enabled device in your store. Using this, for example, the display device in your store can customize and store offers more apt for customers viewing or near the display in a subtle way without too much intrusion into their private data. This is just one of the use cases, but there are a variety of use cases possible using various devices available now to start using this in a more useful manner according to business needs and desires.

More practical and useful data archival

Any transactional system in your enterprise keeps data in the so-called production data store, which is more relevant and needed for data-to-data operation (also known as operational data). However, these historical data pieces are gold mines for the business and their operation. Historical data would give valuable insights into changing business operations and also pave the way for various operational changes in future business operations.

Today, historical data, when not needed or moved away from the transactional data store, is often persisted in hard tapes. The data once persisted in hard tapes is usually ignored and lies there without any usefulness. In place of hard tapes, Data Lakes could be used as an active archival storage for storing data that is considered non-productive. This can be quite useful as it is much easier to bring back this data alive if it lives in the Data Lake, as opposed to hard tapes, which is quite hard to bring back to life.

Compliment the existing data warehouse infrastructure

Analysis prior to Big Data was done in a traditional Data Warehouse setup. Big Data has paved the way for analysis to be done in a more performant manner with a lot of flexibility. However, traditional data warehouses would still exist for a variety of reasons going forward and are not going away soon.

A Data Lake in your organization can augment and support the data warehouse in a variety of ways. A Data Warehouse can be used for a variety of easy canned report generations. The business can create these on the fly using the semantic data warehouse models on top of the transactional data model, which the transactional application deals with on a day to day basis.

Also, certain data warehouse requirements could very well be fulfilled by this Data Lake infrastructure and since they have huge historical data with them, it can be quite useful in many business situations.

Achieving telecom security and regulatory compliance

This is more of an industry specific use case wherein nationwide Telecom companies are driven by regulatory compliance to implement all security protocols for Law Enforcement Agencies for investigation of any cyber crime and to perform occasional audits. These regulations have become much more strict with the advancement of technologies, social footprints and multiple ways by which cyber criminals can perform unethical activities. This has greatly expanded the scope of Telecom companies from regulatory compliance perspective, which today gets into more real-time and percolation driven detection along with batch analysis of network data. The data records can be analyzed in depth to establish a communication graph for every caller over a period of time such that this time series data can be replayed whenever required. These mechanisms prove very useful to Law Enforcement Agencies for their investigations. Here we are discussing massive data that flows through networks of various telecom providers, which may add up to petabytes of data across couple of months. The only way to achieve all the capabilities discussed above is by leveraging Big Data capabilities for data collection, processing and analysis.

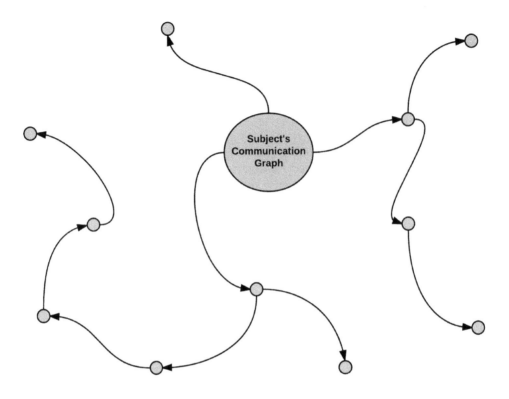

Figure 05: Communication Graph Analysis

Summary

This chapter has intended to give you several data lake use cases to think of. We made sure that we haven't tied any of these use cases to a particular industry. We hope that reading through these use cases gives you enough brain trickles to derive your own use cases for your organization and their operation.

We hope we have successfully sufficient additional use cases, which could be used as an input for you to convey the real value of a Data Lake to your organization's leadership/management team.

Index

C

MicroSTRategy (MSTR) 364
MirrorMaker 257
monitoring components
  about 365
  Apache Ambari 368
multi-broker cluster
  setting up 275

N

NameNode 360
NameNode server 97
National Information Standards Organization
  reference 520
Native Big Data connectors 170, 171
near real time processing layer 55, 100
NodeManager 360
nodes, Elasticsearch
  about 431
  client node 432
  data node 431
  master node 431
Non-Indexed Data 62
NoSQL 31
Nutch 347

O

Object DataBase Connectivity (ODBC) 364
OnLine Analytical Processing (OLAP) 67, 364
OnLine Transaction Processing (OLTP) 22, 67,
  343, 364
Oozie 367
oozie workflow 96
optimizer 296
Oracle Big Data
  URL 170
Oracle JDK
  URL 137
orchestration components 365
Out Of Memory (OOM) 307
output plugins
  URL 422

P

PagerDuty 425
Parquet 498

Pentaho 172
Pentaho Data Integration (PDI) 172
persistent stores 30, 31
personalization
  about 550
  higher degree, achieving 550
personally identifiable information (PII) 348
Pig Latin 362
Pig scripts 96
pluggable external connectors 135
polyglot 533
producer
  configuration 266, 270
  reliability 259
programming interface
  REST interface 258

Q

Query DSL
  about 429
  queries 429
Quickstart
  URL 271

R

RabbitMQ
  about 281
  using 282
raw data 492
RDBMS Data Load 380
Reduce Task 353
regulatory compliance
  achieving 553
relational data stores
  about 63
  distributed data stores 64, 65
Relational Database Management System
  (RDBMS) 16, 21, 30, 115, 313, 532
relational database
  Elasticsearch 433
reliability level, Flume
  best-effort 195
  end-to-end 195
  store on failure 195
remote procedure call (RPC) 109

CPSIA information can be obtained
at www.ICGtesting.com
Printed in the USA
LVHW021915140119
603848LV00010B/498/P

9 781787 281349